Corpus-Assisted Discourse Studies on the Iraq Conflict

Routledge Advances in Corpus Linguistics

EDITED BY TONY MCENERY, *Lancaster University UK*
MICHAEL HOEY, *Liverpool University, UK*

Corpus-Assisted Discourse Studies on the Iraq Conflict

Wording the War

Edited by John Morley and Paul Bayley

Routledge
Taylor & Francis Group
New York   London

First published 2009
by Routledge
711 Third Avenue, New York, NY 10017

Simultaneously published in the UK
by Routledge
2 Park Square, Milton Park, Abingdon, Oxon OX14 4RN

Routledge is an imprint of the Taylor & Francis Group, an informa business

First issued in paperback 2013

Typeset in Sabon by IBT Global.

Library of Congress Cataloging in Publication Data
Corpus-assisted discourse studies on the Iraq Conflict : wording the war / edited by John Morley and Paul Bayley.
    p. cm. — (Routledge advances in corpus linguistics ; 10)
Includes bibliographical references and index.
1. Discourse analysis—Political aspects. 2. Corpora (Linguistics) 3. Iraq War, 2003—Language. I. Morley, John, 1940 Dec. 17–
P302.77.C68 2009
401'.41—dc22
2009015185

ISBN13: 978-0-415-87137-2 (hbk)
ISBN13: 978-0-415-85295-1 (pbk)
ISBN13: 978-0-203-86815-7 (ebk)

Contents

Concordances

Figures

Tables

Acknowledgments

The editors of this volume would like to thank the Italian Ministry of Education, University and Research for the grant which allowed this project to be realized. They would also like to give their warmest thanks to their colleague, Guy Aston, whose expertise as well as his unceasing and meticulous work created the corpus on which the project was based, and whose constructive criticism kept all the contributors on their toes.

The editors also thank: J. R. Martin, P. R. R. White, and Palgrave Macmillan for permission to print Figures 2.1, 2.8, and 2.9, originally published in *The Language of Evaluation: Appraisal in English*, 2005; Guardian News and Media for permission to print in Chapter 10 the article "Civilian Targets", which appeared in the *Guardian* 14/04/2003, copyright Guardian News and Media Ltd. 2003; and finally the *Sun*, for permission to print in Chapter 10 the article "Good Evening: Here Is the Worst Possible News", published on 11/4/2003 under the byline Littlejohn.

Introduction
A Description of *CorDis*

John Morley

0.1. GENESIS OF THE BOOK

This book is the product of the collaboration of a group of scholars in different Italian university institutions which started in 2004.[1] We had a common interest in corpus linguistics, discourse analysis, and institutional and media discourse, though we had all been pursuing rather different lines of research. In 2003 the group put together a bid to the Italian university funding body for a research project which combined our interests. It had the official title *Corpora and Discourse: A Quantitative and Qualitative Linguistic Analysis of Political and Media Discourse on the Conflict in Iraq in 2003*, and became known by the acronym *CorDis*.[2]

Two main elements helped to unify our research: the first was that we were all working on a corpus of texts concerning the Iraq war, the *CorDis Corpus*; and the second was that we were all committed to a methodology which was known within the group as corpus-assisted discourse studies (CADS). We will say a little more about this methodology later. The chapters in this book all derive from research on this corpus and to a greater or lesser extent use the CADS methodology. CADS, like all studies involving corpus linguistics, builds on the work of Sinclair, Hoey, and Stubbs and their names will be mentioned frequently in the volume (in particular, Hoey 2005; Sinclair 1991, 2004; Stubbs 1996, 2001). We would like to pay a tribute to our recently deceased colleague, John Sinclair, to whom all members of our research group owe an enormous professional debt and to whom some of us were linked by ties of friendship. Another unifying factor was that most of the group had a commitment to systemic functional grammar (see, in particular, Halliday 1994), which is the grammatical framework that predominates in the analyses in this book; there was also an interest among members of the group in exploring aspects of stance and evaluation, that is, how speakers and writers 'instruct' their interlocutors on how to interpret their messages (see Hunston and Thompson 2000; Martin and White 2005).

0.2. THE COMPOSITION OF THE CORPUS

The *CorDis Corpus* consists of six related projects. The projects are briefly presented here in an order which reflects an ideal temporal progression. The acronyms refer to the subcorpora which the projects produced. Note that the newspaper project produced three subcorpora corresponding to news stories, editorials, and op-eds.

- Sources of news creation—(a) British House of Commons (*HoC*), (b) US House of Representatives (*HoR*) (Projects 1 and 2).
- News negotiating and mediation—White House press briefings (*WHB*) (Project 3).
- Recounting to the public—(a) television news (*TVNews*), (b) newspapers (*PapNews*), (*PapEds*), (*PapOp*) (Projects 4 and 5).
- Parliamentary inquiry—Hutton Inquiry (*HUTTON*), which touched on the British Government's reasons for going to war (Project 6).

The way the corpus has been marked up allows us to create different groupings or *classes* of texts in order to answer specific research questions. These classes may cut across subcorpora, for instance, all the texts from US papers, whether they are reports, editorials, or op-eds; or they may be parts of one subcorpus, such as the information-gathering section of the Hutton Inquiry subcorpus. We refer to the different ways of dividing up the corpus into classes as *partitions*.

0.2.1. Discourse of the Legislative Assemblies (Projects 1 and 2)

These two projects derive most immediately from work demonstrating that much political action is constituted by linguistic action and as such is a legitimate field of study for the linguist (see Blommaert and Bulcaen 1998; Chilton, Ilyin, and Mey 1998; Fairclough 1995; Geis 1987; Wilson 1990; Wodak 1989). Parliamentary discourse can be considered as prototypical political language and yet it differs from much of what we now call political language because it can only take place in one institutional arena, and in order to participate in it one has to be an elected member of the institution. Previous volume-length studies of parliamentary discourse, which provide a starting point for the project, include Bayley (2004); Carbò (1996); Wodak and van Dijk (2000). This research has shown that a cross-cultural analysis of parliamentary language can be extremely fruitful because on the one hand parliaments in Western democracies fulfil, in and through language, similar functions—they legitimate and/or contest legislative proposals and policy orientations, they subject the executive power to scrutiny, and they represent constituency or other interests—but on the other they differ in terms of their rules and regulations, their representativity, and their accountability. In particular, they are expressions of different political cultures—long-term orientations towards government and general beliefs, symbols, and values (Heywood 2000). The two chapters (2 and 3) by Miller and Johnson and Bayley and Bevitori seek to identify how this political culture in different but allied nations (the US and the UK) is articulated in the discourse of parliamentarians justifying or contesting military intervention.

0.2.2. The White House Press Briefings (Project 3)

The White House press briefings project deals with an extremely recent linguistic-political-media discourse type which evolved in the 1990s in the United States from press conferences (Clayman 1993). Being a new genre, very little has been written about these briefings; indeed, previous work has focused on the genre as a site of political action: Maltese (1992) and Kurtz (1998) have examined, for instance, how the US government attempts to 'spin' its message in times of conflict and the press's reaction to such attempts. Partington's (2003) book-length study is the first work to approach this discourse type using a full range of linguistic tools. One of his main points is that the briefings represent an excellent site for the study of the evolution of a new discourse type. Furthermore, he addresses in some detail how the participants invent ex novo the rules of a novel inter-active 'role-play'; and how they learn to behave both in cooperation but also in competition (the journalists with the president's spokesperson, the podium—and vicariously with the podium's political masters—and vice versa) with the other participants. Riccio's chapter is an example of how a seemingly neutral word, *message*, is spun so that it takes on connotations of menace.

The briefings are, in fact, frequently the arena where White House policy is first aired—sometimes even before it has actually officially been formulated. Moreover, although they are ostensibly a kind of mediation, whereby the White House states its agenda and the press decides how it is going to report it, briefings are also in effect a way for the White House to get its message over the heads of the press directly to ordinary citizens.

It is interesting to note that many major US news outlets have a regular section reporting what goes on in briefings, and this makes the podium a highly recognisable media-political celebrity in his own right.

0.2.3. TV News Discourse (Project 4)

The TV news discourse project focuses on the language of television news and starts from the recognition that, like the rest of the media, TV news is involved in creating what Hall et al. (1981) call 'maps of meaning': that is, the presentation of news to the public in ways that they will understand. As Galtung and Ruge (1981) have it, what is signal and what is noise is not inherent; it is a question of convention. MacDougall puts this more philosophically,

[J]ournalists do not gather news; they construct second order accounts
of reality from materials provided by sources (first order accounts).

(MacDougall 1983:85–6)

The creation of these conventions, which we all recognize, means that the
news stories must conform to criteria of newsworthiness that are accepted
both by the news creators and their audience. It could be argued further
that TV news 'operates within the framework of the dominant value system and therefore helps to maintain the *status quo*' (Selby and Cowdery
1995:144). This aspect of news reporting is central to the television news
project, which investigated the media construction of the conflict in a comparative perspective across four networks representing public and private
channels in the UK, US, and Italy.

Television news also, perhaps predominantly, makes use of images.
Although images are not the direct object of study of either of the chapters
concerning television in this volume, as they are in Lipson's essay in our sister volume, they are the background against which the linguistic analysis is
performed.[3] Here we acknowledge a debt to the pioneering semiotic media
work of Fiske (1987) and Hartley (1982).

It is perhaps strange that so little work has been done on the linguistic
realization of the second-order accounts of the world presented in television news. A few exceptions might be represented by Iedema, Feez, and
White (1994), Fairclough (1995b), Haarman (1999, 2006), and Lombardo (2001, 2004). The chapters by Lombardo and Clark (Chapters 5
and 6), which explore the television data using slightly different analytical approaches, have the virtue of representing a systematic study of this
genre using an extended corpus of texts: they both deal with US and UK
television news programmes.

0.2.4. Newspaper Discourse (Project 5)

The newspaper discourse project, too, starts from a similar acknowledgment of the complex relationship between events and their presentation
through the media. As Chibnall says,

The reporter does not go out gathering news, picking up stories as if
they were fallen apples, he creates news stories by selecting fragments
of information from the mass of raw data he receives and organising
them into a conventional journalistic form.

(Chibnall 1981:76)

The work of Fowler has exercised considerable influence on this part of the
research. In his study of discourse and ideology in the press, he states 'my
major concern is with the role of linguistic structure in the construction
of ideas in the press' (1991:1). Another fundamental text for research on

newspaper discourse is Bell (1991) on the language of news media, which combines the insights of a linguist with the experience of a working journalist, as does White (1997), whose work on distinguishing journalistic discourse types is an important basis for further research. Morley (2004a, 2004b) and Murphy and Morley (2006) have looked at the difference between news stories, editorials, and op-eds. This is the aspect of the research which is followed up in Murphy's chapter on newspapers (Chapter 7).

0.2.5. The Hutton Inquiry (Project 6)

Like the projects on parliamentary discourse and presidential press briefings, the Hutton Inquiry project deals with spoken language in an institutional context, an area of linguistic study set out in systematic form in Drew and Heritage (1992). In July 2003 the British prime minister appointed Lord Hutton to head an inquiry into the circumstances surrounding the death of Dr David Kelly, a scientist working for the government in weapons inspection. A BBC journalist, Andrew Gilligan, claimed that an unnamed source, who was later discovered to be Dr Kelly, had told him that information contained in an intelligence report had been "sexed up" in a government document justifying going to war. Dr Kelly was caught in the cross fire between the BBC and the government and committed suicide under the strain. (cf. note 5 of Chapter 9 for more details.). Here we were working with official transcripts made available on the Hutton Inquiry Web site, http://www.the-hutton-inquiry.org.uk/. The inquiry was directed by Lord Hutton and offers the researcher the possibility of comparing two related but fundamentally different discourse types—information collecting and adversarial probing of the information supplied. Texts which form the basis of research on these discourse types are Grimshaw (1990), Hutchby (1996), and Partington (2003), all of which examine the discourse involved in conflictual situations, particularly in political and institutional contexts. A linguistic analysis of these inquiries presents the opportunity for Taylor to examine a hitherto rarely explored discourse type (Chapter 8).

0.3. MARKUP

The *CorDis Corpus* is a multigeneric corpus containing over five million tokens and about fifty thousand types of both writing and transcribed speech. The corpus brings together eight subcorpora or modules. The construction of a modular corpus brings some practical advantages in that each module can be used independently and could at some moment in the future be added to at will (see Haarman et al. 2002). The corpus was marked up by a team based at the University of Bologna's School for Interpreters and Translators in Forlì, overseen by Guy Aston, as a set of Extensible Markup

Language (XML) documents which conformed to the Text Encoding Initiative (TEI) guidelines. It was designed to be interrogated by *Xaira* (XML Aware Indexing and Retrieval Application), a software developed by Burnard and Dodd at Oxford University Computing Services (see the Web site http://www.xaira.org). The *CorDis Corpus* served as a one of the test beds for the development of that software. It was tagged for part of speech and lemmatized by Rayson's group at Lancaster University, using the CLAWS7 tagset (see Rayson and Garside 1998).

Initially, the markup was seen as being simply ancillary to the work of analysis, which was to come after its completion. In practice, we found that marking up the text was in itself a form of text analysis. This is particularly true of the sections of the corpus containing the *BBC* and *CBS* news programmes. There were no ready-made categories existing for the structure of TV news in the TEI guidelines, and so our divisions had to be based on work already done by members of the research team, in particular by Haarman (see the chapters by Lombardo and Clark on TV news in this volume).

0.3.1. TV News Markup

Some of Haarman's markup codes can be applied to any television news programme;[3] others are specific to the news programmes in the TV news subcorpus which is part of the *CorDis Corpus*. First of all, each news report is indicated as a separate section by the markup. Headlines are then identified and coded; if they appear on the screen, they are also coded for that. Different speakers' utterances are identified, with markup to indicate the identity, sex, and role of the speaker. The default situation is that speakers talk to the camera. If s/he speaks in voice-over, this too is indicated. When the newsreader introduces a reporter's report, this is also indicated in the markup. The reporter's report also includes coding for his/her precise role, whether s/he is a:

- studio reporter
- embedded reporter
- war zone correspondent
- correspondent (e.g., from Baghdad, Washington, Brussels)
- reporter plain and simple.

Different parts of the utterance are marked up as one of the following:

- text spoken by the reporter over video actualities
- text spoken by the reporter to camera
- text spoken by the reporter via telephone link.

Apart from the reporters and studio presenters, other speakers too are identified by their functions, either as:

- legitimated persons: that is, speakers who have the status to speak for others because of their status, e.g., politicians, professors, doctors, experts of some kind
- *vox populi*: that is, members of the public, normally unnamed
- military: that is, members of the military who have not sufficient status to count as legitimated persons.

Where relevant, addressees of utterances are indicated (such as questions asked by a reporter to a legitimated person or a *vox populi*, or by a newsreader to a reporter, or vice versa).

All the codings involved decisions about the importance of these sections of text for the analysis of a television news programme and are the result of research questions formulated by the colleagues working on television news programmes.

Although a considerable amount of time and effort, and a large amount of our research funding, was dedicated to marking up the corpus so that it could be interrogated by the *Xaira* software, we did not abandon *WordSmith Tools*, the software that most of us had 'grown up' with. There were a number of reasons for this, apart from the comfort of familiarity: first of all, we were anxious to get on with our analyses as soon as the corpus existed in an exploitable form and did not want to wait for the lengthy process of the XML, TEI conformant markup to be completed—about forty presentations and papers have been produced in the three years since the project began, many of which will be cited by the authors of the various chapters. Secondly, *WordSmith Tools*, both version 3 (Scott 1999) and version 4 (Scott 2005), produce instantaneous word lists and keyword lists, which are often the birthing point of research questions. And finally, as we were all working with relatively modestly sized subcorpora, on average about a million tokens, of text-only files, it was sometimes possible to add what our markup experts call 'light markup' (see Chapter 1), tailor-made for individual research questions.

A number of corpus linguists, notably Sinclair (2004:190–1), have argued that some forms of markup condition and prejudice later researchers' exploration of the corpus, but we hope to 'use tags en route to the language, and not just stop there', to quote his own words (2004: 191). We believe, as Cirillo, Venuti, and Marchi argue in Chapter 1, that markup favours replicability and enhances the reliability of the research. Careful markup of the rhetorical structure of texts certainly aids the work of comparison between these different parts of the discourse structure.

0.4. COMPARISON

Corpus-assisted discourse analysis, the kind of corpus linguistics embodied in this project, of necessity entails comparison, both at a fundamental ideological level and also in many methodological-practical ways. In general terms, the statement that any given linguistic feature being studied is frequent or infrequent in the discourse type contained in corpus X only has proper contextual significance when corpus X is compared to corpus Y, which normally contains another discourse type. The choice of corpus Y, the comparison or background corpus, needs to be carefully made. We may want to compare a specialized discourse type against general English, in which case our Y corpus will be one of the large corpora of general English, such as the *BNC*. We may, on the other hand, wish to compare one kind of specialized discourse with another kind of, perhaps superficially similar, specialized discourse: we may, for instance, be asking if editorial articles (corpus X) differ from op-ed articles (corpus Y) (see Murphy, Chapter 7). Or we may be interested in diachronic change: it could be that we want to know if White House press conference language has changed since before 9/11 (Riccio, Chapter 4). In this case the X and Y corpora will be of the same discourse type but from different historical moments.

One thing which markup clearly does is allow the researcher to identify quickly and efficiently subparts of a corpus and compare them against one another. We might illustrate this by looking at the newspaper subcorpora. It was decided to divide the newspaper section of the *CorDis Corpus* into three subcorpora—news reports, editorials, and op-eds—because two members of the project group, Murphy and Morley, were already conducting research into the linguistic differences between these discourse types. (This is also an illustration of the observation made by Cirillo, Venuti, and Marchi in Chapter 1 that some elements of the structure of the *CorDis Corpus* were predetermined.)

We then had to decide what other divisions of the newspapers were important for us as researchers. It was fairly obvious that we needed to be able to distinguish the individual newspapers, for instance, the *Guardian* from the *Daily Mirror*. An early piece of research showed differences between the attitudes towards certain aspects of the war of these two newspapers, a left-wing quality and a left-wing popular newspaper (Morley 2005). It was also clear that we wanted to be able to distinguish between UK and US newspapers and between the quality and popular papers as groups, in order to be able to make comparisons between these. As a result of marking up these distinctions it is possible to use the *Xaira* software to make even more precise ad hoc partitions, such as one containing the word *soldiers* in the editorials of US popular newspapers published in a particular week. It would also, for instance, be possible to compare the discourse of all female Democrats with that of all male Republicans. None of us has so far interrogated the corpus in these terms, at least more than informally, but it would be possible and *Xaira* would provide us with elegant histograms or pie charts to illustrate our data.

Another example of the flexibility which *Xaira* affords can be seen in Duguid's work (Chapter 9), where she compares the words which speakers and writers use to report other discourses across all the subcorpora (the Hutton Inquiry, the White House press conferences, Hansard, the House of Representatives, TV news, and the three newspaper subcorpora—editorial, op-eds, and news reports).

As well as inter- and intra-subcorpus comparison, many of the authors of the book make use of large background corpora. The *BNC*, the new version of which can now be searched by *Xaira* software, is the most commonly used as it represents a large, easily accessible and very reliable corpus of texts which allows us to compare our specialized subcorpora with relatively modern general British English.[4] Partington (Chapter 10), instead, references *SiBol 05*, a collection of more than 150 million words of quality English newspaper texts published in 2005. This was more appropriate than the *BNC* for his research as some of the lexical items he looks at are of relatively recent press coinage.

0.5. CORPUS-ASSISTED DISCOURSE ANALYSIS

Tognini-Bonelli has made an important distinction between 'corpus-based' and 'corpus-driven' linguistics (Tognini-Bonelli 2001:10–11). The corpus-based approach uses the corpus as a library of texts to be searched to test preformed hypotheses. In corpus-driven studies, on the other hand, 'the theoretical statement can only be formulated in the presence of corpus evidence and is fully accountable to it' (Tognini-Bonelli, 11). We have to trust the texts. The first approach illustrates what Ellis (1985) calls 'the theory-then-research approach', or deductive reasoning, and the second 'the research-then-theory approach', or inductive reasoning. This is a very important distinction and it is fairly easy to assign most corpus studies to one approach or the other.

Those of us who adopt a CADS approach would argue, however, that one approach does not necessarily exclude the other. What frequently happens is that we generate a word list, read through it, and our intuition tells us that certain words or clusters are going to be interesting. To give a simple example, I composed a word list of four-word clusters from a half-million-word corpus of newspaper news articles on political reporting. This was done with no idea of what, if anything, of interest would come out. The same was done for a half-million-word corpus of editorial articles from the same period and the same newspapers. The 'key-most' cluster for the reports compared to the editorials turned out to be *for the first time*. My intuition, or rather my intuition primed by years of reading newspapers and about newspapers, immediately suggested to me that this was an interesting cluster: it was an illustration of the scoop mentality of Anglo-American newspapers. The next step was to look at the sixteen instances of *for the first time* and check what their function was in the wider context of the whole article. To recapitulate, then, we have three stages in this research:

(1) the software throws up the clusters *for the first* time as being significantly more frequent in news reports than in editorials, (2) intuition tells us there is reason for this, (3) we check by a close examination of texts to see if our intuition is correct.

A less obvious finding came from the four-word clusters of the editorial corpus: the fifth most frequent cluster was *at the heart of*, with a frequency of fifty-eight per million words.[5] The corpus contained editorials from popular and quality English newspapers printed over a period of two years in twenty-seven different articles, so there was no chance that this statistic was generated by some leader-writer's idiolect; its frequency in the whole of the *BNC* was 9.6 per million words. The cluster is clearly characteristic of editorial writing in English newspapers in the early years of the millennium. To this day I have no idea why. It was a purely serendipitous find (see Partington and Morley 2004 for details of this research).

In general, we can say that CADS methodology is predicated on the belief that the combined use of qualitative and quantitative linguistic analysis is not only possible but that their combined application increases the researcher's analytical capacity to an extent greater than would be predicted from the sum of the two methods. As in all forms of corpus linguistics the concordance line remains fundamental and collocations, which we find normally from scanning the concordance lines, are as Hoey so tellingly puts it, 'both pervasive and subversive' (Hoey 2005:3).[6] However, the bare concordance line strips away most of the context of the original utterance, without which the study of features of discourse becomes problematic. As Biber et al. (1999) say,

> [A]lthough nearly all discourse studies are based on analysis of actual texts, they are not typically corpus-based investigations: most studies do not use quantitative methods to describe the extent to which different discourse structures are used.
>
> (Biber et al. 1999:106)

Our solution is to move backwards and forwards—to shunt, to use a Hallidayan term (1961, in 2002:45)—from the concordance line to the wider cotext. Reading vertically allows one to see patterns, but we also need to read horizontally to arrive more securely at meanings.

The first mention of CADS methodology as such is Partington (2004a), and the final chapter of the current work presents some of his further reflections upon its scientific significance. It builds on the pioneering article of Hardt-Mautner (1995) and has been greatly influenced by the concrete examples put forward by Stubbs in two of his volumes (1996, 2001). We also feel an affinity with the work described by Baker in *Using Corpora in Discourse Analysis* (Baker 2006). The methodology has informed the research of most members of the group for some time now. We believe, however, that the current volume is one of the first works that uses CADS methodology to treat a single theme, in this case the Iraq war, in a book-length study.

NOTES

1. These were the University of Bologna, 'LUISS, Guido Carli' in Rome, and the University of Siena.
2. Ministry protocol number 2004105247.
3. There is a sister volume to this book based exclusively on the TV subcorpora of the *CorDis Corpus*, Haarman, L. and Lombardo, L. (2009) *Evaluation and Stance in War News: A Linguistic Analysis of American, British and Italian Television News Reporting of the 2003 Iraqi War*, London: Continuum. This book also deals with Italian TV data.
4. We had no access to the *American National Corpus*.
5. Biber refers to clusters which occur at least 10 times per million words (0.0001 times per hundred words) as 'lexical bundles' and argues that they often characterize discourse types (see Biber et al. 1999).
6. Partington (2003), speaking of the importance of comparison in corpus work, also calls this methodology 'subversive' when he argues that our students can use the corpus to test 'what they have learned from some authority, such as their textbook or teacher? (p. 20)

1 The Making of the *CorDis Corpus*
Compilation and Markup

*Letizia Cirillo, Anna Marchi,
and Marco Venuti*

This chapter sets out to describe how different subcorpora were integrated to form the unified body of texts known as the *CorDis Corpus*. In particular, it focuses on the process whereby *CorDis* was made an XML-valid, TEI-conformant corpus that can be easily interrogated using *Xaira*. In discussing specific examples illustrating the practice of markup, the chapter highlights the import of annotation as a way to enhance reliability of research and (re-)usability of data.[1]

1.1. INTRODUCTION: AN AIR SCOUT VIEW

The *CorDis Corpus* is a large multimode, multigenre collection of political and media discourse on the 2003 Iraqi conflict.[2] It was generated from different subcorpora previously assembled by various research groups for diverse discourse analytical purposes. A more detailed description of its composition can be found in the introduction.

A significant portion of our work was devoted to making the subcorpora into a unified homogeneously encoded corpus which could be interrogated using *Xaira*.[3] Initially the corpus was only lightly encoded by each research group on the basis of specific research objectives and hypotheses. The heterogeneity of data, the specificity of the genres, and the various methods adopted involved the use of a wide range of coding strategies to make textual and metatextual information retrievable by means of available concordance software. It was clear from the outset that marking up the corpus as a whole would entail various levels of pre-encoded and pre-existing interpretation. The main purpose of this chapter is to show the process of standardization and integration whereby a loose collection of texts has become a stable architecture. The TEI Guidelines proved a valid instrument providing for a hierarchical organization of metadata which makes markup part and parcel of the corpus. We will underline that it is precisely the markup which gives the corpus a sound structure favouring the replicability and enhancing reliability of research.

In discussing examples, we will deal with issues like conformity and validity, and we will examine the constraints imposed on data handling by the methodological framework adopted. In particular, we will argue that the crucial role of annotation leads to a reconsideration of the definition of corpus itself, in which special emphasis is placed on markup being the backbone of the corpus rather than a superimposed accessory.

There is a tendency to distinguish between 'markup' and 'annotation' (McEnery, Xiao, and Tono 2006:29), adopting the first term to refer to contextual information (i.e., editorial and descriptive metadata) and the second to refer to 'interpretative linguistic information'. We will here use the two terms interchangeably, since both notions share the same salient qualities for the purposes of our description: they are both *added value* and they both carry *interpretative information.*[4]

Finally, the fact that markup involves a substantial amount of human intervention on machine-processed data has some crucial implications for corpus-assisted discourse studies (CADS), since it permits the combination of qualitative and quantitative research approaches.

1.2. TERRITORY

We will start by introducing the *territory* of our work, providing a short description of the various components of the *CorDis Corpus* in order to highlight some of the difficulties we had to deal with. This overview of the subcorpora will lead to some mainly theoretical considerations of the role of annotation in corpus design, and to an evaluation of the annotation scheme adopted.

1.2.1. *CorDis*: One Corpus/Many Corpora

As implied in the introduction, *CorDis* is an XML, TEI-conformant, POS-tagged, multimode, multigenre corpus containing over five million word tokens (corresponding to about 50,000 types). It is made up of eight subcorpora of texts from the following sources: British House of Commons (*HoC*), US House of Representatives (*HoR*), White House press briefings (*WHB*), television news (*TVNews*), newspaper reports (*PapNews*), newspaper editorials (*PapEds*), newspaper op-eds (*PapOp*), and Hutton Inquiry (*HUTTON*). Further details about the harmonization of metadata will be presented in sections 1.3.2 and 1.3.3. Here we introduce some of the specificities of these subcorpora in order to illustrate the kinds of issues we have encountered.

The subcorpora include a variety of modes of language use occupying different positions on a written-spoken continuum: official transcripts of speech (Hutton Inquiry, Congressional Record, Hansard, White House press briefings, all of which are heavily edited and adapted for publication in written form), unofficial transcripts of speech (TV news programmes, aiming to provide an accurate record of what was said without necessarily conforming to strict conventions of published writing), and published writing (newspaper articles); they also include two main geographical linguistic and cultural varieties—American (Congressional Record, White House press briefings, US newspaper articles, and *CBS* TV news) and British (Hutton Inquiry, Hansard, British newspaper articles, and *BBC* TV news). According to the nature of the texts and to particular research objectives, further specification of these text types had to be made explicit. Thus it was necessary to distinguish between different stages of the Hutton Inquiry (Lord Hutton's opening statement presenting the purpose and the structure of the inquiry, taking of witness statements, cross-examinations) and different types of parliamentary proceedings (e.g., Question Time, statements, speeches, and debates—government or opposition-initiated—just to name a few). To take into account all these aspects, we elaborated a series of categorization schemes. Each of these categorizations provides a different way of dividing up the corpus, known as a *partition*: each partition offers a set of classes in which each individual text can be placed.

Each of the subcorpora also posed specific needs related to the institutional or professional context of the texts, their official status, the discourse setting, and also the particular discourse analytic approach taken by the researchers. Obviously all relevant metadata needed to be encoded in order to make them retrievable by means of dedicated software. Using *Xaira*, which will be described in more detail in 1.3.1, it was possible to instantly select as a subcorpus those texts contained in a particular class of a particular partition. Partitions include *mode* (official transcripts, spoken, and written), *origin* (British vs. American), and *source* (see earlier for the full list). A further partition, *specific*, was used to select each specific source (e.g., a single newspaper or TV news programme) or discourse type (e.g., a debate in the Congressional Record or the Question Time in Hansard), as exemplified in Figure 1.1.

Having outlined the main characteristics of the *CorDis* corpus, we can now move to examine some theoretical and practical issues related to the process of annotation.

1.2.2. The Rationale of Annotation: Marking a Path through the Data

Corpus annotation is the 'practice of adding interpretative linguistic information to a corpus' (Leech 1997:2). This definition stresses two fundamental concepts: when we mark up we *add* information, and in modelling this information we are doing *interpretative* work. Annotation is inserted into the text in order to convey meaning and the operation of reflecting, representing, or creating meaning always implies a selection among a series of possibilities. 'Markup *licenses certain inferences* about the text' (Sperberg-McQueen, Huitfeldt, and Renear 2000: online; original emphasis); each selection privileges some meanings over others and therefore marking up is marking a path through the data.

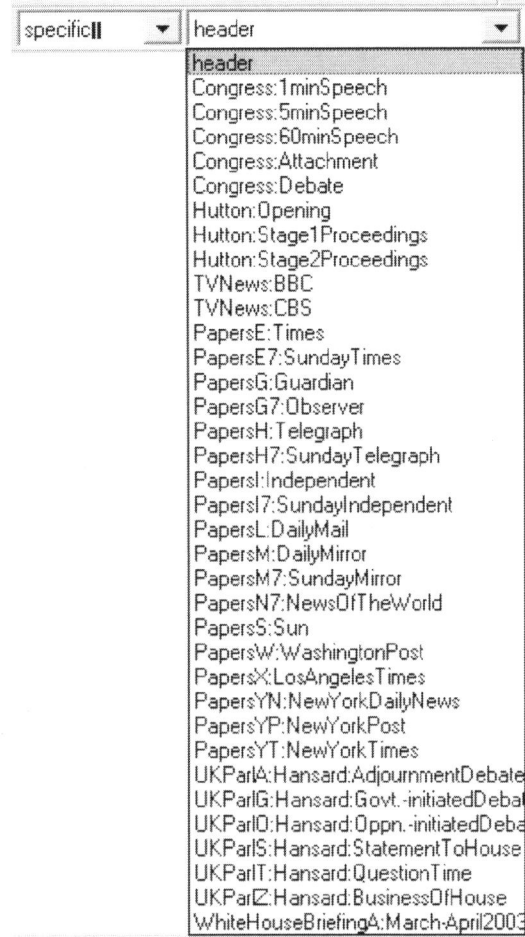

Figure 1.1   Xaira's 'specific' partition for *CorDis.*

Here we argue that annotation, with specific reference to the XML-valid, TEI-conformant markup used in the *CorDis Corpus,* is not merely an accessory to the corpus, a tool that the researcher can use to investigate portions and properties of the texts, but is an intrinsic part of the corpus itself, since it is the annotation that makes the *CorDis Corpus* usable as a whole harmonized and coherent body of texts.

Marking up *CorDis* was crucial for various reasons. These are related both to the general motivations that make the time-consuming task of annotation worthwhile and to the specific nature of the corpus. On the one hand, annotation makes it possible to sharpen the analysis, forcing 'the analyst to test and refine the system of categorization to account for all cases' (Wynne 2005:2), produces more detailed results, and provides a base for replicability of the study and reusability of the data. On the other hand, the *CorDis* project is based on a collection of heterogeneous texts and text types that finds a common core in its topic (Iraq war in 2003) and in the methods of analysis adopted (CADS) which needs to be harmonized in order to work as an organic apparatus.

'Corpora are useful only if we can extract knowledge or information from them' (Leech 1997:4). Markup is *added value* because it makes built-in information retrievable, allowing the user to access knowledge about the data in the corpus that would be lost if it had not been made explicit in the first place through annotation.

Being retrievable, this information/knowledge is also reusable. Markup is also *added value* because it enhances reusability, both in the sense that it makes research easily replicable and in the sense that it makes the data readily shareable by a variety of potential users and for a range of different uses ('[. . .] the annotations themselves spark off a whole new range of uses which would not have been practicable unless the corpus had been annotated', Leech 2005, online). Not only does annotation facilitate the sharing of the corpus as resource, but it also encourages the sharing of analytic tools and of progressive results. Annotation provides a trace of the interpretative work carried out on the texts.

> Metadata plays a key role in organizing the ways in which a language corpus can be meaningfully processed. It records the interpretative framework within which the components of a corpus were selected and are to be understood.
>
> (Burnard 2004:15)

The annotation of a corpus, the selection and application of the tag set, expresses a theory about the texts: deciding which are the important characteristics that make up the identity of a source (in the case of the press, for example, the type of news—editorial, op-ed, report—the type of newspaper—tabloid vs. quality—etc.), or deciding on a unit of analysis for that source (e.g., all the articles from a single newspaper, or a single article) are operations that involve several degrees of selection, thus interpretation.

The mere fact of looking at texts in terms of uses, transforming them from texts to *textual resources* (Atkins, Levin and Zampolli 1994), implies a large amount of interpretative work, precisely because use is interpretation. More specifically, the practice of marking up is interpretation in that it involves a manipulation of the data; the text is preserved in its integrity but we superimpose on it a structure that 'speaks' of the text. The very term *markup* is borrowed from the publishing and printing business, where it indicates the instructions for the typesetter that are written on a typescript or manuscript copy by an editor and in this sense 'compilers have the responsibility typically associated with an editor' (Atkins, Levin and Zampolli 1994:34).

The annotation process is of course supported by automation, but because of the ambiguous nature of language there is a constant need for human intervention and a great amount of manual work needs to be done.

Human beings can disambiguate problems, but as humans we are prone to error and inconsistency and our choices, interpretations, and often compromises have to be specified and checked against a formalized annotation scheme in order for them to be consistent throughout the corpus.

In marking up the *CorDis Corpus*, consistency was our main concern. *CorDis* is a composite corpus, with specific problems: the variety of its text types, different levels of annotation to be managed, and different variables to be equally taken into consideration. We have dealt with differences of origin (British English, American English), differences of genre (judicial inquiry, press briefings, parliamentary debates, print and TV news), and differences of mode (writing, published official transcripts, informally transcribed speech). Originally the six different subcorpora assembled by different research groups already contained some markup on the basis of categories that the original compilers and researchers wanted to investigate but this had not been carried out according to shared norms, was not TEI-conformant, and in many cases had not been consistently applied.

Our goal consisted in consolidating all this in a single corpus, which had to be coherently marked up without losing the information which had been added by these initial attempts. In our operation of interpretation through markup we had to deal with the constraints of pre-existing interpretation, trying to preserve its richness but at the same time negotiating categories and labels. Layers of interpretation start piling up from the moment research objectives are posed, all through the process of corpus design, representation, and, of course, annotation. In addition each step involves the intervention of a number of different people. Each phase and each contribution produced knowledge about the corpus and was therefore part and parcel of the research process, but this compositeness also increased the global complexity, multiplying categories and favouring overlapping of annotation levels. It was therefore essential to strive towards some kind of standardization. 'Standardization of annotation practices can ensure that an annotated corpus can be used to its greatest potential' (Kahrel, Barnett, and Leech 1997:231), and as we will show in this chapter, aiming for TEI conformance gave the corpus a sound structure, enhancing reliability and favouring (re)usability.

1.2.3. Preliminary Information: Markup Language and Annotation Schemes

CorDis is an XML-valid, TEI-conformant corpus. Although it is not our aim here to dwell on technicalities, a few clarifications are in order to explain what these two expressions imply. The data were encoded using XML (extensible markup language), a metalanguage that enables compilers to design their own customized markup conventions for different types of documents. To say that a document (or an entire corpus) is XML-valid means first of all that it must be *well-formed*, that is, it must comply with the rules of the XML syntax. For instance, well-formed documents must be formed of members of a set of elements, each of which may have a set of attributes, and each attribute must be assigned a value. Elements containing other elements or portions of text must be preceded by a start-tag and followed by an end-tag with the forms <elementname> and </elementname>. Attributes and their values must be stated on start-tags, taking the form <elementname attributename1="value1" attributename2= "value2" [. . .]>.

Validity, however, goes beyond well-formedness, as *valid* documents must further conform to a schema of some kind, that is, they have to be formally checked against it. The schema is, trivially speaking, a 'declara-tion' of what markup is allowed/required where a specification of syntax rules. However, if, as we saw in section 1.2.2, encoding consists in making interpretations of a text explicit, then the semantics of the markup should also be specified. It is here that the TEI Guidelines come into play. The guidelines, of which we have employed the P5 version (Sperberg-McQueen and Burnard 2007, online), are intended to provide standards for data inter-change between researchers using different systems and applications and to suggest principles for the encoding of texts in the same format (Sperberg-McQueen and Burnard 2007, online). To be more precise,

> [t]hey provide means of representing those features of a text which need to be identified explicitly in order to facilitate processing of the text by computer programs. In particular, they specify a set of markers (or tags) which may be inserted in the electronic representation of the text, in order to mark the text structure and other textual features of interest.
>
> (Sperberg-McQueen and Burnard 2007, online)

For convenience, tags for the elements and attributes defined by the TEI Guidelines are grouped in 23 modules (cf. Sperberg-McQueen and Burnard 2007, online for the full list), each of which contains a set of declarations used to define elements/attributes and their characteristics. Each module is typically associated with a specific usage; for instance, the module *spoken* is intended for use with transcribed speech, the module *analysis* is designed to provide simple analytic mechanisms, the module *linking* caters for seg-mentation, alignment, and linking both within and between texts, and so on. Modules can be variously combined to form a *TEI-conformant* schema against which documents must be validated.[5] To be TEI-conformant, then, a document must be annotated using the tags that are included in the TEI modules and for which declarations are delivered in the associated schema. Moreover, each TEI-conformant text must necessarily be preceded by a TEI header, that is, an encoded unit of information containing metadata. The header provides a set of descriptions and declarations regarding the document itself and the source it is taken from (e.g., bibliographic data), its profile (categorizations of the text, and, for transcribed speech, informa-tion about the setting and the participants involved), its encoding, and its history of revisions (if any).

So far, we have generally referred to a supposedly *unitary* TEI document/ text. However, a TEI text can also be *composite*, as is clearly the case with a corpus. Although the encoding of a corpus is based on the same principles as the encoding of a single text, the TEI Guidelines specifically provide for annotation of large collections of texts. Customization of markup for a multimode, multigenre corpus like *CorDis* implies using a combination of elements drawn from many different modules, and defining a corpus as a series of <TEI> documents sharing a common TEI header—the corpus header—which includes such information as bibliographic data for the corpus as a whole, the various text categorization schemes employed (what we have termed partitions and their classes), and features of encoding and revision which are shared by all the documents in the corpus. The corpus header is a separate file obtained as a modified version of the standard TEI header. It is a fundamental unit of information, in that besides containing important documentary data it also provides specific processing directives for indexing and searching applications like *Xaira*.

Xaira will be described in some detail in the following section. However, it is worth spending a few words here on the *Xaira* IndexTools Utility. This is used to construct a database which makes the corpus *Xaira*-searchable. Its main function is 'to collect information about the corpus to be supplied additional to that present in any pre-existing corpus header, and to produce a validated and extended form of the corpus header' (OUCS 2006b). Moreover, and more interestingly for the purposes of this chapter, it can be used to run the indexer and test its output. We will shortly come back to *testing*. Suffice it to say here that in addition to the corpus header, and of course the files making up the corpus proper, the indexer requires: a corpus parameter file, which defines the name (of the corpus) and the locations of the files required and to be created by the indexer, another file listing the files making up the corpus, and a bibliography file, which contains 'descriptive metadata about each source text making up the corpus' (OUCS 2006a).

1.3. MAP

Now that the methodological framework has been set, it is our aim to show the path we have constructed through the data, making reference to the practices and tools adopted. The translation of the conceptual architecture into an operative structure sprang from a series of questions concerning the harmonization process. The gradual and recursive annotation work will be illustrated through examples, highlighting some of the problems encountered and the strategies elaborated to overcome them.

1.3.1. Architecture and Tools: Going *Xaira*

We have already discussed the benefits of annotation and we have sketched the characteristics of XML TEI conformant markup, introducing the concepts of well-formedness and validity and their implications in terms of reliability and consistency. A criticism that has been made of the TEI Guidelines is that of being overprescriptive and excessively complicated, and thus not flexible enough. However, the verbosity and rigour of the XML TEI compliant markup language enhance the stability that is indispensable for reusability, and reusability itself may contribute to flexibility.

> Corpora have a long active life, and as technology moves on, it becomes possible to exploit them in ways not envisaged by the original designers. This puts a high premium on *flexibility*. While we cannot predict future research needs, we can predict that there will be such needs. The corpus architecture must be such that it can be adapted to new situations as new research paradigms emerge.
>
> (Ide and Brew 2000:1, emphasis added)

Saying that our annotation aims for stability is not in contradiction with affirming that it grants flexibility. If *flexible* is something that 'is able to change easily and adapt to different conditions and circumstances as they occur' (*Collins Cobuild English Dictionary* 2001), it follows that *flexibility* does not only reside in the characteristics of an object, but it also depends on the potential of the environment. The corpus environment that has been created through a rich annotation multiplies the possible ways in which we can use the data. Annotation is ultimately added value in that it allows us to ask/generate new questions and this generativity is a consequence of the corpus's architecture.

This moves the spotlight onto the tool that was adopted to index, refine, and interrogate the corpus. It has been said that *CorDis* was a complex and composite collection that has been turned into a harmonious corpus. By using *Xaira* features, such as partitions and complex XML queries, we are able to manage *CorDis* modularity and maximally gain from the corpus' rich annotation.

Xaira can handle a considerable quantity of heavily marked-up texts. *CorDis*, as we mentioned before, contains some twelve million XML elements altogether; excluding word and punctuation tags there are 511,773 searchable elements, corresponding to twenty-seven element types.

We will not review here in detail the characteristics of *Xaira*, but we argue that the software carries into the analysis its own logic; therefore, using a different tool implies adopting a different logic. What has changed by integrating and converting the initial light markup into the final XML TEI conformant output is not only the structure and the representation of the data, but the very approach to the corpus. *Xaira* allows us to ask complex and articulated questions and exploit the full potential of annotation. The data can be accessed in a number of ways and the *Xaira* client provides a variety of search possibilities: words, lemmas, phrases, regular expressions, parts of speech, specific XML element tags, and attribute values, any of which can be combined in searches for co-occurrences within the same document or portion of a document, and any of which may be restricted to particular classes of documents.

It is not our intention here to describe in detail the information that can be extracted from *CorDis* using *Xaira*'s search tools, but we would like to exemplify a couple of things that can be done with them and that are particularly useful in querying the corpus:

Creating Partitions

Five different *CorDis* partitions were agreed upon as the corpus was being created, in order to be able to recover the original subcorpora and to analyze transversal salient features (Mode, Origin, Source, Specific and Whoddunit). But as well as using the partitions and classes provided in the markup, it is possible to define alternative ways to classify the corpus texts. This allows the user to reshape the data on the basis of parameters that respond to their specific research interests. Partitions can be created manually, by going through the list of file-names and assigning files to different classes (e.g., tabloid newspapers vs. broadsheets vs. other kinds of texts), or automatically, by using a query to class texts as matching that query or not (e.g., texts which include mentions of 'weapons of mass destruction' against those which do not, or texts which include speech by Tony Blair against those which do not).

Building Complex Queries

Xaira's Query Builder allows us to combine different kinds of query (word/phrase, pattern, XML, part of speech) and to establish different relationships among them. We have to define the *scope* of the query as having to be satisfied within an XML element with particular values on particular attributes, or alternatively within the span of a specific number of words, and one or more *content* nodes that state what we are searching for within that scope. As illustrated in Figure 1.2, content nodes can be linked in various ways: nodes linked horizontally have an OR relation (one or both of the queries represented in those nodes must be satisfied), while nodes connected vertically have an AND relation, whose interpretation is specified (and visualized by the form of the link) as NEXT (the lower query must be satisfied by or before the next word), ONE-WAY (the lower query must be satisfied at any point within the scope following the upper query) or TWO-WAY (the two queries may be satisfied in either order). The structure of the Query Builder interface itself gives an idea of the complexity of the questions that can be asked. The example in Figure 1.2 will search all instances of the lemma *war* immediately followed by a preposition immediately followed by *terror* or *Iraq*, followed by a modal verb, all within a total span of five words.

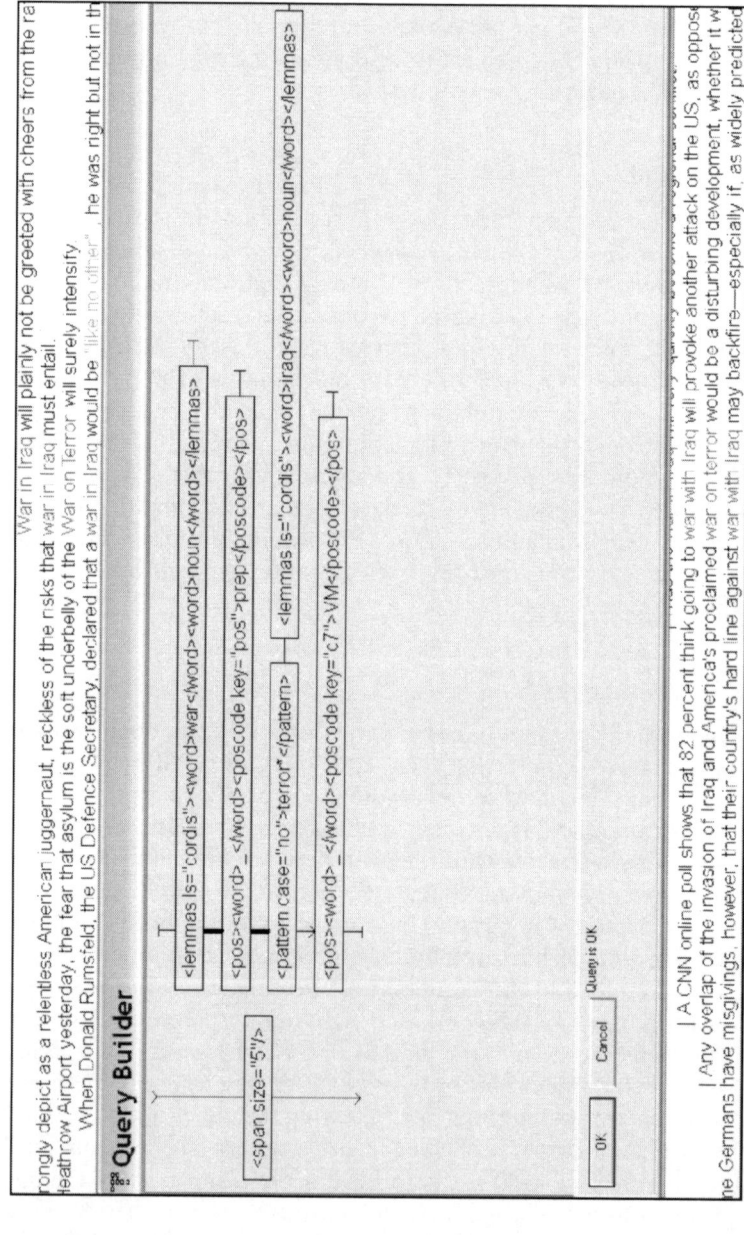

Figure 1.2   Xaira's query builder.

1.3.2. The Practice of Markup: Getting our Hands Dirty

As already mentioned, our main task was to assemble already-existing collections of texts gathered and lightly annotated by various research groups into a unified body of texts. In doing so, the first step we had to take was choosing an appropriate tagset. The composite nature of the object we intended to build required us to draw upon different TEI modules, including the *core* tagset, a combination of *base* tagsets, and some *additional* tagsets (cf. Sperberg-McQueen and Burnard 2007, online; 2.3). By way of a simplification, we can divide the tags used into three main classes: tags containing editorial metadata, tags containing analytic metadata, and tags containing descriptive metadata (cf. Burnard 2004). The first class includes markers used to make interventions like omission or correction explicit (e.g., <gap desc="omitted_from_quote"/>; the second groups structural tags (indicating paragraphs, sentences, words, etc.) and tags used to define style and textual functions (such as emphasis or quotation, e.g., <s> most critics denounced the programme as <q who="_expert"> 'unduly non-intrusive' </q></s>); the third typically provides information related to the context in which the text was produced/received (e.g., <time>10.30 am</time>). In the *CorDis Corpus* most tags belong to the second class; in particular most of them are of the structural kind, ranging from large textual divisions (the <div> tags), through paragraphs, utterances and sentences (<p>, <u>, and <s>, respectively), to words and punctuation marks (<w> and <c>, respectively, with <w> including attributes for part of speech and lemma).[6]

The choice of specific tagsets for the corpus was the first step in a gradual process of standardization, whereby the initial contextual information provided with the texts by the various research groups involved in the project was codified in such a way as to guarantee consistency as well as a reasonable degree of granularity of annotation. This clearly implied ongoing editing work on the corpus, which evolved from the initial *raw texts* and intuitive forms of annotation to the final product, through a series of progressively more refined XML-valid, TEI-conformant versions. Such an evolution can be best appreciated by looking at example (1), following, which is taken from the TV news section of *CorDis:*[7]

(1) a) [Rageh Omaar] (Rageh Omaar Baghdad)
     Finally the war has come to the heart of Baghdad. [. . .] Rageh Omaar, BBC News, Baghdad.

     b) <div2 type="report" resp="reporter:warzone">
     <u who="Omaar_Rageh" sex="m" role="reporter:warzone" dialect="en-GB" type="voiceover">
     <writing type="subtitle"><s n="20"> Rageh Omaar Baghdad</s> </writing>

<s n="21"> Finally the war has come to the heart of Baghdad.</s>
[. . .]
<s n="37"> Rageh Omaar, BBC News, Baghdad.</s>
</u> [. . .] </div2>

(BBC News, 20 March 2003)

Example (1) bears witness to the evolution of the <u> element (hereafter utterance) in *CorDis* drawing on the earliest (1a) and the latest (1b) version of the corpus. [8, 9] In (1a) the contents of square brackets and parentheses correspond to the name of the speaker and the text appearing on screen, respectively. The TV news research groups subsequently added their own customised tags to provide further contextual information indicating the type of news (in this case a report), the person responsible for producing it (a reporter), the speaker (a war-zone correspondent, whose name is displayed as a subtitle), and the relationship between the words he utters and images (in this case voice-over rather than on camera). In (1b) all this information is made explicit and ordered through attribute values, depending on whether it refers to text structure and style (here <div2 type="report" resp="reporter:warzone" and <writing type="subtitle">[. . .] Rageh Omaar Baghdad [. . .]</writing>) or to the speaker (<u who="Omaar_Rageh" sex="m" role="reporter:warzone" dialect="en-GB" type="voiceover">). In other words, the previous intuitive, although not always transparent, tagging has been modified so as to meet the requirements of *perspicuity* and *analyzability* (Leech 1997:25).

Examples (2) and (3), from the Hutton Inquiry and the US Congressional Debates sections of *CorDis,* respectively, further illustrate the markup standardization process:

(2) a) <event desc="Hearing adjourned until 10.30 am the following day"/>

   b) <event type="adjournment"><desc><s n="895"> Hearing adjourned until 10.30 am the following day</s></desc></event>

(Hutton Inquiry, 11 August 2003 afternoon)

(3) a) <event desc="Ms Jackson-Lee of Texas asked and was given permission to revise and extend her remarks"/>

   b) <event type="permission"><desc><s n="131"> Ms Jackson-Lee of Texas asked and was given permission to revise and extend her remarks</s></desc></event>

(House of Representatives, Debates, 5 March 2003)

Here the initial markup (cf. (2a) and (3a)) involved very lengthy and one-off values of the 'desc' attribute. In an effort to streamline the markup, while at the same time preserving the procedural language typically associated with specific contexts, the element <event> subsequently had a 'type' attribute attached to it (cf. (2b) and (3b)), instead of a 'desc' attribute (cf. (2a) and 3a)). This allowed us to create a simple classification of events that could be subsequently used to search the corpus (or, to be more precise, those sections of the corpus made up of official transcripts). The values for 'type' provide immediately identifiable *labels* (i.e., *adjournment* and *permission*) for the events described. In other words, they meet the requirement of *conciseness* of markup as indicated by Leech (1997:25). These events are then fully described in what follows, which is treated as a <desc> element contained within the <event> element, with the original description being preserved as part and parcel of the text proper.

As shown in examples (1)–(3), the streamlining of annotation, that is, ultimately the process whereby tags were made perspicuous, analyzable and concise (see earlier), implied an ongoing *recategorization*, as in the shift from <event desc="xxx"> to <event type="yyy"> in (2) and (3). Recategorizing, however, did not simply mean assigning different labels, but it also entailed rethinking overall classifications and making the necessary changes consistently throughout the corpus. For instance, in line with the TEI guidelines, quotations were divided into two classes. Generally, quotations containing 'material which is marked as (ostensibly) quoted from elsewhere' (Sperberg-McQueen and Burnard 2007, online)—be it direct speech or written extracts, in both cases from a documented source—were marked as <q> with the corresponding attribute 'who' for the speaker being quoted, as in Example (4) from the UK Parliamentary Debates section of the corpus:

(4) <u who="Spelman_Caroline" sex="f" role="Conservative:Opp" dialect="en-GB"> [. . .] <s n="546"> If we do not get a resolution soon, what does the Secretary of State believe will be the legal position of our troops in Iraq?</s><s n="547"> Does she stand by her statement of 26 March that the coalition has no authority <q who="Short_Clare" sex="f" role="Labour:Gov" dialect="en-GB"> to reorganise institutions or establish a new Government</q> ?</s> [. . .] </u>

(House of Commons, Statements, 10 April 2003)

However, if the quotation consisted of 'a passage of written text revealed to participants in the course of a spoken text' (Sperberg-McQueen and Burnard 2007, online), it was tagged as <writing> with the attribute 'who' for the name of the person reading aloud. The 'type' and/or 'script' attributes were used to specify the type and source of the material read aloud (e.g., newspaper articles, UN Resolutions, official records, and the like), and in some cases the 'n' attribute provided the official record for the quoted text, making it possible to univocally identify its source, as in Example (5) from the US Congressional Debates section of *CorDis*.

(5)   <s n="125"> The text of H Con Res 104 is as follows: <writing who="Simpson_MichaelK.Spt" sex="m" role="Republican:SpeakerPt" dialect="en-US" script="resolution" n="H Con Res 104"> <s n="126"> Whereas the United States Armed Forces, a total force comprised of active, National Guard, and Reserve personnel, are now undertaking courageous and determined operations against the forces of Saddam Hussein's regime; </s> [. . .] </writing>

(House of Representatives, Debates, 20 March 2003)

After recategorization decisions were taken and changes made accordingly (manually or semi-automatically using text editors such as UltraEdit), a *revision* and *testing* stage was entered. This stage consisted of a number of operations aimed at guaranteeing uniformity of treatment for features or phenomena of the same kind and avoiding possible mistakes or inconsistencies. As a preliminary operation, to eliminate XML syntax errors and TEI nonconformant markup, each file was validated using the <oXygen/> XML Editor.[10] The *Xaira* Indexer was subsequently run, which made it possible to find mistakes of a different type, that is, those caused by noncompliance with the information specified in the corpus header (e.g., the taxonomy defined for text sources or the list of values corresponding to POS tags). Finally, the *Xaira* Client was used to perform queries that enabled us to 'test' the chosen categorizations, and to spot inconsistencies in the markup used to describe them. Let us consider the already-mentioned <event> example (cf. Examples (2) and (3) previously) by looking at Figure 1.3, which reproduces *Xaira*'s XML query windows.

Here we wanted to identify any remaining instances of 'desc' attributes which we had failed to relabel using 'type'. We therefore launched a simple XML query and we found one occurrence of 'desc', which we proceeded to change to 'type'. A similar procedure was followed for all other elements and attributes that had somehow been recategorized. Once the mistake or inconsistency was spotted and subsequently corrected, the corresponding file/s was/were revalidated and the corpus reindexed.

1.3.3. *CorDis* Markup: Accessory or Backbone?

The examples discussed in the previous section clearly illustrate the evolving markup of the corpus. We now introduce other examples to show how the annotation process, together with the harmonization one, was also a means of creating a harmonized whole, which in return would enhance comparability among the various subcorpora.

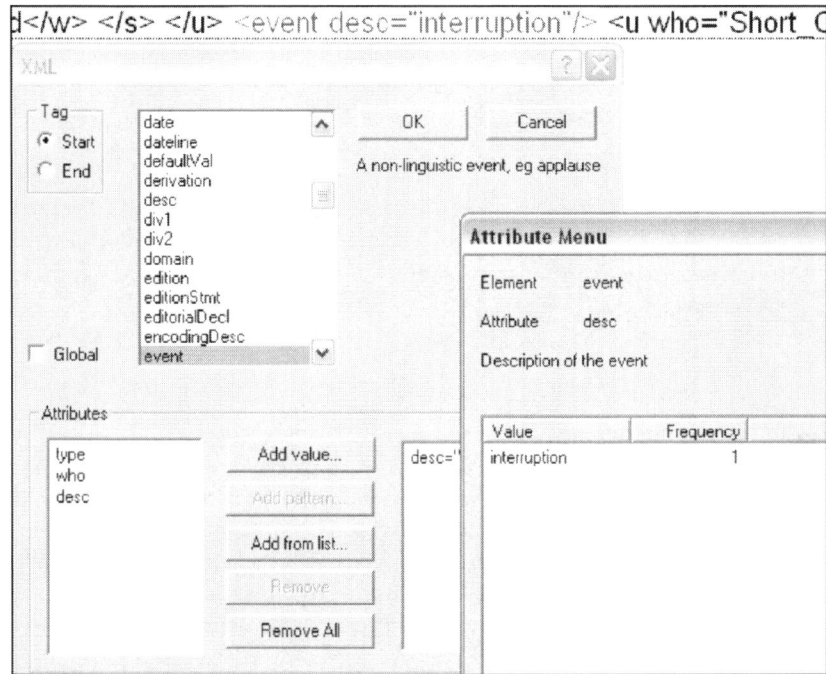

Figure 1.3   Using the *Xaira* Client to 'test' the corpus.

The fact that *CorDis* is centred on a single topic (the 2003 Iraqi war) gives the corpus a highly intertextual nature, explaining why many of the key players involved appear in more than one subcorpus. Given the specificity of each subcorpus, however, some of them play varying institutional and/or situational roles attached to them. For instance, the then British Prime Minister Tony Blair appears in nearly all the subcorpora either as a participant in the interaction or as a quoted source in the media. As a participant in the official transcripts, his role is inextricably linked to the institutional context in which the interaction takes place. Thus he is a member of the Labour government in the UK parliamentary proceedings, as illustrated in (6); he is coded as *witness* (as opposed to *judge* and *counsel*) in the Hutton Inquiry, where, due to the highly formal character of the setting, he is additionally referred to with his full name Anthony Charles Lynton Blair, as illustrated in (7); and he takes on the role of *legitimated person* in the TV news programmes, as illustrated in (8). In particular, this latter choice was motivated by the particular interests of the TV news research group, who wanted to identify utterances spoken by journalists, further classified according to their specific journalistic activity as newsreader, reporter, correspondent, war-zone correspondent, and embedded reporter (cf. example (1) in section 1.3.2) as opposed to utterances spoken by nonjournalists, and demanded that nonjournalists were further classified in *legitimated person, military,* or *member of the public* on the basis of their authoritativeness.

(6)   <u who="Blair_Tony" sex="m" role="Labour:Gov" dialect="en-GB"> <s n="244"> On the nature of the threat, it is the UN Resolution that described Saddam Hussein's programme of weapons of mass destruction as a threat, so that was established by the international community. </s> [. . .] </u>

(House of Commons, Statements, 25 February 2003)

(7)   <u who="Dingemans_James" sex="m" role="counsel" dialect="en-GB" type="question"> <s n="182"> Is there anything from your statement to Parliament that you wanted to emphasise? </s></u> <u who="Blair_AnthonyCharlesLynton" sex="m" role="witness" dialect="en-GB" type="response"> <s n="183"> I think the only thing, as I do in my witness statement to you, is just to emphasise the fact that I make it clear what I perceived the threat to be. </s> [. . .] </u>

(Hutton Inquiry, 28 August 2003, morning)

(8)   <u who="Blair_Tony" sex="m" role="legPerson" dialect="en-GB" type="camera"> <s n="206"> On Tuesday night I gave the order for British forces to take part in military action in Iraq. </s> [. . .] </u>

(*BBC* News, 20 March 2003)

Examples (6)–(8) illustrate how the use of the 'role' attribute makes it possible to retrieve all the utterances by a person with a given role. By specifying the value "Blair_Tony" for the 'who' attribute, we can find all the utterances provided by Blair; if we additionally specify the value "legPerson" for the 'role' attribute, we can find just those utterances provided by him in this role. If we do not specify a value for the 'who' attribute, we can find all the utterances produced by speakers who have that role. For instance, by searching for 'role'="Labour:Gov", all utterances by participants encoded as members of the Labour government will be found. The same applies to other attributes and their corresponding values. Clearly, multiple searches are possible by combining two or more attributes (e.g., searching for utterances spoken by female members of the Labour government, or by male Conservative backbenchers). Similar searches can be performed using the 'type' attribute, which is assigned to utterances in the Hutton Inquiry and the TV news subcorpora. This attribute is used to distinguish questions from responses or other kinds of interaction in the former, and to indicate whether an utterance is spoken with the speaker on or off camera (cf. examples (7) and (1), respectively).

Another useful example of the role of annotation in the harmonization process is the use of what we refer to as *structural* tags. The <div> element was used throughout to identify units of text that matched specific research needs, while still granting consistency. As examples (9)–(11) will show, each subcorpus required specific annotation relating to the nature of the interaction and the role assigned to it within the analytical framework adopted by the researchers.

Hansard, as an official record, required the encoding of all available information to be added by transcribers. Thus a parliamentary session dedicated to oral answers by members of the government consists of a certain number of parliamentary questions and their respective answers, each identified by an official reference number and associated with a topic. As shown in Example (9) following, we adapted the hierarchically arranged structure of numbered <div>s provided by the TEI Guidelines to reproduce the structure of an *Oral answers* sessions preserving all necessary contextual information by means of attribute values. Thus each question is encoded as a separate <div2 type="parliamentary_question"> within a <div1 type="oral_answers"> during which questions are posed to a member of the government (specified by the value of the 'whoto' attribute), with the official reference number indicated as the value of the 'n' attribute and the official subject of the question given by the value of the 'topic' attribute. The adopted structure allows the retrieval of any question using the official reference number, but it also allows the grouping of all the questions addressed on a specific topic, or to a minister or under secretary representing a specific department.

(9) <div1 type="oral_answers" whoto="International_Development">
     <div2 type="parliamentary_question" n="Q1 92204" topic="Sub Saharan Africa">
     [. . .] </div2>
     <div2 type="parliamentary_question" n="Q2 92205" topic="St Helena">
     [. . .] </div2> [. . .] </div1>
     (House of Commons, Question Time, 22 January 2003)

A similar approach was adopted in the markup of the Hutton Inquiry official transcripts. Each session of the inquiry is made up of different kinds of interaction which were coded as values of the 'type' attribute used for each <div2>. Each session could thus be divided up into matters of housekeeping and/or procedural language (*other_interaction*), cross examination of witnesses (*crossex*) of witnesses, and their direct (*direx*) or friendly (*frex*) examination, indicating the person responsible for that interaction as a value of the 'resp' attribute.

(10) <div1 type="session">
      <div2 type="other_interaction"> [. . .] </div2>
      <div2 type="crossex" resp="Gompertz_Jeremy">
      <u who="Gompertz_Jeremy" sex="m" role="consel" dialect="en-GB" type="question">
      <s n="27"> Dr Wells, your background experience first. </s><s> You are a scientist by
      training?</s></u>
      [. . .] </div2>
      <div2 type="other_interaction"> [. . .] </div2>
      <div2 type="direx" resp="Knox_Peter"> [. . .]
      <u who="Knox_Peter" sex="m" role="counsel" dialect="en-GB" type="question">
      <s n="479"> Mr Harrison, could you give the Inquiry your full name? </s></u>
      [. . .]</div2>
      <div2 type="frex" resp="LloydJones_David"> [. . .]
      <u who="LloydJones_David" sex="m" role="counsel" dialect="en-GB" type="question">
      <s n="901"> Mr Hatfield, is your full name Richard Paul Hatfield? </s></u> [. . .] </div2>
      [. . .] </div1>

(Hutton Inquiry, 24 September 2003, afternoon)

Example (11) following shows how the same hierarchical structure was adopted to mark up a TV news transcript according to the interpretative framework chosen for the analysis of this specific subcorpus. Each TV news programme was divided into news items marked up as <div1> elements, and each of these into shorter units of text according to the type of interaction involved. The news item in the example starts with an introduction by the newsreader <div2 type="intro" resp="newsreader">, goes on with a report by a correspondent, is followed by a live exchange between the newsreader and a correspondent, and ends with a report by the newsreader in the studio.

(11) <div1 type="newsitem">
      <div2 type="intro" resp="newsreader"> [. . .] </div2>
      <div2 type="report" resp="correspondent"> [. . .] </div2>
      <div2 type="exchange" resp="newsreader">
      <u who="Edwards_Huw" sex="m" role="newsreader" dialect="en-GB" type="camera">
      <s n ="178"> We'll talk to Matt Frei now who's at the White House. </s>
      <s n="179"> Matt what is your assessment of where we are this evening? </s> </u>

<u who="Frei_Matt" sex="m" role="correspondent" dialect="en-GB" type="camera">
[. . .] <s n="180"> Well the battle is clearly under way but more importantly the White House is also trying to shore up the so-called coalition of the willing. er despite the failed diplomacy of recent weeks. </s>
[. . .] </u> [. . .] </div2>
<div2 type="report" resp="newsreader"> [. . .] </div2> </div1>

(BBC News, 20 March 2003)

The examples provided demonstrate the crucial role of harmonization in the creation of a stable architecture for a unified corpus, mediating between delicacy of annotation and consistency throughout the corpus. Harmonization has two further and intertwined objectives (and effects): consistency and reusability. *Consistency* is needed because of the intrinsic interpretative nature of annotation, and ' . . . because the human analyst is susceptible to error and inconsistency, the mental interpretation of what is correct has to be sharpened and made explicit through the specification of an annotation scheme' (Baker 1997:244). Annotation schemes make categories explicit through the selection of appropriate tagsets, preventing an uncontrolled multiplication and/or overlapping of categories, while at the same time granting categorizations a reasonable degree of delicacy. Being consistently annotated, a corpus is also *reusable*. As pointed out by Leech (2005), corpora are often exploitable for a long time after their origin and in ways not envisaged by their originators. Moreover, 'the annotations themselves spark off a whole new range of uses which would not have been practicable unless the corpus had been annotated' (Leech 2005).

1.4. CONCLUSIONS

The examples analyzed give evidence of the work done on the *CorDis Corpus* and of our attempt to keep a balance between in-depth annotation and global consistency. A reasonable level of detail was needed to bring out the linguistic analysis and keep track of the specific features of each text type and of the relevant differences between genres. On the other hand, for the sake of comparability similar features/phenomena in the various subcorpora had to be treated similarly, meaning that markup had to be often general rather than specific. These two contrasting needs required us to adopt an approach that favours flexibility rather than compliance with rigid standards, and an annotation scheme able to adjust to different research interests and changing research hypotheses.

[I]t's widely felt that standardization of annotation schemes [. . .] is too high a goal to aim at; instead, our goal should be of annotation 'harmonization' [. . .] Such a goal should be easier to attain in a flexible annotation system allowing for both hierarchies of annotation levels and degrees of delicacy in the specification of categories.

(Leech 1991:24)

Finally, the fact that markup involves a substantial amount of human intervention on machine-processed data has some crucial implications for CADS, since it permits the researcher to shift between quality and quantity, thereby preserving both depth and breadth of analysis. Harmonization and consistency of annotation also have the added value of making interpretative choices explicit on the one hand, and favouring comparability on the other. This is an essential feature due to the highly comparable nature of corpus-based analyses in general and of corpus-assisted discourse studies in particular.

NOTES

1. The authors jointly discussed and designed the contents and style of the entire chapter co-authoring section 1.1. However, Letizia Cirillo is mainly responsible for sections 1.2.3 and 1.3.2. Anna Marchi is mainly responsible for sections 1.2.2. and 1.3.1, and Marco Venuti is mainly responsible for sections 1.2.1 and 1.3.3.
2. In the present chapter we refer to multimode rather than multimodal (Baldry and Thibault 2006) since we have not taken into consideration specific multimodal aspects of the communication in the encoding process. In describing the corpus, we thought it would nevertheless be significant to refer to different *modes* (cf. 2.1), as these are relevant categories in corpus design and compilation.
3. *Xaira* (XML Aware Indexing and Retrieval Architecture, developed by Lou Burnard and Tony Dodd, Oxford University Computing Services).
4. In the present paper the term *tagging* is also used, but only to refer to part-of-speech (POS) tagging.
5. For the *CorDis Corpus* we have used a RELAX NG schema (cf. http://relaxng.org/).
6 POS tagging was done using CLAWS7, an application developed by UCREL at Lancaster University. For the purposes of *CorDis*, three sets of attributes were employed for each word: 'c7', which provides the CLAWS category (e.g., RRQ stands for *wh-* general adverb, NN2 stands for plural common noun, etc.), 'pos', which groups these categories under a smaller range of macrocategories, and 'hw', which provides the headword (root) form of the word, as can be seen in the following example ('Where are those weapons of mass destruction?') from the newspaper section of *CorDis*:

   ```
   <sn="35"><wc7="RRQ"pos="adv"hw="where">Where</w><wc7="VBR"
   pos="verb" hw="be">are </w><w c7="DD2" pos="det" hw="those">those
   </w><w c7="NN2" pos="noun" hw="weapon">weapons </w><w c7="IO"
   pos="prep" hw="of">of </w><w c7="JJ" pos="adj" hw="mass">mass
   </w><w c7="NN1" pos="noun" hw="destruction">destruction</w> <c c7=
   "PUN">? </c> </s>
   ```

   For further details see http://www.comp.lancs.ac.uk/computing/users/eiamjw/claws/claws7.html.

7. For the sake of brevity, in 1a and 1b, as in several other examples given in this chapter, a significant portion of text has been omitted and replaced by three dots in square brackets ([. . .]). These are not to be understood as corpus markup.

8. By "utterance" we mean any uninterrupted unit of speech, no matter how long, produced by a single speaker.

9. 1b is in fact a simplified version of the final product for this specific fragment of the corpus, as <w> and <c> tags have been omitted to enhance readability. The same applies to all other examples used in this paper, unless otherwise specified.

10. For further information see www.oxygenxml.com.

2 Strict vs. Nurturant Parents?

A Corpus-Assisted Study of Congressional Positioning on the War in Iraq

Donna R. Miller and Jane H. Johnson

> the orientation of a word among words, the varying perception of another's word and the various means for reacting to it, are perhaps the most fundamental problems for the metalinguistic study of any kind of discourse.
>
> (Bakhtin 1984:202)

This research has had the broad aim of dismantling some recent but common and influential myths about speaker stance in political debate. Its strategy was to gather sufficient evidence to do so, while its main tactics include the congressional corpus (henceforth the *Cordis HoR* subcorpus, or simply *HoR*) creation, its markup and tagging, its interrogation with *Xaira* software, and analysis with a holistic model of speaker evaluation and stance: appraisal systems (Martin and White 2005). Appraisal systems are seen as an integral part of the descriptive and analytical model of systemic functional linguistics (henceforth SFL; Halliday and Matthiessen 2004), part of the lexicogrammar which instantiates interpersonal meanings. The chapter sets out the issue and rationale for the study and discusses briefly the not unproblematic theories and methods informing the research.[1] Corpus design is then presented. In section 2.2, we offer some of the more significant findings of our preliminary explorations, while, in section 2.3, the outcomes of appraisal analysis of segments in the environment of two 'culturally key' search words are marshalled.[2] Some tentative consideration of what we are calling possible 'register-idiosyncratic' features concludes this section.[3] In closing the chapter, we recap some pivotal points of the study vis-à-vis our initial research questions.

2.1. INTRODUCTION, OR LOCATING OUR STUDY

2.1.1. The Issue and Research Rationale

The research issue explored in this paper evolved as a challenge to what cognitivist G. Lakoff alleges in his *Moral Politics* (2002 [1996]:11), that is, that, firstly, conservatives and liberals misread one another due to conflicting moral systems, and that, secondly, these are expressed in what he calls 'lexical metaphors' which he claims are connected to the 'strict father mentality' and the 'nurturant parent' one. The thesis struck us as a dichotomy which, both epistemologically and linguistically, was just a bit *too* neat. In the first place, it is an oversimplified partition of the possibilities for political positioning typically taken up by socio-semiotically constructed 'meaners' (Halliday and Matthiessen 1999:610–11), and then, a too-circumscribed classification of the potential linguistic resources systemically available to construe it. In short, lexical metaphor is hardly the whole story, or even the most relevant part of it. The focal point must be widened, as it is grammar (in the sense of lexicogrammar) that

> creates the potential within which we act and enact our cultural being. This potential is at once enabling and constraining: that is, grammar makes meaning possible and also sets limits on what can be meant.
>
> (Halliday 1992:65).

So then, dissatisfied with Lakoff's mentalist view of things, we reasoned that it would prove much more profitable to hypothesize subtler positional shadings located more usefully along a cline between Lakoff's black-and-white extremes and then to investigate this assumption using a delicate model of speaker evaluation (i.e., Martin and White 2005).

With reference to these 'subtler positional shadings', our research questions were formulated—with the support of previous appraisal analyses of various text types, including parliamentary debate (e.g., Miller 1999, 2002a, 2004, 2007). These also included: (1) the degree to which the clue to the construal of ideology, or 'moral systems', is to be found not solely in the apprais-*er* and his/her ideological stance or even in the appraising lexicogrammar itself, but also in who/what is being appraised, that is, the apprais-*ee*/apprais-*ed*, and (2) continuing attention to what seems to be emerging from this and past studies as the possible register-idiosyncratic options for construing speaker attitude and engagement, as mentioned in our *incipit*.

Of course, greater amounts of evidence than we have gathered to date would be needed before giving definitively reliable answers to these substantial questions. In addition, we are aware of our oversimplistic equation of US Republicans with Lakoff's 'Conservatives' and US Democrats with his 'Liberals'. The advent of 'neocons' on both sides of the fence further muddies what were never crystal-clear waters on this score. Still, we hypothesize that both Republican and Democrat discourses will prove to align with (or alienate themselves from) long-legitimated and indeed naturalized US discourses, but that these discourses will *not* be univocal, but rather fraught with inconsistencies, perhaps even more so in our post-9/11 world order than ever before.[4]

2.1.2. Theory, Methods and Problems in Marrying CL and SFL

In terms of theory, this investigation is firmly located within research into applications of appraisal systems to the study—and SFL theorization—of text types, or *registers*. Since here we cannot presume a knowledge of what these systems are and what they aim to do, a very brief time-out on these is required. But, firstly, some of the problems inherent in the cohabitation of corpus linguistics (CL) and SFL need to be at least broached.

CL and SFL: Strange Bedfellows?

Despite there being a good deal of common ground that sets both of these 'linguistics' apart from formalist approaches to language and traditions which would compartmentalize grammar, semantics, and pragmatics, they are not altogether compatible. To borrow a metaphor from Thompson and Hunston (2006:3–4), there is a 'woods vs. trees' conflict, the holistic, systemic vision of SFL being opposed to CL's '[. . .] innate suspicion of "grand designs" ', with its preference for focussing on the disparate and diffuse. We might say that we identify the 'trees' in an attempt at describing the 'woods'.

Then, there is what Thompson and Hunston point out as a divergence in SFL and CL viewpoints on frequency (2006:5). In short, for the SFL practitioner, what ultimately needs to be *counted*, and accounted *for*, '[. . .] are the abstract categories derived from systems networks, rather than strings of letters or words'. We start with the latter to arrive at the former.

As a result, however, '[. . .] many calculations of frequency can only be done by hand and therefore on smaller amounts of text than corpus linguists are accustomed to dealing with'. We will dub the intensive manual process undertaken for this purpose as being one of 'ticklish trawling' (Miller 2000).

The knotty problem of automatizing meaning analysis in an SFL perspective has been incisively raised by Thompson (2000). 'Is it enough to trust the text?', as Sinclair advises (Sinclair 2004), he asks.[5] Thompson's answer is a qualified negative, as there are also the text-*ees* and text-*ers* to take into account, not to mention the inevitably biased intuitions of the analyst (which, however, '[. . .] we can only be *a*ware, and *be*ware, of— and, of course, declare'—Miller 2007:178).

Moreover, Thompson unearths the knotty problem of consensus, linking it to the difficulty of reading off semantic categories from formal instances in a straightforward way, and points to the identification of transitivity structure as one such slippery enterprise and the object of much debate. Not easily resolvable modelling and analytical problems are at least in part the result of what he suggests is a 'tension' between the notional, 'commonsense' terms the category descriptions typically draw upon—like it or not—and the grammatical evidence upon which the identification of the categories must be made to rest, however these may conflict with the notions. Such tension and resulting dissension vexes appraisal theory and analysis as well.

Indeed, to bring all this back to the global interpretative framework of our study, not only is there disagreement on category assignment, but in-built interpretation fuzziness abounds. As appraisal values are invariably culture-specific (one thing we *do* agree on), widespread accord on the distinction between explicit attitude, or its textual 'inscribing', and implicit attitude, or its 'invoking', and even on *what* attitude it is that is being inscribed or invoked, and what wording it is that is doing it, is, perhaps unavoidably, elusive.[6]

All of this is of course tantamount to an admission that our approach to this research is not invulnerable, or without its hazards. The issue of representativity will be confronted below in section 2.1.3. Although the computations performed in section 2.2 are fully retrievable and replicable with access to the corpus, those for the appraisal analysis in section 2.3 are not, as the corpus was not tagged for these categories.[7] But now to a brief gloss of the systems we are employing in analysis.

Appraisal Systems, and What We Would do With Them

Firstly, it may be useful to define in brief the term *system* as adopted in the SFL framework. Quite simply, it refers to the paradigmatic ordering in language, to the patterns, as Halliday and Matthiessen (2004:22) put it, '[. . .] of what *could go instead of* what'. It therefore contrasts with 'structure', which is the syntagmatic ordering, or the '[. . .] patterns, or regularities, in what *goes together with* what'.

Figure 2.1 is a schematic overview of the systems (see also Chapter 5, this volume). The attitude system is subdivided into those of affect, judgement and appreciation. Affect deals with language resources for expressing speakers' *emotions*. Judgement, a major system in parliamentary or congressional debate as we will see, is used for enacting *moral assessments of human behaviour*, whereas appreciation has to do with *evaluating products and processes* (rather than *human* behaviour).

The engagement system is modelled in a Bakhtinian dialogic perspective on speaker and hearer positioning (White 2003). Here, the basic distinction is between the *dialogic heterogloss*, which acknowledges the diversity associated with all utterances, and the *undialogized monogloss*, which ignores that diversity. Heteroglossic engagement, however, can act either to dialogically *contract* the speaker's position away from alternative ones (i.e., to reject, counter, rule them out, etc.), or to *expand* that stance towards those of others (i.e., to entertain, acknowledge, be open to them, etc.).

Graduation comprises language resources for *up- or downgrading* or otherwise adjusting the *intensity* of meanings.

The real trick of course is to see how all these systems *interact* to construe evaluation in this text type, because interact they do. Such a venture continues in the wake of research into linkage between the typical rhetorical aims of congressional debate, seen as ritualized 'deliberate dispute'

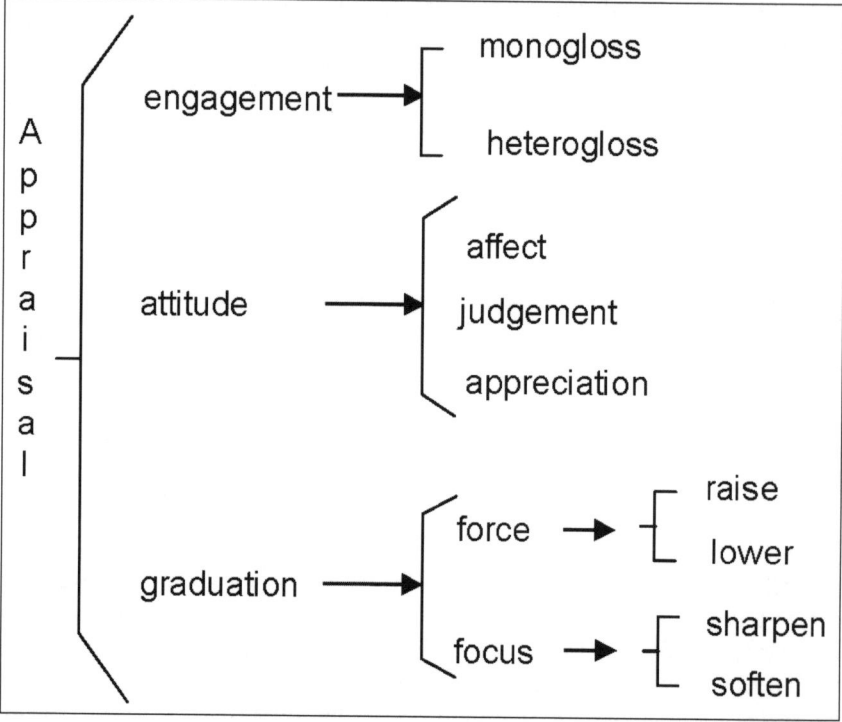

Figure 2.1   An overview of appraisal resources (from Martin and White 2005:38).

(Adams 1999), and patternings of resources typically used to achieve these. Ultimately, we would like to add to the growing bank of knowledge of the resources which are typically used for intersubjective positioning in parliamentary/congressional debate, and so contribute to the development of the instantiation cline proposed by Martin and White (2005:164), with particular reference to what they dub 'stance'.

Very ambitiously perhaps, we would also aim to look at our findings in the light of the semi-historical conflict between that very particular American 'virtue', so often extolled by de Tocqueville in his *Democracy in America* (1835–1840), of 'self-interest', and that of 'classic republican virtue', or what we will be calling, more simply, a concern with the 'common good'. As political scientists remind us (cf. Diggins 1984), these have always coexisted as equally respectable and dominant cultural values in the United States. The conflict roughly dates from the eighteenth century's Great Awakening's clash between evangelicals and rationalists and can be traced through to the Federalist and Anti-Federalist debate over the Constitution and beyond. The tension between these two coexisting conflicting poles is even the topic of metadiscursive debate between historians of the American Revolution over the philosophical input which carried most weight with the Founding Fathers in their construction of US institutions. It is undeniably also the contradictory cornerstone of 'the American Dream' (Miller 2006b). In speaking of conflicts and clashes, of course, we to some extent locate ourselves within the critical discourse analysis (CDA) tradition, that is, performing analyses that are aimed at revealing how lexicogrammar promotes hidden and ideologically 'suspect' agendas.[8]

The study is corpus-assisted, primarily qualitative, but also quantitative. This means that, although we agree that 'Not everything that counts can be counted, and not everything that can be counted counts' (as a sign in Einstein's office at the University of Princeton is said to have read), we do believe that patterns of ways of saying, and thus of meaning, 'count', and so that they may usefully be counted.

Much research involving corpora has tended to focus on fairly small chunks of language, limited by the width of the standard computer screen and so normally displayed as concordances of roughly ten to fifteen words. This practice is of restricted use for the kind of discourse analysis we are interested in. However, and as this volume itself amply testifies, corpora are being increasingly exploited to examine more extensive stretches of text for the purposes of investigating discourse. Early illustrations of using corpora for these wider research purposes include Hoey (1997) and Conrad and Biber (2000), to name just three of the better-known scholars, but also include authors contributing to this volume such as Miller (1999), Bayley (1999), and Partington (2001). Among their other advantages, '[. . .] corpora are a very useful tool for the critical linguist, because they [. . .] can be used to identify explicit meaning' (Hunston 2002:123).

The key word just cited for us is indeed 'meaning', which often, and regrettably, tends to get lost in many corpus-driven, -based, and even no more than -assisted studies. In short, we are not proposing that counting is at all *enough*, or that context, together with cotext, do not count in the analyst's 'reading' speaker evaluation and positioning. They do. Indeed, any word class can construe any of the appraisal systems, either positively or negatively, but appraisal is *not* merely a question of single words, or even multiword expressions, or phraseology, in single clauses. Its interpretation very strongly relies on *logogenesis*, or what SFL means by the expression 'semantic prosody', that is, the 'cumulative groove' (Coffin and O'Halloran 2005) of meaning patterning being dynamically construed over stretches of text—a potential snare for even corpus-assisted study, admittedly.[9] Such 'grooves' may be usefully likened to Hoey's ninth type of lexical priming, what he calls 'textual semantic associations' (2005:13), with the proviso that these obviously result from grammatical, as well as lexical, patternings.

So what, in sum, we are positing is that corpora can usefully be used to 'shunt' (Halliday 2002 [1961]:45), from clause, or concordance line, to text, and also intertext, using the corpus as a kind of 'echo chamber' (Thompson and Hunston, 2006:13) in which to focus, economically, on certain, circumscribed, apparently preferred, and so, perhaps, 'probabilistic' (Halliday

1992, 1993) patterns of actualized meaning potential, much in the same way as Miller (2006a) works towards doing.

2.1.3. Research Design: The Corpus

The following sections describe how our own corpus was compiled and provides the rationale for the markup of certain elements.

The corpus of raw material consisted of the transcribed texts of all 135 sessions of the US House of Representatives for the whole of the year 2003, part of the 108th Congress, texts which are freely available in electronic form from the official Congressional Record Web site.[10] The total raw corpus thus collected consisted of seventeen million tokens, with almost sixty thousand different word types.

Since our focus was the language used in relation to the Iraq war, a subcorpus, henceforth referred to as the *HoR* subcorpus, was created using *WordSmith Tools* 4.0 (Scott 2005) to search semi-automatically for occurrences of *Iraq**. The House of Representatives sessions consisted of various clearly identifiable stages and some of these, though featuring repeated references to Iraq*, were discarded in advance as being irrelevant to our study. One example was the prayer, coming at the beginning of every session. Our final subcorpus instead included relevant one-minute speeches, each completely self-contained, as well as five-minute speeches. There were also sixty-minute speeches, alternating recognition between the parties and delivered by the designees of the majority and minority party leaders. These three types were introduced with the standard formula, as follows:

> The SPEAKER pro tempore. Under a previous order of the House, the gentlewoman from California (Ms. WOOLSEY) is recognized for 5 minutes.

and involved a single speaker each time. We may thus describe them as monologues. Since our focus was on the transcribed spoken text, we also included the full debates on resolutions or amendments.

Written or Spoken Text?

The question is an important one. As Slembrouk (1992) makes clear, any transcription that fails to account for the prosodic features that only an audio-video recording of the speech event can provide is necessarily an imperfect representation of the modality that speaker intonation construes. It also fails to provide extralinguistic multimodal information. Thus, the transcription of the sessions may only be described as a 'broad transcription', in that it distinguishes '[. . .] different speakers' utterances, dividing these into sentences or prosodic units, and dividing the latter into words, with a disambiguation of homophonous elements with distinct orthographical forms' (Aston and Burnard: 1998:26).

But such transcription essentially suffices for our purposes. In fact, there are certain characteristics of this 'contaminated' text type that lessen the import of Slembrouk's criticism (Miller 1999:390–91). Foremost among these is that a more appropriate description of the speeches included in the Congressional Record would be 'previously prepared', rather than 'transcribed from spontaneous speech'. For example, the one-minute, five-minute, and sixty-minute speeches often included statements such as:

> Mr. Speaker, I would insert at this point my full statement in the RECORD

indicating that the speaker was not improvising but reading, or rewording, from a pre-prepared script in order to fit the salient points into the restricted time allotted. Since it was never clear from the transcript to what extent this was taking place—because *ad hoc* references might be made to previous speakers in the same session, for example—these were all classified as 'spoken' text, to distinguish them from instances where the speaker expressly quoted from other written sources.

The subcorpus thus compiled consisted of 1,394,163 words in utterances.

Breakdown by Party, Sex, and Role

The 108th Congress consisted of 440 Representatives, as in Table 2.1.

Of the total number of representatives in the Congress, 376 (85 per cent) featured in the *HoR* subcorpus. Of these, 183 were Democrats (that is, 87 per cent of the Democrats entitled to speak did so about Iraq), 191 were Republicans (83 per cent of those entitled to speak about Iraq did so), and one was an independent. The clerk, Jeff Trandahl, was included in the subcorpus, but used only procedural language, in line with his institutional role. From now on we will be counting only those utterances made by elected representatives.

The participants in the *HoR* subcorpus are divided according to sex as in Table 2.2:

Table 2.1 Members of the House of Representatives in the 108th US Congress 2003–2005

Party	Male	Female	Total
Republicans	209	20	229
Democrats	167	43	210
Independent	1	–	1
Overall totals	377	63	440

Table 2.2   Number of Participants in the *HoR* Subcorpus According to Sex and Party

Party	Male	Female	M+F
Republican	176 (92% of Republicans; 47% of House)	15 (8%; 4% of House)	191
Democrat	145 (79% of Democrats; 38.5% of House)	38 (21%; 10% of House)	183
Independent	1	—	1
Clerk	1	—	1
Total	323 (86%)	53 (14%)	376

Division by sex in the subcorpus reflects the gender ratio in the House of Representatives in general and is thus not significant. We might thus infer that Iraq was an issue that both sexes felt equally strongly about, one way or the other. The speakers were also tagged where relevant for the roles they performed within the 108th Congress. This meant that utterances by, say, the Democrat minority leader, Nancy Pelosi, could be selected either according to name or to role, as could those by the various chairpersons.

Additional Considerations

For the purpose of tracking references to previous speakers, and thus speeches in support of or countering particular views, it was decided to include a particular identity attribute wherever another representative was mentioned within an utterance. The convention used in the House of Representatives was to refer to other representatives by area of election, with nominal identification added in brackets by the transcriber, for example:

> as my colleague, the gentleman from Virginia (Mr. Scott), just spoke about minutes ago.

We considered it important to be able to distinguish where necessary between a representative's own words and those 'borrowed' from others (endorsed or unendorsed material attributed to outside sources), so it was decided to mark this material specifically as 'writing' to distinguish it from the 'spoken' nature of the subcorpus proper, subdividing it further into six different categories of written material (report, newspaper, letter, resolution, amendment, quotation).

In addition, in order to be able to distinguish idiosyncratic speech from the procedural language which is part of congressional *modus operandi*, but still not transcribed speech, for example:

The clerk read the resolution

a different markup convention was used for this.

Breakdown of Tokens in Utterances in Subcorpus According to Text Type

Since we are dealing with distinctions between Republican and Democrat speech, we have used the number of tokens in their utterances as our gauge, for the reasons specified in greater detail in the Introduction and Chapter 1 of this volume. Henceforth, any mention of numbers of tokens will refer to these, unless otherwise specified.

Table 2.3 gives details about the utterances of the representatives in the *HoR* subcorpus.

The contributions from either side of the House to the different speech types reflect the proportions of Republican and Democrat speech, *except* in the case of the five-minute speeches, where the Democrats dominated, producing 75 per cent of tokens. One might hypothesize that ordinary members of the Democratic Party were more inclined to intervene at this length on the subject of Iraq than their Republican counterparts, who, on the contrary, produced slightly more one-minute contributions—pithy and to the point.

Considering the contributions of both Democrats and Republicans to the *HoR* subcorpus as a whole, Table 2.4 shows that the Republicans, though greater in number in the Congress, had slightly less to say about Iraq. The Democrats were slightly fewer overall but more loquacious.

Table 2.3   Tokens in the Different Speech Types of the *HoR* Subcorpus

Speech Type	No. Tokens	No. Tokens in Reps <u>	No. Tokens in Dems <u>
One-minute speeches	23,387	12,760	10,627
Five-minute speeches	141,260	35,222	106,038 (75%)
Sixty-minute speeches	571,888	269,651	302,237
Total monologic speeches	**736,535**	**317,633**	**418,902**
Debates	657,628	286,955	370,673

Table 2.4   Tokens in Utterances in Partition According to Party

Participants	Tokens
Republicans	604,588 (43% of total)
Democrats	788,118 (57%)
Independent	458
Iraq subcorpus of Congressional Record	1,394,163

The proportional contribution of men and women appears to correspond to the ratio of males to females present in the *HoR* subcorpus (see Table 2.5). However, a breakdown of the total tokens, considering *both* sex and party, does show up some interesting differences (see Table 2.6)

As mentioned earlier, the Democrats as a whole say more about the war in Iraq. The Democrat males, though making up 38.5 per cent of the total speakers in the subcorpus, produce 43 per cent of the tokens. Democrat females (10 per cent of the total speakers) produce slightly more than would be expected too, with 13 per cent. Only the Republican women are significantly underrepresented in the subcorpus, making up only 4 per cent of the total speakers and producing just 1.6 per cent of the tokens.

Table 2.5   Tokens in Utterances in Partition According to Sex

Participants	Tokens
Males	1,186,002 (85% of total tokens in subcorpus)
Females	208,161 (15%)
Iraq subcorpus of Congressional Record	1,394,163

Table 2.6   Tokens in Utterances in Partitions According to Sex and Party

Participants	Tokens
Male Republicans	583,703 (41.8% of total tokens in subcorpus)
Female Republicans	21,716 (1.6%)
Total Republicans	605,419
Male Democrats	601,673 (43%)
Female Democrats	186,445 (13%)
Total Democrats	788,118
Male Independent (total)	458 (0.03%)
Total House Representatives	1,393,995

The Representativeness of the HoR Subcorpus

Our subcorpus may be considered fully representative of congressional discourse on the topic of the war in Iraq in a particular period in time (2003).

In relation to what Mauranen calls 'notional representativeness', in other words '[. . .] the capacity of the subcorpus to answer the questions put to it' (Mauranen 2001), we would expect our subcorpus to be able to answer our specific questions on the notions being investigated within the 2003 House of Representatives discourse on the war in Iraq, the 'contextual configuration' (Hasan 1978) of which can be sketched as follows.

In terms of the contextual variables of the register being investigated, Miller (2004:275–6) describes the 'field' of the discourse, that is, the nature of the congressional speech event, as institutionally legitimated alignment and/or alienation among elected representatives. These, in this specific case, are 'deliberately disputing' (Adams 1999) the conflict in Iraq in 2003. With reference to the 'Tenor', these are speakers of high social status whose discourse role is to argue positions which will most likely be in line with the party and/or the local electors they 'represent'. The addressees of interventions include other representatives, the US public and media, and may on occasion be even more inclusive, for example, comprising the leaders and interest groups of foreign nations. With reference to the 'Mode' of discourse, the 'channel' can be said to be, originally, phonic, though obviously at least pre-scripted/rehearsed, but, as said earlier, we are working with quasi-written versions of the speech events. The 'medium' of the message oscillates on a cline between both the 'written-ness' and 'spoken-ness' extremes (Halliday 1989 [1985]). In general we can say that the text type we are dealing with is deliberative and argumentative, and that its global rhetorical aim is composite: in Jakobson's terms (1960), referential primarily, but also emotive (at least apparently), conative, and even metalingual/textual.

2.2. THE STUDY: BEGINNINGS

In this section we recount some of the more significant findings of our preliminary explorations of the subcorpus. We recall at this point that our study consisted in examining, with the appraisal framework, the use of two 'culturally key' search words in the subcorpus: how they function to construe speaker attitude and positioning with regard to certain war-related behaviours, with the ultimate purpose of revealing whether there is any systematic difference in the way Democrats and Republicans use these words and if that difference is not more complex than Lakoff's hypothesis posits.

2.2.1. The Node Words Examined

Our initial starting point for comparing and contrasting what Lakoff dubs the 'strict father' mentality of the conservatives—our Republicans—and the 'nurturant parent' mentality of the liberals—our Democrats—was Lakoff's own descriptions of the two worldviews and indeed his own lists of recurrent words and phrases (Lakoff 2002:30 ff.). The following are the lexemes Lakoff identifies as belonging to the two 'moral systems', though he does not specify whether to do so he used computational tools.

Conservative Discourse

authority; backbone; breakdown; character; common sense; competition; corrupt; decay; degenerate; dependency; deviant; discipline; earn; elite; enterprise; freedom; get tough; hard work; heritage; human nature; individual responsibility; interference; intrusion; lifestyle; meddling; property rights; punishment; quotas; reward; right; rot; self-indulgent; self-reliance; standards; tough it out; tough love; traditional; virtue; wrong.

Liberal Discourse

alienation; basic human dignity; big corporations; biodiversity; care; concern; corporate welfare; deprivation; diversity; ecology; ecosystem; equal rights; free expression; health; help; human rights; nutrition; oppression; pollution; protect; respect; right; safety; social forces; social responsibility; support; wrong.

Using Thesaurus Classifications

Although only words in use can be said to truly *mean*, mapping culturally keywords against Roget's Thesaurus' semantic categories can be a useful step in corpus studies, as Miller (2004) and Lukin (2006), following Halliday (1978:79 ff.), have shown. An initial semantic field classification of these words in relation to the class framework set out in *Roget's Thesaurus* (Dutch 1962 [1852]), even though uncontextualized, provided a valuable starting point in selecting the search nodes to focus on.

Interestingly, according to Roget's classifications, many words belonging to *both* Lakoff's 'moral systems' have something to do with the exercise of 'volition' (conservative category 75 per cent vs. liberal 63 per cent), and to some extent with the emotion, religion and morality spheres (23 per cent vs. 21 per cent); but only the 'nurturing' liberal category has words having anything to do with the semantic field of 'intellect': for example, 'care' in the sense of solicitude (9 per cent).

Initially, selection of the node words according to frequency alone proved problematic. By way of example, the generation of a frequency list showed that the most frequently occurring of the preceding listed words was *care*, at position 1,076. However, a closer look at the actual occurrences of *care* showed that a good 65 per cent of these were part of the nominal group *health care* and its synonyms, and tended to be merely included, with no explicit expression of speaker attitude or stance, in a list of policy areas. For this reason, it was decided to make a manual selection of the node words to be analyzed.

A number of different node elements, including *common sense*, and *right* as in *do right by*, were initially included in our explorations, and could well prove worth pursuing (some findings are reported in Johnson 2006). However, the most interesting preliminary results came from investigation into two words in particular, each representative of one of Lakoff's categories. We thus selected these, and examined each occurrence in a segment of text expanded from the concordance line until attitude construal towards something/someone was perceptible. The two words were:

> *protect*: conveying the 'nurturant parent' ideal hypothesized by Lakoff for the 'Liberal'—our Democrat,

and

> *punish*: typical of the 'strict father' approach to government of 'conservatives', our Republicans.

With regard to Roget's categories, the semantics of the two words plainly conflict:

> *protect*
>   Class V: Voluntary Powers; Section II: Prospective Volition; 3. Contingent subservience

vs.

> *punish*
>   Class VI: Moral Powers; Section IV: Moral Affections; 5. Institutions

Though we cannot reproduce lengthy synonym lists here, it struck us in reading them off that these notions may be glossed in terms of 'goodness' vs. 'righteousness', or, still more biblically, in terms of 'mercy' vs. 'justice', or even with regard to those parallel competing discourses of 'self-interest' and 'classical Republican virtue', or what we are calling the 'common good'.

The scope of our research required making a rigid selection of the nodes to be examined further. Thus we decided to limit examination to the most frequently occurring lemmas and, on the basis of this, isolate the phraseology in which they were mainly to be found. In order to do this, we initially made a frequency list to distinguish the various word forms.

The total number of occurrences of the root search nodes are given in Table 2.7, along with a list of the different lemmas found, divided according to party as well as the subtext type they come from.

Table 2.7   Raw Frequencies of Lemmas and Word Forms of the Search Nodes in the Different Partitions

Lemma	Word Form Class	Tot. Monologic Speeches		Debates		Overall Raw Total	
		D	R	D	R	D	R
protect	verb	84	66	193	119	277	185
		20	13	17	19	37	32
		18	21	55	38	73	59
		3	3	7	10	10	13
	noun	50	18	90	52	140	70
		—	2	—	—	—	2
		—	—	1	—	1	—
	adjective	18	1	16	3	34	4
		1	—	1	1	2	1
Totals		194	124	380	242	574	366
puni	verb	2	—	3	7	5	7
		1	2	1	4	2	6
		—	1	1	—	1	1
		—	—	—	—	—	—
	noun	1	7	—	1	1	8
		—	2	2	1	2	3
	adjective	1	—	2	7	3	7
		—	—	1	2	1	2
		—	3	—	—	—	3
Totals		5	15	10	22	15	37

The relative frequencies calculated across the subcorpus show that, as Lakoff indeed expected, Democrats *do* talk about 'protecting' more than Republicans, while the Republicans talk about 'punishing' more than Democrats. But of course there is more to it than that, as we will presently see.

Most Frequently Occurring Phraseology

At this stage all irrelevant occurrences such as proper names, quotations, repetitions, and titles were removed. Drawing on the work of Biber and Conrad on lexical bundles, ('[. . .] the most frequent recurring lexical sequences; [. . .] usually *not* complete structural units, and usually not fixed expressions' [Biber and Conrad 1999:183]), the cluster option of the *WordSmith Tools* suite was used, and proved useful, in automatically

Table 2.8 Grammatical Breakdown of Relevant Occurrences of *to Protect* in the Five-Minute Speeches, Divided by Party

Grammatical Category	Democrat	Republican
Hypotactic (Purpose) clause	14	2
Embedded qualifier	1	1
Nominalized 'Act'	—	1
Projected idea	1	3
Projected locution	1	—

highlighting common phraseologies. It should be said here that, given the size of our corpus, we were able to disregard the finer distinction Biber and Conrad make between lexical bundles and clusters.

The most frequent form of *protect* was the to-infinitive form. Just by way of example, Table 2.8 gives a grammatical breakdown of *to protect* in the five-minute speeches, the first we investigated, as we explain in section 2.3.

As can be seen, most of the instances function as purpose clauses; thus it was decided to focus on these.

As regards the search node **puni**, both Democrat and Republican occurrences included verbal and nominal groups, as well as the qualifiers and classifiers within the latter. In any case, there were few enough instances of all word forms of **puni** for us to examine them all.

2.2.2. Exploratory Analyses and Outcomes

Reference Corpora Comparisons

We first investigated collocates of the nodes in two other reference corpora, to see if this would give us a more reliable idea of what was typically being appraised. For this purpose, collocates in the *CorDis HoR* subcorpus were compared with the *British National Corpus* (100 million words), and a relatively small corpus (335,000 words) taken from a larger collection of US presidential speeches and televised debates which took place between 1961 and 2004, put together by Paul Bayley. Table 2.9 gives the comparative figures for the three corpora.

In the *BNC*, *punishment* is usually classified, with frequent occurrences of *capital punishment*, *corporal punishment*, and *physical punishment*, whereas in both the US presidential speeches and the *HoR* subcorpus, it tends to be pre-modified with epithets: for example, *arbitrary/collective/ inhuman punishment* (*HoR* subcorpus); *tougher/severe punishment* (US presidential speeches). This shows that evaluations were indeed being made in the two latter corpora, in line with what we would expect from political, and, more specifically, congressional discourse.

Table 2.9 Relative Frequencies of Search Nodes across Three Corpora

	Corpus	Relative Frequency (per 100 Tokens)
puni	HoR subcorpus	0.003
	US presidential speeches	0.001
	BNC	0.004
protect	Corpus	Relative Frequency
	HoR subcorpus	0.02 (of which 89% are *to protect*)
	US presidential speeches	0.05 (of which 55% are *to protect*)
	BNC	0.005 (of which 74% are *to protect*)

As regards the verb complement, the 'goal' of punishing in the Iraq subcorpus emerged immediately as more specific than in the other two corpora, with frequent examples being:

punish the Syrian people
punish the people of Iraq
punish the Iraqi murderers
punish innocent Americans
punish American workers

In the US presidential corpus, the 'goal' is much more general, for example, 'punish those who commit violent acts', and there are no explicit references to Americans. Interestingly, this node is used overwhelmingly by Bill Clinton (eleven out of the seventeen occurrences).

As regards *to protect*, if we focus on the nominal group collocates to the right as indicative of what is being appraised, we could perhaps expect this to tell us what is or was in the forefront of the political agenda in the *HoR* subcorpus and the US presidential corpus. For example, in the US presidential corpus, we have instances of the following phraseology:

protect (our/the) rights security /freedom/privacy
protect (our/this) country/heritage/nation
protect (our/American) children/citizens/families/future generations/ the unborn

A party breakdown in the US presidential speeches corpus certainly highlights a fairly predictable difference in priorities, with the Democrats (forty-five occurrences) focussing on:

protecting *the environment /the countryside*
                   the coastline
                   areas of natural beauty

while Republicans (fewer, twenty-nine, occurrences) were more concerned
with:

protecting   *the homeland*
              our citizens
              our country
              the unborn

It is also remarkable that while the period diachronically considered
in this corpus included that of the Vietnam war, no references to this
particular event emerged from an examination of right collocates of
protect.

In contrast, the concerns of both Democrats and Republicans as to what
should be protected in 2003 emerge in these examples of frequent right collocates for *to protect* in the *HoR* subcorpus:

America/our homeland/our country/(the) nation
our citizens
our troops/soldiers
(the) lives/people

Given that the US presidential speeches corpus deals with a much wider
variety of topics, the differences are not surprising.

However, as it should not be assumed that the right collocate is actually
what is being appraised in cotext, it is important to examine the occurrences in larger segments of text before any generalizations can be made.
Indeed, frequency of occurrences alone can provide only a starting point
towards seeing how these culturally key nodes are being used. So at this
point we took up the tools of appraisal theory to systematically investigate
the means by which the speakers in our subcorpus express their feelings
and take their stands towards these. Through appraisal analysis, differences, but also similarities between the identities, or 'personae' (White
2003), which Democrats and Republicans construct for themselves with
reference to these notions began to emerge.

2.3. APPRAISAL ANALYSIS FINDINGS

We have constantly pointed to the quandaries involved in our study and
we now need to add to these. The task of analysing all instances of **puni**
was, as said, doable, whereas the idea of doing the same for all instances of
to protect was, in the first place, daunting, and then, and more essentially,
worked against what we wanted to be a sample that was statistically and
contextually as comparable as possible to that for **puni**. How we went
about dealing with this dilemma is detailed following.

2.3.1. What Democrats and Republicans Appraise and how

In this subsection we will be reporting our attitude system findings, first for *puni* and then for *to protect*, focussing on not only the resources for construing such attitude, but also, as said, on the appraiseds/appraisees as well as on the appraisers, and the polarity (positive or negative) of their voices. Space restrictions preclude extensive in-depth illustration of analytical procedures. In addition, we will be briefly discussing the difficulties of deciding whether appraisal is inscribed, that is, explicitly construed, or invoked, that is, implicit. In section 2.3.2, we offer select results of analyses for speaker stance with reference to the engagement system and, in 2.3.3, some considerations of register-idiosyncratic mechanisms.

One significant if unsurprising finding is that the appraisal system which can be most regularly identified as being construed is judgement, which, as already remarked, is deployed for enacting moral evaluations of human behaviour with respect to what people ought, or ought not, to do, and typically with a practical view to actually controlling such doings (Miller 2007:162–3). It is not that other systems are *not* construed, but rather that, in most cases, even these can be seen to be contributing to the overall judgement in play (cf. Miller 2004), as we will see.

The reasons judgement (and in particular the more seriously 'ethical' judgement category of 'social sanction: propriety') is the dominant attitude system in evidence are fairly obvious: (1) the making of war in Iraq is the overall behaviour being focussed on and war is a life-and-death phenomenon, having, in our Western liberal worldview, highly ethical implications and, (2) both *puni* and *to protect*, in themselves, point to behaviours which are always already ideologically, and so evaluatively, that is, attitudinally, *saturated*, and so 'primed', in Hoey-esque terms, to appraise in certain ways (Martin and White 2005:19, 23, 24).

puni

We will now take a comparative look at how Democrats and Republicans use the node form *puni* which, according to Lakoff, should be the marker of a more 'conservative', or 'strict father' style. The relevant instances are thirty-three, divided between six Democrat and twenty-seven Republican occurrences. An immediate caveat is that the percentage of Democrat data is simply too scant to be statistically significant, but it does bear out Lakoff's suggestions.

As has been said and as Figure 2.2 undeniably shows, Republicans talk about *punishing/punishment* a lot more than Democrats do—despite the Democrats talking more, globally, than Republicans in the subcorpus. They also appraise *puni* in a greater number of domains.

However, polarity (+/–), juxtaposed with just *what* is being appraised, immediately introduces some crucial fine-tuning. In Figure 2.3, it is clear that the Republicans are *not* always in favour of 'punishing'. Most of the

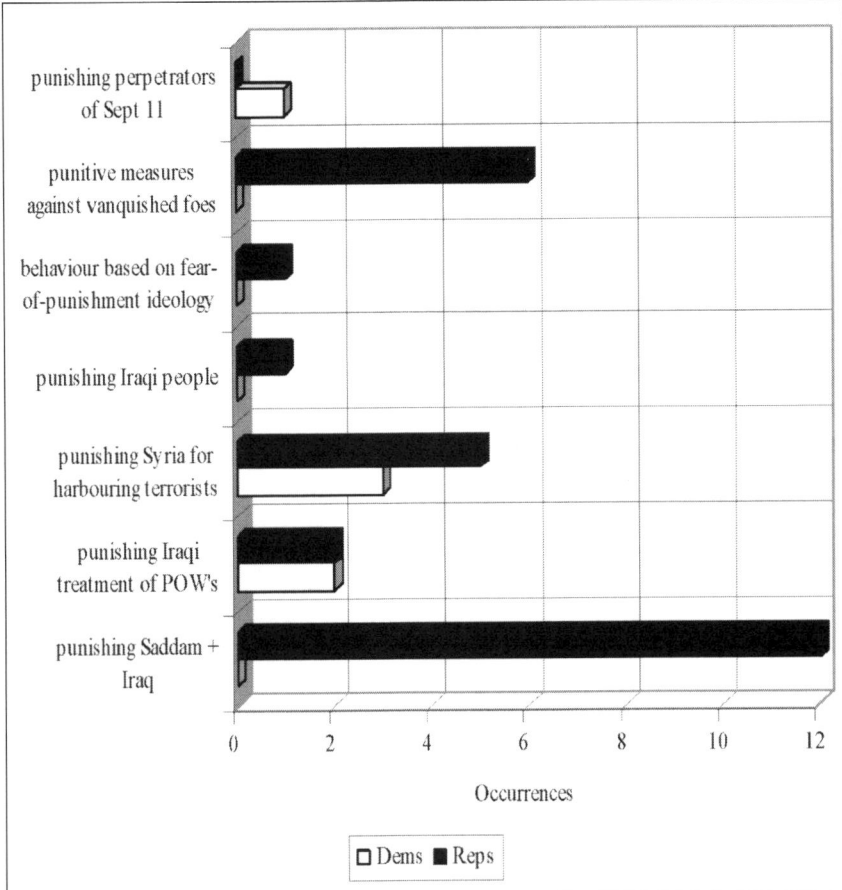

Figure 2.2 What Democrats and Republicans appraise with **puni**.

negative instances regard passing punitive measures against the United States' vanquished foes: that is, the post–World War I Versailles Treaty debacle *docet*. But neither do Republicans judge punishing the Iraqi people at all positively. Most—but not all—see punishing Syria for harbouring terrorists as a good thing to do, and they are unanimous on punishing Iraq for its mistreatment of POWs and, in general, Saddam for the long list of abuses they repeatedly mention.

Following are some examples: firstly, of negative judgement on punishing Syria, and the Iraqi people, in which Republicans sound like 'typical' Lakoff-esque liberals—almost the nurturing parents indeed!

(1) Syria needs not face this type of **punitive** legislation.

(Dana Rohrabacher, Republican, 15 October 2003)

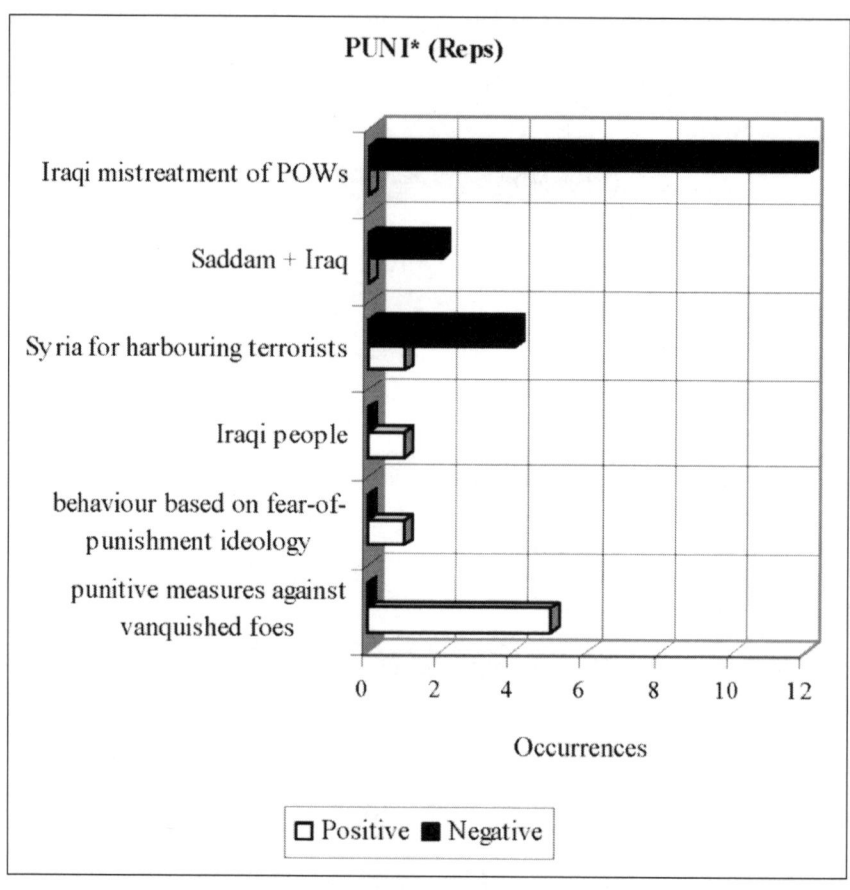

Figure 2.3   Positive vs. negative Republican judgement of **puni**.

(2)   They were victims [. . .] Therefore, it is critical that they [the Iraqi peo-
ple] not be **punished** or made to pay for the actions of their oppressor.

(Ileana Ros-Lehtinen, Republican, 16 October 2003)

This last segment clearly signals its negative judgement with the objectiv-
izing 'it is critical that', and its –polarity. It also illustrates how the negative
appreciation inherent in the culturally keywords 'victims' (as a result of an)
'oppressor', and the reader-hearer empathy they thus typically trigger, adds
to the weight of the negativity of the judgement being construed.

More true to expected form is the following positive Republican judgement on punishing Syria, an exemplary instance of Republican tendencies
towards moral hyperbole, here using the biblical metaphor of people with
blood-soaked hands who, according to Isaiah (59, 1–4), deserve to be cut
off from the Lord. Interestingly, there are two Republicans, a man and a
woman, who use this metaphor. This, by the way, is the woman.

(3) The blood of Americans is on their hands, and for this, they must be called to task. They must be **punished**.

(Ileana Ros-Lehtinen, Republican, 15 October 2003)

However, there is one extremely loquacious Republican—a certain Mr. Paul—who is also quite the intellectual. His is the only voice to construe judgement on the *sui generis* category labelled in Figure 2.2 as 'behaviour based on fear-of-punishment ideology'. The following is a corroborative segment of the extensive intervention, the negative polarity of which is only observable over a longer stretch of text, however:

(4) Ledeen explains why God must always be on the side of the advocates of war: 'Without fear of God, no state can last long, for the dread of eternal damnation keeps men in line, causes them to honor their promises, and inspires them to risk their lives for the common good'. It seems dying for the common good has gained a higher moral status than eternal salvation of one's soul. He goes on to say: "*Without fear of punishment, men will not obey laws that force them to act contrary to their passions. Without fear of arms, the state cannot enforce the laws* [. . .] to this end, Machiavelli wants leaders to make the state spectacular. [our emphasis]

(Ron Paul, Republican, 10 July 2003)

Paul's point is that the ideology, and psychology, that the United States is basing its call to arms against terror on is flawed at its roots, a position that is in clear conflict with example (3) above, and one that not even most Democrats would have dared to voice in 2003. He is arguing for 'the Christian doctrine of a Just War', vs. a pre-emptive one (see Chapter 3, this volume). He also clearly does not think much of the rhetoric of the 'common good'.

The few Democrat instances of judgement on *punishing* are, for the most part, and unexpectedly, positive. Reading off Figure 2.4, we can see that no Democrat contests that Iraqi mistreatment of US POWs should go unpunished. Two want to 'get' Syria for harbouring terrorists, but one begs to differ. And, of course, punishing the perpetrators of 9/11 is uncontested.

The following is an illustration of Democratic negative judgement on Iraqi mistreatment of US POWs that is 'strict' enough to please even Lakoff's Conservatives.

(5) we have expressed our commitment that those who do not [act according to the Geneva Convention regarding our POWs] will be **punished, however long it takes us to find them and bring them to justice.**

(Tom Lantos, Democrat, 26 March 2003)

And their negative judgement on punishing Syria is, as we have seen, also shared by some Republicans:

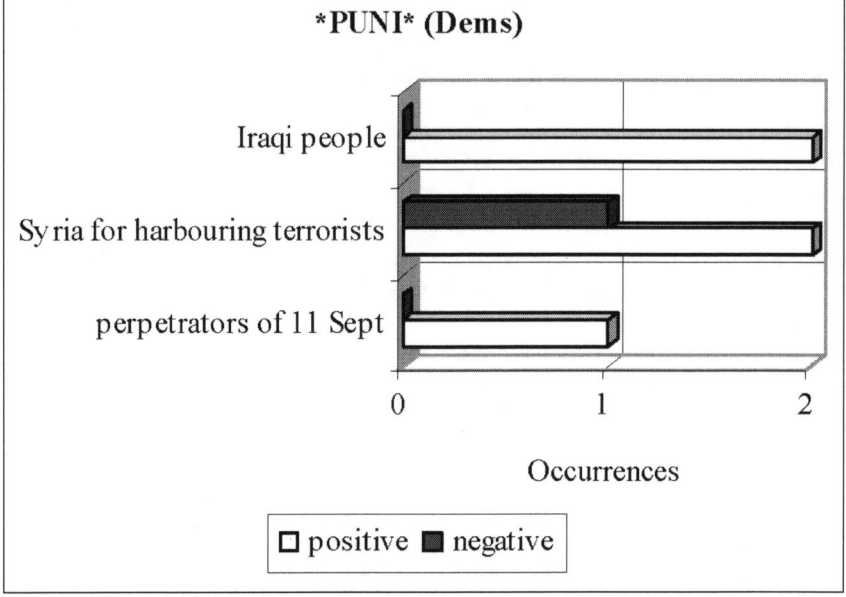

Figure 2.4   Positive vs. negative Democrat judgement of *puni* .

(6)   Our aim is to become partners with Syria in the war on terror, not to make Syria an enemy, not to **punish** the Syrian people.

(Danny K. Davis, Democrat, 15 October 2003)

To be noted is the grammatical parallelism (Jakobson 1960) in evidence here, and ubiquitous in this corpus, as is typical in political rhetoric. Miller (1999, 2000, 2002a, 2007) suggests that this regular repetition of equivalent grammatical units is a common 'token', or 'flagger', of attitude, which is also often conflated, as here, with the semantics of countering and denial linked to the contextual variable of 'deliberate dispute'. [11] As such, she proposes that such resources may be seen as possibly register-idiosyncratic appraisal mechanisms.

Here is an example of wholehearted Democratic support for punishing, although, as will be seen, Democrats also argue for keeping the attacks of 9/11 distinct from the misdeeds of Saddam and Iraq.

(7)   All Americans were united in the desire to seek justice by finding and **punishing** the perpetrators of September 11.

(Tammy Baldwin, Democrat, 16 October 2003)

The issue of the implicitness or explicitness of appraisal construal, not just in the environment of node *puni*, but also in general, requires further reflection. At the start of this section, we introduced the notion of 'satura-tion'. The full potential richness of the term, and its implications for the fuzziness of readings of inscribed and/or invoked appraisal, has been, as far as we are aware, only ever theorized by White. In a posting to the Appraisal discussion list (AppraisalAnalysis@yahoogroups.com), on 14 January 2005, he suggested a sliding scale of saturation according to which *mob*, say, would be decidedly more saturated (in terms of negative evalua-tion) than *crowd*, but much less so than *rabble*. He appended, however, an important caveat which, despite intensive modelling efforts, still needs to be kept in mind:

> we can classify locutions which are highly saturated attitudinally as evaluatively 'explicit', and within appraisal analyses as attitudinal 'in-scriptions'. However, [. . .] we have to allow that there may be no clear-cut boundary between the evaluatively 'overt/direct' and the eval-uatively 'covert/indirect', that is to say, no clear-cut boundary between evaluative 'explicitness' and 'implicitness'.

> (White, Appraisal list posting
> [AppraisalAnalysis@yahoogroups.com], 14 January, 2005)

Despite essentially agreeing with White on this point, we did painstakingly attempt to calculate Democrat and Republican explicitness and implicit-ness on the basis of the typical mechanisms hypothesized as construing the difference. The results for *puni* were that Democrats selected for inscribed (explicit) appraisal twice as much as for implicit wordings, while the Republican data, much greater, more than reversed this finding. If the number of Democrat instances had been more significant, we might have tentatively concluded that they 'beat around the bush' less, if that is what explicating attitudes can be said to 'mean'.

In our interpretation, however, we were doing our scholarly best *not* to let our knowledge of the US cultural paradigm push us excessively towards the category of inscription. In short, we attempted, perhaps mistakenly, to discount the culturally saturated semantics of certain conventionalized ways of speaking. Thus, for instance, in this further example of Republican negative judgement on punitive measures for vanquished foes:

(8) Now, we learned that lesson because after WWII, instead of imposing **punitive** measures on the losers, we came up with the Marshall Plan.

(Henry J. Hyde, Republican, 15 October 2003)

we interpreted the judgement here not as being explicitly inscribed, but as invoked, and, in particular, as 'afforded' by the factual ideational meanings being instantiated here and in the cotext. We might have simply read men-tion of the Marshall Plan as inscribing such judgement, as a co-member of Congress would be likely to do. The reader position adopted is, in short, a vital factor. As a result, our findings on explicitness and implicitness must be seen as skewed and subject to variation. Trusting the saturation more, and thus seeing appraisal as being inscribed, would undoubtedly make for different results.

To Protect

Recalling the quandary regarding the creation of a sample of instances of this search node that would be statistically and contextually comparable to that for *puni**, our first step was to analyze all instances of *to protect* in the five-minute speeches, as their total number—twenty-six—was conveniently analogous to that of relevant occurrences of *puni**. We became concerned, however, that these came from what were all fairly brief monologues, after discovering that the *puni** data came exclusively from the sixty-minute speeches and full debates, almost twice as many from the latter (seventeen vs. thirty-two of all instances). Our at least partial solution was to *re*select occurrences for analysis. We now chose these randomly from the debates, which contain 209 of the 322 corpus occurrences of *to protect*, and did so in proportion to the normalized frequency of the total Democrat and Republican occurrences of *to protect* over the whole subcorpus: this being approximately 63 per cent for the Democrats—against approximately 37 per cent for the Republicans. Thus, twelve Democrat and eight Republican instances were randomly chosen for analysis, fewer than the relevant *puni** instances, but for a good reason.

We had already seen from a spot check that the numbers would not stay the same (as they did with the *puni** data, as *all* instances were analysed). And in fact they did not; they grew, and did so due to a phenomenon inherent to expanded concordance line instances, that is, other occurrences of the search forms may then be found in the cotext. But in this case they also grew due to the to-infinitive form being searched for, which made for the not infrequent occurrence of identical paratactically linked infinitives in the same environment, even within the same clause-complex, usually with 'to' being deleted. Such growth may be (another) argument for their 'keyness', or their power to signal 'aboutness' in the corpus. The initial twelve Democrat and eight Republican instances became seventeen to eleven, a total of twenty-eight, not too unlike the relevant *puni** instances, thirty-three. This is all to be kept in mind, then, with reference to the results of the analyses offered following. All findings concern the *second* set of data created unless otherwise specified.

Once again the dominant appraisal category construed is judgement and again, invariably, the subcategory of social sanction: propriety prevails. Figure 2.5 sets out the identifiable domains of such judgement and the relative Republican and Democrat figures. At first glance, yet again, Lakoff would appear to be right. Democrats *are* more concerned with protecting, even with reference to conventional Republican interests such as US troops/

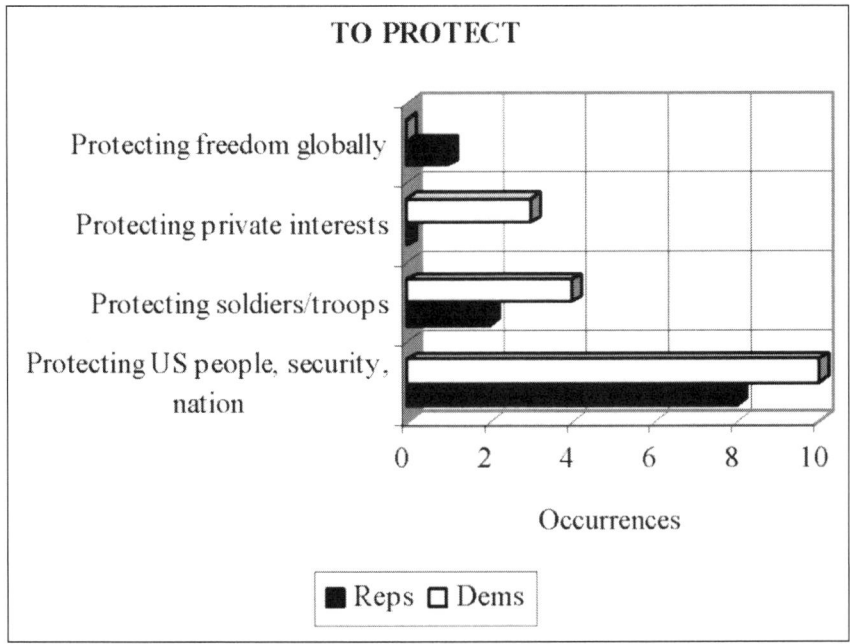

TO PROTECT

Figure 2.5 What Democrats and Republicans appraise with *to protect*.

people/nation. Their complete absence from the domain of 'protecting freedom globally' was, however, intriguing, as is their total *monopoly* of the typical Republican concern for 'protecting private interests'.

As we have already seen with **puni**, adding the +/–polarity factor to a consideration of what is being appraised sheds light on such incongruities. This time we will look at the breakdown for Democrats first, in Figure 2.6.

'Private interest' protection is judged exclusively negatively, three times, and on the same subject. One example is:

(9) Mr. Chairman, I find myself in disbelief that the same Delta Airline executives who could spend $25 million **to protect** their pension trust funds said today in Killeen, Texas, in my district, that they cannot afford to continue air service *during a time of war* to the community that is the home of the only two-division Army installation in America, Fort Hood. [original Congressional Record emphasis in italics]

(Chet Edwards, Democrat, 3 April 2003)

With reference to the semi-historical conflict between 'self-interest' and a concern with the 'common good' that we also aim at tracking, this is an unequivocal example of how typical Liberal Democrat rhetoric champions

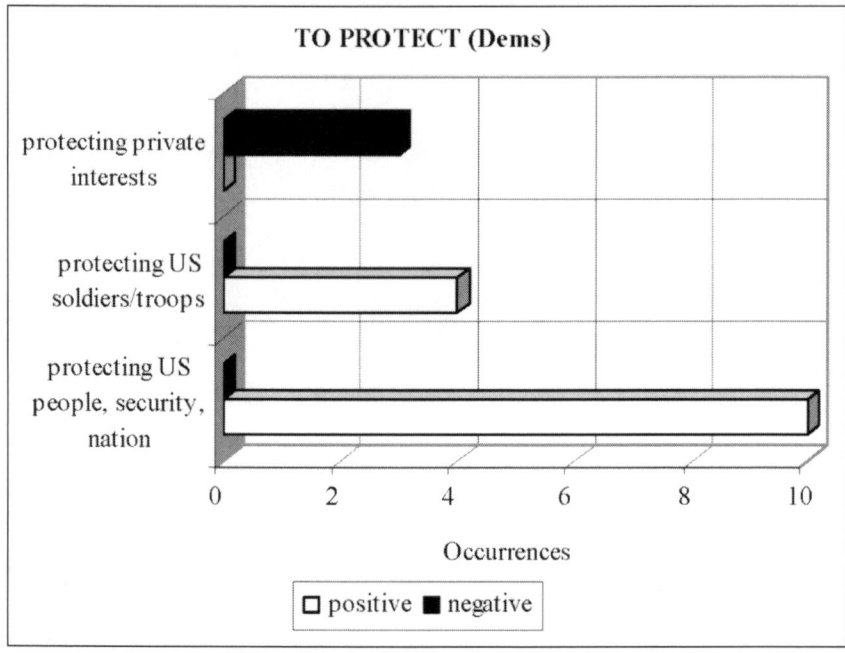

Figure 2.6   Positive vs. negative Democrat judgement of *to protect*.

the collective over the individual. Indeed, the statistically largest Democrat domain of protecting 'US people, security, nation' reveals a constant concern with protecting 'our own', 'at home'. In the following example, it pairs up with a concern with US troops abroad.

(10) While making sure our forces are secure abroad, we must also strive **to protect** our people at home.

(Lucille Roybal-Allard, Democrat, 3 April 2003)

Once again we witness other appraisal categories contributing to the judgement being construed. The nominal group 'our people at home' is at least implicitly signalling the speaker's positive affect towards what 'must' be protected. In short, it is not only ideational meanings which 'afford' appraisal; 'supporting' appraisal systems, and so interpersonal meanings, do the same.

We have still to account for the Democrat absence from the category labelled 'protecting freedom globally'. As a step towards explaining this, we look at Republican judgement of 'to protect. Figure 2.7 shows the breakdown of Republican occurrences according to domain and polarity, all, *pace* Lakoff, positive.

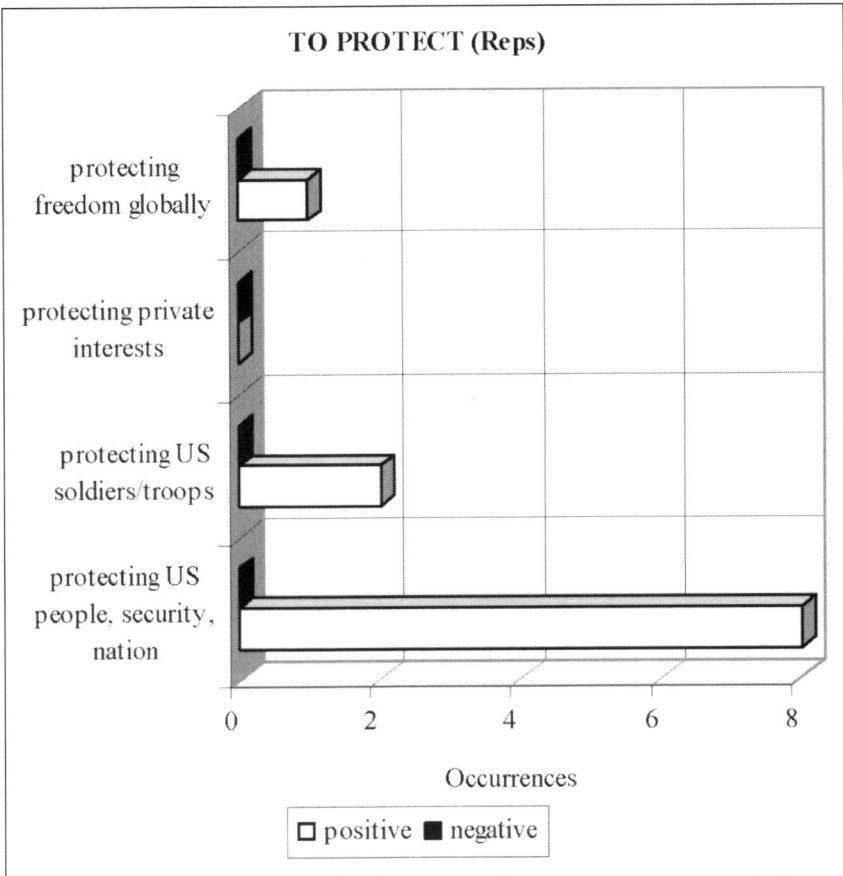

Figure 2.7 Positive vs. negative Republican judgement of *to protect*

The one instance of what we have classified as global protection is the following:

(11) Mr. Chairman, thousands of our Nation's troops woke up today with the express task of defending our country against Saddam Hussein's reign of terror in order **to protect** the safety and freedom of his people, neighboring countries and other nations like ours across the globe.

(Peter Hoekstra, Republican, 3 April 2003)

And note how the 'task of defending' the United States is, unquestionably, represented as having the aim of protecting the people of the nation that war is being waged on, Iraq, as well as its 'neighboring countries and other nations *like ours* across the globe' (our emphasis).

Inclusiveness is not quite total and this is but one instance in limited data. A better idea of the nature of this extended 'global' protection may be had if we exploit an occurrence from our initial five-minute speech data. This also illustrates two appraised domains missing in the new data: judgement on 'attacking Iraq for the purpose of protecting the US' and 'Multilateral protection'. Unsurprisingly, on the first of these Republican judgement is positive while on the latter it is negative.

(12) There is a great danger in so elevating the trappings of international consultation and the rituals of multilateralism that they become a surrogate for our true purpose: we have **to protect** ourselves and the world by disarming Saddam Hussein.

(Tom DeLay, Republican, 28 January 2003)

The argument mockingly counters the chiefly Democratic appeal to *diplomacy* running through the corpus. The Republicans generally have no time for that, labelling multilateralism, as here, the potential deterrent from 'our true purpose' (i.e., 'to protect ourselves and the world'). Neither have they any doubt about the proper means for achieving that purpose: 'by disarming Saddam Hussein'. As forecast previously, such rhetorical certainty contrasts with Democrat doubts on the propagandized linkage between 9/11 and Saddam. Once more this emerged only, but strongly and repeatedly, in the five-minute speech data. As this assessment is recurring and constructs an insurmountable hurdle between the sides regarding their evaluation of just *who* and *what* should be protected, it will be cited below. Here it is paired, as it indeed usually is, with Democrat negative judgement on extending protection beyond US borders.

(13) The question, and it is the only question that matters, is this: Did the threat posed by Saddam Hussein rise to the level of an imminent threat to national security or even to a grave and gathering danger? So far nothing leads to that conclusion [. . .] But the 200 young Americans who have died and continue to die, one died last night, did not pledge their lives to make the people of Iraq better off. They pledged **to protect** the United States of America from real threats to our security. They died believing that they did.

(Jim McDermott, Democrat, 15 July 2003)

Once more, the semantic intensification resulting from grammatical parallelism reinforces the judgement being construed, as the co-presence of another appraisal category (graduated appreciation: '*real* threat to *our* security') also does. Again the Democrats see protecting the United States positively, but the explicit exclusion of the 'other' here is introversive, if not isolationist. The 'common good' the Democrats pay at least lip service to is consistently all-American and clearly confined within its boundaries, whereas the magnanimous global protection aggressively sponsored by the Republicans is more universal, all-inclusive, a rhetorical justification of the US crusade against terror, which also means, for them, against Saddam.

On explicitness vs. implicitness of appraisal instantiation in the environment of *to protect*, our findings were quite surprising: notwithstanding intentionally allowing our reading to be more swayed by 'saturation' this time around, we found *more* implicitness than in the **puni** data, which, recall, showed nearly twice as much explicit inscription in Democrat utterances than in those of Republicans. The results of analysis of the second set of data for *to protect* actually gave us 100 per cent implicitness for Republicans and 75 per cent for Democrats. The findings may be considered more reliable in the case of the Democrat data, which are decidedly greater for this search node, but one still needs to ask oneself what other factors may be responsible for this disparity.

A comparison with the first set of five-minute speeches *to protect* data only muddies the waters further. The Democrat preference for invoked (implicit) appraisal rises to 85 per cent, while the Republican figures for explicitness are the highest here across all three sets of data: nearly 50 per cent. Again, and for various reasons, our findings on explicitness and implicitness must be seen as too unstable to be very significant. The speakers, however, are for the most part *not* the same in the different sets of data, so that perhaps we need to bring in the question of 'individual' speaking styles, something we tend to eschew dealing with, but which may just count for something.

2.3.2. How Democrats and Republicans Take their Stands

In this subsection, our findings on speaker stance involving resources for intersubjective positioning will be selectively reported. As said earlier, the basic distinction in the engagement system is twofold: we classify utterances that make no reference to others' voices or points of view as 'monoglossic', and, as 'heteroglossic', those that do give space to dialogic alternatives (Martin and White 2005:99–100). This latter category is then broken down into contracting and expanding mechanisms, according to the degree to which utterances are closed or open to alternative speaker positions. Figure 2.8 maps these categories.

Of course this is a patent over-simplification, both of a very complex interpersonal phenomenon and of the system that has been modelled to account for it. As evidence we provide an overview of the delicacy of the system of heterogloss in Figure 2.9.

It must remain beyond the scope of this chapter to do more than gloss our findings for the subsystems of contraction and expansion, as we cannot adequately sum up their grammatical resources and semantic functions. A word will be said, however, about the potential effects of the use of the monogloss, or the bare, unqualified statement.

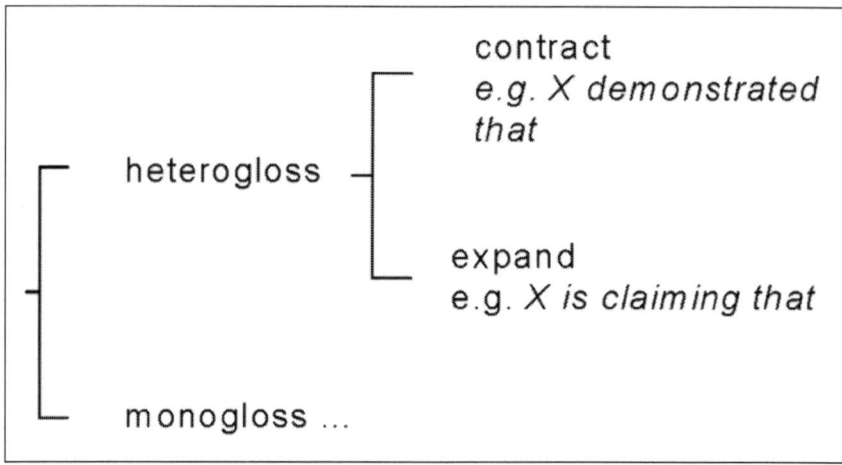

Figure 2.8   Engagement: monogloss vs. heterogloss: contract and expand (from Martin and White 2005:104)

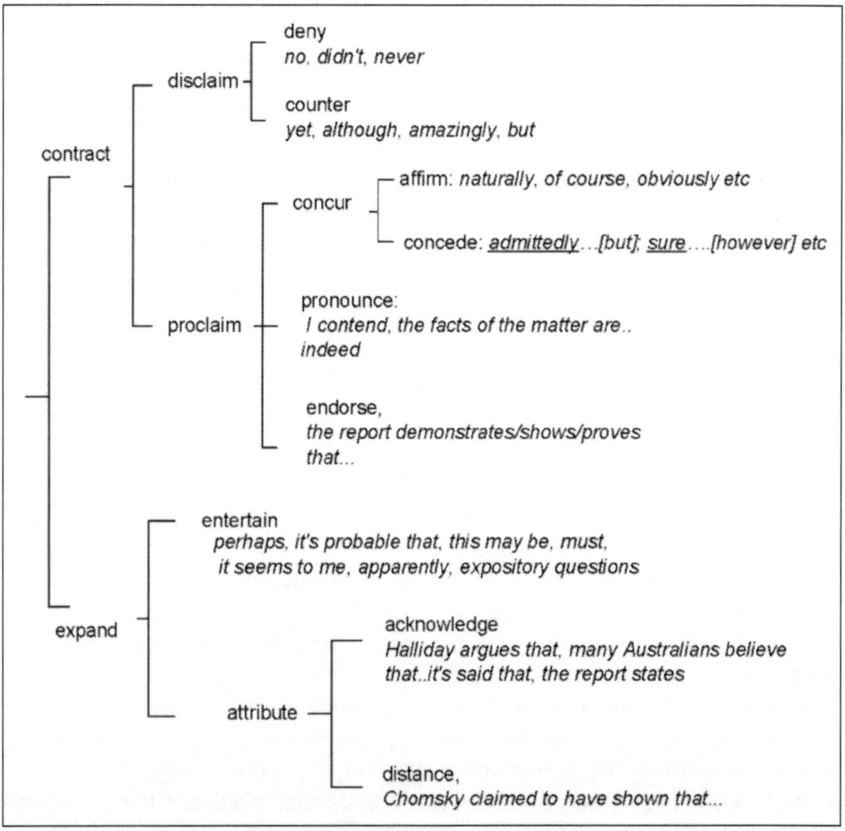

contract

   disclaim

      deny
      no, didn't, never

      counter
      yet, although, amazingly, but

   proclaim

      concur

         affirm: *naturally, of course, obviously etc*

         concede: *admittedly...[but]; sure....[however] etc*

      pronounce:
      I contend, the facts of the matter are..
      indeed

      endorse,
      the report demonstrates/shows/proves
      that...

expand

   entertain
   perhaps, it's probable that, this may be, must,
   it seems to me, apparently, expository questions

   attribute

      acknowledge
      Halliday argues that, many Australians believe
      that..it's said that, the report states

      distance,
      Chomsky claimed to have shown that...

Figure 2.9   Engagement: the heterogloss system (from Martin and White 2005:134).

Monoglossic assertions, as White (2003) points out, construct the speaker as having the status and moral authority not only to assert and assess, but also to do so in a way which chooses *not* to recognize, and hence to suppress, alternative viewpoints. They are essentially non-negotiable. At the same time they construct a special relationship between the textual voice and its modelled hearer/readership. This is because the monogloss is frequently associated with the assumption that speaker/writer and audience operate with and agree on the same beliefs and values. As a result, a relationship of solidarity and concurrence is being forged between the speaker's position and that of those who hear/read it. As a further result, the 'cost' of denying such alignment for the latter can be high.

As any parliamentary/congressional body is the *locus* of institutionalized confrontation, however, these general hypotheses must be somewhat rethought, and in terms of the specific contextual variable, broached in section 2.1.3, of the Tenor of this text type in its US spatial setting. As Miller (2004:275–6) notes:

> the discourse role of a Representative is to present arguments that presumably either: i) represent those of the majority of the voters that elected them to the House, or ii) correspond to those of the party in whose ranks they were elected. Both of these presumed dicta are influential in determining speaker positioning, and yet neither is invariably followed. Despite division along party lines, some Representatives see their role (discursive and non-) as being more independent of party and partisan positions; thus, a more personal Tenor (vs. the institutional) is almost always contemporaneously there, and tolerated. With reference to other Representatives [the role is] to express and 'reason' one's opinions, often explicitly agreeing/disagreeing with previous speakers (intratext). Yet, within the House itself, alignment or alienation on debated issues appears to be generally pre-established, rather than being the expected or the effective outcome of the persuasive powers of Representatives.[12]

Thus, the status and moral authority being presumed with a bare statement in the congressional context is *an already officially acknowledged one*, and the (at least) dual nature of the audience (comprising hearers *on* the speaker's side and others lawfully opposed to it) means that there will be a largely pre-established number of hearers in agreement, but also in disagreement, with that statement. Moreover, the costs of dissent are minimal, because institutionally legitimated, indeed conventional. Perhaps that is one reason why congressmen and -women are, to a considerable extent, monoglossic.

Remembering that we have many more Republican than Democrat utterances in the environment of *puni*, both parties tend to select for heteroglossic stance, with reference to punishment at least; nineteen out of twenty-seven Republican, and four out of six Democrat utterances—that is, 70 and 66 per cent, respectively—are heteroglossic, as can be seen in Figure 2.10.

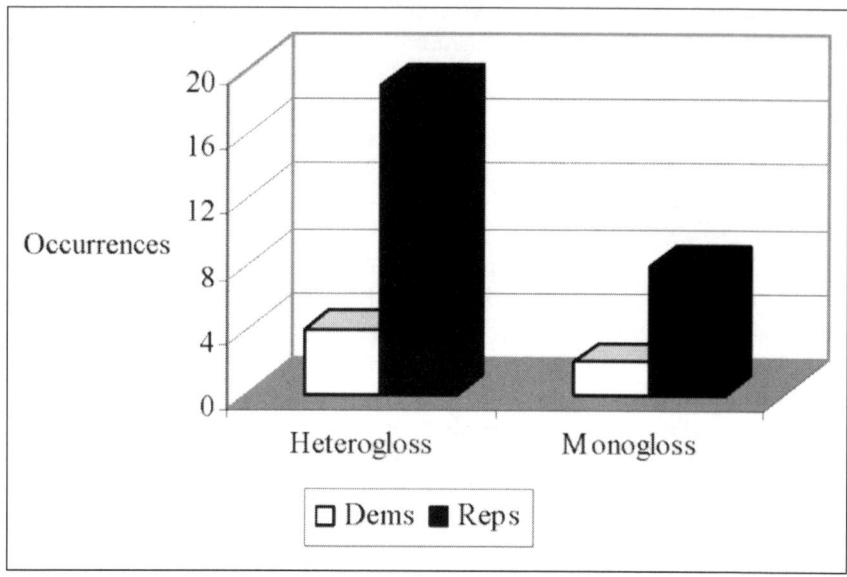

Figure 2.10   Heterogloss vs. monogloss in the environment of *puni*.

The following instance of positive judgement on punishing Iraqi mistreat-ment of POWs contracts, and proclaims: pronounces, by personalizing (*'my hope'*). This rhetorical construal of solidarity between speaker and hearer '[. . .] against some dialogic adversary' is typically exploited in political speechmaking (Martin and White 2005:130).

(14) It is my hope that this Congress and the IC [International Commu-nity] will send a strong signal to the Iraqis that if they do not up-hold the Geneva Convention and treat our troops humanely [. . .] the Iraqis will be sought, caught and they will be **punished** as war criminals.

(Sam Johnson, Republican, 26 March 2003)

Concerning the subcategories, findings will be briefly reported: all Demo-crat utterances are contractions and, within these, the overwhelming major-ity (75 per cent) are disclamations, with a preference for denial (67 per cent). Given the register, we repeat, the semantics of countering is always implicit—that is, countering the other side's already expressed, or at least presumed, opinions.

The data for Republican subcategories, because more numerous, are slightly more significant. Similar to the Democrats, in 95 per cent of cases contraction is favoured. Within contraction, there is a more than two-to-one preference for proclamation, rather than disclamation. Within proclamation, we have a fairly even proportion of pronouncements and endorsements. And within disclamation there is again a two-to-one option for denial, as opposed to countering, but, once more, the semantics of countering are to be seen as being implicitly in place.

Stance options rarely remain invariable for more than two running clauses. But a counter–example from the Republicans, containing a series of monoglosses that cumulatively assess punitive measures against vanquished foes negatively, is:

(15) After World War I, we had the Versailles Treaty. It was **punitive**. It spawned resentment in Germany. The result was World War II.

(Ralph Regula, Republican, 16 October 2003)

And once again another attitude system—negative appreciation of the Treaty here—serves to invoke, interpersonally, the judgement being construed.

The results for the *to protect* engagement analysis are very different, as can be seen in Figure 2.11.

Recalling that the proportion in the environment of **puni** was only 2:1 in favour of heterogloss, Democrats select heterogloss decidedly more often in the environment of *to protect*—a full fifteen times to two, and these two monoglosses occur in contiguous clauses in the same utterance; this is also an example of how one node occurrence became two:

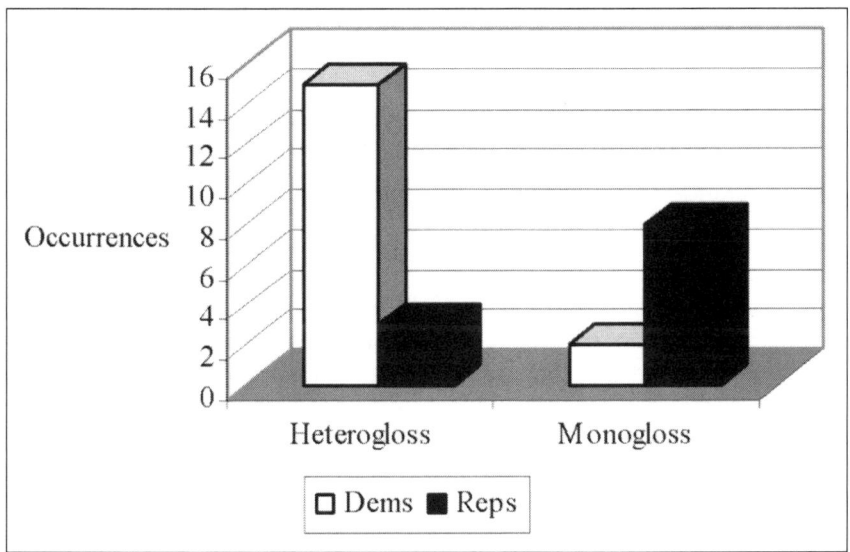

Figure 2.11 Heterogloss vs. monogloss in the environment of *to protect*.

(16) At home the Coast Guard continues **to protect** our shores and ports. On Monday, March 17, the Secretary of Homeland Security initiated Operation LIBERTY SHIELD to increase security at our Nation's borders and **protect** our critical infrastructure and key assets.

(James L. Oberstar, Democrat, 20 March 2003)

Yet the scanty number of Democrat **puni** data must, again, be kept in mind.

Republicans, however, opt for the monogloss in nearly 73 per cent of their utterances (eight of the eleven instances of *to protect*). One instance, replete with the kind of lexical metaphor (or better, metonymy) said to 'provoke' evaluation, is the following positive judgement of support of US troops:

(17) My gratitude and prayers are with the 270,000 brave American troops at war **to protect** the American people, including 2,512 Minnesota National Guard and Reserve Troops. Mr. Speaker, politics stops when war starts. It's time for all members of this body to take off their political hats and put on their American hats in support of our troops. At time of war, there are no Republicans, no Democrats and no Independents, only Americans.

(Jim Ramstad, Republican, 20 March 2003)

As is often the case where lexical metaphor is in evidence, however, *grammatical* metaphor is as well (Halliday and Matthiessen 2004:586–658). There would clearly be more 'congruous' ways of saying what is being said here. For instance, rather than representing *my gratitude and prayers* as nominalizations which 'accompany' the troops, it would be more congruent to say that *I am grateful to and praying for* them. Moreover, rather than represent *political* versus *American* backing as *hats* to be, materially, taken on and off, the semantics might be lexicogrammatically remapped as something like *We need to stop thinking in a partisan fashion and make the well-being of our troops our first priority*. In this way the cognitive and causative processes involved in this latter instance would be explicitly realized and the classifiers 'political' and 'American' in the original 'hats' metaphor would become, more congruently, the recommendation of a different manner of thinking. But then, of course, these would no longer be monoglosses.

Keeping in mind that there are more data for Republicans in the case of **puni** and for Democrats in the case of *to protect*, in our first five-minute speech *to protect* sample, later abandoned for the reasons discussed earlier, the proportion of Republican heterogloss selection was also decidedly lower than in the **puni** data. But Democrat findings were quite different: rather than the decided penchant for heterogloss found in the second *to protect* sample, the heterogloss vs. monogloss proportion that emerged in the first sample was an equal 50:50, still, however, in contrast to the 2:1 Democrat preference for heterogloss in the **puni** data.

The findings on subcategories of heterogloss for the *to protect* data for the Democrats are in part similar to and in part quite different from those for **puni**. Contraction is still the most selected category (down slightly from 100 to 92 per cent), but the disclamation: proclamation ratio is nearly exactly reversed from what it was for **puni**—now 34 and 76 per cent, respectively.

The Republicans prove to be more consistent: contraction remains the preferred subcategory, going up from 95 to a full 100 per cent, and the disclamation: proclamation ratio is similar (for **puni**, 32:68; for *to protect*, 40:60).

In the first *to protect* data findings there was more subcategory variety, due to there being more instances of rhetorical questions and quoted and reported attribution. Once again an example from those initial findings illustrates another divisive domain of judgement which is missing from the second *to protect* data: 'unlimited spending to protect the US', on which Democrats were consistently negative and Republicans, positive.

(18) You cannot separate war from America's ability to meet the needs of our own people here at home. We need to ask the questions: Why does America have hundreds of billions to ruin the health and take the lives of innocent people in Iraq but no money to provide health care for all Americans? Why would America spend hundreds of billions to retire Saddam Hussein, but no money **to protect** the retirement security of its own people? Why does America have money to blow up bridges over the Euphrates River in Iraq, but no money to build up bridges over the Cuyahoga River in Cleveland? The path America must take is one of peace which leads to prosperity.

(Dennis J. Kucinich, Democrat, 8 January 2003)

This is also a further illustration of the Democrat concept of a strictly American—and so 'self-interested'—'common good'.

A reasonable-sounding hypothesis accounting for the distinctions between the findings in the two *to protect* samples is that five-minute speeches, despite their brevity and the time limit set on them, are decidedly more pre-prepared and thus more carefully constructed to include: (1) just what the speaker wants to include and (2) diverse, and more uncompromising, ways of taking a stance towards it. The debates are for the most part on bills, motions, reports, and so on, which one argues are to be supported, or not.

2.3.3. On Possibly Register-Idiosyncratic Resources

Another caveat is immediately necessary. The 'possibly' in this section's title is there to stress that no properly *'probabilistic'* claims about register-idiosyncrasy can be made without having performed much more extensive quantitative studies on this corpus and carefully selected reference corpora (Halliday 1993:24). What follows are thus tentative generalizations.

Throughout the report of appraisal analysis findings earlier, we have continually, if not wholly systematically, pointed to possibly register-idiosyncratic attitude and engagement mechanisms at work. Miller (2007), having such register-idiosyncrasy as its prime research aim, marshals such attitude and engagement resources in a more orderly fashion, and on the basis of wider-ranging research into the question. There it is suggested that 'tokens' of speaker evaluation in the functional variety of parliamentary/congressional debate are typically multiple, densely intertwined, and functionally interdependent and this study has confirmed that proposal. Included were features such as mood selections (and rhetorical questions/'suggestions'), 'we'/'our' forms, grammatical metaphor, 'facts' (Halliday and Matthiessen 2004:470 ff.), grammatical parallelism, and thematic progression, at least some of which we have noted in operation here as well. There, too, it is proposed that, due to the contextual variable of 'deliberate dispute', the countering of alternative viewpoints intra/intertextually would appear to be an inherent parliamentary/congressional way of meaning and that disclaim: denial resources seem typical means for doing this (cf. Bevitori 2007). Moreover, it is proposed that 'softening' strategies, including higher numbers of heterogloss instantiations, are linked to what may be seen as a typical congressional 'etiquette' of 'false' deference to adversaries (cf. Bayley 2007). Subtle irony, for one, often calls for something more than a bare statement, indeed means pulling out the rhetorical stops. A good example from a Republican, ridiculing the rhetorical and intellectual ineptitude of a Democrat member, is the following:

(19) Mr. Chairman, reclaiming my time, I understand what the gentleman is saying, but oftentimes what one intends in a very simple amendment is not really the effect. Now, if the gentleman is talking about no further military action without a declaration of war, and I think that is what he is talking about, because Article I, section 8 refers to declaring war, let me make the point that the United States has not declared war since World War II. Korea was a massive war, but there was no declaration of war. Vietnam was a massive war, but there was no declaration of war. We worked on resolutions passed by the Congress to authorize the President to take whatever steps necessary **to protect** American interests or whatever the purpose was at the time.

So what I am suggesting is that this is a mischievous amendment for those who are opposed to this war in Iraq. They certainly have a right to oppose the war, and I wish we did not have to go to war as well. But I know that if we do not take care of the problem before it gets out of control, then it becomes out of control.

(C. W. Young, Republican, 3 April 2003)

Though time precludes an account, we hope that at least some of the myriad attitude and engagement mechanisms at work in the preceding segment will be, by now, evident.

2.4. IN CLOSING

As we admitted from the start, our investigation has been fraught with 'fuzziness', which, however, is an inevitable part of what must be a dynamic, and so necessarily unstable, process of language (system and instance) description. Still, much remains to be done.

It will be recalled that our essential aim in this chapter was to engage with Lakoff's hypothesis on political positioning and prove it to be an over-simplification. Essentially what he posits are two separate and conflict-ing 'moral systems' for conservatives and liberals. These, he proposes, are expressed through 'lexical metaphors' belonging, on the conservative side, to the 'strict father mentality' and, for the liberals, to the 'nurturant par-ent' one. We mistrusted the theory as leaving out too much: for example, not only condensing the complexity of politically positioned social sub-jects' ways of making meaning, but also abridging the store of linguistic resources at their disposal for doing so.

To be able to categorically say we've 'won' our challenge to Lakoff, investigation of many more of his 'strict father' or 'nurturant parent' lex-emes, and more instances of them in more corpora, would, by rights, be needed. However, in terms of our basic research questions, we can already say that the results of this corpus-assisted analysis have shown that Lakoff's hypothesis is, as suspected, too neat.

Firstly, we have observed that the meaning of these two culturally key concepts—*protect* and *punish*—is highly indeterminate and can only be investigated in extensive co- and con-text. Secondly, we have seen how speaker attitudes also very much depend on *what* is being appraised and that domains of appraised behaviours are varied and variously nuanced. Evaluatively, Democrats and Republicans freely cross party lines, though of course this is no surprise, as they are not subject to the kind of pressure that is customary in British parliamentary practice to toe those lines. Thirdly, we have seen that speaker attitudes are, as was posited, construed in an ample choice of ways, that is, that it is certainly not only what Lakoff calls lexical metaphor that provides evidence of such 'mentalities'.

So, then, we have shown that the conflicting positions of 'strict fathers' and 'nurturant parents' are not mutually or consistently exclusive to mono-lithic categories one can easily label 'liberal' or 'conservative'. Oversimpli-fying ourselves, we might say that we have discerned how Democrats tend to eschew **puni** and aim *to protect*, and would do so in the interests of the 'common good', but that that 'common' is invariably 'local' and so almost, indeed, 'self-interested': they would look after their own. Republi-cans undoubtedly engage more with the semantic field of **puni**, but not simply to side with it. And they too would *protect*, but righteously and globally, and oftentimes by means of punishing.

A full-text, exclusively qualitative analysis would not have allowed us to examine ways of evaluating these behaviours in almost a million and a half words spoken over a year of congressional sittings, and to say certain, hopefully significant, things about them. We've only been able to attempt to do this by wedding qualitative to quantitative methods that let us use our corpus as a kind of 'echo chamber' to focus, economically, on apparently preferred ways congressional speakers have of taking their stand.

NOTES

1. Although this paper is the product of continuous co-operative research, parts 2.1 (2.1.1, 2.1.2), 2.3, and 2.4 may be largely attributed to Miller; 2.1.3 and all of section 2.2 are to be credited to Johnson.

2. For a working definition of 'keyness', see *Wordsmith Tools* 4.0 online manual: http://www.lexically.net/downloads/version4/html/index.html?keyness_definition.htm (last accessed 16 June 2007). What we propose here is a distinction between 'corpus' and 'cultural' keyness, as these concepts do not necessarily overlap. Simply because a word does not emerge as being significantly 'key' in a text or corpus, which is what we mean by the former term, does not mean that it is not, in the context of culture in which the text or corpus is produced, but also in the text or text-collection in which it comes to our notice itself, an indicator of highly significant meanings. Our notion of cultural keyness is not dissimilar to that of Stubbs (1996, 2001), and Mahlberg (2007), though it would be only proper to link up to the seminal notion as first proposed by Williams (1976 [1983]). Quite fortuitously, we have discovered that what we are calling 'corpus keyness' is being developed in the comparable terms of 'computer keywords' by Mahlberg (2009 and personal communication), who thus focuses on the instrumentation rather than the site of interrogation. She also introduces a third category of keyness, 'textual', which, in the context of corpus research, we have simply conflated with 'corpus'. But avoiding the term *textual* is also in the interests of averting confusion with the well-established metafunctional category in our SFL framework. Keeping the meanings of the metalanguage we use straight must, we believe, be prioritized.

3. The term *idiosyncratic* strikes us as being more precise than *specific*, and for at least two reasons: there is always a certain amount of overlap between the material and social contextual variables governing diverse registers; furthermore, the system, or total meaning potential of a language, may be immense, but it is not infinite. Thus it is predictable that what may be seen as 'idiosyncratic' to one register will rarely be the exclusive property of that register.

4. We are using the term *discourse* to mean '[. . .] the process of language in some recognizable social context' (Hasan 2004:16).

5. Sinclair had given the keynote lecture with the same title at XVII International Systemics Conference in Stirling, Scotland, in 1990.

6. As Geoff Thompson has also wisely observed (personal communication), 'At the simplest level there's a broad division between "wordingers" and "meaningers" in deciding on what Attitude is being expressed', meaning that the former would focus on the innate connotations of word(ings) and the latter on the general evaluative thrust of the text. The 'middle path' is of course possible and what we would aim to walk: never overlooking how the text is worded, but recognizing that meaning/evaluation units are never mechanically mapped onto isolated words.

7. The experience of Don (2007) dissuaded us from a task whose replicability was, at best, transient, even for the primary analyst. She had even developed her own software for the labour-intensive job of tagging and computing, only

to find, as the work advanced, that '[. . .] the context which included me as analyst had changed also' (personal communication). Our further discussion of the snares of appraisal analysis in section 2.3 underwrite Don's belief that '[. . .] the methodology is replicable, but the findings may not be, since appraisal is about semantics and that is dependent on context and all that that entails'.

8. CDA has been conscientiously theorized and practised at least since Kress and Hodge (1979). Names that have been most widely connected to this and the critical linguistics tradition include Fowler (1988, 1996), van Dijk (e.g., 1993), Fairclough (e.g., 1995a), Caldas-Coulthard and Coulthard (e.g., 1996), Toolan (1997) and Wodak (e.g., 2006). Its often incompatible ideological bases have also been scrutinized (Miller 1993). Baker (2006) has explicitly put forth the issues involved in marrying DA and CDA to corpus methods, a marriage that many have been celebrating in their own work for some time, however (cf., e.g., diverse studies in Bayley [ed.] 2004). Positive discourse analysis (PDA), proposed as a 'corrective' to CDA, would shift the focus of attention *away* from semiosis in the service of abusive power and reconsider 'power' with respect to the way it '[. . .] circulates through communities, as they re-align around values, and renovate discourses that enact a better world' (Martin 2004:30; see also Miller and Turci 2006). Both approaches are, in our view, needed and should be seen, to borrow a favoured Hallidayan image, as opposite sides of the same analytic coin.

9. Logogenesis is '[. . .] the unfolding of the act of meaning itself: the instantial construction of meaning in the form of a text [. . .] in which the potential for creating meaning is continually modified in the light of what has gone before [. . .] using logo(s) in its original sense of "discourse"' (Halliday and Matthiessen 1999:18).

10. The Congressional Record is available at http://www.thomas.loc.gov/ (last accessed 22 June 2007).

11. The appraisal model currently hypothesizes various ways in which attitude may be implied, or invoked; one of these is by intensifications which are said to 'flag' it (cf. Martin and White 2005:61–8).

12. For more on the important distinction between 'institutional' and 'individual' Tenor, see Miller (2002b:122–3).

3 'Just War', or Just 'War'
Arguments for Doing the 'Right Thing'[1]

Paul Bayley and Cinzia Bevitori

> We should work out the right thing to do, whatever anyone else may say.
>
> (Tony Blair, House of Commons, 12 March 2003)

This chapter will make a corpus-assisted discourse analysis of the language used by the British government in the House of Commons in 2003 concerning the war in Iraq. It will first comment briefly on some of Tony Blair's public statements on the doctrine of international law and subsequently will set out the basic principles of just-war doctrine. After a brief description of methods and materials, it will investigate whether the discourse of the government, in arguing its case to use 'all necessary means' to disarm Iraq to the House of Commons, contains traces of just-war theory. The final section will focus on the discourse of just one member of Parliament, Claire Short, who was both a government member and a backbencher in the year under study.[2]

3.1. INTRODUCTION

3.1.1. Tony Blair's 'Just War'

The decision of the British government, sanctioned by Parliament on 18 March 2003, was unquestionably one of the most controversial in recent British history. This has been amply recognized by the then Prime Minister Tony Blair, as illustrated by the following extract from a speech made in his Sedgefield constituency on 5 March 2004, nearly a year after the invasion of Iraq. Blair began by conceding that:

(1)   No decision I have ever made in politics has been as divisive as the decision to go to war to in Iraq.

(Tony Blair, 5 March 2004)

But he was, and has since been, relentlessly consistent in the defence of his decision to participate in a preventive war, on the grounds of the tangibility of the threat posed by the Iraqi regime in particular, and by international terrorism in general, and of the moral duty to face it:

(2) The global threat to our security was *clear*. So was our *duty*: to act to eliminate it [my emphasis].

(Tony Blair, 5 March 2004)

However, the preventive (or pre-emptive) use of force could possibly, but not necessarily, be considered contrary to the norms of international law governing armed conflict according to which self-defense and/or response to aggression are the only justifications for military action. Blair was of course hardly unaware of this and, referring back to a speech he had made in Chicago on 24 April 1999, he said that, even before 11 September 2001, he was:

(3) already reaching for a different philosophy in international relations from a traditional one that has held sway since the treaty of Westphalia in 1648; namely that a country's internal affairs are for it [sic] and you don't interfere unless it threatens you, or breaches a treaty, or triggers an obligation of alliance.

(Tony Blair, 5 March 2004)

He was thus theorizing the right to go to war to correct injustice in a sovereign state. During the Chicago speech (see also Fairclough, 2005), which went under the title of 'Doctrine of the international community', Blair, speaking of the 'humanitarian' intervention in Kosovo, said:

(4) This is a *just war* [my emphasis], based not on any territorial ambitions but on values. We cannot let the evil of ethnic cleansing stand. We must not rest until it is reversed. We have learned twice before in this century that appeasement does not work. If we let an evil dictator range unchallenged, we will have to spill infinitely more blood and treasure to stop him later.

(Tony Blair, 24 April 1999)

There are, then, clear connections between the 1999 and 2004 speeches.[3] In the latter, Blair argued that the doctrine of international law needed revisiting and hypothesized that the use of military force in order to liberate an oppressed people was, or at least should be, justified:

(5) It may well be that under international law as presently constituted, a regime can systematically brutalize and oppress its people and there is nothing anyone can do, when dialogue, diplomacy and even sanctions fail, unless it comes within the definition of a humanitarian catastrophe

(though the 300,000 remains in mass graves already found in Iraq might be thought by some to be something of a catastrophe). This may be the law, but should it be?

(Tony Blair, 5 March 2004)

Nonetheless, in the same speech he repeated what he and members of his government had affirmed on numerous occasions in the House of Commons in 2003:

(6)   And I accept, incidentally, that however abhorrent and foul the regime and however relevant that was for the reasons I set out before the war [. . .], regime change alone could not be and was not our justification for war. Our primary purpose was to enforce UN resolutions over Iraq and WMD.

(Tony Blair, 5 March 2004)

Despite Blair's general frankness, he seems to be rather coy on two points. On the one hand he was making a case for rethinking the bases of international law, and just-war principles, and yet on the other he was claiming, in the specific case of Iraq, to be acting in order to 'enforce' UN resolutions. In example (5) he hedges the question of whether the situation in Iraq amounted to a humanitarian catastrophe which would have justified military intervention, attributing this idea to some unspecified thinkers— *might be thought by some*—while in example (6) he expresses in a concessive clause his appraisal of the Saddam regime—*abhorrent and foul*—but denies that this was the 'justification for war'. The adverbial *alone*, however, allows us to conclude that it was a secondary justification.

In order to cast some light on how the British government justified military action in the solemn setting of Parliament, and also in order to verify what contribution a corpus-assisted discourse analysis can make to an analysis of institutional language and international relations, the following sections will make a linguistic analysis of the discourse of the British government in the House of Commons in 2003, measuring up its arguments against the framework of just-war doctrine, as well as against the discourse of other members of Parliament (henceforth MPs). It is not our purpose, of course, to establish whether the war was or was not 'just' (this is a task for the historian and the political scientist; see, for example Enemark and Michaelsen, 2005) but rather to look at the discourse to see whether the British government, explicitly or implicitly, construed their actions as conforming to just-war principles or whether they were testing new frontiers in international law.

3.1.2. Just-War Theory

Not all wars, or theories of war, are based on the concept of a just war. Pacifists would consider a just war a contradiction in terms and oppose military action in any circumstances. Realists argue that moral principles should not be employed in the field of international relations, either as descriptions or prescriptions; according to them, foreign policy is conducted by nation-states on the basis of their national interests.

Just-war theory is associated with religious thought and while it can be traced back to Aristotle and Cicero, it is systematically linked to the work of Augustine (354–430) and St. Thomas Aquinas (1225–1274), in two phases in which Christianity made a doctrinal move from pacificism to a position according to which warfare could be justified in certain circumstances and in certain forms. It was given much attention between the fifteenth and eighteenth centuries, and was revived in the second half of the twentieth century—see, for example, Walzer (1977), and Orend (2000). Most just-war models are based on two major categories: *jus ad bellum*, the justice of resorting to war, and *jus in bello*, the justice of conduct of the war, although some include *jus post bellum*, justice in the transition from war to peace. Many of the criteria set out in the first two categories have been encoded into international laws, such as The Hague Treaty and the Geneva Convention. According to the principle of *jus ad bellum*, a war should have a 'just cause', and be fought for a 'right intention'; it should be declared by the 'proper authority', be a 'last resort', there should be a 'high probability of success', and the benefits should be 'proportional' to the cost in human lives (Christopher 1994:87–96). Among the *jus in bello* principles, the means of conduct of the war should be 'proportional' to its ends, and it should 'discriminate' between combatants and noncombatants (Beer and Hariman 1998).

The various criteria in this framework are clearly interrelated and, according to the doctrine, in order for military action to be considered just, all of them must be satisfied. As they stand, they are extremely vague; adjectives such as *just*, *right*, and *proper* could cover a myriad of meanings. Moreover, while some if not all have been codified into international law through which they have had their meanings defined, the criteria often seem futile. For example, the *jus in bello* principle of 'discrimination' has been encoded into The Hague Convention (1907), which, among other things, establishes that 'The attack or bombardment, by whatever means, of towns, villages, dwellings, or buildings which are undefended is prohibited' (section 4, article 25), and yet no political or military leader has appeared before an international tribunal to answer to what has been a frequent practice since the convention was ratified. 'Proper authority' has been taken to mean the authority of a sovereign nation-state according to the laws or conventions of that state. Most nations have procedures through which war can be legally declared. In the United States, for example, the Constitution vests Congress with the power to declare war (article 1, section 8, clause 11) and yet the wars fought in Korea and Vietnam were never authorized by the legislature. In fact, since the Second World War, wars have rarely been declared, but merely waged.

In these instances, the problem is that principles which have been codified into law have not always been respected, and perhaps this should be of no surprise—almost by definition, laws are disobeyed since otherwise they would not be necessary. However, there are also problems of interpretation. Let us take 'just cause'; the main just causes for war are self-defence against aggression and the defence of other nations from aggression. Aggression may take different forms, from border skirmishes to full-scale invasion, and so one may ask what kind of aggression justifies a war. But what of pre-emptive military action to prevent an anticipated aggression? It could be argued that anticipating an attack with a first strike may satisfy the principle of 'proportionality'. What evidence of a clear and imminent danger is required to justify a first strike? Which institutions are authorized to certify the existence of such a threat? Another and more tenuous just cause of war is to prevent a gross violation of civil rights. In such a case there is a conflict between the sovereignty of states and the role of international law. Who is to judge the severity of the violation and to certify that the cause is just? Similar problems arise with 'proper authority'; although this has referred to the authority of the state, most nations have freely become members of a supranational organization, the United Nations, whose charter, in Chapter 2, Article 4 states:

(7)   All Members shall refrain in their international relations from the threat or use of force against the territorial integrity or political independence of any state, or in any other manner inconsistent with the Purposes of the United Nations.

(Charter of the United Nations, 1945)

This would suggest that the UN, not the nation-state, has supreme authority to decide on the appropriate response to an act of aggression or a threat. But the language of the law is characterized by indeterminacy; meanings can be open to interpretation. To take the case of British government's legal arguments on the use of military force in Iraq, the foreign secretary argued on more than one occasion that:

(8)   We have made it clear throughout that we **want** a **second resolution** for political reasons, because a consensus is required, if we can achieve it, for any military action. On the legal basis for that, it should be pointed out that resolution 1441 **does not require** a **second resolution**.

(Jack Straw, 10 March 2003)

In other words, any military intervention in Iraq had already been authorized by the UN. Indeed, a corpus query for *the authority* in the discourse of the government in the House of Commons yields fifty-seven instances of *authority* as an abstract noun, all collocating with *the United Nations* or *the UN*. Of these, thirty-three collocate with material processes, typically nonfinite, or nominalizations in the semantic area of *upholding* (in the case of military action) and four with an antonym—*undermining*—in the case of no military action. Concordance 3.1 illustrates twenty of these.

o that in a way that most **upholds** the	authority of the UN. If such a vote takes plac
military action, it is essential that the	authority of the UN **be upheld**. If such action
already, that decision, **upholding** the	authority of the UN, was justified on 18 Marc
plate the use of force **to back up** the	authority of the UN. The regime was brutal, th
now doing is seeking **to enforce** the	authority of the United Nations when it said
nd thereby **the maintenance** of the	authority of the United Nations. From the outs
Union—and, above all, **maintain** the	authority of the United Nations, that we shoul
The motion was there **to uphold** the	authority of the United Nations as set out in re
3 votes—on the need **to uphold** the	authority of the United Nations as set out in
to use military action **to back up** the	authority of the UN. We might not like it, but
y action is necessary **to maintain** the	authority of the UN to deal with the problem,
deal way to proceed is **to back up** the	authority of the UN and make progress on Isra
mplate military action **to enforce** the	authority of the UN. On the question of the de
ch action is necessary **to enforce** the	authority of the UN. We must be willing to co
g to use military force **to back up** the	authority of the United Nations. That is the rig
ncibly committed to **backing up** the	authority of the United Nations this time, not
e United Kingdom **must uphold** the	authority of the United Nations as set out in R
ects, will continue **to undermine** the	authority of the UN and directly affects my w
omfort to tyrants and **emasculate** the	authority of the United Nations. It is for these
s regime, but an **undermining** of the	authority of the United Nations, the rearmame

Concordance 3.1 Concordance of *authority*: uphold or undermine.

These patterns of meaning that government ministers were repeatedly uttering might be stretching the boundaries of interpretation, especially when one considers that operative paragraph 4 of Resolution 1441 reads:

(9) *Decides* that false statements or omissions in the declarations submitted by Iraq [. . .] and failure by Iraq at any time to comply with, and cooperate fully in the implementation of, this resolution shall constitute a further material breach of Iraq's obligations and **will be reported to the Council for assessment**.

(UN Resolution 1441, 8 November 2002)

The meaning of this seems transparent: a second resolution, after assessment by the Security Council, would have been required before any subsequent action was taken. However, the government never cited this paragraph in the Commons, although it made thirty-seven references to the term *serious consequences*, from paragraph 13, which reads:

(10) *Recalls*, in that context, that the Council has repeatedly warned Iraq that it will face **serious consequences** as a result of its continued violations of its obligations

(UN Resolution 1441, 8 November 2002)

Clearly, if we were to ask whether 'serious consequences' can be legally interpreted as 'military action' (in accordance with the foreign secretary, who, on 21 January, told the House: 'The words "serious consequences" have only one meaning—the use of force'), a linguistic analysis of these two paragraphs would need to be founded on the intertextual resources of legal doctrine and jurisprudence, which would go far beyond our present remit.[4] However, we will illustrate, albeit briefly, one example of how this interpretation of the term was explicitly contested in the House:

(11) MARK HENDRICK (Labour backbencher): What does the hon. Gentleman take the words "serious consequences" to mean if it is not military action?
ELFYN LLWYD (Plaid Cymru, parliamentary leader): According to diplomatic language and the way in which previous resolutions have been drafted, those words do not authorise military action. Any expert on legal interpretation would confirm that.

(22 January 2003)

In section 3.2, we shall focus on the more common-sense *jus ad bellum* factors of 'just cause' and 'right intention'.

3.2. JUST-WAR DISCOURSE IN THE HOUSE OF COMMONS

3.2.1. Materials and Methods

Considering the value-laden nature of the discourses which we will analyze, and considering the fact that the analyst is inevitably part of the analysis, a brief statement of our sociopolitical positioning is pertinent. In the first place, we were both opponents of the war in Iraq, on grounds of principle— we did not believe it represented a case of 'last resort', for example—and of opportunity—we thought that the war would be ultimately difficult to win and that it would be more likely to breed terrorism than to defeat it. At the same time we were uncomfortable with the centrality of the notion of sovereignty within international law according to which any government is free to act in any way it desires towards its subjects or citizens—the poverty of which was illustrated by the horrors of the 1990s, in Rwanda and the Balkans. Having said this, the chapter might seem to be an exercise in what Martin (2007:85) has disparagingly (or 'uncharitably') called 'Watergate linguistics', 'the idea that by exposing language in the service of power we are contributing to a better world'. To this we would answer that we hope to approach our data with open minds and with a certain humility as regards the 'rights' and 'wrongs' of the question, and that there is still room to investigate the language of power, especially in a setting in which these rights and wrongs were both endorsed and contested.

The analysis will take into consideration one form of political language, parliamentary discourse. Although parliamentary discourse is a form of language that belongs to a small and closed discourse community in the

UK, although the British Parliament's importance in the decision-making process has been eroded by the strength of political parties, which can normally expect to marshal the support of their MPs in divisions, and although the role of the British Parliament as the institution where UK government activity is scrutinized has been diminished by the role of the media, we do believe that the what is said on the floor of the House of Commons is of significance because of the symbolic role it plays in the liberal concept of democracy and because its discourse may be said to demarcate which meanings can and cannot be made at the symbolic centre of Western democracies. In the case of the Iraq war, the role of parliamentary discourse is particularly important. Firstly, although, according to the British constitution, war making is a royal prerogative and therefore one of the discretionary powers of government, 10 per cent of parliamentary time in 2003 was dedicated to the conflict. The discourse role of MPs was either to justify or to contest military action and they expressed strong and explicit points of view. Secondly, the hold that political parties normally exercise over their MPs was broken during these debates as 139 Labour MPs voted for an amendment against the government's stance on the war.

The basic questions of methodology, corpus design, markup, and tagging procedures have already been dealt with in the Introduction and Chapter 1 of this volume and most issues can be taken as given. This paper will draw on corpus linguistic literature (e.g., McEnery and Wilson 2001), the descriptive framework of systemic functional grammar (Halliday 1994), work that has tried to reconcile these two traditions (Thompson and Hunston 2006), appraisal theory (Martin and White 2005), and previous work on parliamentary discourse (Bayley 2004). We would, however, like to briefly comment on how we mean to interpret 'corpus-assisted discourse analysis' and on the structure of the House of Commons subcorpus (henceforth the *CorDis HoC* subcorpus, or simply *HoC*).

The data have been analyzed using the procedures traditional to corpus linguistics, but because the *HoC* subcorpus is relatively small, because it was compiled by ourselves, and because the software permits access to full texts, we have also been able to read our subcorpus, and the process of shifting back and forth between the corpus data and the full texts permits the analyst a twofold gaze. Corpus data provide decontextualized information about lexical, grammatical, and semantic patterns; they also indicate entry points to the full texts for a more detailed discourse analysis. This allows us to examine examples in finer detail, locating them in their extra-linguistic and linguistic context, through which it is possible to discern how speakers construe the issues they are addressing, how they enact their multiple roles and status through discourse, and how their interventions fit into the textual framework of parliamentary events. However, it must be admitted that time and space limits do not permit more than a shift back and forth between corpus and text, providing fuller examples but a rather limited discourse analysis; although we hope that much will be achieved, it is also clear that much will be omitted.

The *CorDis HoC* subcorpus was derived from a simple corpus of all the 152 sittings of the House of Commons held in 2003, amounting to approximately 9,800,000 tokens according to the counting procedures of *WordSmith Tools 4.0*. By using the plotting function of *WordSmith*, seventy-three 'events' dedicated to the Iraqi question were identified and isolated, thus creating a subcorpus amounting to approximately 980,000 tokens, encompassing the discourses of 412 MPs. By parliamentary 'events', we mean moments of the parliamentary timetable dedicated to particular discursive activities, such as Question Time, Statements to the House (and the ensuing discussion), or government-initiated debates, and so on.

The subcorpus is a transcription of a speech event and is thus rather different from the speech event that it represents and there are many linguistic features missing (intonation, for example) and probably embellishments (Slembrouck 1992).

The official record also contains information of a metatextual nature such as headings, column references, and so on. However, the markup procedures used have allowed us to examine only the tokens that were recorded as being uttered on the floor of the House. As a consequence, references to the size of the subcorpus will be in terms of 'words within utterances', and cross-corpora comparisons will be based on counts using similar procedures.

The number of 'words in utterances' in the *HoC* subcorpus amounts to 960,293. Of these, members of the government uttered 358,472. Government members were, discursively, highly disciplined; only seventeen of them (out of almost one hundred sitting in the House of Commons) spoke during these events, and they did so only on the basis of their departments' remit, enacting their roles within the limits of their institutional responsibility. Moreover, the lion's share of governmental discourse was taken on by the three major players: the prime minister, the foreign secretary, and the defence secretary. Between them, they were responsible for the utterance of 244,273 tokens.

3.2.2. Right Intentions—Helping the People of Iraq

There are many ways by which one can begin to query a corpus. Traditional corpus linguistic studies typically begin by looking at frequent and polysemic lexemes. Because of the nature of this particular investigation, we shall begin with words, or co-selections of words, which are likely to carry significant sociopolitical meanings. Given the title of this paper, an obvious but interesting point of entry could be provided by a search for the nominal group *just war*. However, it turns out to be a very marginal phrase, occurring only fifty-five times in the entire *CorDis Corpus* and only fourteen times in the *HoC* subcorpus (plus two instances of *just wars* and one of *unjust war*). The word form *war*, on the other hand, as might be expected, is much more frequent. In the entire *CorDis Corpus* its relative frequency is 0.283 per 100 tokens, while in the *HoC* subcorpus it is a little lower, but still a high 0.232 per 100 tokens. However, a search isolating the discourse of members of the British government (in what we will call the government partition) reveals a relative frequency of only 0.069, a rather spectacular difference. What is more, of the 246 instances of *war* in government discourse, seventy-seven were representing things other than the 2003 conflict (such as *Gulf War, war criminals, prisoners of war, cold war, Second World War, First World War, Vietnam War, War Pensions Agency, Falklands War*). This relative 'silence' regarding war would be of interest in itself—within our methodology, comparative infrequency may be just as revealing as comparative frequency. However, we shall begin with the investigation of frequent lexical items and phrases.

Two of the most frequent lexemes in the *HoC* subcorpus are *Iraq* (including *Iraq* and *Iraqi*) and *people*. This is, of course, predictable; a search for *Iraq* defined the subcorpus itself, and *people* is a very frequently occurring lexeme in any corpus. They also tend to be frequently co-selected, once again quite predictably; a general corpus such as the *British National Corpus* (henceforth *BNC*) shows that the phrase *the people of* is nearly always contiguous with a place name. Behind this rather unsurprising finding lie some more interesting data. Let us take the nominal group *people of Iraq*, which is less frequent than *Iraqi people* in the entire *CorDis Corpus* but has a higher relative frequency (calculated per 100 tokens) in the *HoC* subcorpus than in any other, as Figure 3.1 shows.

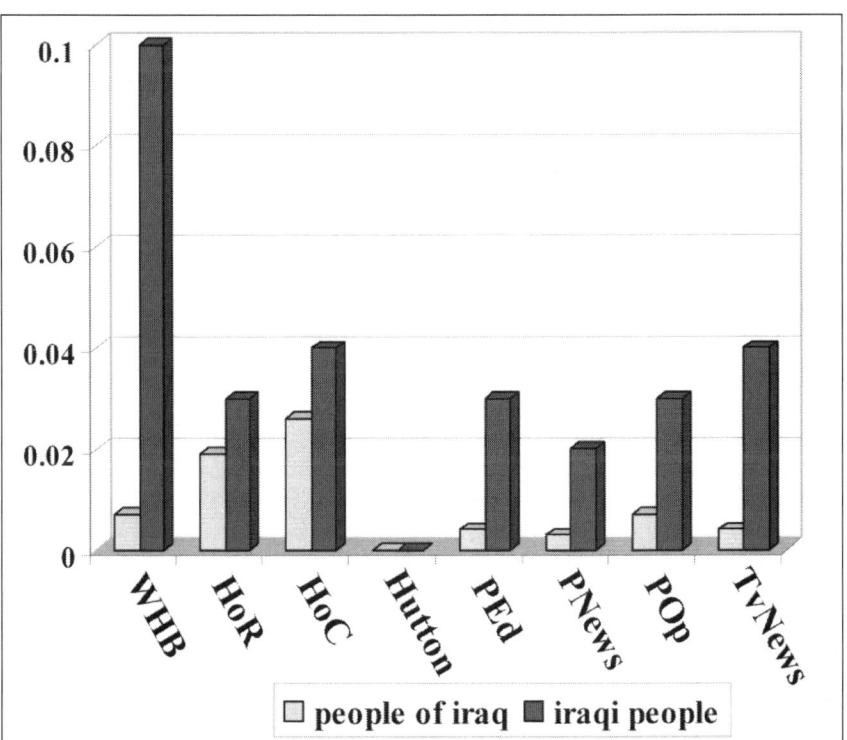

Figure 3.1   Relative frequency of *people of Iraq* and *Iraqi people* per 100 tokens.

In the *HoC* subcorpus, the relative frequency of the phrase is 0.033 per 100 tokens in the discourse of government members while it is 0.022 in the discourse of all other MPs. Adding to this the observation that of all the different kinds of 'event' that the corpus markup identifies, the one in which *people of Iraq* is selected most frequently (0.038) is the 'Statement to the House', an event during which a government minister, with the permission of the speaker of the House, makes a speech whose function is purportedly to inform the House on some activity of the executive, followed by a question-answer session. The 'Statement' is the parliamentary occasion during which the government exercises greatest control over the discursive agenda. On the contrary, in the 'event' during which the government exercises the least control, 'Question Time', the relative frequency of *people of Iraq* in government utterances is 0.018. All these numerical data seem to point to the possibility that the government's discourse was systematically construing a particular stance towards *the people of Iraq*, which seems to emerge also from a close reading of some key documents just before the war began. For example, during a tense Question Time on the eve of the commencement of hostilities, the prime minister said:

(11) Let me make it quite clear that our quarrel is not with the **Iraqi people** because the **Iraqi people** are the principal victims of Saddam Hussein.

(Tony Blair, 19 March 2003)

With this clause, which reverberates throughout the subcorpus, Blair makes a net distinction between the *Iraqi people* and their leader. A systematic look at semantic patterns which emerge from concordances reveals that the government's stance went beyond having 'no quarrel' with the Iraqis but rather it positioned the government as their 'benefactor'. We suggest, moreover, that the government reserved the postmodified form *people of Iraq* to construct a discourse of caring and empathizing, while the adjective plus noun phrase *Iraqi people* was used predominantly for the discourse of empowerment. In forty-three of the 117 instances of *people of Iraq* in the government partition, the Iraqis are either construed, through recurring transitivity patterns, as the beneficiary of a process of *helping, benefiting, providing* or of an agnate prepositional phrase (*for the benefit of*), as the recipient of a process of *giving*, or the complement of a causative process of *enabling* or *allowing* them to *build, rebuild,* or *restore*. Concordance 3.2 displays a sample of twenty instances of what might be called a semantic motif of 'helping' and which, in terms of just-war doctrine, can be seen as an affirmation of the government's 'right intentions' (see also Chapter 9, this volume, Concordance 9.8, drawn from a different subcorpus).

In some of these examples, the 'gift' of which the Iraqis would be beneficiaries was something quite concrete—'humanitarian relief', for example (see section 3.3), but more significantly the use of its oil. The phrase *for the*

le, and our priority is to **look after**	the people of Iraq and **help them to restore** the
t that the first **beneficiaries** will be	the people of Iraq. The Prime Minister has spok
to be used more widely to **benefit**	the people of Iraq. That will initially have to h
tion and other purposes **benefiting**	the people of Iraq. On Sunday, an important st
and for other purposes **benefiting**	the people of Iraq. The assistance fund will be s
ing to **provide a better future** for	the people of Iraq. Long-term security is the ke
build up the wealth available for	the people of Iraq. There is no reason why that
looks to **secure a better future** for	the people of Iraq. Our fight is not with the peo
o **provide humanitarian relief** for	the people of Iraq and to **support them in reco**
ran. All of us need to unite **to give**	the people of Iraq a **better future** and to work t
ent that we are **providing to help**	the people of Iraq. As one who supported the d
Hillsborough was how best to **help**	the people of Iraq **build a stable and prospero**
have set about the task of **helping**	the people of Iraq **to build a more secure, pro**
and will be used **for the benefit** of	the people of Iraq. There is also substantial fur
have to be used, **for the benefit** of	the people of Iraq. The war was never about oil
to be settled now **for the benefit** of	the people of Iraq. It sets out important principl
can be used **only for the benefit** of	the people of Iraq. That, too, will be audited. It
al community **in order to support**	the people of Iraq in **rebuilding** their country, t
ge all major players **in supporting**	the people of Iraq **to rebuild** their country. The
rget that is **of long-term benefit** to	the people of Iraq. I associate myself with the e

Concordance 3.2   Concordance of the *people of Iraq*: helping.

benefit of the Iraqi people was part of the motion that the House debated on 18 March, when the government asked the House's approval to take 'all necessary means':

(12) [. . .] in the event of military operations requires that, on an urgent basis, the United Kingdom should seek a new Security Council Resolution that would affirm [. . .] the use of all oil revenues **for the benefit of the Iraqi people**.

(Government motion, House of Commons, 18 March 2003)

In parliamentary language, as indeed in general language, certain expressions echo over large stretches of discourse—references to prior discourse in the House are a distinctive discursive feature (Bevitori 2005)—and in fact this seven-word cluster recurs fourteen times (eleven by members of government), and eight times in the variant form *for the benefit of the people of Iraq* (five by members of government). It was, clearly, part of the government's rhetorical strategy to highlight its 'right intentions' and rebut the accusation that the motive for the war was to gain control of Iraq's oil resources. Other 'gifts' were rather more abstract, such as the promise of a *better future*:

(13) Overall, our campaign looks to secure a better future for the **people of Iraq**. Our fight is not with **the people of Iraq**. There can be no greater demonstration of that than the efforts that we are making to provide

1. can the Secretary of State assure us that the awarding of the contracts will be fair and, as the money will come from the oil trust fund, in the long-term interests of the **people of Iraq**?
2. Most people would accept that the current situation, however imperfect, is an improvement for the **people of Iraq**.
3. However difficult or uncomfortable, we will take action to protect our freedoms, children and people, liberate the **people of Iraq** and build a world of peace and security where trust can be rebuilt in a future that we all must share.
4. the fact that one of the most murderous and brutal tyrannies has been destroyed? That, in itself, is a victory for not only the **people of Iraq**, but humanity as a whole.
5. If we take action that involves the use of our own weapons of mass destruction in a horrific onslaught against the **people of Iraq**, that, too, has to be put on the moral scales. Half the people whom we are going to kill are children.

The discourse of Conservative backbenchers (95,764 tokens in 521 utterances), on the other hand, as is fitting for a party in opposition, was characterized principally by the motifs 'we support the war but the government is not doing enough' (1), 'support our troops, who are helping the people of Iraq' (2), but the search also reveals two rather maverick propositions—'we are against the war' (3), and 'we were in favour of the war, but only with the backing of the UN' (4).

1. To date and to my serious regret, the Government have refused to take that simple but practical step, which would not only bring immediate relief to sufferers, but show the **people of Iraq** that we were genuinely committed in practical terms, through deeds as well as words, to their successful and secure future.
2. I also endorse the glowing and justified tribute that the right hon Gentleman paid to our troops and to the other British nationals who are working day after day in the public interest of the **people of Iraq**.
3. It sends a clear message to the Government that we are not yet convinced that the time has come to commit the lives of British troops, or to wreak death on the innocent **people of Iraq** in pursuit of their leader.
4. There is no doubt that we have removed an evil dictator who was oppressing the **people of Iraq**. I have every sympathy with those inside and outside Iraq who sought his removal. However, the case should have been made to the international community and executed under the auspices of the international institutions that we have spent half a century building up.

Liberal Democrat backbenchers (32,760 tokens in 207 utterances) belonged to the only national party clearly opposed to the war and this opposition transpires manifestly in the way that the *people of Iraq* were construed in their discourse. There are not many examples but they may be divided into three classes: 'are the Iraqis really benefiting?' (1); 'we are not communicating with the Iraqis' (2); and 'the Iraqis are deprived of resources' (3).

1. Is that not wholly contrary to the assurances that oil export revenue would be used exclusively for the benefit of **the people of Iraq**?
2. the deployment will obviously send out a positive message to our allies and, I hope, a message of determination to the Saddam regime, what message does the Secretary of State imagine it will send to **the people of Iraq**? Is he satisfied that enough is being spent by the US and UK Governments in telling **the people of Iraq** the true position and what problems they face?
3. I hope that the Hon Gentleman is right, but that does not negate my point that economic sanctions have stopped **the people of Iraq** getting the food that they need, and we have taken the blame for it.

These comparative results indicate that the discourse of backbenchers was heteroglossic, while the discourse of the government was monoglossic and gave the impression of being scripted and orchestrated, or at the very least highly coordinated. Although we do not have the space to make detailed comparisons across the various corpora, similar findings can be found in the discourses of the US executive and legislature. The use of *the people of Iraq* in the White House briefings is not dissimilar to that of the British government (with a greater emphasis on empowerment), while in the House of Representatives it was far more varied.

A search for the nominal group *Iraqi people* in government discourse yields some rather different results; like *people of Iraq*, it was used more frequently by government members than other MPs (0.062 as opposed to 0.032), although looking at the *CorDis Corpus* as a whole, it was much more frequent in the White House briefings (*WHB*) subcorpus (see Figure 3.1). It is possible to find the 'helping the Iraqi people' motif, although the 'help' that is being offered is typically ensuring 'political empowerment', and as such, even though it serves as a demonstration of 'right intentions', it construes another kind of just-war argument related more to *jus in bello* and *jus post bellum* rather than *jus ad bellum*. In fact, unlike the more generic 'helping' examples, all examples of the 'empowerment' motif were uttered after the opening of hostilities, although the prime minister anticipated it during a half-hour session of Question Time on the day before the armed conflict began. In answering a question put by the then leader of the opposition inquiring of his plans 'to put in place a civilian representative Government in Iraq', he neatly fitted together all the different meaning patterns associated with the nominal group in the discourse of the government that we have seen so far.

(14) We have set out a vision statement for Iraq and the **Iraqi people**, and it might help if I highlight one or two of its aspects.[5] First, we will support the **Iraqi people** in their desire for 'a unified Iraq within its current borders', and we will protect their territorial integrity. Secondly, we will protect their wealth, and I repeat again that any money from Iraqi oil will go into a UN-administered trust fund for the benefit of the **Iraqi people**. There should be freedom in 'an Iraq which respects fundamental human rights, including freedom of thought, conscience and religion and the dignity of family life', and there should be freedom from the fear of arbitrary arrest. There should also be an 'Iraq respecting the rule of law, whose government reflects the diversity and choice of its population', and who help to rebuild Iraq, for **the Iraqi people**, on the basis of unifying the **Iraqi people**. Those principles of peace, prosperity, freedom and good government will go some way toward showing that if there is a conflict and Saddam Hussein is removed, the future for the **Iraqi people** will be brighter and better as a result.

(Tony Blair, 19 March 2003)

The Minister who most frequently used the 'empowerment' motif was the foreign secretary, Jack Straw, and the preferred event was the Statement of the House. The following sentence concordance lines are drawn from two statements he made to the House on 10 April (1–2) and 28 April (3–6):

1. It is our *guiding principle* that, as soon as possible, Iraq should be governed by the **Iraqi people** themselves. [my italics].
2. It will work with the interim authority in the early stages, but we hope that such external institutions will be replaced relatively quickly by internal institutions that will be run for, by, and from the **Iraqi people** themselves.
3. As well as meeting humanitarian and other essential needs, and starting the process of physical reconstruction, *a key objective* of the coalition is to support a viable political process that allows the **Iraqi people** to create representative, democratic government for themselves. [my italics].
4. Secondly, it would create a constitutional framework to prepare the ground for the election of a democratic Government run by the **Iraqi people** themselves.
5. Of course there are problems associated with this dramatic change for the **Iraqi people** after more than 20 years of coping with a brutal and vicious regime, but a new and representative Iraqi Government, run by the **Iraqi people** and for the **Iraqi people**, will help to guarantee this freedom for future generations.
6. But within that, we *have to* establish strong and robust political institutions in Iraq, and to have some confidence and faith in the **Iraqi people** to run their own government—a confidence and faith in their ability that the dictator Saddam Hussein never had. [my italics].

The semantic pattern is realized grammatically in a number of ways; for example, the use of non-finite material processes such as *determine, take control, take responsibility*, finite material processes such as *run*, both in active or passive voice but always with *Iraqi people* as actor, and finally material processes such as *hand over* and *move* with the government or the allies as actor. The will of the government is expressed by causative and desiderative verbs such as *we must ensure* and *we ultimately want*. This combination of patterns was not discernible in the discourse of other groups in parliament, and was clearly a fundamental part of the government's rhetorical strategy. 20 of the 62 instances are illustrated in Concordance 3.3.

There is one final semantic motif associated with *Iraqi people*, and it is one that is echoed also in the discourse of backbenchers: 'the regime is brutal'. Among backbenchers the 'brutality' argument was frequently used in the rhetorical form of a concession ('I don't like Saddam, but'), as in the following example, which constitutes a premise to an antiwar argument.

(15) There are things on which we all agree. We can all agree that Saddam is **duplicitous**; there is no doubt about that. We can all agree that he has failed to meet, and has tried to avoid, his obligations under UN resolutions for many years. We can all agree that his regime is **brutal** and **ruthless**, particularly towards his own people.

(Richard Burden, Labour backbencher, 11 March 2003)

Grammatically, the motif is realized by a number of features: for example, adjectives expressing negative judgment of the regime—*pitiless, terrible,*

resses the fundamental right of the	Iraqi people to **determine their own political fu**
ture. We must also ensure that the	Iraqi people feel **involved in this reconstructio**
bringing forward the day when the	Iraqi people can **take full control of their own**
the elements necessary to allow the	Iraqi people **to run their country.** As I indicate
e achieved, we ultimately want the	Iraqi people **to take responsibility for their ow**
out the principle that we want the	Iraqi people **to take control of their own affair**
\e, Iraq **should be governed by** the	Iraqi people **themselves.** We therefore support t
t will be **run for, by, and from** the	Iraqi people **themselves.** The right hon Gentlem
sure that Iraq **is run by and for** the	Iraqi people **themselves.** As President Bush and
tive Iraqi Government, **run by the**	Iraqi people **and for the** Iraqi people, will help t
ve some confidence and faith in the	Iraqi people **to run their own government**—a c
aq—though, in the end, it is for the	Iraqi people **to determine** under the new structu
ll goal: **to hand sovereignty to** the	Iraqi people as quickly as possible in conditions
o create the conditions in which the	Iraqi people can **take responsibility for the gov**
iftly to **moving sovereignty to** the	Iraqi people. That is one of the aims of part of t
to hand over control of Iraq to the	Iraqi people and then safely leave that country. T
ponsibility and **sovereignty to** the	Iraqi people, but it would be irresponsible for us
e a **rapid transfer of power to** the	Iraqi people. That process has been started. As I
sure that it **is led by Iraqis**—by the	Iraqi people **themselves.** The process of transitio
t of Iraq **to be handed over** to the	Iraqi people. We want that to happen as quickly

Concordance 3.3   Concordance of *Iraqi people*: empowerment.

appalling—verbs expressing negative appreciation of the regime's behaviour—*they have [. . .] terrified*—and verbs and nouns expressing the affective condition of the Iraqi people—*suffering, suffered, frustration*. Twenty of the twenty-four instances of this collocation pattern in the discourse of the government are displayed Concordance 3.4, providing an apt transition to the next section, which will deal with arguments for a 'just cause'.

3.2.3. Just Cause: Regime Change or Disarmament

As was pointed out in the first section to this chapter, the position of Tony Blair towards 'regime change' as a just cause for war was not entirely clear. He argued that it should be a just cause in general terms, but fell short of claiming it as a just cause for this particular war. This can be confirmed in the corpus. A search for the nominal group *regime change* in the *HoC* subcorpus yields ninety-eight examples, only four of which were uttered by government members. Among nongovernment MPs, value orientations were highly variable. Take, for example, the following two examples drawn from the same debate and both from Labour backbenchers.

(16) I have supported **regime change** in Iraq since long before it was popular to do so. We argued that that man and his country would be a threat in years to come if we went on selling weapons to him and doing business with him. We all made a big mistake in doing that, but that does not change the fact that he must be dealt with now.

(John Smith, Labour backbencher, 22 January 2003)

e of **pitiless terror**. That is how the	Iraqi people live. Leave Saddam in place, and th
the 21st century, and meet it; of the	Iraqi people, **groaning under years of dictator**
illed by the Saddam regime. The	Iraqi people will begin to enjoy the freedom and
olly **unnecessary suffering** for the	Iraqi people Last November, the UN Security C
sequence of that will be freeing the	Iraqi people from **the terrible burden** and huma
the overwhelming majority of the	Iraqi people—but for the **appalling intimidation**
inimises **the suffering** of ordinary	Iraqi people, **brutalised by Saddam**; to safeguar
confidence of the Iraqi people. The	Iraqi people have **been terrified**. More than half
the **regime that has terrified** the	Iraqi people and **impoverished** the nation for tw
manitarian relief. For a generation,	Iraqi people were **starved** of information both a
only be used for the benefit of the	Iraqi people, or to compensate **other victims** of t
lly aware of the **frustrations** of the	Iraqi people—**frustrations** that existed in greater
ncern have been the **attacks** on the	Iraqi people themselves, including the assassinat
which demonstrates how much the	Iraqi people **suffered under Saddam**. I apprecie
roceeds used for the benefit of the	Iraqi people, rather than **stolen or squandered**,
used of various **crimes against** the	Iraqi people: they should be allowed to get on wi
d those around him rather than the	Iraqi people, who themselves have been his **vict**.
t with the Iraqi people because the	Iraqi people are the **principal victims** of Sadda
le who will rejoice most will be the	Iraqi people who will be free of **a murderous ty**

Concordance 3.4 Concordance of *Iraqi people*: brutality and suffering.

(17) The Americans say that weapons of mass destruction, not **regime change,** are the issue. Sometimes they change their minds; we hear different versions. We must ask ourselves, why we would bomb Iraq if some weapons were found. Why have we sent the inspectors in? Have we not sent them in to destroy the weapons if they find any? Why do we have to slaughter hundreds and thousands of innocent civilians if we can get at the weapons and contain the regime?

(Alice Mahon, Labour backbencher, 22 January 2003)

The following list of examples all come from the government (prime minister, Blair 1, 4 and 5, foreign secretary, Straw 2, defence secretary, Hoon 6–9, and parliamentary under-secretary to the Foreign Office, O'Brien 3). They comprise all instances of utterances containing *regime change* in government discourse, together with the relevant instances of co-selections of *regime* with the lexeme *remove*, and they are displayed in chronological order.

1. The argument about **regime change** has not changed. I have always said that the purpose of any action has got to be the **disarmament** of Iraq of weapons of mass destruction. That is the purpose, but the nature of the **regime** is relevant in two ways. First, **weapons of mass destruction** in the hands of a regime of this brutality are especially dangerous. (25 February 2003)
2. I do not like the Saddam Hussein regime—I regard it as one of the most revolting and terrible regimes in the world—but the focus of 1441 is not **regime change** per se, but the **disarmament** of Saddam's **weapons of mass destruction.** (26 February 2003)
3. Our aim is not **regime change,** but if Saddam Hussein does not **disarm,** we may have to **change** the **regime** in order to **disarm** him. If he remains in power with **WMD,** there is no question but that he will continue to murder his own people and to threaten the region. (11 March 2003)
4. I have never put the justification for action as **regime change.** We have to act within the terms set out in **resolution 1441**—that is our legal base. But it is the reason why I say frankly that if we do act, we should do so with a clear conscience and a strong heart. (18 March 2003)
5. It is the case that if the only means of achieving the **disarmament** of Iraq of **weapons of mass destruction** is the **removal** of the **regime,** then the **removal** of the **regime** of course has to be our objective. (19 March 2003)
6. As I have said, and as the Prime Minister made clear yesterday, we are seeking to remove weapons of mass destruction from Iraq. However, with the expiry of the ultimatum to the regime and to Saddam Hussein, the means of achieving that will be through the **removal** of the **regime. The removal** of the **regime** will be the specific focus of our military operations. (20 March 2003)

7. Our objectives remain as set out in the document placed in the Library of the House yesterday: to **remove** the Iraqi **regime** and its **weapons of mass destruction**. (21 March 2003)
8. As my right hon Friend the Prime Minister has made clear, it will be the **removal** of Saddam Hussein's appalling **regime** which will ultimately lead to Iraqi **disarmament**. (26 March 2003)
9. Above all, we are committed to seeing through what we have begun— **removing** the **regime** that has terrified the Iraqi people and impoverished the nation for two decades. (3 April 2003)

There are several observations to be made on these examples, beginning from one of a temporal nature; the pivotal proposition is 4, made on the day when the government asked the Commons' (unnecessary) imprimatur to go to war, while the final example was uttered a few days before the downfall of the Saddam regime on 10 April. It is quite transparent why the discourse changes after 18 March; once the decision to go to war had been made, the objective inevitably became the removal of Saddam. Secondly, *regime change* or *removal* is co-selected with *disarmament* and/or *weapons of mass destruction* in all utterances but two, although no. 4, however, does refer to *resolution 1441*, which in the language of the government amounted to the same thing. What seems to emerge is that regime change and disarmament are posited as two alternative 'just causes', with a government preference for the latter, at least at the beginning. However, on 11 March, *regime change* becomes a means to achieve the ends of disarmament. This concept is repeated on 19 March, and with the adverbial *of course* it reaches the status of an obvious, taken-for-granted proposition. On 21 March, both *regime change* and *disarmament* are put together and identified as objectives, while on 3 April, with military action in full swing, removing the regime becomes a *commitment* to be *seen through*, with *disarmament* slipping out of the picture altogether.

Nos. 2 and 4, uttered by Straw and Blair, respectively, are interesting because they seem to suggest a carefully orchestrated rhetorical strategy (see Chapter 9, this volume). They share semantic and grammatical features; both of them deny that regime change is the objective of eventual military action, both pronounce that the aim would be *disarmament*, in the first example, and *resolution 1441* (which amounted to the same thing), in the second, and both of them centre around a concessive relationship marked by the adversative conjunction *but*. The order of concessive and dominant clause, however, is reversed; Straw begins by expressing a negative judgement of the Saddam regime in a concessive clause, and proclaims the aim of the government in the dominant clause. [6] Blair, on the other hand, denies that regime change is his personal justification for action in a concessive clause and, in the final and dominant clause, expresses his happiness (affect, in Martin and White's terms) at what would be a felicitous, but merely secondary, consequence of military action—regime change.

In rhetorical terms, then, the government's foregrounded 'just cause' was the disarmament of Saddam's arsenal of weapons of mass destruction, while removing the regime was merely a means to achieve this, which brings us inevitably to the question of Saddam's alleged stock of weapons of mass destruction, the evidence of which, in the words of Jack Straw, was 'overwhelming':

(18) The **evidence** in respect of Iraq's possession of **weapons of mass destruction**, chemical and biological **weapons** and **weapons** programmes, and its readiness to develop a nuclear **weapons** programme, is overwhelming.

(Jack Straw, 13 February 2003)

A search for the word *weapons* in the *HoC* subcorpus yields 1,962 occurrences (relative frequency 0.20 per 100 tokens), 899 of which appear in the cluster *weapons of mass destruction* (0.094), along with a further forty-seven occurrences of the acronym *WMD*. Relative frequency in *HoC* as a whole is slightly higher than in the government partition, probably for a number of reasons. Many MPs did endorse the government's stance on the nature of the threat and voiced this frequently. However some opponents of the war tried to overturn the government's stance, construing the Anglo-American alliance as both possessors and users of such weapons. For example:

(19) Has my right hon. Friend drawn up contingency plans for the plight of the children, when they are subjected to such terror bombing with **weapons of mass destruction**?

(Alice Mahon, 10 March 2003)

Perhaps more significantly, as the year passed and doubts about the government's intelligence information and its dossiers began to emerge, the government's use of *weapons* diminished while that of other parties increased. Isolating the longest parliamentary events, debates, the highest relative frequencies for *weapons of mass destruction* are found in the debate initiated by the Liberal Democrats on 4 June (0.26), and the two debates initiated by the Conservatives on 16 July and 22 October (0.16 in both). All three debates were on motions calling for, in one form or another, an official inquiry into the government's handling of its intelligence. In these three debates, there were a total of 189 occurrences of *weapons of mass destruction*, only twenty-four of which uttered by government members.

The position of the Liberal Democrats had been clear from the outset; it had been opposed to military intervention. The Conservatives, on the other hand, had explicitly endorsed the government's position on weapons prior to the war:

(20) hon. Members on both sides of the House continue to make it clear
that this is a conflict not with Islam, but with a gangster who has
weapons of mass destruction and who needs to be dealt with.

(Michael Ancram, shadow foreign secretary, 26 February 2003)

And it had explicitly endorsed the use of force:

(21) There are matters at stake that rise above party politics. It is **the duty**
of the Government to act in the national interest, and it is **the duty** of
the Opposition to support them when they do so. The Prime Minister
is acting in the national interest today. That is why he is entitled to our
support in **doing the right thing**.

(Iain Duncan Smith, leader of the opposition, 18 March 2003)

However, on 22 October, on one of the allotted 'opposition days', the
shadow foreign secretary, Michael Ancram, spoke of:

(22) the **manipulation** of intelligence and **misrepresentation** of what was
intelligence and what was not; [. . .], **questionable** information and
statements about **weapons of mass destruction**, both before and after
the war.

(Michael Ancram, 26 October 2003)

Some Conservative backbenchers, notably Kenneth Clarke, were more
forthright. For example:

(23) I am astonished to hear the Foreign Secretary using language worthy
of George Orwell to describe how we went to war at a time when we
knew that there were no **weapons of mass destruction** posing a threat
to anybody.

(Kenneth Clarke, Conservative backbencher, 22 October 2003)

To return to government discourse, a query for instances of *weapons* in the
speeches and responses of the prime minister reveals a relative frequency
of 0.25, the highest among government members (once every 2 minutes 40
seconds on average, calculating a modest 150 words per minute) and 0.14 for
weapons of mass destruction. Blair's discourse on *weapons* was characterized not just by the frequency of the term but also by its attention to detail. In
what was certainly his most important speech to the Commons on the Iraqi
question, on 18 March, it is possible to find: *biological weapons, nuclear
weapon, missiles; VX nerve agent production equipment; 10,000 litres of
anthrax; 6,500 chemical munitions; 80 tonnes of mustard gas; sarin, botu-
linum toxin and a host of other biological poisons; an entire Scud missile
programme; 550 mustard filled shells and up to 450 mustard filled aerial*

bombs; and *a so-called dirty radiological bomb* plus twenty-one mentions of *weapons of mass destruction* and four *WMD*. These weapons of mass destruction were, according to Blair on 18 March, 'a real and present danger to Britain and its national security', a proposition which would on its own constitute a 'just cause' for a pre-emptive, rather than a preventive, war. This kind of argument was developed by Foreign Secretary Jack Straw. He uttered the word *peace* 101 times, most of them with reference to the Middle East in general in clusters such as *peace process* and *peace in the Middle East*. When he focused more specifically on Iraq, the recurring cluster (thirty instances, nineteen of which collocating with *threat*) was *peace and security*, a binomial which highlights the notion that 'peace' is not merely the absence of 'war' but also the absence of 'threats' and that it can only exist in the wider context of 'security' for peoples and nations.

Clearly, for Blair, the proposition that Saddam was a real and present danger constituted the central part of his argumentation and as such he was arguing in terms of just-war categories. As the following four examples show, he insisted that not using force was *weakness, folly and weakness, indulgence, feebleness,* and *permanent incapacity,* and that such weakness would lead not to *peace* but to *conflict*. The grammatical choices combine in such a way that in terms of the appraisal category of engagement, Blair's discourse is 'contracting', in Martin and White's terms (2005: 122–4), which means that he 'proclaims' and entertains no alternative points of view. He construed the scenario in term of absolute certainty—*no one will ever believe us, it will simply be, will only mean that when the conflict comes, the surest way,* and absolute necessity—*this indulgence has to stop.* Moreover, the weakness would lead to a future conflict that would be *more bloody, less certain and greater in its devastation*, which neatly slips in a further just-war argument: 'proportionality'—conflict now will reduce inevitable damage in the future. Less explicitly, but see the probable allusion to Munich 1938 (see also example (4), earlier) in example (26), Blair also invokes the 'last resort' condition.

(24) That is why a signal of **weakness** over Iraq is not only wrong in its own terms. Show **weakness** now and **no one will ever** believe us when we try to show strength in future [. . .] No one wants conflict. [. . .] But if, having made a demand backed up by a threat of force, we fail to enforce that demand, the result will not be **peace or security**. It **will simply** be returning to confront the issue again at a later time, with the world less stable, the will of the international community less certain, and those repressive states or terrorist groups that would destroy our way of life emboldened and undeterred.

(Tony Blair, 3 February 2003)

(25) This is not a road to **peace**, but **folly and weakness** that **will only mean** that **when the conflict comes**, it is more bloody, less certain and greater in its devastation.

(Tony Blair, 25 February 2003)

(26) The tragedy is that the world has to learn the lesson all over again that **weakness** in the face of a threat from a tyrant is the surest way not to **peace**, but—unfortunately—to **conflict**.

(Tony Blair, 18 March 2003)

(27) Our capacity to pass firm resolutions has only been matched by our **feebleness** in implementing them. That is why this **indulgence has to** stop—because it is **dangerous: dangerous** if such regimes disbelieve us; **dangerous** if they think they can use our **weakness**, our **hesitation**, and even the **natural urges** of our democracy towards **peace** against us; and **dangerous** because **one day they will** mistake our innate revulsion against war for **permanent incapacity.**

(Tony Blair, 18 March 2003)

3.3. *JUS IN BELLO.* THE CASE OF CLARE SHORT

The acrimonious debate on the Iraqi issue in the House of Commons in March 2003 and the unfolding events following the attack saw the resignation of two members of the cabinet. The former leader of the House, Robin Cook, resigned the day before the US and UK allied forces officially launched the war against Iraq, on 17 March 2003, and Clare Short, secretary of state for international development, had at the time already announced, or, as the press put it, 'threatened', that she would leave the government following Cook's example, but opted to stay in office for two more months before coming to her final decision to resign on 12 May 2003.[7]

Clare Short provides us with a vantage point for observation as remarkable differences emerge from a comparison of her discourse with that of other members of the government. The aim of this section is to compare and contrast Short's discourse with that of the government, as far as the principles of *jus in bello,* or justice in the conduct of war, are concerned. The questions we shall pose include: how does Short's discourse differ from that of the government on the question at issue? What do regular and, above all, irregular patterns tell us about her discourse? What kind of resources are used throughout the texts in order to negotiate attitude (Martin and White 2005) and how are meanings construed as regards the just-war principles and, in particular, *jus in bello*? Finally, how can corpus-assisted discourse analysis help us investigating a speaker's individual positioning? In the conclusion, discourses on war across the subsections of the *CorDis Corpus* will be compared and contrasted, focusing in particular on two of the other transcribed subcorpora, the House of Representatives (*HoR*) and the White House Press briefings (*WHB*).

In order to examine the differences (and similarities) between the government's and Short's discourse, the key words were first computed, comparing the Short partition, amounting to 29,517 'words in utterances', to the larger government partition (358,472) by using the *Keywords* facility of the programme *WordSmith Tools 4.0*. The data show that the keywords running through Short's discourse are in the semantic area of international development and assistance, either with specific reference to contingent resources, for example, *food, supplies, preparations, programme*, and so on, or to institutions (*UN, the World Bank*). For the purpose of analysis, we shall focus only on the top keyword (according to keyness): *humanitarian*.[8]

3.3.1. The Semantics of *Humanitarian*

Figure 3.2 illustrates the relative frequency of *humanitarian* in *CorDis* as a whole, in the *HoC* corpus and two of its partitions, the government (excluding Short), and Short. The frequency of the term is significantly higher in the *HoC* corpus compared to *CorDis* as a whole; in fact, 53 per cent of all instances of *humanitarian* in *CorDis* are from the *House of Commons*. However, what is most salient is the extraordinary high occurrence of the term in the Short partition compared to both the government and the *Hoc* corpus.

The term *humanitarian* is problematic for a number of reasons. In the first place, it is a word that is used only when there is, or is likely to be, some kind of tragic circumstance in the real world. Moreover, while semantically it would appear to be an inherently neutral word, when we look at it as part of a wider unit, it can be seen that it is semantically associated with both positive and negative attitudinal assessments; on the one hand, it is associated with words expressing positive appreciation of the practical concern for providing aid and protecting people's lives and rights. However,

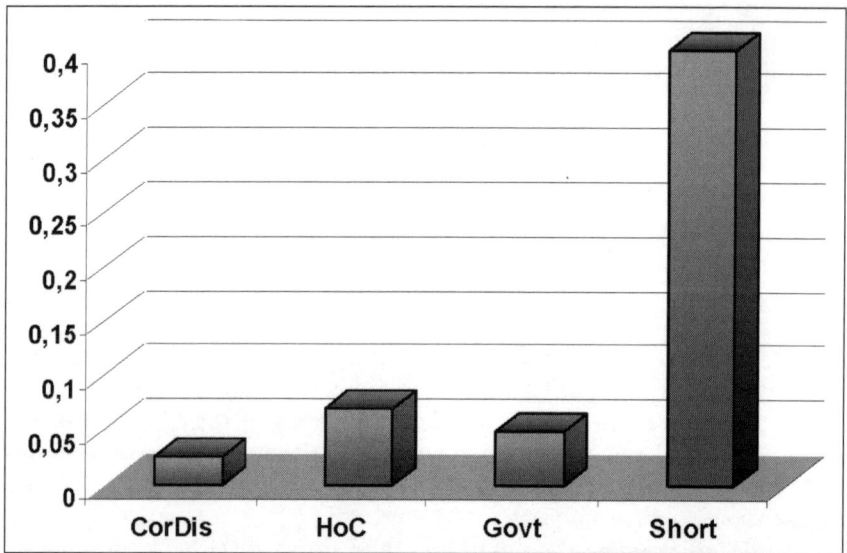

Figure 3.2   Relative frequency of *humanitarian* per 100 tokens across *CorDis*, *HoC*, and two of its partitions: the government (excluding Short) and Short.

on the other, *humanitarian* has negative semantic associations which high-light the impact of the tragic event on its victims. A close inspection of the concordances of *humanitarian* in the Short partition reveals three distinct meaning patterns:

1. the first foregrounds positive actions on behalf of victims and carries positive semantic orientations towards 'providers', *e.g., I hope that a united effort to provide **humanitarian** relief for the people of Iraq and to support them in reconstructing their country will help to bring that about;*
2. the second highlights future or present negative consequences of an event and carries with it negative semantic associations; *e.g., That is the most horrifying **humanitarian** possibility;*
3. finally, the third, which may be classified as institutional, typically refers to agencies, organisation, etc., *e.g., The Office of Reconstruction and **Humanitarian** Assistance.*

Figures 3.3 and 3.4 illustrate the distribution of the meanings of *humanitarian* in the Short and in the government partitions according to the three different collocation profiles. Noticeably, *humanitarian 1* is the most fre-quent in both partitions, covering 87 per cent of all instances in the latter and 58 per cent in the former. In contrast, *humanitarian 2* is much more frequent in the Short partition:

As far as the relative frequency of the occurrence of the lexeme in the two partitions is concerned, *humanitarian 2* is almost exclusively concentrated in the Short partition, 0.13 compared to 0.002 in the government partition. How-ever, *humanitarian 1*, although well documented in Short's discourse with a relative frequency of 0.25 per hundred tokens versus 0.05 in that of the gov-ernment, seems to be typically produced by the other government members.

As far as *humanitarian 1* is concerned, the semantic motif running through-out the texts may be labelled as 'duty to provide relief'. Typical collocates on the right hand of the node include: *relief, supplies, effort,* and *reconstruction,*

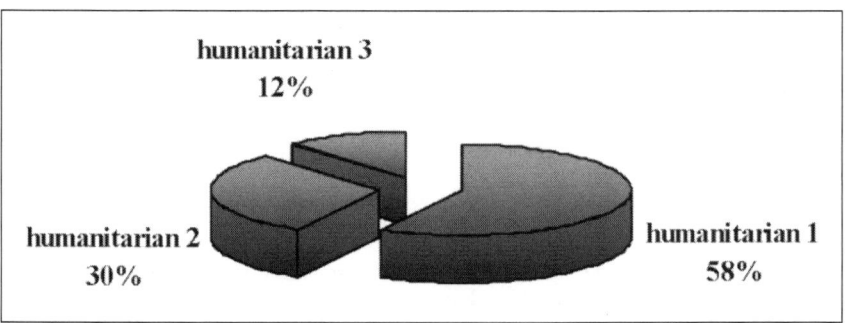

Figure 3.3 Distribution of the three collocation profiles in the Short partition.

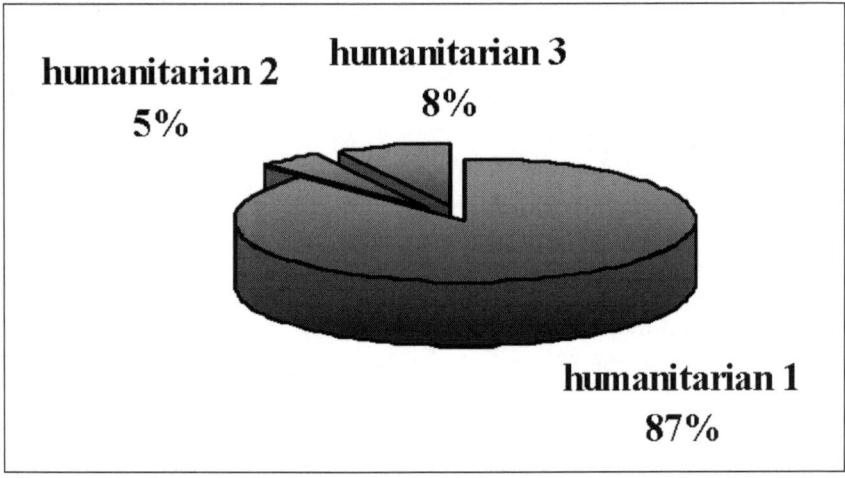

Figure 3.4   Distribution of the three collocation profiles in the government partition.

often associated with the material processes *provide, help, care for,* and combined with modal meanings of obligation and/or necessity. Not surprisingly, this is the most frequent meaning associated with *humanitarian 1* in Short's discourse; as a member of government, Clare Short had institutional duties and it is of no surprise that her lexical preferences should reflect her political remit. Concordance 3.5 illustrates a sample of twenty of the instances of *humanitarian 1* and its typical collocates in the Short partition:

play our part in any international	humanitarian **effort,** but no one should be compl
Iraq as an occupying power with	humanitarian **responsibilities and duties** to kee
l as the **immediate provision** of	humanitarian **relief** and the maintenance of civil
are in place to **provide** adequate	humanitarian **relief** and that proper preparations
rnational community behind the	humanitarian **and reconstruction effort** in Iraq.
the **immediate responsibility** for	humanitarian **support** for the people of Iraq in t
ng the conflict and **to ensure** that	humanitarian **relief and support** for reconstructi
pe that a **united effort to provide**	humanitarian **relief** for the people of Iraq and to
um of civilian casualties, a good	humanitarian **effort and a rapid reconstruction**
ations the coalition has **duties** of	humanitarian **care** until such time as things are s
or the UN system to be involved in	humanitarian **relief**—that is **a duty** everywhere a
and it will be possible to **deliver**	humanitarian **supplies** throughout the country.
to all international treaties and	humanitarian **obligations.**
aq now, so that they **can bring in**	humanitarian **supplies.**
egime to co-operate, in which case	humanitarian **aid and reconstruction** would stil
vide US **supplies** in the emergency	humanitarian phase
longer be in the lead in **providing**	humanitarian **supplies**
Our forces **have been providing**	humanitarian **assistance** in the areas that they oc
civilians are properly **cared for**	humanitarian **terms,** given the situation in
responsibility for co-ordinating	humanitarian **support,** in accordance with huma

Concordance 3.5   Concordance *of humanitarian 1* in the Short partition.

Although generalizations across groups of texts are revealing about patterns and tendencies, a shift from concordance to text allows us to look at discourse more closely, and to partly explore how texture is construed as the text unfolds. What emerges from the analysis of more contextualized stretches of discourse of *humanitarian 1* is the strong and rather predictable co-selection of *humanitarian care* and *relief* with modal meanings of duties and obligations. Example (28) illustrates that two relevant international agreements are frequently cited: the Geneva Conventions and The Hague Treaty, which, as already noticed earlier, according to scholars of just-war doctrine, are seen to embody some of its principles, as they set the standards of international law for humanitarian concerns and, in particular, for treatment of prisoners of war (3rd convention) and the protection of civilians during war (4th convention):

(28) As I have made clear—repeatedly, I had thought—under the Geneva convention and the Hague regulations the coalition has duties of **humanitarian care** until such time as things are safe, when the UN will return and take over the role.

(Clare Short, 10 April 2003)

The analysis of *humanitarian 2*, on the other hand, construing meanings of negative appreciation, is what seems to most typify Short's discourse. Typical semantic associations, as illustrated in Concordance 3.6, include: *catastrophe, disaster, crisis, risk, nightmare*, in conjunction with resources of graduation (*serious, severe horrifying*), which act to intensify meanings, frequently combining with modal meanings of possibility.

As has been said, the	humanitarian situation is already a **tragedy**.
are in touch with it on all **possible**	humanitarian scenarios.
I should like to set out the	humanitarian **risks**. There is a **very serious risk**
ups, that fighting **could result** in a	humanitarian **nightmare**.
avoid what would otherwise be a	humanitarian **disaster**.
That is the **most horrifying**	humanitarian **possibility**.
ows the complexity of the **possible**	humanitarian **disasters** that **could** occur if there
top of all of that, the international	humanitarian system is **under considerable stra**
urces and those of the international	humanitarian system are therefore **strained**.
s, but through the UN, to minimise	humanitarian **harm** and as speedily as possible r
st-cold war era, in which one finds	humanitarian **crisis** and military action side by s
reports of an **increasingly serious**	humanitarian situation in Baghdad.
remember that there is **a severe**	humanitarian **crisis** in the west bank and Gaza st
When	humanitarian **catastrophes** occur, those that co
ple of Iraq are **already suffering** a	humanitarian **catastrophe**.
he military giving consideration to	humanitarian **risks**—and there have—I have to t
n trying to get the world to face the	humanitarian **risks** and make preparations.
panies to deal with **the immediate**	humanitarian **crises**.
as been involved, especially in the	humanitarian **crisis**.
ad in neighbouring countries, so the	humanitarian **crisis** is also less bad there, althou

Concordance 3.6   Concordance of *humanitarian 2* in the Short partition.

A word of caution is needed here for the term *crisis*, which, despite carrying negative assessments, is different from all the other negative instances in the concordance as it refers to some generalized current or present situation; it is clear, however, that Short's 'humanitarian' discourse tends to point to the future, warning of the likelihood of a potential crisis. Furthermore, if we expand one of the concordance lines, it can be observed how meanings tend to accumulate and be intensified drawing on resources of graduation.

(29) I should like to set out the **humanitarian risks.** There is a very serious risk, **if there was** military action and there was not good organisation, that large-scale ethnic fighting **could** break out in the country. There has been deep repression. With the different ethnic groups, that fighting **could** result in a **humanitarian nightmare.** Any preparations for military action have to take account of that. There needs to be order and stability in the country to avoid what **would** otherwise be a **humanitarian disaster.**

(Clare Short, 30 January 2003)

The extract brings us to a debate initiated by the opposition at a time preceding the declaration of the war by the allied forces. The cumulative effect, through which Short fervently warns of the possible tragic outcomes of war, might be seen as a kind of 'saturation'—a type of prosodic realisation (Martin and White 2005:20) which is conveyed through the repetition of modal meanings of possibility/probability (*could*) embedded in *if*-conditional clauses (*if there was*) of the foreboding consequences; what is more, this tends to co-occur with the use of intensified lexis (*very serious risk, large-scale ethnic fighting, deep repression, nightmare, disaster*). This extremely negative collocation profile occurs very rarely in the government partition, once Short's discourse has been deleted. In the speeches of the foreign secretary, the defence secretary, and the prime minister—who produced most of the government talk on Iraq—*humanitarian 2* is selected only seven times, out of a total of 134 instances of the token. In Blair's discourse the words *humanitarian* and *crisis* or *catastrophe* do not tend to cluster. Moreover, concordance lines from the speeches of these ministers show that the negative appreciation of the humanitarian situation is largely construed through causal relationships, in which the past regime or Saddam Hussein is posited as major cause. Compare, for example, instances of *humanitarian catastrophe* and *humanitarian crisis* in examples (30) and (31):

(30) I have been involved in discussions with the Secretary-General of the United Nations about the **humanitarian crisis** that has existed in Iraq for the past 12 years, and about the circumstances that would arise if military action had to be taken.

(Jack Straw, 26 February 2003)

(31) The **humanitarian catastrophe** that we have seen over very many years in southern Iraq and indeed elsewhere in Iraq is entirely the responsibility of Saddam Hussein's regime and the brutal repression that it has caused to the people there.

(Geoffrey Hoon, 31 March 2003)

In example (30), the that-clause following the node *humanitarian crisis*, by which Straw implicitly points to Saddam's regime, stands in antonymic opposition to the more mitigated 'circumstances' that would arise in case of 'military action'. In (31), during Question Time, Saddam's regime is construed by the defence secretary through attitudinal resources of negative judgment to express moral sanction: *humanitarian catastrophe* and *brutal repression*.

To sum up, by comparing the two partitions, the following observations can be made. First of all, the word *humanitarian* has a higher relative frequency in the Short partition than in the government one: about 39 per cent of the occurrences in the government partition belongs to Short (119 out of 307), corresponding to a relative frequency of 0.4 per hundred tokens, and this is remarkable, especially if the data are compared both to the *CorDis Corpus* as a whole, in which the lexeme has a relative frequency of 0.025 per hundred tokens, and to a larger reference corpus, such as the *BNC* (0.0004 per hundred tokens—see also section 3.3.2). In terms of collocates, whereas the positive semantic association of the 'providing relief' motif is predictably frequent in both partitions, the overwhelming negative semantic associations in the concordance combined with modal meanings of possibility typically characterize Short's discourse. We may thus draw the conclusion that while the government emphasized the necessity to perform 'good' actions, Short also emphasized the possibility or likelihood of negative consequences, possibly related to the just-war principle of proportionality.

3.3.2. *Humanitarian* in the *CorDis Corpus*: Comparing Discourses on War

As has been said earlier, *humanitarian* was selected more frequently in the House of Commons than in any of the other institutional arenas represented in the corpus—almost 50 per cent of the 1,305 instances in the *CorDis Corpus* were uttered by MPs. Interestingly, the *HoR* subcorpus—the other parliamentary module in the *CorDis Corpus*—has, excluding *Hutton*, which has none, the lowest number of occurrences. See Figure 3.5:

As far as collocates are concerned, *aid* is most frequent in the *CorDis Corpus* as a whole, with a total of 258 co-occurrences, and is immediately followed by *relief* and *assistance*. A comparison with the *BNC* confirms this finding, although a closer investigation of patterns reveals a rather different picture. While the meaning pattern highlighting positive semantic associations is still present, features expressing negative appraisal, such as the phrase *under the guise of* or *playing politics with*, or the adjective *lethal*

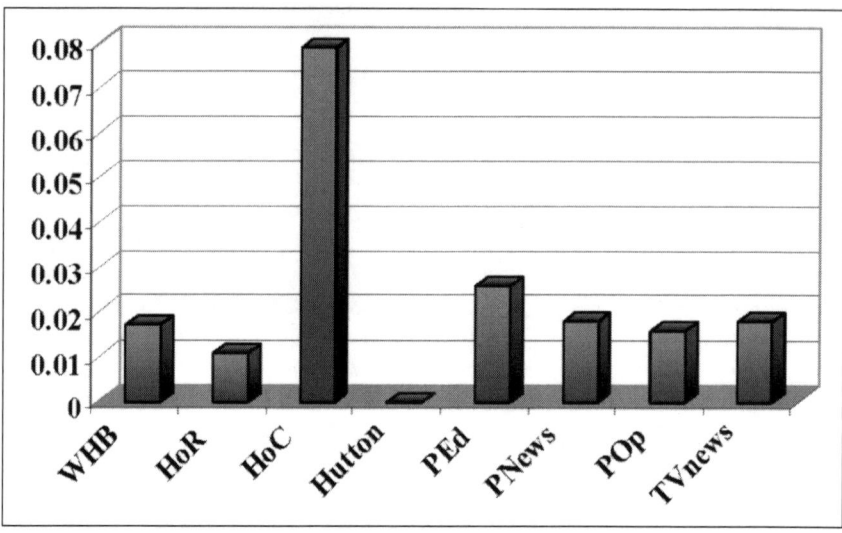

Figure 3.5   Relative frequency of *humanitarian* across the *CorDis Corpus*.

were found in the co-occurrence of *humanitarian* and *aid*. This suggests that its meaning is tied to political interests and that 'good actions' disguise other interests. The presence of 'scare quotes' (see 1 and 2 following) points in the same direction. Here are some examples:

1. The appeal appears to be aimed at preventing further American 'humanitarian aid' to the contras.
2. In 'The Tale of the Turnip', Yevgeny Yevtushenko writes about the virtual annexation of Russia by capitalist influences under the guise of 'humanitarian aid'; Andrei Voznesensky laments the bloodshed in Tbilisi in 'Candles and Tanks'.
3. Until the authorities in Sarajevo decide to stop playing politics with humanitarian aid and decide to stop depriving their own people of food, we won't be able to deliver, UNHCR spokeswoman Sylvana Foa said in Geneva.
4. She said the Serbs' agreement to let the convoy move on would not affect the UNHCR's decision, announced on Wednesday, to suspend relief operations for Bosnia-Herzegovina because all sides in the conflict there were playing politics with humanitarian aid.
5. The Bosnian Serbs are using humanitarian aid as a military weapon and the Bosnian government and Croatian groups are using it as a political weapon.
6. It was technically already unnecessary, for money for both lethal and humanitarian aid had been voted by Congress a matter of days before.
7. The 11-tonne arms shipment to Croatia, in crates marked 'humanitarian aid', had been intercepted in Hungary on Nov. 30.

It goes without saying that that the materials composing the *BNC* are set in a particular time frame in which historical contingencies, such as the intervention in Balkans, can skew the data. It would therefore be wise to be cautious of *BNC* queries for 'content' words that have take on a particular cultural salience in relatively brief historical periods. Corpora are in fact very sensitive to time of collection and sample. To give an example, a search for the word *ethnic* in the *BNC* gives us 2,317 occurrences, fifty of which collocating contiguously with *cleansing* compared to 700 collocating with *minority/ies*. In contrast, in COBUILD *Collocations on CD-Rom* (COBUILD 1995), drawn from the *Bank of English*, *ethnic* co-occurs with *cleansing* 933 times in 10,078 instances, compared to 936 with *minorities* and 812 with *minority*.

The comparison with the other modules of the *CorDis Corpus* will be restricted to some aspects of two other transcribed subcorpora: *HoR* and *WHB*.[9] As far as the former is concerned, the analysis of the collocation profiles of the word confirms that *humanitarian* 2 is rather infrequent in the House of Representatives; only seventeen out of 152 occurrences belong to this meaning pattern, with *crisis* as the most frequent collocate. Only in one instance, however, does the meaning pattern express a truly negative appreciation of the consequences in the event of war, when a representative voiced his opposition to the war against Iraq through a series of questions (see 1 following). In contrast, the majority of instances of *humanitarian* 2 within this domain are typically found in no-negation clauses through which the *crisis* is denied (2–3). What is more, even where the denial is not present, the roots of the *crisis* are construed elsewhere: *famine, AIDS,* and so on, or they point to the September 11 attacks (4):

1. How will we deal with the **humanitarian crisis** that inevitably will follow this war?
2. No **humanitarian crisis** grew as a result of the combat operations, and although they have a long way to go, the hospitals remain open and functional.
3. Their judicial system is functioning. Food distribution is occurring. There was **no humanitarian crisis** in Iraq. Their hospitals are functioning, below standards, but far better than they were before; and, most importantly, 4¼ million children were immunized.
4. Not 2 years ago, a terrorist group inflicted terrible damage on the American people through the acts of 9–11. This was a huge **humanitarian tragedy,** but as well a $2 trillion impact on our economy. This $87 billion funding request is dwarfed by the negative economic impact of the toll of 9–11. Some may argue that the $20 billion should be loaned to Iraq.

An analysis of the *WHB* subcorpus confirms these findings. Out of the eighty-five occurrences of *humanitarian* found in the White House briefings, 66 belong to the discourse of the podium; of these only twelve (see Concordance 3.7) collocate with negative words—*crisis* and *problem*; but

issues and working together on	humanitarian **crises** around the world, **such as AID**
d Afghanistan to addressing the	humanitarian **crises, such as AIDS and famine,** and
unity, in this case to deal with	humanitarian **crises.**
ake certain that there was **not a**	humanitarian **crisis** in the north, they had talked
No	humanitarian **crisis** has developed.
And **no**	humanitarian **crisis** has resulted in the north.
k very hard to avert any type of	humanitarian **crisis** in the north.
nt expressed concern about the	humanitarian **crisis** in the western province and a
There is **not a widespread**	humanitarian **crisis** in Iraq.
re are pockets of Iraq that have	humanitarian **problems** to be worked through
Much of the	humanitarian **problem** in Iraq **existed because of Sa**
	Humanitarian **problems that Saddam Hussein creat**

Concordance 3.7 Concordance of *humanitarian 2* in the White House press briefings.

more importantly, these patterns typically co-occur either in no-negation mood structures, through which the existence of the crisis is denied, or followed by an embedded clause attributing the cause to Saddam.

3.4. CONCLUSIONS

In this chapter we have sought to make a corpus-assisted discourse analysis of the discourse of the British government on the Iraq issue in 2003 with the purpose of investigating how the 'divisive' decision to go to war was justified in the parliamentary setting. It is a case study and its findings do not tell us anything new about language as a whole, but about a particular discourse in a particular setting. It could be argued that similar findings could have been made with a more fine-grained discourse analysis of one particular speech. For instance, example (14), from a speech by Tony Blair, encapsulates all the discourse of the government. But looking at the whole backdrop of the subcorpus has allowed us to compare and contrast competing discourses, to investigate how arguments changed over time, and to isolate the rather individual voice of one member of the government.

We shall now, by way of conclusion, very briefly summarize the most relevant outcomes of the study. In the first place, what emerges very clearly in the analysis of the government's positioning on 'the right thing to do', as regards two just-war principles in the category of *jus ad bellum*, 'right intentions' and 'just cause', is that the cluster *people of Iraq* and *Iraqi people* tend not only to occur more frequently in the government's discourse compared to rest of the House but they also, and more importantly, reveal quite distinctive semantic motifs and meaning patterns in the affirmation of the government's 'good' intents. Moreover, as far as the 'just-cause' principle is concerned, the investigation of the noun group *regime change* in co-selection with both word forms of the lexeme *remove/al* and the cluster *weapons of mass destruction,* both in Blair's and in the government's discourse, are indications of how the 'just-cause' argument in favour of military action was construed by the government.

In the last section, the analysis of the lexeme *humanitarian*, emerging as the top keyword in the discourse of one selected government member, Clare Short, and foregrounding the principle of *jus in bello*, has revealed the presence of distinct meaning patterns. Despite a number of similarities with the government, however, Short's 'humanitarian' discourse was found to be characterized by a negative collocation profile through which the likelihood of negative consequences of the war event are emphasized. This contrasts also with the investigation of the lexeme in two of the other transcribed corpora, the Congressional Record and the White House Press briefing, in which the occurrence of negative semantic associations is very rare, and indeed they typically construe a denial.

NOTES

1. This part of the title is borrowed from the newspaper section of the *CorDis Corpus* and was a headline in the *New York Times* of 9 March 2003.
2. Although this study is the result of intense collaboration between the two authors, sections 3.1 and 3.2 are to be attributed to Paul Bayley; sections 3.3 and 3.4 to Cinzia Bevitori.
3. Transcripts of both speeches can be found on the Web site of 10 Downing Street: http://www.number-10.gov.uk/output/Page5.asp. Documents last accessed on 7 July 2008.
4. Professor Marco Balboni (personal communication), however, has informed us that interpretation in international law is based, firstly, on 'literal meaning' and the context and purpose of the judicial instrument, and finally on the intentions of the deliberating body, in this particular case the UN security council. This militates against the government's position. Moreover, in authorising military action, the UN uses the formula 'all necessary means' and not 'serious consequences'.
5. The 'vision statement' was a government document published on 17 March 1993. The quotation marks indicate citations from the document. At the time of writing it can be found at http://www.number-10.gov.uk/output/Page3283.asp, access date 5 April 2006.
6. The terms *judgement, appreciation*, and *affect* are used in the sense of Martin and White (2005).
7. See, for example, BBC news on 12 March 2003 at http://news.bbc.co.uk/. Accessed on 10 April 2006.
8. The keywords tool allows the user to set different parameters. In the present study, the log-likelihood statistical test has been used. A comparison of the data with the chi-square test, however, has not shown any significant difference in the ranking.
9. The other transcribed subcorpus, the Hutton Inquiry, contains no occurrences of *humanitarian*.

4   White House Press Briefings as a Message to the World

Giulia Riccio

> Words are actions, and they make things happen.
>
> Hanif Kureishi,
> *Intimacy.*

This chapter explores possible links between the George W. Bush administration's doctrine of unilateralism—one of the pillars of its foreign policy—and the carefully studied discourse strategies that the rhetorical defence of such a position requires. In particular, the chapter focuses on features of the discourse of the White House press briefings, which represent the main official communication channel between the White House and the outside world. A corpus of all the briefings and gaggles (informal meetings between podium and press) dating back to the first term of the Bush administration (2001–2005), collected as an extension of the *CorDis* briefings subcorpus, was investigated following the approach of corpus-assisted discourse analysis, and focusing in particular on one lexical item that at first blush does not seem to carry any particular ideological weight—the noun *message* in its singular and plural form—in order to uncover *non-obvious* meanings of the word in the context of the briefings, and highlight its prominent role in the Bush administration's propaganda.

4.1. INTRODUCTION

4.1.1. Unilateralism and Discourse Strategy

At the end of the cold war, the United States of America was left as the world's only military superpower. As such, it has been involved in numerous military operations abroad: in the Persian Gulf, Kosovo, Afghanistan, and Iraq. In the cases of the 1991–92 Gulf War and of the 1999 Kosovo conflict, US troops and allies fought under the mandate of an officially recognized international organization: the UN in the former case, and NATO in the latter.

The foreign policy pursued by the George W. Bush presidency represented a turning point: Iraq was invaded without a UN or NATO mandate by a so-called coalition of the willing, a multinational force led by the United States. In terms of its political agenda, one of the pillars of the current administration's foreign policy is unilateralism—a term that has come back into vogue with the advent of George W. Bush, taking on a new meaning: the United States arrogates to itself the right or duty to carry out unilateral military intervention in other sovereign states when multilateral solutions are not possible.

The rhetorical defence of such a position presupposes the need for carefully studied discourse strategies, and the present study focuses on these, as they are realized in the main official communication channel between the White House and the outside world: White House press briefings. In particular, briefings held during George W. Bush's first term as President (January 2001–January 2005) were collected for analysis.

4.1.2. White House Press Briefings

White House press briefings are news conferences held almost daily by the White House press secretary, the administration's chief spokesperson, generally referred to as 'the podium'. They take place at either the White House or the location the president is visiting. The White House press secretary is usually—but not always—appointed from among the ranks of the governing party, and already has experience as a spokesperson. In particular, during Bush's first term as president, the role was first covered by Ari Fleischer (January 2001–July 2003) and, when he retired, by his former deputy, Scott McClellan (July 2003–May 2006).

A report on the White House Press Office released on the occasion of the Clinton-Bush transition indicates the following four principal roles for the press secretary: 'information conduit, constituent representation, administration, and communications planning', while his constituents are identified as 'the president, the White House staff, and news organizations' (Kumar 2000:ii). In practice, through its briefings, the White House delivers official information and announcements about the president's daily schedule, the administration's decisions and policies, and responds to journalists' questions.

Partington—who examined the relationship between the White House and the press during the Clinton presidency—describes the briefings as 'a particularly fascinating genre of institutional talk in which the two parties involved, the podium and the press, have very different interests and aims in life, which are in conflict on several levels' (Partington 2003:vi). However, many commentators argue that, since the late 1990s, the briefings have become a sort of show (Cooper and McKinnon 2005), in which the unexpected is unlikely to happen, largely due to the fact that podium and journalists know each other so well that they are able to predict each other's moves.

Nevertheless, although the briefings may be rather routine from the point of view of the press, they are undoubtedly extremely interesting as an object of linguistic investigation, particularly as regards the communicative strategies by which the world's only superpower imposes its vision of the world on the global audience through the globalized media system.

The scope of the briefings, indeed, goes well beyond the mere interaction between podium and press: they are one of the main ways the White House communicates with the world. The White House uses briefings to send messages to two sets of addressees: not only the worldwide audience reached by the globalized media, but also, and perhaps more importantly, other nations—enemies as well as friends—governments, international organizations, and so on. The briefings thus have considerable significance in both the domestic and the international political context.

4.1.3. Theoretical Framework, Materials, and Methods

The methodology chosen for this study combines corpus linguistics and discourse analysis, a combination intended as a contribution to the burgeoning field of corpus-assisted discourse studies or CADS (Partington 2004a:11–19). It is in this very recent tradition that this chapter's main research hypothesis finds its roots: this study intends to investigate whether the Bush doctrine of unilateralism requires the White House to deploy a particularly careful discourse strategy. This hypothesis has been explored by selecting and examining—through the observation of both corpus data and single portions of text—a specific discourse feature in the White House press briefings of the first term of the George W. Bush administration.

A corpus was assembled comprising all the briefings and 'gaggles' available on the White House Web site for the aforementioned time span.[1] The earliest briefing dates back to 24 January 2001, three days after the president had entered office, while the most recent one took place on 19 January 2005, the day before the president swore in for his second term.

The above-described White House Press Briefings corpus (henceforth *WHPB* corpus) can be regarded as an extension of the *CorDis* White House press briefings (henceforth *WHB*) subcorpus. The *WHPB* corpus contains 3,427,379 tokens in 699 texts, while the *CorDis WHB* subcorpus contains 511,791 tokens in 98 texts. The two corpora were compiled in a different fashion: while the *WHPB* corpus covers a complete four-year time span, the *CorDis WHB* subcorpus covers a total of eight months divided into four blocks of two months each, collected from 2003 to 2005.[2] The *CorDis WHB* subcorpus is XML-marked-up for speaker and speaker role, while the *WHPB* corpus is still awaiting full markup. The *Xaira* software, especially designed for processing marked-up text, was used with the *CorDis Corpus*, whereas *WordSmith Tools* 3.0 was used for performing operations on the *WHPB* corpus.[3,4] This latter, however, is currently being marked up following the *CorDis* pattern; the new version of the corpus will be used for future investigations.

While the analysis presented in this chapter is mostly based on the larger *WHPB* corpus, the *CorDis WHB* subcorpus—richer in information due to the markup—was used to carry out various comparisons and obtain additional data.

4.2. THIS STUDY: WHITE HOUSE PRESS BRIEFINGS AS A MESSAGE TO THE WORLD

4.2.1. One Word as a Starting Point

The first step in this research was the preparation of the keywords list for the *WHPB* corpus, calculated using *WordSmith*'s keywords tool. The collection of all spoken English texts contained in the *British National Corpus (BNC)*, whose frequency list in *WordSmith*'s wordlist format is freely available from Mike Scott's Web site, was used as the reference corpus to determine the corpus keywords.[5] As recommended by Scott (1998:70), the word list chosen as reference was obtained from a corpus three times larger than the *WHPB* corpus (9,852,249 tokens).

Predictably, most keywords from the *WHPB* corpus were found to refer to the political issues discussed in the briefings (for example, *Iraq*, *security*, *terrorism*, *weapons*, *war*, *economy*, *tax*), and to the protagonists of the main events of the time (such words as *president*, *Saddam*, *Bush*, and *Democrats*). However, in order to shed light on the subtle and perhaps covert discourse strategies adopted by the White House, I decided to investigate the use of a lexical item that does not directly relate to the issues dealt with in the briefings. I chose the word *message*—together with its plural form, *messages*—not only because it is found among the corpus keywords, but because, at first sight, this might appear an *innocent* word, which does not carry any particular ideological weight.[6] However, as Tognini-Bonelli says, 'words often carry an ideological weight that we sometimes guess, but very rarely prove' (2001:123). I set out to see whether corpus techniques could in fact be of use in explaining the ideological weight of such an item.

Communication between the United States and the rest of the world is explicitly described in the briefings in terms of messages (of which the briefings themselves constitute a fundamental example):

(1) JOURNALIST: What are you doing here at the White House to make certain that Iran or North Korea or any other countries are not taking advantage of the situation while we're so heavily engaged in Iraq?
MR. FLEISCHER: Well, our nation is a large one and is able to honor its commitments globally, even with the action that is taking place in Iraq. The **message** to North Korea, as you well know, has been a diplomatic **message**, a **message** that is being pursued in a multilateral fashion. [. . .] The United States carries out its **messages** daily, not only to North Korea and to Iran, but to other nations, on a host of issues, with whom we have important trade obligations.

(21 March 2003)

4.2.2. *Message** in the White House Press Briefings Corpus: General Statistics

As suggested by the keyness data, the frequency of both *message* and *messages* in the *WHPB* corpus (1,161 and 98 tokens, respectively) is significantly higher than in other general and specialized corpora.

As shown in Figure 4.1, the lexical item *message* is significantly more frequent in the *WHPB* corpus than in the whole *CorDis* corpus—despite its similarity to the *WHPB* corpus as to its topic—while in the *CorDis WHB* subcorpus the relative frequency of *message* is slightly higher than in the larger *WHPB* corpus. Furthermore, the difference is striking when the relative frequency of the item in the *BNC* is observed, *message* being more than five times more frequent in both the *WHPB* corpus and the *CorDis WHB* subcorpus.

As regards speaker roles and the use of *message(s)* in the *WHPB* corpus, a comparison was carried out by creating two separate concordances of *message**. This task is of course much easier if one uses *Xaira* and an XML-marked-up corpus, while in the present case—in the absence of markup for speaker roles—a very lengthy and complicated procedure was required:

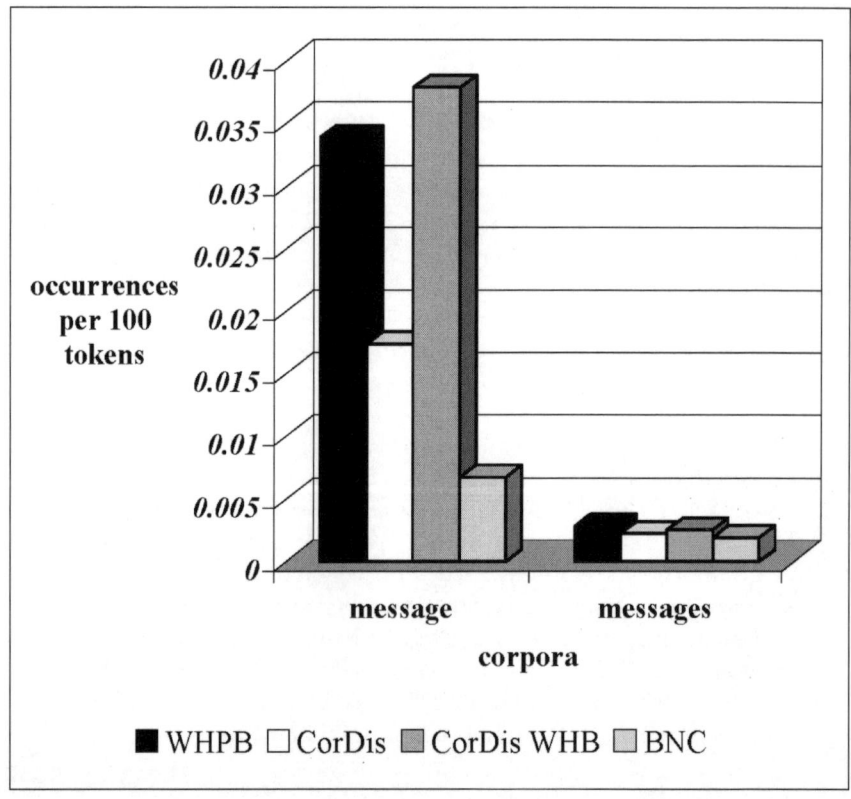

Figure 4.1   Message*: relative frequencies compared.

Table 4.1   Absolute Frequencies of *Message** in the *WHPB* Corpus Compared by Speaker Role

Token	Podium	Press
Message	732	425
Messages	62	36

two identical concordances containing all the occurrences of *message** were generated using *WordSmith*'s concord tool, and single concordance lines had to be examined with their cotext to find out whether the node word had been uttered by the podium or by the press; all occurrences in the press's words were deleted from one file, while occurrences in the podium's words were deleted from the other, so as to obtain two distinct concordance files for press and podium.

Table 4.1 shows that about two out of three occurrences of *message* and *messages* in the *WHPB* corpus are found in the podium's words. However, this is not necessarily significant from a statistical point of view, as the total number of words uttered by the podium and by the press cannot be automatically calculated in a non-marked-up corpus.

These proportions can, however, be checked in the *CorDis WHB* subcorpus, where a practically identical number of utterances is found for press and podium—the briefings being by nature a matter of questions and responses—but where the podium's utterances are in fact much longer than the press's: in the *WHB* subcorpus the podium speaks three times as much as the press. The normalized frequency data calculated in this way and shown in Figure 4.2 indicate that *message* and *messages* are more frequent

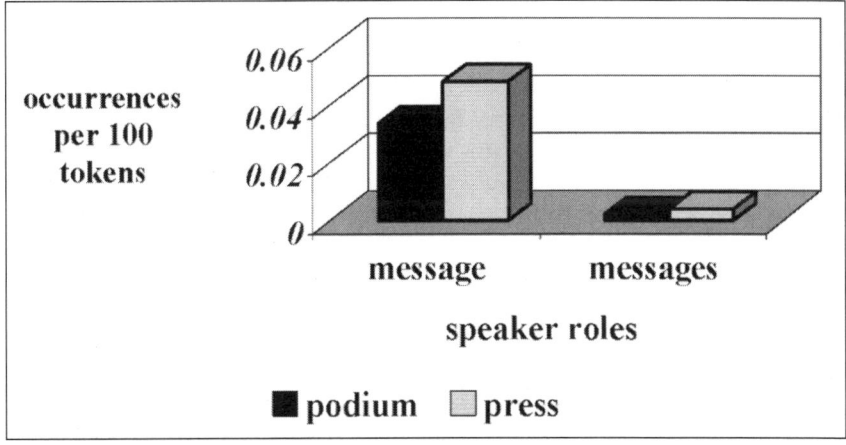

Figure 4.2   Relative frequency of *message** by speaker role in the *CorDis WHB* subcorpus.

in the words of the press than in those of the podium, at least in the *CorDis WHB* subcorpus.

Such a comparison will be further investigated in the following sections of the present paper, where the concordances of *message** for podium and press in the *WHPB* corpus are compared, in order to check whether specific patterns recur only in the podium's words or in those of the press, which might well imply that different sets of participants in the White House press briefings typically employed different discourse strategies.

Another aspect that was investigated in this study is the way the use of the word *message** varies in time. The *WHPB* corpus was divided into four sections, on a chronological basis. Three major world events which occurred during George W. Bush's first term as president and affected US foreign policy were chosen as watersheds dividing one phase from another.

Thus, the corpus was divided into sections according to the following criteria:

1) from George W. Bush's inauguration as president to the day prior to the 9/11 attacks (21 January 2001–10 September 2001);
2) from the 9/11 attacks to the day prior to the beginning of major military operations in Iraq (11 September 2001–19 March 2003);
3) during the invasion of Iraq by a US-led multinational force until Bush's declaration of 'mission accomplished' (20 March 2003–1 May 2003);
4) from Bush's declaration of the end of major combat operations in Iraq until the end of his first term as president (2 May 2003–20 January 2005).

Table 4.2 shows the total number of occurrences and relative frequency of *message* and *messages* in each chronologically divided section. Normalized frequency data, also highlighted in Figure 4.3, indicate that our node word occurred much more frequently in the year and a half prior to the invasion of Iraq, and during the invasion itself.

Such data can be confirmed and enriched by the frequency data for *message* and *messages* in the four blocks that constitute the *CorDis WHB* subcorpus, of which the first contains the briefings dating back to the days of the invasion. Normalized frequency data for the singular and plural form (see Figure 4.4) show the podium tended to use the words *message* and *messages* more often during the initial invasion phase and less frequently later on, while journalists spoke in terms of *messages* more and more as years went by. It needs to be remembered that the *CorDis* subcorpus only covers a small period of the first term of the Bush presidency. However, data obtained from this corpus are interesting as they hint at phenomena that can be studied on a larger scale in the *WHPB* corpus.

Beyond the raw statistics, one of the aims of the current study is to ascertain whether variations are apparent in the discourse strategy regarding the use of *messages* in the briefings at different points in time and, if possible, to appraise their significance.

Table 4.2   *Message** in the WHPB Corpus: Variation in Time

Phase 1—before 9/11

Token	Absolute frequency	Podium	Press	Relative frequency per 100 tokens
Message	134	74	60	0.0279
Messages	9	7	2	0.0019

Phase 2—before the invasion of Iraq

Token	Absolute frequency	Podium	Press	Relative frequency per 100 tokens
Message	637	428	209	0.0446
Messages	64	41	23	0.0045

Phase 3—during the invasion of Iraq

Token	Absolute frequency	Podium	Press	Relative frequency per 100 tokens
Message	86	72	14	0.0524
Messages	15	12	3	0.0091

Phase 4—after the end of major combat operations

Token	Absolute frequency	Podium	Press	Relative frequency per 100 tokens
Message	300	158	142	0.0221
Messages	10	2	8	0.0007

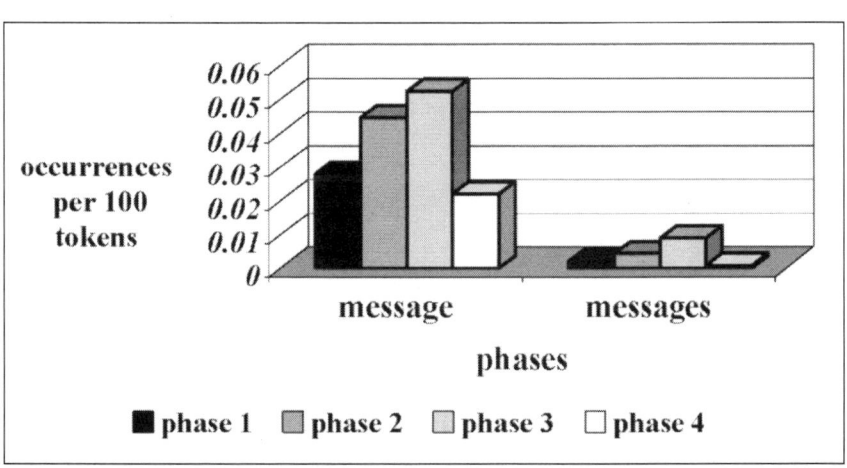

Figure 4.3   *Message** in the WHPB corpus: variation in time.

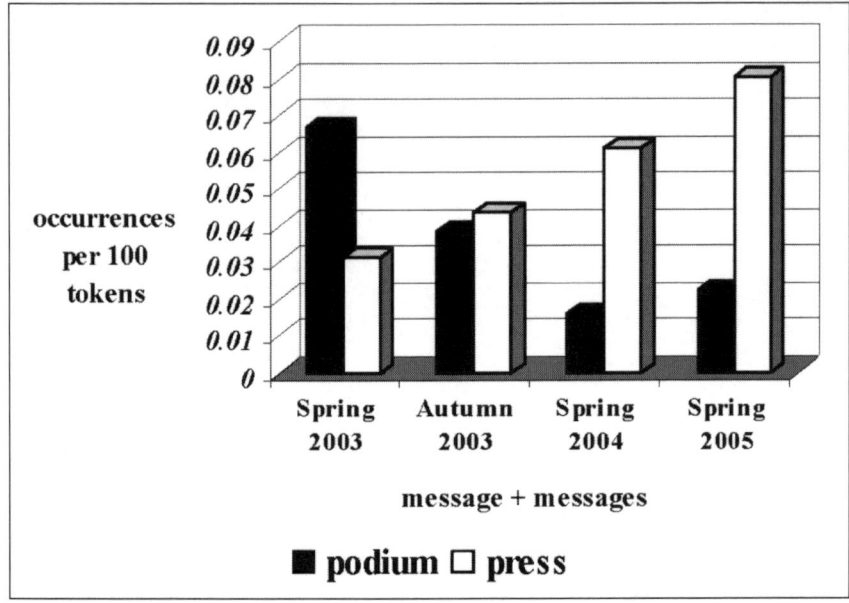

Figure 4.4   Message + messages in the *CorDis WHB* subcorpus: speaker role and variation in time.

4.2.3. Research Questions and Analytical Procedure

As mentioned earlier, by investigating the role played by the lexical items *message* and *messages* in the White House press briefings, this study intends to shed light on the briefings as communicative events involving numerous actors on the US domestic and international scenes.

The relevant research questions, then, can be set out as follows:

- Who are the participants (addresser, addressee) in this particular communicative situation?
- How are messages characterized? Do different ways of characterizing messages correspond to different contexts, including political ones?
- What are messages about?
- Is there a link connecting political strategy, communicative strategy, and the way this word is used?

In order to provide an answer to these analytical questions, a concordance including all occurrences of *message* and *messages* in the *WHPB* corpus was generated using *WordSmith*'s concord tool. Subsequently, the collocates of our node word were grouped according to five categories, which were regarded as significant in regard to the aforementioned research questions:

- nouns or names of people;
- geographical and nationality adjectives and nouns;
- personal pronouns and possessive adjectives and pronouns;
- verbs;
- adjectives.

4.3 PARTICIPANT ROLES IN THE BRIEFINGS: ADDRESSERS, AND ADDRESSEES OF MESSAGES

4.3.1 Collocate Lists

Participant roles in the briefings as communicative events were outlined, in the first place, by compiling lists of nouns, personal pronouns and possessives, geographical nouns, and adjectives that collocate with *message** in the *WHPB* corpus (see Tables 4.3, 4.4, and 4.5). Many of these words were

Table 4.3   Collocates of *Message** in the *WHPB* Corpus: Nouns or Names of People (Excluding Nationality Nouns)

Token	Absolute frequency
President	221
President's	155
People	71
World	46
States	38
Congress	32
Nations	24
House	21
Administration	20
Hussein	19
Saddam	16
Secretary	16
Way	15
Bush	14
Laden	14
War	13
Democrats	12
State	12
Vote	12
Country	11

Table 4.4   Collocates of *Message** in the *WHPB* Corpus: Geographical and Nationality Adjectives and Nouns

Token	Absolute frequency
North	37
Korea	30
American	28
Iraq	17
Israel	15
America's	12
Syria	12
Americans	11
Arab	10
Iraqi	9
Iran	8
Koreans	8
Afghanistan	7
America	6
Chinese	6
India	6
Palestinians	6
Pakistan	4

Table 4.5   Collocates of *Message** in the *WHPB* Corpus: Possessive Adjectives and Pronouns and Personal Pronouns (Including Variation by Speaker Role)

Token	Absolute frequency	Podium	Press
it	148	110	38
he	142	80	62
I	110	82	28
you	108	43	65
his	106	62	44
we	77	55	22
they	56	43	13
our	37	36	1
them	25	11	14
their	23	17	6
your	23	3	20
him	16	6	10

expected to refer to the participants in this communicative situation, either in the role of addressers or of addressees of a message. In some cases it was also felt to be interesting to break down frequency data in order to compare occurrences found in the podium's words and in those of the press.

4.3.2. The President as Addresser/Addressee of Messages

President (also with possessive *'s*) stands out in Table 4.3 as the noun that most often collocates with *message** in the *WHPB* corpus. *President* and *President's* occur 221 and 155 times, respectively, as collocates of *message** (collocation span: 5L, 5R), the former most frequently in the second position to the right of *message** (seventy-one times), the latter almost always (131 times) found to the immediate left of *message**, in the phrase *the President's message* that introduces the president's positions or views.

A concordance of *President's* in the whole *WHPB* corpus shows that *message* is indeed one of the most frequent words found to the immediate right of *President's*, together with numerous other nouns introducing the president's opinion, such as *position, view, proposal, remarks, opinion, approach, reaction, words, statement*—an indication that communication in the briefings concerns, above all, the president's opinions and positions. The president, indeed, is portrayed as the main addresser of messages in the briefings, rather than the addressee.

In 267 cases out of 376, that is, 71 per cent of total co-occurrences of *President('s)* and *message**, the president is explicitly mentioned as the addresser of the message, in such patterns as:

- *the President's* [adjective or other pre-modifier] *message* (140 cases);
- *message* [adverb] *from [the] President* (21 cases);
- *message [that] the President* [verb: send/deliver/bring/convey etc.] (41 cases);
- *[the] President [Bush]* [verb: send/give/have etc.] (24 cases);
- *what [kind of] message [you think] [does] [the] President [Bush]* [verb: have/deliver/send]? (8 cases);
- *message of [the] President [Bush]* (5 cases).

In contrast, in twenty-six cases only (less than 7 per cent of the total) is the *President* the addressee of the message. Patterns include:

- *message to [the] President [Bush]* (4 cases);
- *message for [the] President [Bush]* (2 cases);
- *message [that] the President* [verb: hear/receive/agree with] (6 cases);
- *the President [verb: hear] the/that/this/a message* (6 cases).[7]

In addition to this, as Baker suggests, 'when carrying out searches on a particular subject (particularly a noun), [. . .] it might also be the case that it is referred to numerous times with determiners [. . .] or pronouns [. . .]. [. . .] It is important that these cases of anaphora [. . .] are taken into consideration' (2006:89–90). Other cases where the addresser or the addressee of a message can be identified as the president were therefore looked for in a search for co-occurrences of the concordances of *message** and *he/his*. These are, respectively, the most frequent pronoun (excepting *it*, which does not refer to people) and possessive adjective that collocate with *message** (see Table 4.5) and we hypothesized that they referred to President Bush in most cases in the briefings, where much talk regards presidential activities and policies. The hypothesis proved to be correct; in seventy-six out of eighty-eight occurrences of *his message* or *his* [adj.] *message*, the possessive refers to the president. Seventy of these can be added to the count of cases where the president is the addresser—the remaining six had already been counted as co-occurrences of *message** and *President('s)* (e.g., *the President in his message*).

Furthermore, in the concordance of *message** co-occurring with *he*, seventy-one more cases were found, excluding those already counted, where this pronoun refers to the president, and where he is either addresser (fifty-seven times) or addressee (fourteen times). *Bush* also co-occurs with *message** fourteen times in the corpus, as shown in Table 4.3. These occurrences, however, have already been counted earlier, since in the briefings *Bush* is never mentioned without his title, *President*.

As regards speaker roles and variation in time, *President*, *President's*, *he* and *his* mainly co-occurred with *message** in the podium's words during the prelude to the invasion of Iraq (ninety, ninety-two, forty-five, and thirty-six occurrences, respectively), when the Bush administration was striving to obtain from the UN Security Council a resolution explicitly authorizing the use of force.

In total, then, in the *WHPB* corpus there are at least 394 distinct cases where the president is portrayed as the addresser of a message, while in forty cases only is he the addressee—a quite significant ratio as it provides clues about the direction the communication in the briefings mainly travels: obviously from the administration towards the rest of the world, but with a high level of personalization, as about one-third of all messages in the briefings is presented as coming from the president in person.

Furthermore, sometimes the president is the implicit addresser of the message, in such cases as those where the president's policies are presented as actively conveying a message on behalf of the president, as in the following excerpt, where the tax plan is sending a message, which actually comes, once again, from the president:

(2)   Mr. Fleischer: Tomorrow **his tax plan** appears on its way to passage. [. . .] And the President believes that **it starts to send the right message** to the country that he meant what he said when he ran on tax relief.

(7 March 2001)

4.3.3. Messages and the Administration

The high level of personalization of communication in the briefings is also indicated by the relatively rare co-occurrences of *administration* and *message** (twenty cases; see Table 4.3). In twelve of these cases *administration* is the addresser of a message, only three of which occur in the podium's words, a very low figure compared to the aforementioned data concerning the president as addresser.

Thus, the podium tends to present the president rather than the whole administration as the pivot of the White House policies and communications, probably because the credibility of the administration needs to be established in the first place by giving as much prominence as possible to the figure of the president.

4.3.4. Our Message, Whose Message?

At times, however, it is harder to find out exactly who the message actually comes from. This is particularly the case with *we*, when it collocates with *message** (seventy-seven times; see Table 4.5). In twenty-three cases the pronoun refers to the addresser of the message and in eighteen cases to the addressee (respectively, eighteen and fourteen of which occur in the podium's words).

Moreover, the two-word cluster *our message* occurs sixteen times in the corpus, exclusively uttered by the podium.

But who *we* and *our* refer to is not always clear. This ambiguity strategy exploits the intrinsic twofold nature of this pronoun, which can be either inclusive or exclusive. Whether the audience or other people are intended to be included in or excluded from the communicative act is often left unclear in the briefings. The antecedent of *we* (and *our*) in this context may be the US administration (exclusive *we*), but also the American people or the US and its allies, or even such abstract groups as 'the civilized world' or 'the international community' (inclusive *we*). A concordance (see Concordances 4.1 and 4.2) is of little help in disambiguating the reference. Larger portions of text need to be analyzed to find out whether the reference is vague or not.

Iranian people. **We** continue to get the	message across about the importance of I
Iraq? Mr. Fleischer: **We** have made the	message clear to Iran. But let me state
errible message to send. **We** must send a	message of unity, of strength, and of re
r to promote human rights. And that's a	message that **we** will continue to emphasi
ring terrorists. So that's a very clear	message that **we**'ve sent. Q If I could
r have not yet done. Are **we** sending any	message to the North Koreans, either pub

Concordance 4.1 Sample from the concordance of co-occurrences of *message** and *we* (5L, 5R): 'we as addresser of a message'.

United States? Mr. Fleischer: Again,	our message is that the future of Iran w
e and those who work in mail rooms. And	our message has been consistent, it has
Clellan: I think that the Chinese heard	our message very clearly. Again, we will
ance, and no more game playing. That is	our message to Saddam Hussein. Q Scott
x. We have to be vigilant, and that is	our message to the American public. When
ese things? Mr. McClellan: I think	our message to the rebels, or the so-cal
s meeting with parties in the region.	Our message is very clear to the Palesti
els in Haiti's political system. And so	our message has been very clear that we

Concordance 4.2   Sample from the concordance of *our message*.

In some cases the antecedent of the pronoun clearly emerges from the cotext, as in the following excerpt, where the podium, questioned about a US official position, replies using the exclusive first-person plural pronoun:

(3) JOURNALIST: But does **the United States** approve or disapprove of this action?
MR. FLEISCHER: The **message** that **we** have given, unequivocally, is that we support the choosing of the next leader of Iraq by the people of Iraq, from both inside and outside Iraq

(28 February 2003)

Sometimes, in contrast, an involvement of the American people or even of the so-called international community in the Bush administration's policies and positions is deliberately sought and underlies the podium's statements, as in the following example:

(4) JOURNALIST: Scott, you said this morning that terrorists shouldn't be allowed to think that they can influence elections or policy. Do you think that that was the case in Spain?
MR. McCLELLAN: Terrorists want to intimidate. They want to shake the will of the civilized world. And as you heard from the President earlier, they cannot. **The United States** remains **strong** in our **resolve** and in our **determination**. **The civilized world** remains **strong** in its **determination** and its **resolve**. **We** will continue to pursue this war on terrorism and bring those terrorists to justice before they can carry out their attacks. [. . .] I think it is the wrong **message** to send to make those suggestions. It is a terrible **message** to send. **We must** send a **message** of **unity**, of **strength**, and of **resolve** in the war on terrorism. Terrorists want to break our will and resolve. They want us to cut and run. There is no negotiating with terrorists.

(16 March 2004)

The preceding text is part of a long discussion about the then recent victory of the Spanish Socialist Workers' Party (*PSOE*) in the general election in

Spain, and Zapatero's intention to withdraw Spanish troops from Iraq. The Madrid bombings, which had occurred on 11 March 2004, were said to have influenced the election results. By looking at the whole exchange, two possible antecedents for the first-person plural pronoun used by the podium to identify the addresser of a *message of unity, of strength and of resolve* can be found: *the United States* and *the civilized world*, which are the subjects of two parallel and almost identical sentences, both containing a noun (*resolve*) and an adjective (*strong*) which are subsequently mentioned to characterize the message that must be sent. Both the United States and the civilized world, thus, might be the antecedent of *we*, in this case. The selection of words here could be construed as presenting the unspecified 'civilized world' as having the duty, indicated by *must*, to share with the United States the *message of unity, of strength, and of resolve* against terrorism.

In general, a certain degree of vagueness is present when the addresser of a message is expressed by the first-person plural pronoun. Only in some cases does the cotext help in identifying the antecedent of the pronoun, which is usually the US administration. When, in contrast, the antecedent cannot be identified, this pronoun could be construed to mean that the message is shared by the American people as a whole, or by even vaguer collective entities such as the aforementioned 'international community' and 'civilized world'.

4.3.4. America, the United States, and the American People: Different Patterns in Sending/Receiving Messages

Interesting observations can also be made about messages sent or received by *the US, America* or *the American people. America* (also with possessive *'s*) co-occurs with *message** eighteen times. While only twice is *America* the addressee of a message (*America's men and women* in one case), both times sent by the president, *America* is presented as the addresser of a message seven times. The cluster *America's message*, in particular, occurs six times. The content of America's messages is usually left unspecified: it is perhaps taken for granted that these messages are intended to communicate American values around the world. Such values are explicitly mentioned in two cases, where America's message is specified to be one *of hope and opportunity* or *of idealism and hope*. Also the addressees of these messages are only vaguely defined, and generally referred to as *the world* or *other nations. America's message*, thus, appears to be used as a rhetorical device rather than being a real communicative act, since the US administration chooses to present its policies as based on a set of values that the world needs to share.

Most co-occurrences of *American people* and *message**, in contrast, see the *American people* as addressee (nine cases out of sixteen). The addresser here is usually the president, who speaks to his people mainly in the role of commander in chief, as in the following case, dating back to two days before the attack on Afghanistan began:

(5) JOURNALIST: I'm just saying, does the President not have a responsibility to sit down and tell the American people it's very likely we're going
to be attacked when we begin hostilities?
MR. FLEISCHER: John, **the American people** have heard that **message
from the President**, that threats remain.

(5 October 2001)

Only twice is *the American people* the addresser of a message in the *WHPB*
corpus, but in one of these it is *the President* who *is carrying the American
people's message to the Congress*, while in the other, reported next, the message comes both from the American people and the American government:

(6) MR. FLEISCHER: The President also today signed an executive order to
create the White House Office of Global Communications, which is a
reflection of the importance the President attaches in this modern era to
communicating worldwide **the message of the American people and the
American government**, particularly as we face a war involving terrorism
and other great issues involving diplomacy and the importance of communicating America's **message** of idealism and hope around the world.

(21 January 2003)

Significantly enough, in this announcement *message* appears once again to
be the podium's favourite word to indicate the way the United States communicates with the world in a strategic way, in particular on the international scene, and in the context of the war on terrorism.

As far as *the United States* is concerned, this cluster co-occurs with *message** thirty times, while in eight cases the acronym *the US* is found. In
twenty-two cases *the United States* or *the US* (eighteen and four cases,
respectively) is sending a message, while in just five cases are they receiving
it. Concordance 4.3 shows that when the United States is the addresser of
a message, the addressee is usually either unspecified *people around the
world* or any US opponent (*the Taliban, Iran, that armed opposition*). It is

---

ilitants. Does the United States have a   message for Israel on that? Mr. McClel
uestion. Is the United States sending a   message to Iran? Have they done that in
to get the very clear understanding and   message from the United States and from
and that unless he get a clear and firm   message from the United States that this
Iraq. The United States carries out its   messages daily, not only to North Korea
e Northern Alliance. The United States   message will continue to be consistent w
for Afghanistan. But the United States   message to the Taliban could not be more
of power. Why wasn't the United States'   message to that armed opposition, look,
d in the region, and deliver a straight   message from the United States governmen
for people around the world to hear the   message of the United States. And I thin

---

Concordance 4.3 Sample from the concordance of co-occurrences of *message** and
United States (5L, 5R): 'United States as addresser of the message'.

also significant that most of those citations where *the United States* is the addresser (fourteen out of eighteen) date back to the phase that preceded the invasion of Iraq.

Different ways of referring to the people or nation that George W. Bush represents as the president, that is, *the American people, America, the United States*, thus correspond to different patterns in sending and receiving messages. While *the American people* is generally presented as receiving messages from the president rather than sending them to anyone, *America* as a nation is shown as addressing the world by communicating its values and ideals. *The United States*, in contrast, is presented as the addresser of messages usually directed to its opponents. The existence in the briefings of two types of message that partly overlap—a set of diplomatic messages conveyed by *the United States* as a state, and a set of messages about values and ideals, conveyed by *America* as a nation—points to a mechanism illustrated by George Lakoff, who defined it as the State-As-Person System:

> A state is conceptualized as a person, engaging in social relations within a world community. Its land-mass is its home. It lives in a neighborhood, and has neighbors, friends and enemies. States are seen as having inherent dispositions: they can be peaceful or aggressive, responsible or irresponsible, industrious or lazy.
>
> (Lakoff 1991: online version)

It is clear from this case that the construction of participant roles in such an event as the communication of messages is not left to chance: it is taken for granted that the people of America not only support the administration in conveying its messages, but the whole nation is construed as participant in this communicative act.

The following example illustrates how a characteristic discourse pattern underlies the presentation of *America* and *the United States* as addressers of messages in the briefings:

(7) JOURNALIST: Were you able to follow-up on the New York Times story that you have a new disinformation campaign going on, or being planned against the allies?
     MR. FLEISCHER: I've looked into this, and let me say to you there is widespread recognition throughout the administration that **the United States** has an important role in the world in better communicating **America's message** of hope and opportunity. It is important that it is a **message** that is shared throughout the world, in friendly nations and other places, as well.

     (16 December 2002)

Here, indeed, it is *the United States* that communicates *America's message*. The administration thus seems to be arrogating to itself the role of presenting to the world the message the people intends to send. The mention of abstract concepts and values such as *hope* and *opportunity*, however, rather than merely expressing the American people's communicative needs, is a typical feature of American political discourse, generally used to avoid discussing a specific issue or problem.

There are also cases where a US message is conveyed through another state, person, or institution acting as an intermediary.

(8) JOURNALIST: There's a new GAO report that is critical of public diplomacy efforts by the United States. How is that effort going in Iraq, the effort to inform the Iraqi people? Is **the U.S. message** getting across?
MR. MCCLELLAN: Well, I think that it's always important to make sure that we are communicating the steps that we are taking in Iraq to improve the infrastructure, improve stability and security in the country, and transfer responsibility to the Iraqi people. I think **the Iraqi Governing Council** is playing more and more of a role in getting that **message** across.

(16 September 2003)

The Iraqi Governing Council, being the provisional government of Iraq consisting of Iraqi political, religious, and tribal leaders appointed to manage the transition of Iraq to elections, was at least formally not supposed to be speaking on behalf of the United States and conveying their messages.

Other instances of people or groups functioning as addressers of messages, who either officially represent the United States or actually send a message on behalf of the US administration, are: *government experts and officials, the US troops in Iraq, the President of the National Association of Letter Carriers.*

4.3.5. Messages and the World

Another interesting collocate of *message** in the WHPB corpus is *world*, which co-occurs with the node word forty-six times. *World* as a collocate of *message** is almost exclusively found in the podium's words (forty times), never before the September 11 attacks and mainly (thirty-seven times) during the prelude to the invasion of Iraq—that is, at a time when communication between the United States and the world, expressed in terms of messages, was a particularly important business: the Bush administration and its allies were striving to obtain support from the UN for military intervention in Iraq. Thus, in the perspective of launching a unilateral attack, it was vital to give the audience the impression that the US-led war on terrorism, far from being unilateral, was supported by peoples and nations throughout the world.

Most citations refer to messages sent *around* or *throughout the world* by the president or by the United States (the cluster *around the world* co-occurs with *message** twelve times). At times, however, the *world* is presented as the addresser of a message. Highly ambiguous are cases where the addressee is Saddam Hussein and the United States purports to be speaking on behalf of the whole *world* (or *world community*). In particular, the use of *world* as the addresser of a message can only be justified when it is backed by a stance taken by the UN, by a multilateral treaty ratified by most nations in the world, or by a mandate given by countries all over the world to the United States or a coalition to try to settle a controversy. Nonetheless, in the same way as the use of the phrase *international community*, analyzed by Norman Fairclough in a recent study (Fairclough 2005), is becoming more and more widespread in the discourse of international relations in the twenty-first century, and is frequent also in the *WHPB* corpus, so the *world*, in the discourse of the White House, turns into an active participant on the scene, in this case in the transmission and reception of messages.

The following excerpts date back to a time when it was not clear yet whether a UN resolution would explicitly authorize the use of force in Iraq:

(9) MR. FLEISCHER: I think the President has been very serious. And hopefully, Saddam Hussein will get the **message** that **the world community, through the United Nations,** has called on Saddam Hussein to disarm, and as the President said, he will either disarm or the United States will lead a coalition to disarm him. That's a serious **message**. It's not a bluff. And perhaps as a result of it being such a serious **message**, Saddam Hussein will indeed get that **message** and disarm peacefully.

(6 January 2003)

(10) JOURNALIST: Ari, the President, in the days leading up to the adoption of that resolution, spoke in **very clear language.** He said that this was Saddam Hussein's final chance [. . .]. Unless you see a complete change of heart before that January 27th deadline, is the President prepared to tell his representatives at the United Nations to say, game over?
MR. FLEISCHER: I think Saddam Hussein needs to get the **very clear understanding** and **message** from **the United States** and from **the world** that he needs to disarm, that this is indeed serious.

(17 January 2003)

Again, the wording here is meaningful since, as noted previously, US diplomatic effort was reaching its peak at that time, in the attempt to obtain support from the UN for the invasion of Iraq. Thus, in the first excerpt *the United Nations* are portrayed as an intermediary (indicated by *through*) between *the world community* and *Saddam Hussein,* while in the second *the United States* and *the world* appear to be speaking with one voice.

An extreme case of vagueness is one in which *the world* is the addresser and *people around the world* are the addressees:

(11) MR. FLEISCHER: The **message** of democracy is often stopped as a result of nations that don't have a free press or an open press, nations that don't welcome ideas. And that's always a challenge for democracy; it's always a challenge for the **message** of the **world** to be received by people around the **world**. Not everybody is as tolerant, as open as the United States.

(16 December 2002)

In this ambiguous utterance, the message is actually a product of the US administration, but it is presented as being sent by the world and received by the world itself, so that it suggests that the whole world agrees with the United States and endorses its policies.

4.3.6. Events and Policies Sending Messages

In other cases, events or even abstract concepts and values function as the addresser of a message in the briefings. In these cases the communicative situation is entirely metaphorical. The degree of literalness in the use of message in the corpus ranges from Osama bin Laden's pre-taped messages, to messages of condolences America received from world leaders after September 11, to the less literal meaning described until now (e.g., *the President's message about the creation of a Palestinian state*), up to the fully metaphorical meaning we have just mentioned.

Abstract nouns and events presented as sending messages in the briefings include, among others; *the use of force against Iraq*; *actions by the US and its allies*; *today's event*; *this vote*; *today's unemployment report*. In the briefings events are thus assigned an interpretation functional to the US administration's worldview, and turn into active participants in international relations, endowed with awareness of the consequences of their occurrence. This mechanism is illustrated by the following excerpt:

(12) MR. FLEISCHER: **All of these actions by the United States and our al- lies**—and we have worked every step of the way with our allies—**have,** I believe, **sent an unmistakable message** to regimes that are seeking or that possess weapons of mass destruction: these weapons do not bring the benefits of security, as the President stated; they bring isolation and unwelcome consequences.

(19 December 2003)

4.3.7. Other Sets of Participants

Coming back to Tables 4.3 and 4.4, a number of other nouns or names of people as well as of geographical and nationality adjectives and nouns that collocate with *message** can be supposed to indicate other participants (addressers/addressees) in the communicative situation analyzed. They can be grouped into two categories.

First of all, there are words referring to countries, peoples, international organizations, leaders, and other protagonists on the international political scene, apart from already mentioned ones: *Korea* (30), *Koreans* (8), *Iraq* (17), *Saddam* (16), *Hussein* (19), *Osama* (10) *bin* (12), *Laden* (14), *Israel* (15), *Syria* (12), *state* (12), *country* (11), *leaders* (10), *Arab* (10), *terrorists* (10), *Iraqi* (9), *Iran* (8), *Sharon* (8), *Taliban* (8), *Afghanistan* (7), *Muslim* (7), *Arafat* (6), *Chinese* (6), *India* (6), *Palestinian* (6). Most of these words refer to nations and people that are regarded as US opponents or accused of being unsupportive of the US-led war on terrorism.

Other nouns refer to American institutions, parties, politicians: *Congress* (32 occurrences), *White* (13), *House* (21), *Democrats* (12), *Senate* (9), *Senator* (8)/*Senators* (3), *Republicans* (7).

When the addressee of a message is explicitly mentioned, it generally immediately follows the node word and is preceded by *to*. Therefore, the list of collocates for *message* to*, sorted by the second word to the right (2R), then to the third (3R), will show the most frequent addressees of messages. In this way, messages appear to be frequently directed to countries that the United States considers as rogue states, and to people who are dictators and terrorists: *North Korea, Saddam Hussein, Iraq, Syria, terrorists*. Interestingly, however, sometimes the White House sends messages to people, countries, and institutions that are not US antagonists, such as the UN, the Perm Five (permanent members of the UN Security Council), the UN inspectors in Iraq, European governments opposing the invasion of Iraq. In the following section, features of messages sent to US antagonists and to apparently friendly nations, people, and organizations will be compared in order to explore possible analogies in the way these two sets of participants are addressed in the briefings.

4.4. RECURRING PATTERNS AND RECURRING STRATEGIES

4.4.1. Responsibility in the Transmission of Messages

Coming back to the collocate lists for *message**, a number of the verbs that collocate with our node word (see Table 4.6) belong to the semantic fields of transmission (*send*: 207 occurrences; *get*: 73; *receive*: 41; *give*: 36; *convey*: 30; *deliver*: 18; *carry*: 11) and perception (*hear*: 68)—quite predictable associations indeed, as a message needs of course to be transmitted from an addresser to an addressee.[8] What is noteworthy, however, is that some verbs that collocate with *message** (*hear**, *convey**, *deliver**, *continue**) are almost exclusively uttered by the podium (significant figures are highlighted in bold in Table 4.6), and two of these (*hear** and *convey**) occur especially when the attack on Iraq was looming, while *continue** is a typical collocate of *message** in the podium's discourse in the post-invasion phase. Before the attack, thus, the podium insisted on the conveyance

Table 4.6   Collocates of *Message** in the *WHPB* Corpus: Verbs (Including Variation by Speaker Role)

Token	Absolute frequency	Podium	Press
send	87	38	49
think	85	64	21
sending	61	32	29
get	45	27	18
sent	41	29	12
heard	33	29	4
going	32	15	17
received	26	25	1
said	25	16	9
hear	23	22	1
trying	23	4	19
continue	22	22	0
conveyed	22	20	2
sends	18	11	7

of messages and on the need for addressees to hear them, while after the invasion, and especially during the presidential re-election campaign, he emphasized continuity in US policies and communicative strategies.

Apart from verbs of transmission and perception, the verb *hopes* also often collocates with *message** (fourteen times). In all of these cases the subject is the *President* and the verb indicates his hope that the transmission of the message will be successful, as in the following case:

(13) JOURNALIST: Does the meeting today with the Iraqi Americans reflect a concern on the part of the administration that it needs to do a better job of countering the negative public relations backlash that's evident now across the Middle East and much of the Muslim world?
MR. FLEISCHER: The answer is unequivocally no. But, certainly, the **President hopes** that **people everywhere in the world** will **listen** to the **message** of these Arab Americans and these Iraqis who saw firsthand what a brutal dictatorship Saddam Hussein has led, the torture that he has used to stay in power. And I think you're going to **hear** a very welcoming **message** about why it's so **important** for the United States and the coalition to be successful at ousting Saddam Hussein. I think it's a **powerful message**, and it's a **message** the **President hopes** will be **heard**.

(4 April 2003)

What is mainly emphasized is thus the addressee's responsibility to actually receive and correctly interpret the message, while the addresser is relieved from any responsibility, having done their best in the communicative act.

4.4.2. Topics of Messages: Terrorism and Weapons of Mass Destruction

Collocate lists are of little use when it comes to identifying the topic of messages in the briefings and any linguistic pattern related with such topics; wider portions of cotext need to be analyzed for this purpose. A large number are found in this way to relate more or less directly to terrorism, dictatorship, and weapons of mass destruction. Most excerpts from briefings reported in this chapter, indeed, are examples of this kind of message. Such messages are mainly directed to non-democratic governments or to those suspected of supporting terrorist organizations or of possessing chemical, biological, or nuclear weapons.

The content of these messages is often expressed through various recurring linguistic patterns. In particular, the lexical items *important* and *importance* are found in this context, in patterns that include *message that it's important for* [addressee] *to* [action to be taken] (e.g. *all parties to adhere to the cease-fire*) and *message about the importance of* [addressee + action to be taken] (e.g. *Iran acting as a nation that assumes its proper place in the world*).

In another recurring structure in this context, *need* to* is followed by a verb phrase such as the following:

- *comply with their international obligations;*
- *do their part to create peace;*
- *end the nuclear weapons program;*
- *examine their ties to terrorists;*
- *speak out and counter terrorism.*

Using such a wording implies that those addressed have to change behaviour, not because the United States is threatening them with negative consequences unless they do so, but because of an absolute moral need for them to disarm or stop supporting terrorist networks. Thus, the United States justifies its imposition—at times, but not always, backed by the United Nations—in moral terms, as though they had been assigned the task to bring justice to the world.

Need to, in particular, is not only frequently found in the company of *message** in the briefings, but is actually quite frequent in the whole corpus, and significantly more frequent there than *must*, a modal that shares shades of meaning with *need to*. While *must*, when it is used deontically, refers to an obligation imposed by the speaker (the wording *Saddam Hussein must disarm* would imply that the speaker is trying to force him to do so), *need to* reflects a moral need imposed by the circumstances, independent of the speaker's will (*the Iraqis need to disarm for the sake of peace*). Indeed, the subjects of *need* to* in the briefings are usually rogue states, terrorists, or opponents of the United States, which confirms that the high frequency of this verb in the corpus can be ascribed to its presence in specific contexts, aimed at imposing US policies by showing them as the best possible option in an absolute sense, for the world's sake.

Coming back to the recurring patterns I mentioned before, in the following excerpt the different wordings chosen by press and podium stand out:

(14) JOURNALIST: Ari, Secretary of State Powell warns Pakistan of consequences if it continues to help North Korea with its nuclear program. What consequences—if they are continuing?

MR. FLEISCHER: And I think if you take a look what the Secretary said, he also made clear that it is not continuing. And he did not define what that would be. We will continue to work, press that **message** with Pakistan, as well as other nations around the world about the **importance** of **making certain** they do not take any steps that could destabilize that region.

(26 November 2002)

While the journalist talks explicitly in terms of warnings and consequences for Pakistan unless they stop supporting North Korea's nuclear program, the press secretary uses the phrase *message about the importance of making certain* to express in a milder way what is actually a threat.

In the following excerpt, by contrast, the message is expressed more explicitly:

(15) JOURNALIST: Does the administration believe that the IRA is a terrorist group, or the new IRA, or the Real IRA?

MR. FLEISCHER: Certainly, the Real IRA is listed on the official list of terrorist groups. But I think the President said what he said for a reason. He is sending a **message** and he's rallying a coalition, that those who engage in terrorism and those who harbor terrorists **need to be worried** about the actions that our government will take.

(19 September 2001)

However, even here, no clear reference is made to the nature of the actions which the United States might take.

What emerges here is that the underlying message expressed in the briefings looks more like a threat than an innocent, neutral communicative act. Concordancing the *WHPB* corpus for *threat* shows, indeed, that this lexical item is never chosen by the podium to refer to actions performed by the United States, although the administration does often threaten people, states, and organizations with negative consequences in briefings, as shown earlier—as a matter of fact, no one in the world has more adequate military and economic means than the world's first superpower to represent a threat to someone else.

The lexical item *threat* is actually found in the briefings to refer to threats that other people or groups (e.g., Saddam Hussein or terrorist organizations) pose to the world. This, however, is quite predictable, as *threat* generally refers to an external situation, and *threaten* is not a performative verb (see Bayley, Bevitori, and Zoni 2004). The communicative function of expressing a threat, in contrast, is generally expressed through euphemisms, and the threat is likely to be the more understated, the greater the power of those expressing the threat.

Talking in terms of messages in the briefings is actually a way of expressing threats in an understated way. In addition to this, *message* is often accompanied by phrases that shift responsibility away from the White House for what was just stated, either because emphasis is placed on the addressee's responsibility to understand the message and take necessary measures, or because the message is expressed as if it were descending from an unknown superior moral entity.

The next section will shed further light on the ways messages are characterized in the briefings, in particular through adjectival choices whose recurrence reinforces the hypothesis that *message* here is a sort of euphemism for *threat*.

4.5. WAYS OF CHARACTERIZING MESSAGES

4.5.1. Adjectives that Collocate with *message**

Table 4.7 Collocates of *Message** in the *WHPB* Corpus: Adjectives (Including Variation in Time and by Speaker Role)

Word	Total occurrences	Podium	Press	Before 9/11	9/11 to invasion of Iraq	During invasion of Iraq	Post-invasion of Iraq
clear	44	41	3	6	17	1	20
important	28	26	2	2	18	4	4
taped	27	27	0	0	27	0	0
same	26	24	1	5	15	1	4
strong	19	18	1	2	9	2	6
consistent	18	17	1	2	9	0	7
other	17	8	9	2	7	1	7
wrong	14	10	4	1	2	0	11
right	14	13	1	2	1	1	10
powerful	13	12	1	1	9	2	1
specific	11	9	2	0	7	1	3
mixed	10	0	10	0	8	0	2

The adjectives that most frequently collocate with *message** in the *WHPB* corpus are shown in Table 4.7 and can be grouped into two categories:

- adjectives expressing positive evaluation, associated with the semantic fields of strength (*strong*: 19 occurrences; *powerful*: 13), correctness (*right*: 13), relevance (*important*: 28; *serious*: 5), unambiguousness (*clear* 44; *consistent* 18; *unmistakable*: 4), all of which are typical of the podium's discourse;
- adjectives expressing negative evaluation, or belonging to the semantic field of inconsistency (*wrong*: 14 occurrences; *mixed*: 10 occurrences).

The ways these two sets of adjectives are used by podium and press to characterize different messages in communicative situations involving different participants in the briefings will be analyzed in the remaining part of this study.

4.5.2. Clear Messages

Clear is the adjective that most frequently collocates with *message** in the *WHPB* corpus (see Table 4.7), and this co-occurrence is typical of the discourse of the podium (forty-one cases out of forty-four), both in the phase that preceded the invasion of Iraq and after Saddam Hussein had been removed from power. A concordance of *message** with *clear* as context word allows the identification of recurring patterns such as the following:

- *a clear and firm* **message;**
- *the President made his* **message** *clear;*
- *the very clear understanding and* **message;**
- *a simple and clear* **message;**
- *our* **message** *is very clear;*
- *the* **message** *he's sending loud and clear;*
- *a clear, consistent* **message** *universally;*
- *an effective, clear, unmistakable* **message.**

Thus, *clear* associated with *message** collocates in turn with other adjectives with a similar meaning, and is often reinforced by *very*. *Clear*—very frequent throughout the corpus—is indeed the adjective most frequently modified by *very* in the *WHPB* corpus (933 times). The high frequency of co-occurrence is not surprising: it is frequent also in the *BNC*, where *very* is the second most frequent adverb collocate of *clear*. It is more surprising, in contrast, that *quite*, which is the most frequent adverb collocate of *clear* in the *BNC*, only has seventeen co-occurrences with *clear* in the *WHPB* corpus. It is also worth mentioning that, in comparison to

BNC, the frequency of *very clear* is extremely high in the *WHPB* corpus (0.000584 occurrences per 100 tokens in the *BNC* and 0.027279 per 100 tokens in *WHPB*). Whereas other chapters in this book report outstanding differences between *CorDis* and general corpora as far as frequencies of words with a specialized meaning are concerned (see *humanitarian*, for example, in Chapter 3, this volume), the difference here regards a much more common phrase. Investigating the reasons behind its recurrence in the White House press briefings is beyond the scope of this chapter; it might be interesting, however, to explore them in the future.

Coming back to *clear*, this adjective appears to be mainly used to characterize *messages* sent by the United States or the president to either North Korea, Iraq (and Saddam Hussein), or Iran—the 'regimes that sponsor terror', termed the 'axis of evil' in Bush's 2002 State of the Union address— or to other US antagonists. Near-synonyms of *clear* that co-occur with *message**, sometimes also together with *clear*, are used in similar ways.[9] *Unmistakable* is found in the *WHPB* corpus only together with *message*, and also paraphrased once in *let there be no mistake about it; let it be a strong message and a very clear message*); likewise *unequivocal* (and the corresponding adverb *unequivocally*) occur with *message*. Both adjectives imply that the addresser has done everything possible to make the message as clear as it can be. Thus, the addressee is presented as the only participant responsible for the success of the communicative act. In the same way, *plain* and *simple* are also used, alone or combined with *clear*, as well as such phrases as *make sure they understand/receive/hear it*; in the context of this communicative event, these and similar phrases share the same function as *clear*, *unmistakable* and *unequivocal*.

4.5.3. Powerful Messages and Strength Beyond Challenge

Messages in the briefings are also *powerful* or *strong*, two adjectives that co-occur with *message** in nineteen and thirteen cases, respectively, the vast majority of which in the podium's words. The strength of a message refers to the effect it has on the addressee. These adjectives here express the US attitude on the scene of international relations: the attitude of the world's only superpower, which can afford to display maximum strength when addressing other actors. In a briefing dating back to the day before Bush's final ultimatum to Saddam Hussein expired, *powerful* is also found in combination with *deterrent*, which reinforces the function of such a message:

(16) MR. FLEISCHER: And the President also believes that the use of force against Iraq will similarly send a **powerful deterrent message** to terrorists around the world that the United States will do what it takes to prevent terrorist attacks against our country.

(19 March 2003)

4.5.4. Important Messages

Other adjectives such as *important* and *serious* repeatedly highlight the importance of the messages sent in the briefings, as already mentioned in section 4.4.2. *Important* and *serious* are also typical collocates of *message** in the podium's discourse (twenty-six occurrences out of twenty-eight and four out of five, respectively), and characterize messages sent by the United States or the president, an adjectival choice which emphasizes that the message should be taken seriously and dealt with immediately. This is explicitly stated in a briefing already reported earlier (excerpt 9). While US aircraft carriers were travelling to the Persian Gulf, the White House insisted that everything possible was being done to avoid war in Iraq. Thus, when asked about the seriousness of such statements, the podium pointed out that the US messages were *not a bluff.*

4.5.5. Consistent Messages and Unilateralism

Messages sent by the United States are also described in the briefings in terms of their consistency: the idea of the US administration insisting on certain messages as time goes by is emphasized by the co-occurrence of the adjective *consistent* (eighteen times) with *message**, also combined with other adjectives, by the verbs *continue* and *remain* and by the adjective *same* (e.g., *the President's message remains the same*; *we will continue to send that message*).

(17) MR. FLEISCHER: I think we've continued to send a **consistent** series of **messages** to North Korea that North Korea has chosen to ignore.

(13 January 2003)

The US unilateral approach to international relations implies, indeed, that a stance taken will remain the same in time although circumstances may have changed.

4.5.6. The Right Message vs. The Wrong Message

Interestingly, the two antonyms *right* and *wrong* also collocate with *message**, and, once again, both of them mainly in the podium's words (thirteen out of fourteen times and ten out of fourteen, respectively). The opposition between *the right message* and *the wrong message* in the briefings corresponds to an opposition between different addressers, addressees, and topic of the messages.

So, just as with the other adjectives expressing positive evaluation, *right* also characterizes messages sent by the White House, especially regarding domestic issues, as shown by the concordance of *the right message* in Concordance 4.4. Thus, such a phrase may be used to express the superiority

> reeding ground for terrorists. Is that the right message to be sending? Mr. M
> efforts of parents and coaches to send the right message to our children. Drug
> esident believes that it starts to send the right message to the country that he
> f grants. It's important that we send the right message with this legislation
> ive energy plan because that will send the right message to our energy markets

Concordance 4.4   Sample from the concordance of *the right message.*

of the Bush administration's policies compared to those of the Democrats, and to outline successes achieved by this administration.

Again, as *the right message* emphasizes the rectitude of the current administration's policies, the White House chooses the phrase *the wrong message* to indicate the dangerous consequences that may arise if the policies of the administration's opponents (European governments opposing the Iraq war as well as anti-intervention Democrats) were adopted in fighting terrorism. A *wrong message* is, for example, the withdrawal of Spanish troops from Iraq after the 2004 Madrid bombings, a decision the podium regards as an encouragement for terrorists:

(18) MR. MCCLELLAN: Terrorists cannot think that they can influence elections or influence policy. That is **the wrong message** to send. That's why we must redouble our efforts and take the fight to the terrorists.
JOURNALIST: But I wonder, and I think we're all kind of wondering about the **message** that is being sent from the Spanish elections. You say it would be **a terrible message** if the terrorists were to assume that they had influenced the Spanish elections. Well, that's not a **message**, is it? It's a **fact**. The terrorists influenced the Spanish elections.
MR. MCCLELLAN: I'm not the one who does the analysis of elections. But I will point out the facts. And it is **the wrong message** to let terrorists think that they can influence policy.

(16 March 2004)

4.5.7. Negative Characterization of Messages

The case of *wrong* illustrates the radical difference between contexts where adjectives expressing negative evaluation are found in the briefings and contexts where adjectives expressing positive evaluation are found. Adjectives expressing negative evaluation characterize messages sent by opponents of the Bush administration or of the United States, and such an adjectival choice can be accounted for in strategic terms as presenting these states and people and their policies as completely unreliable. Otherwise, these adjectives are found in questions, when journalists challenge stances taken by the White House by highlighting ambiguity or negative aspects in them.

When the addresser is a US enemy, the impossibility for the world to share the message they sent is often emphasized:

(19) JOURNALIST: Yesterday, you told us that Baghdad imams called for holy war violence, the drowning of Bush and Blair was opposed by one unidentified imam in Kuwait. And my question is, have there been any other imams or mosques who have publicly disagreed with these calls for holy war and drowning of Bush and Blair?
MR. FLEISCHER: I think you can rest assured, Lester, that the **message** that you expressed from Baghdad is **not a message shared** by Muslim leaders around the world.

(19 March 2003)

Similarly, when the UN is the addresser of a message in the briefings, this generally happens in a negative context: the UN's failure to support US foreign policy is presented in terms of the dangerous consequences of such behaviour; the UN is presented as sending rogue states messages of tolerance, instead of warning them:

(20) MR. FLEISCHER: If the UN does not enforce the resolution, the **message** to Iraq will be one **of laissez-faire**, that it is okay to have the weapons you have.

(11 March 2003)

The same happens with those European governments that refused to support the war in Iraq. For example, the podium chooses the interrogative form (*What **message** are these three countries in Europe sending to the people of Turkey?*) to express his disagreement with the message expressed by Belgium, France, and Germany, who blocked the NATO decision to place defences against Iraq in Turkey.

But also when the UN, European governments opposing the war, and other apparently friendly states, people, and organizations such as the Perm Five and the UN inspectors in Iraq are the addressees, rather than the addressers, of messages, as mentioned in section 4.3.7, interesting patterns can be observed. Despite the difference in status between them and the people and states that are more generally found to be the addressees of messages coming from the White House—rogue states, terrorists, unfriendly regimes—similar messages are sent to both sets of addressees. This may be seen as evidence that the UN and anyone else practically opposing the US strategy, or causing the pace towards war to slow down, are implicitly described in the briefings as though they were on the wrong side in the war on terrorism.

In a briefing dating back to a few weeks before Iraq was invaded, the podium harshly criticized the lack of support the United States received from the UN Security Council.

(21) JOURNALIST: This morning the President said, again, that he doesn't think he needs this resolution. Is that **message** intended—what is that intended to do? Because it could be the signal to other countries that you're—either get on board or the train is leaving; less a **message** about what he thinks is important, as a signal to them, that now is your last opportunity.

MR. FLEISCHER: Well, the President's **message** is **this is a chance for the United Nations to be relevant.** There is no question about it. After all, if the United Nations passes a resolution that says, Iraq must disarm immediately, and then the United Nations says, immediately really means 12 years, what kind of signal are they sending to the next proliferator? What **message** are they sending about the ability of the international system to maintain the peace and fight proliferation? And this is why the President has changed the equation in New York, and he has said it is important for the United Nations to have value and to have meaning for resolutions to be backed up. Otherwise, it's a paper society. It's not a meaningful society to keep the peace. That's what's at stake here.

(25 February 2003)

In this as well as in another briefing, the adjective *relevant* is used to describe how the Bush administration thinks the UN should be; however, the mere fact that a single member of the UN has the power to make such a statement indicates that this organization is anything but relevant in the eyes of the United States, and has such limited power in the context of the Bush doctrine of unilateralism as to be defined *a paper society*.

4.6. CONCLUDING REMARKS

The use of the word *message* and of its plural form *messages* in the George W. Bush administration's press briefings has been shown in this study to respond to specific discourse strategies linked with the Bush doctrine of foreign relations.

Addresser/addressee patterns have been identified by examining briefings as communicative events in which messages are sent and received. The most common pattern has been found to include the president, the US administration, and a usually unspecified *we* as the addresser of messages, while the addressees are frequently opponents of the United States. In particular, the podium characterizes messages in different ways depending on the addresser and the addressee as well as on the context in which the communicative event takes place.

By analyzing both the ways messages sent by the United States to their opponents (Iraq, North Korea, terrorist organizations, etc.) are characterized and the topic of such messages, it has been shown that this word is used in this context as a euphemism to express a threat. The use of message(s) in this sense was particularly frequent in the briefings in the phase that preceded the attack against Iraq. In this period especially, the UN and the European governments not supporting the Iraq war were addressed using the same lexicogrammatical patterns as when addressing opponents.

It was thus shown that the lexical item under investigation, rather than being a common, innocent word, plays a prominent role in White House propaganda. This can be regarded as an interesting example of how *invisible* discourse strategies in political and media discourse are worth exploring by combining corpus tools and techniques and the discourse-analytical approach. It is an instance of how, as Partington contends (2003:7; 2008:190–91), CADS techniques can uncover what he calls *non-obvious* meanings in a particular discourse type, that is, meanings not easily accessible to other forms of discourse analysis.

NOTES

1. http://www.whitehouse.gov/news/briefings (accessed 18 July 2005).
2. March–April 2003; September–October 2003; March–April 2004; March–April 2005
3. http://www.oucs.ox.ac.uk/rts/xaira/.
4. http://www.lexically.net/WordSmith/index.html (accessed 7 July 2007).
5. http://www.lexically.net/downloads/spoken.zip (accessed 18 July 2005).
6. *Message* is found at position 161 in the keywords list, keyness 1,549.4.
7. In the remaining cases, either *President* refers to other presidents, or the president is mentioned in the content of the message, or *President* and *message** are found in different utterances or sentences.
8. Verb forms are lemmatized.
9. http://www.whitehouse.gov/news/releases/2002/01/20020129-11.html (accessed 7 July 2007).

5 Positioning and Stance in TV News Reporting of the 2003 Iraq War

The Anchor on CBS and the News Presenter on BBC

Linda Lombardo

This chapter aims to take a corpus-assisted discourse analysis approach (Partington 2004a) to TV news reporting on the 2003 war in Iraq applying the theoretical tools of Martin and White's (2005) appraisal systems. The text under analysis is the discourse of the anchor on CBS and, for purposes of comparison, the news presenter on BBC during a month of war reporting beginning on March 20, 2003. Of particular interest is the way in which linguistic resources are used by the anchor/news presenter to adopt a stance towards the value positions being advanced by the text and to position themselves with respect to the audience each one construes, resulting in the creation of an appropriate professional 'persona' within the given socio-cultural context. Quantitative and qualitative methods are used to identify systematic patterns on the two broadcasters, particularly with respect to representation of the following: the war, US/UK military casualties, and Iraqi civilian casualties.

5.1. INTRODUCTION

5.1.1. Social Context

Teubert (2005:13) speaks of public discourse in the United States since 9/11 as 'homogenized discourse' in that the broad consensus established between media and administration has 'filtered out certain undesirable ideas', discouraging the pluralist negotiation of meaning characteristic of a democratic discourse community. This is certainly true of US TV news reporting of the 2003 war on Iraq (see Aday et al. 2005; Allan and Zelizer 2004a; Cunningham 2003; Dimitrova et al. 2005; *Project for Excellence in Reporting* 2004; Ravi 2005). On the other hand, the *BBC* was accused of having an antiwar bias and commissioned a study, which was carried out by researchers at Cardiff University (Lewis et al. 2003), and which absolved it of these accusations. It is interesting to note that, in comparison with a divided public in the UK, on the day before the attack an *ABC-Washington Post Poll* reported that 71 per cent of the American public supported the war on Iraq, which grew to 80 per cent in a survey reported in the *Washington Post* on April 5, 2003. The spiral created by the reciprocal influence between social context and media discourse is evident.

5.1.2. Research Objective

The present study will make a linguistic analysis of anchor/news presenter discourse on these two highly respected national news programmes to see how such significant differences in reporting are constructed through language. Adopting a corpus-assisted discourse analysis methodology (Partington 2004a), which combines a more quantitative corpus linguistics approach through the application of specialized software (*WordSmith Tools,* Scott 1999) with a qualitative discourse and critical discourse analysis approach, the study will make use of the theoretical tools of appraisal systems with particular reference to resources of 'intersubjective stance' as outlined by Martin and White (2005). They are concerned with 'the linguistic resources by which speakers/writers adopt a stance towards the value positions being referenced by a text and with respect to those they address' (Martin and White 2005:92). Appraisal theory is informed by Bakhtin's/Voloshinov's notions of dialogism and heteroglossia under which 'all verbal communication, whether written or spoken, is "dialogic" in that to speak or write is always to reveal the influence of, refer to, or to take up in some way, what has been said/written before, and simultaneously to anticipate the responses of actual, potential or imagined readers/listeners' (Martin and White 2005:92). In this dialogic perspective, of interest is the extent to which speakers/writers acknowledge prior speakers/writers and the ways in which they engage with them (that is, whether they present themselves as agreeing or disagreeing, as being undecided or neutral with respect to them and their value positions) and also the signals speakers/writers provide about how they expect their listeners/readers to respond to the proposition and the value position it advances. More specifically:

- Are key propositions formulated monoglossically ('bare' assertions) or heteroglossically (with reference to an external source)?
- If monoglossically formulated, are propositions presented as 'taken for granted' or 'at issue'?
- If heteroglossically formulated, is the speaker/writer's stance contractive (excluding or constraining alternatives) or expansive (actively allowing for alternative positions)?

If a value position is presented as one which can be taken for granted for a particular audience, the speaker/writer is aligning themselves with the 'envisaged', 'imagined', or 'ideal' audience. If the speaker/writer's stance is dialogistically contractive or expansive, they are construing alignments and anticipating responses from their addressees.

An analysis will be made of the utterances of *CBS Evening News* anchor, veteran journalist Dan Rather, and, for comparative purposes, those of the news presenter on *BBC News at Ten*. The linguistic analysis aims to compare the utterances by the anchor on *CBS* and the news presenter on *BBC* with respect to:

- the extent to which they introduce external voices, foregrounding attribution, and the ways in which they align themselves with the text they present, thus creating their own authorial identity or discursive 'persona';
- the kind of TV audience which they construe and interact with, positioning this audience in turn through the construction of communities of shared feelings, values, and attitudes;
- the ways in which these positionings are achieved linguistically: through 'affect', 'judgement', and 'appreciation' (positive or negative evaluations of what is expressed), modality (the commitment to what is expressed but also the positioning with respect to other voices and other positions), and 'intensification' or 'vague language' (the force and clarity of assertions).

Attention is also given to the ways in which the anchor/news presenter positions self and TV viewers by means of implicit evaluation (Iedema et al. 1994).

5.1.3. Corpus and Methodological Approach

The partitions, or subsections, of the *CorDis Corpus* to be analyzed were drawn from the *TVNews* subcorpus composed of transcriptions of a month of *CBS* and *BBC* TV news reporting from the outbreak of the war on Iraq reported on March 20, 2003.[2] I shall be focussing specifically on two smaller partitions, the *CBS* anchor partition and the *BBC* news presenter partition. From Table 5.1 it can be seen that while the *BBC* partition is larger than that of *CBS*, *BBC* news presenter discourse accounts for a

Table 5.1 Anchor on *CBS Evening News* and News Presenter on *BBC News at Ten*

Channel	Total no. of programme	Total no. of spoken words[2] in programme	Total no. of words of anchor/news presenter discourse	Anchor/News presenter discourse as % of total discourse
CBS	21	59,045	18,965	32%
BBC	28	103,806	22,437	22%

lower percentage of tokens in the partition than does anchor discourse in the *CBS* partition, which is in keeping with the 'star' status of the anchor on US TV news in comparison with the traditionally more impersonal and 'institutional' status of the news presenter on *BBC*.[1]

The empirical tools of corpus linguistics in the form of *WordSmith Tools* (Scott 1999) are used: for making word lists and frequency counts; for generating concordances which give all instances of the use of a particular item in the corpus with the possibility of retrieving the full context; and for calculating keywords to see which words appear significantly more frequently in the corpus under study than they do in a reference corpus used for comparative purposes.

Martin and White's (2005) appraisal theory, concerned with evaluation in discourse, is outlined briefly and schematically here as a point of reference for the subsequent analysis of the data (see also Chapter 2, this volume). The three interacting domains are 'attitude', 'engagement', and 'graduation'. Attitude is concerned with feelings, judgements of behaviour, and evaluation of things. It includes three categories: 'affect' (resources for construing emotional reactions to behaviour, text/process, phenomena); 'judgement' (resources for assessing behaviour, which is admired or criticized, praised or condemned); and 'appreciation' (resources for construing the value of things, including text/process and natural phenomena). The category of judgement is further divided into 'social esteem (having to do with normality, capacity, tenacity) and 'social sanction' (having to do with veracity and propriety).

The domain of 'engagement' has to do with devices for construing audience, alignment/disalignment, and solidarity with socially constituted communities, and Martin and White refer to this as 'intersubjective stance' (2005:97). Engagement has two main categories: monogloss, which refers to a proposition that does not recognize dialogistic alternatives, and heterogloss, which refers to a proposition that makes reference to other voices or viewpoints. Heteroglossic propositions are further divided into 'contraction' and 'expansion'. Contraction is associated with resources which close down dialogic alternatives either by disclaiming (denying or countering) or proclaiming (concurring with, pronouncing, or endorsing) the content of what is being communicated. Expansion, on the other hand, involves resources which keep dialogic alternatives open by entertaining (typically via some form of epistemic modality) or attributing to an outside source (either acknowledging or distancing from) the content of what is being communicated.

The third domain is 'graduation', which has to do with resources for adjusting the degree of an evaluation by raising or lowering, upscaling or downscaling degrees of positivity or negativity or, in terms of engagement, the degree of the speaker's intensity or investment. It is further subdivided into 'focus' and 'force'. Focus refers to resources for sharpening (for example, by indicating prototypicality) or softening (typically through the use of hedges and vague language), while force refers to resources for intensifying and quantifying.

Also of interest here is work by Iedema et al. (1994) on the language resources which enable journalists to be perceived as 'impersonal' or 'objective' by avoiding the expression of judgement and modality which introduce elements of 'subjectivity'. Their system of 'authorial voice' distinguishes the reporter voice typical of 'hard news' reporting (maximum 'objectivity') from the correspondent voice typical of the field-specific expert (elements of 'subjectivity') and the commentator voice typical of editorializing (maximum subjectivity) on the basis of the language which is used. Reporter voice is constructed as impersonal—the voice of the institution—through the absence of commitment to the truth value of a statement, the expression of only indirect or implicit judgement or causality, and reference to what others have said but not to their mental processes. It can express indirect judgement by means of the use of non-core lexis and certain kinds of intensified language or of 'tokens of judgement' (Martin and White 2005:61–8), which involve the use of language that describes a behaviour in such a way as to elicit a value judgement in the receiver of the message. Correspondent voice is characterized by the expression of explicit judgements of 'social esteem' (Martin and White 2005:53) (about capacity and inclination, fate and resolve), by reference to others' mental processes (what they think, know or believe) and the explicit expression of a cause-effect relationship. Commentator voice is distinguished by the use of a personalized and individualized voice, deontic modality, and by the expression of both judgements of 'social esteem' and of 'social sanction' (about truth and ethics) (Martin and White 2005:53). In the analysis that follows, of particular usefulness will be Martin and White's concept of 'tokens of judgement' as a form of implicit judgement.

5.2. QUANTITATIVE AND QUALITATIVE ANALYSIS

The first step in examining the data was to use a more quantitative approach in order to get an overall view of similarities and differences in the *CBS* and *BBC* partitions. Using *WordSmith Tools* (Scott 1999), frequency lists were generated and then a keyword list created, showing which words occur significantly more frequently in one subcorpus than in another. Among the keywords in *CBS* anchor talk as compared with *BBC* news presenter talk are: *US*, *big*, *war* (175 occurrences vs. 108 on *BBC* with a keyness of 0.25 log likelihood). Among the words with negative keyness for *CBS* are: *British*, *American*, *talk* (39 occurrences on *BBC* vs. only three on *CBS* with a negative keyness of 0.32). Out of a total of thirty occurrences of *big* on *CBS*, more than half (eighteen) collocate with *picture* (*the/tonight's big picture*) and almost all of these (sixteen occurrences out of eighteen) refer to the news from the correspondent at the Pentagon, who puts the war 'into context' for viewers, usually at the beginning of the programme, thus 'framing' all the news that follows. Concordance 5.1 shows these concordance lines for *big picture*.

e. We start at the Pentagon where David Marin has tonight's	big picture. Dav
tonight we go to CBS's David Martin at the Pentago for the	big picture. Dav
David Martin, live at the Pentagon with the	big picture. No
of the war in an effort to connect the dots, we offer you the	big picture with
e turn again to CBS's David Martin at the Pentago with the	big picture. Dav
r. We start with David Martin at the Pentago with tonight's	big picture. Dav
CBS's David Martin at the Defence Department for Tonight's	big picture. Dav
st, David Martin at the Pentago with tonight's overview, the	big picture. Dav
erview from the Pentago. CBS's David Martin has tonight's	big picture.
CBS National Security correspondent David Martin, has the	big picture.
o the pentago for an overview. CBS's David Martin has the	big picture.
National Security correspondent David Martin has tonight's	big picture.
as the latest hopes of official Washington about that, and the	big picture of the
e tonight at the Pentagon where CBS's David Martin has the	big picture.
n the arrest of a key player in the Saddam regime in tonight's	big picture

Concordance 5.1   Sample from concordance of *big picture* in *CBS* anchor discourse referring to news from the Pentagon.

On *BBC*, there are forty occurrences of the keyword *talk*, thirty-two of which are addressed to the television audience in a structuring move, mostly to prepare them for a live exchange: *we can talk (now) to* (sixteen), *let's talk to* (ten), *we'll talk to* (one), *he can't talk about* (two), *he's not allowed to talk about* (one); these last two introduce a pre-recorded exchange with an embedded reporter. There is also one occurrence of *we had all that talk about* and one of *to talk about* used in reference to news actors in the news presenter's introduction to a reporter's prepared report. The remaining occurrences (eight) are used by the newsreader to address the correspondent in a live exchange in structuring moves like: *can we talk about* (two), *let's talk about* (one), *when you talk about* (one), *all the talk of* (one), *they are likely to talk* (one) and *good to talk to you* (two). The frequency with which the word *talk* is used reflects the importance of the news presenter-reporter exchanges that are conducted on behalf of the TV audience and provide them with more information about what is happening, both in terms of updates and of interpretations, explanations, evaluations, and predictions (see Haarman 2004). Concordance 5.2 shows the first fifteen concordance lines in chronological order with the word *talk*.

The fact that information is more 'controlled' and less 'spontaneous' on *CBS* is borne out by the fact that there are almost no live exchanges between anchor and reporters (a live exchange being defined as at least two speaking turns by each participant); typically, the introduction to a pre-recorded report begins with a statement and even where the reporter is supposedly reporting 'live', the anchor opens with a general question about what is happening to which there is no follow-up.

In fact, of the seventy-two occurrences of *you* in the discourse of the anchor on *CBS*, only four are addressed to a reporter, while sixty-three are addressed to the TV audience. On the other hand, in *BBC* news presenter discourse the situation is the exact opposite: of the 143 occurrences of *you*,

el. Well, let's	talk about some of those concerns there with Andrew Marr, in
Well we can	talk to Matt right now, he's at the White House. Erm, Matt, when
Well, let's	talk live to Rageh Omar, who's in Baghdad now. Rageh, on the o
Well, let's	talk to Ben Brown, now, who's in southern Iraq tonight. Ben, c
Well we can	talk now to our Washington correspondent Tom Carver. Ah, T
and we can	talk now to Ben Brown in Baghdad. Ben, those questions about
ago. We can	talk to Rageh Omaar who's er who can join us on the phone. Ra
dad, we can	talk to Rageh now, he's on the line. The Iraqi authorities are m
ight. We can	talk to him now. Andrew, could you tell us, then, in your view
tonight, let's	talk to our world affairs editor John Simpson. John, the Ameri
today. Let's	talk to Rageh Omar, our correspondent who's there. Rageh, to
ities. We can	talk to Rageh now. Rageh, what is the latest there on the bomb
rkish capital,	talk to your correspondent Jonny Dymond. We mentioned the K
Qatar we can	talk to our correspondent there Nicholas Witchell. Nick, what
and we can	talk to John live now in northern Iraq. John, we saw you injured

Concordance 5.2   Concordance of *talk* in news presenter discourse on *BBC*.

137 of them are addressed to a reporter while only six are addressed to the TV audience (see also Ferrarotti 2009 and Lombardo 2007b). Thus while the *BBC* news presenter speaks to reporters on behalf of the TV audience, the *CBS* anchor addresses the audience directly in a *we* and *you* relationship of expert to public, very often to structure the presentation of news and to underline the (difficult) role of the news team as in:

- *(now) we('ll) take you to/inside*
- *we begin by taking you*
- *to bring you clear/comprehensive/accurate/solid coverage*
- *we give you an update*
- *we have a full summary of the war for you*
- *we offer you the big picture*
- *we can't tell you [. . .], what we can tell you*
- *we try this night to put the war in context for you*

From these general and more quantitative considerations, what seems to distinguish the two broadcasters is, on the one hand, the *CBS* anchor's explicit 'framing' of the news via information from the Pentagon, and on the other, the *BBC* news presenter's focus on dialoguing with correspondents in live exchanges. These differences imply a very different kind of speaker-audience relationship, which bears further examination.

5.3. QUALITATIVE ANALYSIS

5.3.1. Representation of the War on *CBS* vs. *BBC*

Given the keyness of the word *war* in anchor talk on *CBS*, it was decided to proceed by doing a more qualitative analysis to identify the concordances with *war* which seemed to be typical of the reporting on *CBS*. A careful examination of all the concordances with *war* on both broadcasters provides evidence of a systematic 'labelling' of the war which only takes place on *CBS*. Concordances which label the war are shown as sentence concordances following (1–5); they have been edited to allow for more cotext, the cotext being essential for determining meanings.

1. Good evening. It's just about one-day old now *the US-led war to disarm Saddam Hussein and liberate Iraq.* (20 March 2003)
2. *The US war to disarm Iraq and oust Saddam Hussein* intensified dramatically today. (24 March 2003)
3. *Besides ridding Iraq of chemical and other outlawed weapons,* main goals of the war include bringing Iraqis freedom and food. (24 March 2003)
4. *The war against Saddam Hussein's Iraqi regime* is entering its second week tonight. (26 March 2003)
5. Tonight, US ground forces have started to fight in the biggest challenge yet in *their war against Saddam Hussein.* (1 April 2003)

The first thing to notice about the concordances labelling the war in anchor discourse on *CBS* is the way in which the motivation for the war (which is, except for no. 3, that of disposing of a tyrant) is presented as 'taken for granted' through its encoding in a series of nominal and verbal phrases (in italics). They are examples of presupposition, where the speaker aligns with the addressee, who is construed as sharing the value position which is presented as fact. Number 3 includes the presupposition of eliminating weapons of mass destruction and a monoglossic proposition which leaves no space for alternative interpretations and adds a humanitarian element to the war. Associations of the war with freedom and with liberation (*liberate* and *freedom* in nos. 1 and 3, and the alliteration *freedom and food* in no. 3) constitute judgements of 'social sanction' related to ethical behaviour.

Through a non-electronic reading of the entire *CBS* anchor partition, other instances of defining war goals were found, without the word *war* in the cotext (examples (1) to (5)).

(1) One of the goals of the US invasion of Iraq is to kill or capture Saddam Hussein.

(20 March 2003)

(2) Still ahead on the *CBS* Evening News concern and pride on the home front for *loved ones fighting to make Iraq free of Saddam.*

(20 March 2003)

(3) Updating you now on *Operation Iraqi Freedom.*

(20 March 2003)

(4) Three weeks after the United States launched *an attack on Iraq to oust Saddam Hussein*, the US military declared that his collapsing government no longer controls the capital.

(9 April 2003)

(5) Looking beyond Baghdad today, US military planners know they have a lot more work to do *to erase and replace the regime of Saddam in Iraq*.

(9 April 2003)

Here too affirmations are presented as 'the facts' in the impersonal language style of 'hard news' reporting, where the truth value of statements is assumed, as is the existence of an audience who would not contest the positive values and the pro-war position constructed by the text. The war is also associated with positive emotions, *pride* and *loved ones* in example (2), and with positive judgement, *free* and *freedom* in examples (2) and (3). In example (5), the attribution to US military planners is in Iedema et al.'s (1994) correspondent voice in that the anchor reports on a mental, not a verbal, process (*know*), thus implying that he knows what US military are thinking, which would also account for the 'bare assertion' we saw in sentence Concordance no. 5 (*main goals of the war include bringing Iraqis freedom and food*). This perception of closeness to the US military is further reinforced by the anchor's use of the military's language as in *Operation Iraqi Freedom* in example (3) and *to erase and replace* in example (5). Here again, as in the selected concordances with *war*, the texts are monoglossic and their contents presented as factual.

Unlike *CBS*, concordances with the word *war* in *BBC* news presenter partition do not include any kind of unattributed labelling of the war itself (nos. 1–2, following).

1. *Britain and America say* they've made dramatic progress in *the war against Saddam Hussein*. (24 March 2003)
2. As fears grow that the war in Iraq could last for months, *Mr Blair and President Bush have underlined* their determination *to topple Saddam Hussein*. (27 March 2003)

Only these two instances of labelling or defining the motivation for the war were found, both of which occur within attributions, to the British and American military in no. 1 and to US and British political leaders in no. 2 (in italics), and both report a verbal process (Iedema et al.'s reporter voice). From a non-electronic reading of the *BBC* news presenter partition, an instance of defining war goals was identified without the word *war* in the cotext (example (6), in italics).

(6) Good evening. *The massive military operation to topple Saddam Hussein* is now underway.

(20 March 2003)

However, it occurs at the opening of the programme on the first day of war reporting and is never repeated in the data.

Other references to reasons for the war, in this case to the thorny question of the presence of weapons of mass destruction in Iraq, can be seen in examples (7) and (8) (in italics).

(7)   *CBS* anchor: Despite their secretive nature, special ops [. . .]. Among their many missions now, preparing a way inside Baghdad and *trying to locate the weapons of mass destruction they expect to find somewhere in Iraq.*

(7 April 2003)

(8)   *BBC* news presenter: It's exactly 4 weeks since the war began in Iraq but *the search for weapons of mass destruction and for Saddam Hussein have so far proved fruitless.*

(17 April 2003)

Notice the way in which the anchor on *CBS* takes distance through attribution in example (7) (*they expect to find*), although the choice of the reporting verb *expect* by the anchor on *CBS* suggests a speaker who is knowledgeable about what the American military is thinking and doing. On the other hand, in example (8) the news presenter on *BBC* recalls a fact which has already been established and expresses negative appreciation of the search for these weapons (*fruitless*), with *but* signalling the shift from the usual to the conflictual (Iedema et al. 1994:253), perhaps implying that this failure is unexpected after such a significant period of time.

Both the concordancing of the word *war*, and a non-electronic reading of the transcripts of the two partitions, turned up some significant differences in the way in which the progress of the war is reported. Examples (9)–(12) are taken from the *CBS* anchor partition.

(9)   In *a notable success* today US forces captured many key facilities in Iraq's southern oil fields preventing sabotage by Iraqi troops.

(21 March 2003)

(10) Facts on the ground indicate that overall from a military standpoint *the invasion continues to go well.*

(24 March 2003)

(11) Good evening. As the war against Iraq heads into a third week, tonight *there is major progress and a stunning battlefield victory to report.* The US military says two key Republican Guard divisions protecting Baghdad have been beaten so badly they are quote "no longer credible forces".

(2 April 2003)

(12) *The four week battlefield victory here was an impressive success for the US military,* but as *CBS* News correspondent Richard Roth reports to-night from a US airbase in Germany, *one of the most dramatic successes of the war,* the rescue of seven American POWs, very nearly failed.

(16 April 2003)

In reporting on the way the war is going, the anchor on *CBS* frequently expresses positive evaluation (in italics) without citing specific sources of information, as can be seen in examples (9), (10), and (12). The clearly monoglossic propositions (examples (9) and (12)) and the implicit align-ment with the US military sources cited (examples (10) and (11)) all convey a single 'truth' to an audience which does not hold alternative views. In example (10) the impersonalized construction (*facts on the ground indi-cate*) serves to obscure subjectivity. Words like *notable, major, stunning,* and *impressive* contribute to the overall effect, which is that of an upscaling of attitude that construes the speaker as maximally committed to the value position being advanced and thus strongly aligns the audience into that same value position.

This is very different from the reporting of the same kind of news by the news presenter on *BBC* (examples (13)–(16)).

(13) Good Evening. *Britain and America say they've made dramatic prog-ress in the war against Saddam Hussein.*

(24 March 2003)

(14) Well, *the Prime Minister says 'a huge amount', in his words, has al-ready been achieved in the war, and that it's generally going to plan.*

(26 March 2003)

(15) Good evening. *The British forces in Iraq have claimed their biggest victory of the war so far. They say they've, in effect, taken control of the big town,* not far from the key city of Basra. *The British say it's a decisive move forward* on Day 12 of the campaign.

(31 March 2003)

(16) Good evening. *The American forces in Iraq say they've made huge prog-ress* today in their advance towards Baghdad. *They now claim they're within striking distance of the capital,* barely twenty miles to the south. *The Americans also insist that two divisions of the Iraqi Republican Guard are no longer credible forces. The Iraqis say there's no truth in the American claims.* So, *this seems to be the picture* tonight.

(2 April 2003)

All evaluation of the progress of the war is attributed (in italics). Military or political sources are cited by means of the 'neutral' reporting verb *say* or the word *claim/claims* (and perhaps also *insist*) is used by the newsreader to take distance from the source. In example (16) an alternative source is cited (*the Iraqis*) and uncertainty is expressed (*seems to be*). The consistent use of attribution implies an acknowledgment of the possibility that the various parties to the conflict may hold contrasting and conflicting versions of events, all of which can be entertained. Downscaling of attitude through repeated attribution (*'a huge amount', in his words*) construes the speaker as having no (or only a tenuous) investment in the value position being referenced.

In fact, in the overall context of war reporting on *BBC* the news presenter does not hesitate to express, on occasion, an explicit negative judgement of specific allied actions, as in example (17) (in italics), which reports the erroneous bombing by an American plane of a Kurdish convoy.

(17) Good evening. A day of *coalition advances in Basra and Baghdad have been overshadowed* tonight *by the worst case of so-called 'friendly fire' since the war began.* [. . .]. John, we've seen many of these friendly fire incidents in the last few weeks. *It seems extraordinary* that with all the high-tech gadgetry on display these days, *this is still happening.*

(6 April 2003)

In addressing the TV audience, the news presenter's choice of the verb *overshadowed* and the superlative adjective *worst* serves to upscale the effect of the negative evaluation expressed in the monoglossic affirmation, while the expression *so-called* implies a criticism of the military euphemism *friendly fire*. In addressing the reporter (veteran war correspondent John Simpson, who was injured in the incident), the use of the quantifier *many* adds force to the problematicity of the issue in question. The 'social esteem' judgement of 'usuality' (*extraordinary*) is used here in a negative sense along with *still*, which seems to counter the contention by the military that modern technological warfare with its 'surgical attacks' and 'smart bombs' can prevent 'unnecessary deaths'. The news presenter entertains this proposition (*it seems*) and introduces into the dialogue a potentially critical voice.

Another striking difference in the anchor/news presenter discourse on the two broadcasters has to do with way they introduce the reports of the American military's entry into Baghdad on 9 April 2003. First we will examine the examples taken from *CBS* anchor discourse (examples (18)–(19)).

(18) *Without fanfare, with scarcely a shot fired, American armor rolled into the center of Baghdad today and began liberating the city as Iraqis celebrated in the streets.*

(9 April)

(19) Ahead on the *CBS* evening news, striking sights and sounds from *a day of liberation, for the people of Baghdad.*

(9 April)

Here the *CBS* anchor in the war zone and his substitute in the television studio in New York both give a positive evaluation of the American military action, expressing an explicit judgement of 'social sanction' (*liberating/ liberation* as examples of ethical behaviour), and an expression of positive affect in the reaction of Iraqis (*celebrated*). In a context of 'liberation', the adverbials of circumstance *without fanfare* and *with scarcely a shot fired* function as 'tokens of judgement', presenting a positive image of the discretion on the part of the American soldiers and of their ability to avoid unnecessary bloodshed.

On the other hand, the *BBC* news presenter paints a more complex and problematic picture (examples (20)–(23)).

(20) Good evening. *American tanks have rolled into central Baghdad bringing to a dramatic end Saddam Hussein's 24 years in power.* Three weeks after the war began *American troops were greeted by cheering crowds of Iraqi civilians* in several parts of the capital. *But the war is not over yet.*

(9 April 2003)

(21) *Should we point out Rageh* that of course Baghdad is a city of millions of people, some 5 million, there were maybe thousands on the streets today. *What should we read into the fact that most of the Iraqi people who are in Baghdad certainly weren't on the streets.*

(9 April 2003)

(22) The White House said today's events showed a thirst for freedom across Iraq. *That's not the view across the Arab world of course where there's still massive resentment at the American and British invasion.*

(9 April 2003)

(23) Well, that's the focus in Downing Street. Er, let's go to the White House. Matt, erm, *will Mr Bush be working at all hard on re-building relations in the Arab community, or, frankly, will he just not bother?*

(9 April 2003)

In example (20), the news presenter uses a more 'reserved' descriptive approach in an 'x but y' construction which tempers the positive impact of the event (in italics). The evaluative lexis (*dramatic, cheering*) is positive but does not entail a positive moral judgement of the action as it does on *CBS*. In example (21), through negation he disclaims the proposition (reported in the US media) that there is a massive turnout by ordinary Iraqis (*certainly weren't on the streets*) and, by means of a rhetorical question (*should we point out*) and a leading question (*what should we read into the fact*), he seems to invite the Baghdad correspondent to present an alternative view of this event.

In example (22) the news presenter underlines the conflicting interpretations of events, disclaiming the universality of the American viewpoint through negation (*that's not the view*), and constructs an interlocutor who has the same knowledge as he does and who is aware of these divergences (*of course*) and an audience which is potentially divided over the issue of the war itself. The word *still* seems to counter the expectation held by the allies that the war would improve the situation in the Middle East. The quantifier *massive* adds force to the negative evaluation of events attributed to those in the Arab world. In example (23), by means of another question (a leading question?), he alludes to potential discrepancies between the British and American positions on relations with the Arab world. The choice of *at all hard* seems to set up a negative response. The stance adverbial *frankly* is more characteristic of conversation (Conrad and Biber 2000) or editorials (Morley 2004a) than news reporting, and *not bother* is an example of colloquial lexis used as an amplifier, which is further intensified by the adverbial *just*.

Throughout, the *BBC* news presenter seems to recognize as potential participants in the dialogue those who hold positions contrary to the positions of the British and American governments. It can also be said that he sometimes positions his audience to challenge (particularly US) military propaganda and 'information management'. Dialogic space is expanded through the use of rhetorical questions or leading questions, which seem to be employed to raise the possibility that some other proposition holds and which construe an audience of observers with reservations, doubts, and criticisms about the war.

This is in contrast with the way in which the war is represented by the *CBS* anchor, who uses monoglossic propositions ('bare assertions') and presupposition to affirm a definition which justifies the war. He expresses unattributed positive emotion (affect) on the part of the Iraqi people, favourable evaluation of the progress of the war (appreciation), and positive implicit and explicit judgement, including both judgements of 'social esteem' and of 'social sanction'. Through the unattributed use of military euphemism and reporting of a mental process, he aligns himself and the television audience with the US military in unquestioning support of a war to dispose of a tyrant. While the style of the *BBC* news presenter seems to alternate between reporter voice for the reporting of specific events and correspondent voice for analysis and prediction in live exchanges with reporters, that of the *CBS* anchor touches on commentator voice in its expression of judgements of 'social sanction' through the unattributed use of words like *liberation/liberate* and *freedom/free*.

5.3.2. Representation of US/UK Military Casualties on *CBS* vs. *BBC*

Another area of significant reporting differences on the two broadcasters is that related to the representation of US and UK military casualties. Let us begin with examples from *CBS* anchor partition (examples (24)–(30)).

(24) *They gave the last full measure of devotion to their country. We honour their memories and we send our condolences to their families.*

(21 March 2003)

(25) Coming up next on the CBS evening news, voices of the wounded. For the first time some of *those who now wear the red badge of courage* describe it, the pain and the shock of what they passed.

(27 March 2003)

(26) Speaking to marines today at Camp Lejeune, North Carolina, President Bush saluted *the Americans who gave their lives.*

(3 April 2003)

(27) When President Bush sent American servicemen and women to war, *the entire nation went with them.*

(4 April 2003)

(28) We *dedicate this broadcast to our fellow Americans who have died fighting in the war* so far, and especially this night to David Bloom, *the great young NBC news correspondent who died here at the weekend covering the war.*

(7 April)

(29) Arlington National Cemetery *where so many heroes of America's wars are buried, is now the final resting place for a hero of the Iraq war.*

(10 April)

(30) The president awarded Purple Hearts to a dozen of the troops and saluted *their dedication and loyalty.*

(11 April)

In reporting on allied military casualties, the anchor on *CBS* uses war rhetoric, positive evaluation, and the first person plural *we* to align himself with the message he is conveying, to express solidarity with the troops and to construct an interlocutor who shares the same patriotic views. In example (24), most of the first sentence (*they gave the last full measure of devotion*) is taken directly from Lincoln's Gettysburg Address. The *we* used here to refer to the news team could also be interpreted as inclusive of the TV audience. The tone is personal (*we send our condolences to their families*). In example (25) *the red badge of courage* not only gives a positive evaluation of the actions of the soldiers, but also alludes to a famous novel about war the title of which, at least, would be familiar to all Americans.[3] In examples (26) and (30), which also recall the language of the Gettysburg Address, the recognition of heroic sacrifice (*who gave their lives, dedication and loyalty*) is not explicitly attributed to President Bush and thus it is impossible either to dissociate from these voices or (without investigation) to affirm that these words were used by Bush.[4] In this way, the speaker can be perceived as aligned with the content of the text. The monoglossic proposition expressed in example (27) constructs the American people as having a unitary position in support of the troops. Examples (28) and (29) are further instances of the way in which the news team itself considers those who have died in the war as heroes, including the use of the rhetorical phrase *their final resting place*, which again echoes the Gettysburg Address ('as a final resting place for those who here gave their lives'). Through the ambiguous *we* and *our* viewers are encouraged to identify with the speaker on the basis of co-citizenship. *The Iraq war* is clearly placed within the sphere of *America's wars* and its heroes along with all the others in American history. There is a systematic expression of positive judgements of 'social esteem': *honour, dedicate, great, heroes, hero, dedication and loyalty*. Throughout, there is an aligning of viewers with the US military, and a common pro-war position is taken for granted.

Notice how differently the news presenter on *BBC* reports similar events (examples (31)–(37)).

(31) Well tonight speaking for the first time since the major assault started *President Bush praised what he called the great skill and bravery of the American forces.*

(20 March 2003)

(32) Well in a televised address to the nation tonight the Prime Minister confirmed that he had given the order to send British servicemen and women into battle. *He said the fate of many nations rested on their courage and their determination.*

(20 March 2003)

(33) This morning *the Prime Minister, Tony Blair, paid tribute to the eight British servicemen* who *died in last night's crash. He said they were courageous men who deserved our gratitude.*

(21 March 2003)

(34) *Downing Street has expressed deep sadness at the deaths of seven servicemen in a helicopter collision over the Gulf.*

(22 March 2003)

(35) Ten bodies were brought back to RAF Brize Norton in Oxfordshire, where *a sombre ceremony was held in their honour, attended by grieving families and friends.*

(29 March 2003)

(36) The bodies of eleven British servicemen have been flown back from the Gulf. [. . .] *They were given full military honours in a special ceremony at RAF Brize Norton, in Oxfordshire.*

(8 April 2003)

(37) HMS Arc Royal is due to return soon, and *there were emotional scenes at an RAF airbase in Fife today, as four Tornado fighter planes arrived home.*

(11 April)

In examples (31)–(34), the intensified favourable evaluations and affect expressed are all scrupulously attributed to external sources, *President Bush, the Prime Minister,* and *Downing Street.* In this way, the most that can be said is that the news presenter acknowledges what is said. In examples (35)–(37), passive or impersonal constructions are used to present the information in a more descriptive 'reporter voice', also through the adoption of an 'official' formal register with phrases, such as: *in a sombre ceremony, in their honour, grieving families and friends, full military honours, in a special ceremony, there were emotional scenes.* Like the news presenter, the audience is positioned outside the text as observers of the events and of the evaluations. The explicit attribution to third parties of all value judgements, while presented in a highly acceptable reporter voice style, seems nonetheless in the overall context to construe an audience which might view these value positions as problematic, one which might potentially question, resist, or reject them.

5.3.3. Representation of Civilian Casualties on *CBS* vs. *BBC*

The last area of significant reporting differences that will be discussed here has to do with the representation of civilian casualties by the two broadcasters. First of all, it should be said that the term *civilian casualty/ies* can be considered in itself a 'token of judgement', in that it would normally elicit a negative social evaluation. It is used twice by the anchor on *CBS,* once on 26 March after the first market bombing in Baghdad (example (38)), and once on 8 April, the day before the 'fall of Baghdad' (example (39)).

(38) The Iraqi government says the blast killed fourteen people and wounded about thirty others, *the worst civilian casualty toll yet known in Baghdad. The US suggest Iraq's own antiaircraft fire may have hit the area.*

(26 March 2003)

(39) Good evening. The American military says it owns the skies of Iraq tonight, and on the ground even in the heart of Baghdad, American forces are battering increasingly desperate Iraqi defenders, *but civilian casualties are mounting*, and it's an open question whether Saddam Hussein survived the latest air strike against him.

(8 April 2003)

In example (38), the negative judgement associated with the term *civilian casualty* is dissociated from the allies through a probable assignment of responsibility to the Iraqi military. In example (39), it appears in an 'x but y' construction, signalling a shift from positive to negative, where it seems to be included in a series of speculations that might be positively construed.

Notice the difference in the way this term, and the equivalent one *civilian losses*, is treated in news presenter discourse on *BBC* (examples (40)–(41)).

(40) *But the coalition was dogged by further claims of civilian casualties* today, *this time* in a bombing attack on the town of Hilla south of Baghdad.

(1 April 2003)

(41) James Robbins is with me once again to discuss the day's events. Let's start with the Pentagon, James. *They clearly found it necessary tonight to tackle this issue of civilian losses.*

(1 April 2003)

Here civilian deaths are treated, not only as a negative consequence of war, but as an issue in itself, one which provokes debate about the war, including potential criticism of allied actions requiring an explanation. In example (40), the non-core lexeme *dogged* in *dogged by* has an amplifying effect, as do *further* and *this time*, and in example (41), *they clearly found it necessary* and *to tackle this issue* imply that it is a question that is difficult to resolve but which cannot be avoided.

In reporting on civilian casualities, there are two expressions which are used only on CBS: *unintended casualties* (used to refer to the journalists killed by US fire at the Palestine Hotel), and *civilians [. . .] caught in the crossfire* (used to refer to Iraqi civilians who are innocent victims of the fighting). Overall, it can said that while in CBS anchor talk civilian deaths are never under focus and are presented as an inevitable side effect of war, in *BBC* news presenter discourse they seem to be constructed as an issue which has the potential to divide the government, the military, and public opinion.

For further illustration, let us look at how the bombing of a Baghdad market on 28 March was reported on the two broadcasters, beginning with *CBS* (example (42)).

(42) Earlier, *Iraq said the US bombing today killed at least fifty-eight peo-ple in a crowded Baghdad market.* New York Times correspondent John Burns is in the Iraqi capital and *I asked him about those Iraqi claims.*

(28 March 2003)

Here the speaker distances himself from the Iraqi assignment of responsibility for civilian deaths to the United States (*said, claims*). His voice is present in the first-person pronoun through which he takes upon himself the respon-sibility of soliciting a report from an American journalist in Baghdad. The report which follows, while not assigning responsibility, does confirm that civilians have been killed; it is brief and fragmented (possibly due to editing by *CBS*), and ends with: "[. . .] umm whoever was responsible for this, this was clearly a very large tragedy." There is no follow-up by the anchor on *CBS*.

The references to this episode in *BBC* news presenter discourse are pre-sented in examples (43)–(44).

(43) *Iraq says at least 50 people were killed tonight in a massive explosion in one of Baghdad's markets. Local people are blaming an American Cruise missile. An Iraqi doctor said he counted 55 bodies at one of the city hospitals. There's been no comment so far on the explosion from coalition central command.* America is sending at least a further 120,000 troops.

(28 March 2003)

(44) And James Robbins is with me now to discuss today's developments. Well, James, *another tragedy in Baghdad, another explosion in what looks like being a residential area.*

(28 March 2003)

In example (43), the impression is that of an attempt by the news presenter to cite all available sources of information. *Local people* signals an infor-mation source which could be interpreted as carrying credibility, and the reporting verb *blame* includes a negative evaluation by that source. The doctor's statement seems to corroborate that of Iraqi sources. In example (44), the use of repetition (*another*), along with words expressing strong negative appreciation of the event (*tragedy,* an example of inscribed or direct negative appreciation, *explosion in [. . .] a residential area,* an example of invoked or implicit negative appreciation), suggest that allied actions which result in civilian deaths have become a real problem. The modal construction *looks like being* signals that this proposition (that the explosion occurred in a residential area) is being entertained. A bombing in a residential area can be considered in itself a 'token of judgement' in that it implies a behaviour to which a negative evaluation would normally be attached. *To discuss* announces an intention on the part of the news presenter to expand the dialogic space to include other voices on this topic.

Another episode where *CBS* and *BBC* differ in their mode of reporting is that of the 'checkpoint shooting', reported on 31 March, in which Iraqi women and children were killed by US soldiers. Examples (45)–(47) demonstrate differences in the reporting by anchor and news presenter on the two broadcasters, beginning with *CBS*.

(45) Iraqi fears will not be eased by word of a tragic incident today near Najaf. *US central command says a van approached the US army checkpoint and failed to stop even when warning shots were fired. Fearing another car bomb attack, the American troops opened fire on the vehicle killing seven Iraqi civilians, all women and children.* Night thirteen of the war.

(31 March 2003)

What is interesting to note here is that in reporting the most important motivation for the shooting, the fear of another car bomb attack, an official information source is not repeated and thus the information could be attributed to the anchor, who in this way shows his knowledge and understanding of the need felt by US soldiers at the checkpoint to protect themselves. American soldiers are portrayed as people and as connected with 'the good Iraqis' with whom they share the same emotion (*fears/fearing*). Responsibility is 'technically' assigned by the US military command to the victims since their vehicle *failed to stop even when warning shots were fired,* and the incident is *tragic,* also because in the general picture of the war it is exactly the opposite of what the US military says it is trying to do in Iraq. This version can be contrasted with the account by the news presenter on *BBC* in examples (46) and (47).

(46) In the past few moments we've been getting details of a shooting near Najaf in central Iraq. *Some civilians were killed and two injured when American forces opened fire on a vehicle which apparently failed to stop at a checkpoint.* Nicholas Witchell is at US Central Command in Qatar.

(31 March 2003)

(47) Well Matt was referring there to America's most senior military figure General Richard Myers who tonight expressed his regret to the families of the 7 Iraqi women and children killed yesterday in a shooting at a checkpoint. He said the loss of any innocent life was tragic. *But the coalition was dogged by further claims of civilian casualties* today, *this time* in a bombing attack on the town of Hilla south of Baghdad. David Shukman's report contains images of the dead civilians.

(1 April 2003)

In example (46), only the hard facts are presented (in italics) with the dynamics of the incident still unconfirmed (*apparently*). The focus is on the civilian deaths through the passive construction typical of 'hard news' stories. On the following day (example (47)), the incident is connected with another bombing in which civilians were killed (*further claims, this time*) and presents the issue of civilian casualties as problematic. The images of dead civilians can be considered a 'token of judgement', likely to elicit a negative evaluation from viewers.

The last two examples contrasting the information presented by the anchor/news presenter on the two broadcasters regard the incident of 8 April in which several journalists reporting from the Palestine Hotel in Baghdad were killed by US fire. Example (48) is the way the story was introduced by the anchor on *CBS*.

(48) There were also *unintended casualties: an American tank trying to take out what the US military said were snipers, fired on the hotel where most foreign journalists are staying, killing two and wounding three.* Another journalist was killed when the office of the Al Jazeera television network was hit.

(8 April 2003)

In this example, the motivation for the shooting (*to take out what the US military said were snipers*) is included in the reporting of the news item, as was the case with the report of the checkpoint shooting. The focus is placed, thematically and grammatically, on the American tank, not on the victims, and the narrative construction serves to 'explain' what happened and why. The point of the whole narrative is given by the expression *unintended casualties*.

Example (49) shows the same story as it was introduced by the news presenter on *BBC*.

(49) Vital buildings, including the Planning and Information Ministries, were bombed by coalition planes. *But the Americans also shelled one of the hotels occupied by Western journalists, and two cameramen were killed.* A third journalist died in a missile attack on the offices of Al Jazeera Television.

(8 April 2003)

Here, the shooting is presented without a motivating factor, leaving open the possibility of error on the part of the Americans. The 'x but y' construction seems to suggest a positive evaluation of the actions preceding the 'x' and a negative evaluation (*but [. . .] also*) of those which follow it.

The greater focus placed on civilian casualties in news presenter discourse on *BBC* can also be seen in its reporting of the devastating effects of the bombings on a young Iraqi boy as shown in example (50).

(50) The *doctor in Baghdad treating the twelve-year-old Iraqi boy who lost both his arms in a bombing raid has said his wounds are so severe it would be a mercy if he died.*

(13 April 2003)

The attribution to a medical expert leaves little doubt about the severity of the boy's injuries and, at the same time, allows the news presenter to remain in perfect reporter voice style.

In summary, on *CBS* the anchor presents episodes of civilian casualties in one of two ways: either without definitively assigning responsibility or in a narrative which provides an explanation justifying the allied action. After the first two weeks of reporting, an impression is created of the inevitability of civilian losses, as the unavoidable side effect of a necessary remedy, through the use of language like *caught in the crossfire* and *unintended casualties*. Taken together, these communication strategies constitute a reading of events from a single though evolving viewpoint, one favourable to the allies and with no conflicting alternatives.

On the other hand, on *BBC* the news presenter in his initial accounts tends to present the 'hard facts', with appropriate attributions and indications of uncertainty where warranted. In a follow-up, however, he often focuses on the problematic aspects of these episodes, principally on the death of innocent people as an unresolved 'issue' and the possibility of error with tragic consequences. He seems to view as part of his own role that of entertaining alternative propositions to those presented by British and American official sources.

5.4. CONCLUSIONS

Through first a quantitative and then a qualitative approach to corpus-based discourse analysis, the study presented here has attempted to illustrate the striking differences between the ways the war was reported by the key figure of the anchor on *CBS* and the news presenter on *BBC*. The news presenter on the *BBC* seems to alternate between a 'hard news' style in reporter voice for reporting events and an investigative journalism style in correspondent voice for discussing related issues in live exchanges with reporters. He operates in the first instance against a backdrop of alternative voices and viewpoints where he foregrounds attribution and expands dialogic space through acknowledgment and distancing, and in the second he contracts and expands the dialogue, also through the use of expository questions, in order to challenge information provided predominantly by American and British official sources. He entertains propositions at odds with some of their affirmations, also through opposition (denial and negation). He uses 'tokens of judgement' and judgements of 'social esteem' but not of 'social sanction'. By entertaining alternatives, he constructs an audience that is potentially divided and he seems to include in the dialogue those who hold contrasting positions. The news presenter's 'persona' is that of the journalist who tries to provide the public with diverse and contrasting viewpoints, and he is sometimes sceptical of the information provided by official sources. On occasion, there is (at least implicit) criticism of the Bush administration and, perhaps, of the war itself. This is in line with the findings of Clark (2007) and Haarman (2006), whose linguistic analysis indicated an antiwar stance on the part of *BBC*-embedded reporters and correspondents, respectively.

The anchor on *CBS* reports the news in what is apparently a reporter voice style, but frequently operates against the background of a monoglossic text in which it is impossible to distinguish his own voice from that of the American military and political institutions. In comparison with *BBC*, there are fewer voices introduced, less foregrounding of attribution, and greater certainty expressed by the speaker, in what is a less heteroglossic perspective. Pro-war evaluations are frequently presented as matter-of-fact, and the use of presupposition suggests that the anchor and his audience are in agreement. The anchor tends to be aligned with the text he presents, and expresses implicit evaluation through 'tokens of judgement' and intensified language and explicit evaluation through 'social esteem' judgements and (less frequently) 'social sanction' judgements. Attributed and unattributed value positions are presented as familiar and unproblematic to the audience that is construed as a single voice in support of the war and in solidarity with allied troops. The speaker's interpersonal style and rhetorical strategies are in keeping with the role of the journalist in times of perceived national crisis, which risks conflation with that of the 'patriotic citizen' (Zelizer and Allan 2002:12) and refrains from asking 'why' questions and from reporting dissenting 'marginal' views. It seems to be an example of how the fear of 'a nation at risk' has led to what has been called 'the death of detachment as a guiding ethic for the press after September 11, 2001' (Zelizer and Allan 2002:16). It is in keeping with the findings of previous studies comparing *CBS* coverage with that of *TG5*, a private Italian channel, (Lombardo 2007a) and with that of BBC (Lombardo 2009). The present study is meant to underline the responsibility of communication professionals in providing information in such a way as to expand the space for public discourse and public debate in the interests of a democratic society.

It is worth noting, however, that in her lexicogrammatical analysis of how the military action and the behaviour of the two sides were represented, Clark (Chapter 6, this volume) illustrates similarities in the way in which the war was reported on both broadcasters. She argues that there is a tendency on the part of both broadcasters to avoid the *us* versus *them* dichotomy and to report on troop movements and advancement in such a way as to render the war abstract and obfuscate its horrors. This being said, the focus in the present study on evaluation, attribution, and audience alignment, and in particular on the discourse of the anchor/news presenter, a role which tends to characterize the programme in the United States and functions as a probe in live exchanges with reporters on BBC, goes a long way toward explaining the differences that have been presented here.

More generally, corpus-assisted discourse studies would seem to have a significant role to play in tracing and documenting what Martin and White (2005:9) refer to as 'the reading that is "naturalized" by the overall trajectory of the meanings in a text.' It is hoped that research of the kind presented here can cast further light on the linguistic processes through which media messages are shaped in order to create greater awareness of how these messages are constructed and can provide tools for deconstructing them.

NOTES

1. *BBC* was recorded everyday while *CBS* was only recorded from Monday to Friday; there was also more space devoted to advertising on *CBS,* at the expense of news reporting.
2. The number of spoken words does not include the words written on the screen, which would increase the CBS partition by 1,762 words and the BBC partition by 2,102 words, CBS anchor text by 116 words and BBC news presenter text by 22 words, with the resulting proportion of anchor/news presenter discourse to total text of 31 per cent for CBS and 21 per cent for BBC.
3. Although the novel *The Red Badge of Courage* by Stephen Crane is dramatically different from the typical bestseller novel glorifying war, and is even considered by some to be antiwar, it is felt that when cited this way in the context of *CBS* reporting on the Iraq war, it has a clearly positive connotation for the average TV viewer and serves to situate this war within American culture and history, and indeed within the same Civil War context as the Gettysburg Address. Evidence of Dan Rather's intent to use this expression as positive evaluation can be seen in his introduction to the reporter's story following a commercial break: 'Some of the Americans wounded in the war are now being treated at hospitals in Germany and they are telling how they got their battle scars. In some cases they didn't think they'd live to tell their tales. CBS's Lara Logan is in Germany and has their stories of fear, pain and bravery.'
4. In the Gettysburg Address we find 'those who here gave their lives'. The lexeme DEDICATE occurs six times in the Gettysburg Address out of 278 words.

6 'Either You are with Us, or You are with the Terrorists'

How UK and US Television News Reported the 2003 Iraq Conflict

Caroline Clark

Among the numerous controversies which arose from the Iraq war was that which related to the media—its role and its reporting. Lombardo, in the previous chapter, found striking differences in how the war was reported by the *CBS* anchor and the *BBC* news presenter. This chapter, on the other hand, discusses whether, and the extent to which, TV news in the UK (*BBC*) and in the US (*CBS*) may have differed in their coverage of the conflict by looking in particular at how the two sides and the military action were represented.

6.1. INTRODUCTION

In the lead-up to the Iraq war of 2003, the Pentagon and the armed forces became increasingly aware of the importance of the role the media were likely to play, and strategies were devised to cope with the inevitable frustration of media groups trying to access the conflict, with the aim of subjecting to public scrutiny what was predicted, in many circles, to be a controversial war. There was unprecedented media involvement both in the planning of their role and in the vast numbers of journalists mobilized once the war was under way. These included nearly seven hundred reporters embedded with coalition forces, who were accompanied by greatly improved technology which allowed access to areas where land logistics were extremely complex. It also permitted an immediacy whereby news could be instantaneous—that is, an extreme reduction in the spatial and temporal distance between the event and the public—which affected how the information was conveyed and presented, and how it was received by home audiences.

Previous analyses of TV news reporting (Knightley 2004; Media Tenor 2003) have suggested that there were significant differences between the major US and UK broadcasters' coverage of events in Iraq, differences to be found in how the coalition and Iraqi regime, military action, and the plight of civilians were reported. These differences were also said to lie in how the conflict was framed, in the wider issues broached, and in the language used by political figures and various expert commentators.

This corpus-based study of how the two channels, *BBC* and *CBS*, presented the war to their viewers attempts to answer the question of whether audiences on either side of the Atlantic witnessed the 'same' war. The principal research questions relate to whether the perceived difference between the US and UK reporting is evident in the *BBC* and *CBS* partitions of the *TVNews* subcorpus. The degree to which reporters were 'with us or with them' is explored, that is, whether the purported difference between the two news services can be linked to a representation of the 'sides'—a simplistic dichotomy often found in traditional war rhetoric.

The chapter describes a number of linguistic analyses of the two partitions of the *TVNews* subcorpus containing transcriptions of the *BBC* and *CBS* news services which were broadcast over a twenty-eight-day period commencing with the 'Operation Iraqi Freedom' invasion on 20 March 2003. The analysis outlines how the war was framed by the two channels, how the coalition and Iraqi regime were represented, and what 'picture' of the conflict resulted. The methodology adopted is, as elsewhere in the book, that of corpus-assisted discourse studies (CADS) (Partington et al. 2004), as outlined in the introduction to the volume. The corpus was marked up conformant to TEI standards (see Chapter 1, this volume) and subsequently analysed using the *Xaira* and *WordSmith Tools* software.

George W. Bush's now infamous words: 'either you are with us, or you are with the terrorists', expressed a 'false dilemma', a logical fallacy whereby two options, one of which is deemed unacceptable, are proposed as mutually exclusive, thus denying the opportunity to entertain alternative views.[1] This false dilemma has often been heard in conflict situations, and war reporting in particular. The reporter not recognized as being 'with us', or viewing the conflict from 'our' point of view, will be accused of being 'with them', working against our interests, a stance considered to be just short of treason. The middle ground in war reporting is often therefore absent, and a distinct dichotomy can emerge in the form of 'sides', which may undermine the possibility of 'objective', 'neutral', and 'detached' reporting.

This same false dilemma has been the basis of criticism (and praise) for the reporting of the conflict in Iraq. As Partington (Chapter 10, this volume) points out, the role of the media in Iraq was a controversial question in Parliament, perhaps more so in the UK than the United States. The British news media, the *BBC* in particular, were the target of 'an attack led by the British government on the role of particular news organizations in undermining its case for the war' (Brookes and Lewis 2004:283).

Some elements of the media, particularly in the United States, were accused of taking a blindly patriotic, aggressively pro-war stance. Others were seen as betraying the coalition cause by in fact 'being with the terrorists', that is, by reporting events from the Iraqi perspective, or simply by questioning the coalition's version of events, revealing mistakes and detaching themselves from the coalition cause. In both cases—criticism of an antiwar stance, and equally, criticism of being aggressively patriotic—the notion of 'objective reporting' seems to be mistaken for 'dallying with the enemy'.

The Pentagon was well aware of the frustration of the media in trying to access the conflict: 'the build-up to war had taken so long and the issues had been so extensively debated that the media was determined that this would be the most thoroughly reported war of modern times' (Knightley 2004:528). To a certain extent it was 'thoroughly reported'; however, many questions were also raised about the coverage—not least the perennial problems 'associated with allegiance, responsibility, truth and balance' (Allan and Zelizer 2004b:3).

6.1.1. *BBC* and *CBS* News Coverage

The basis of this study is the oft-cited view that the American and British television reporting of the events in Iraq were very different; views which are found in the fields of media studies and sociology, often without any supporting quantifiable evidence. Media Tenor (2003), in a study of the coverage of the Iraq war in five countries including the United States and UK, found that 'there were significant differences in the war coverage', including the portrayal of death, military action, and casualties. According to Knightley (2004:541) 'the reporting of war was very different on both sides of the Atlantic', a view partially supported by Brookes and Lewis (2004:298), who claim that British broadcasters 'did not submit to the kind of cheerleading that characterised much of the US network coverage'.

Generally, US networks were seen to take an overt pro-war stance whereby any duty of impartiality was undermined by patriotic duty; they were effectively in the hands of the Pentagon according to the then director general of the *BBC*.[2] Nor was the *BBC* above criticism, being assailed from both ends of the spectrum: attacked by those supporting the war for what was considered its 'antiwar' coverage, and opponents of the war for being too close to the government's pro-intervention stance, a debate which also resounded throughout the Hutton Inquiry (see Chapter 8, this volume). The *Sun* newspaper accused the *BBC* of treating 'any old drivel put out by Baghdad [. . .] as gospel' (Littlejohn 2003). In turn, the *BBC* commissioned a report to respond to these, and similar, assertions which concluded that there was 'little evidence to support the widespread claims that the *BBC*'s coverage was anti-war' (Lewis et al. 2003:27), findings which were echoed in the *Guardian* (4 July 2003): 'far from revealing an anti-war *BBC*, our findings tend to give credence to those who criticised the *BBC* for being too sympathetic to the government in its war coverage'. There is, however, other evidence that the *BBC* stance was not pro-intervention (see Clark 2007). The *CBS* too was criticised by some more conservative institutions for not giving enough prominence to positive developments during the war, for spreading pessimism in viewers, and giving the impression that the Iraq campaign was 'falling apart' (Media Research Centre 2006).

6.1.2. Research Questions

Based on the assumption that such a widely perceived difference between the US and UK coverage of the same events in Iraq must necessarily be evident in the news reports, it could be hypothesized that the American network *CBS* would be actively pro-war and patriotic, while the *BBC* would be more neutral and balanced in its reporting. The main research question is therefore aimed at investigating whether there were any differences in reporting the conflict, and if there were, the extent and nature of these differences.

The presumed differences between US and UK reporting should also lie in the portrayal of the sides involved in the conflict, as well as in the reportage of military action. These differences would reflect a fundamental us/them dichotomy, the same dichotomy which was found in the political and press arenas surrounding the conflict, and would lead to a second research question. With reference to discussions in media studies, and to the work of van Dijk (1988, 1998), I will explore how the two news services represent *us* and *them*, that is, whether the purported difference between the two channels lies in the representation of *us* as essentially good, morally sound, and magnanimous and *them*, Iraq, as fundamentally bad and morally depraved.

6.2. MATERIALS AND METHODS

The television news subcorpus (*TVNews*) is part of the much larger body of texts created for the *CorDis* research project. The *BBC* and *CBS* partitions of the subcorpus were investigated separately and compared using *Xaira* (version 1.23) and to a limited extent, *WordSmith Tools* 4.00 (2005). It should be noted that the *TVNews* subcorpus is smaller than the others in the *Cordis Corpus* and covers a narrower time span. Other subcorpora within the *CorDis Corpus* were used for comparative purposes, in particular the newspaper subcorpora (see Chapter 7, this volume).

The study is based on the transcriptions of the news services—that is, the words uttered by newsmakers and newsworkers. According to the methodological framework adopted, the texts cannot be decontextualized, and it should be remembered that the audio and visual aspects of the reports are part of the context and neither should be disregarded; in this regard, all recordings have been viewed and re-viewed throughout the research. Studies of the visual portrayal have been carried out by various scholars, who have discussed the synchronicity, or fit, of the visual and verbal texts (see Haarman and Lombardo 2009; Lipson 2007).

The news services can be broken down into three levels of analysis: the news programme as a whole (that is, the selection of stories and/or avoidance of particular issues), the story itself (the individual story in the context of the entire news programme), and 'within' the story (that is, the structure and utterances to be found within the story), the latter being the focus of this research.

6.2.1. Corpus Data

The *BBC* and *CBS* partitions of the *TVNews* subcorpus comprise news reports as aired by these two broadcasters over the twenty-eight-day period from 20 March to 17 April, 2003. The first period of twenty-one days ended with the so-called Fall of Baghdad on April 9. The subcorpora partitions of reports include material for a further eight days of the immediate postwar period when there was a distinct shift in reporting angle, in particular in the representation of Iraqi civilians, as the question of law and order arose. The *TVNews* subcorpus comprises the *BBC* partition (105,908 words), drawn from the corporation's 10 p.m. news programme, and the *CBS* partition (60,807 words), drawn from its 6 p.m. news service. This total number of words includes the small proportion (2–3 per cent) of written text appearing on screen as pull-throughs or titles.[3]

The considerable difference in the size of the two subcorpus partitions does not affect the findings of the research since results are expressed in relative frequencies. The number of words in the *CBS* partition is about 30 per cent less than the *BBC*, reflecting the intrusion of advertising breaks which reduce the thirty-minute programme to about twenty minutes of news (based on a rate of 140 words per minute, as measured by a random sampling of the subcorpus).

Although the United States sent 85 per cent of the coalition troops to Iraq, the viewers of its prime TV channel heard around 30 per cent less news about the conflict on any given day compared with *BBC* viewers. The *CBS* televised an average of six to seven news stories in each service compared with eight for the *BBC*, resulting in approximately 450 and 535 words per story, respectively, which points more to a rather different structuring of the news service than any difference in content or angle.

The conflict was presented through the collective utterances of newsreaders, political leaders, military commentators, embedded reporters, and even members of the public. For a more sensitive analysis of the content of the news services as a whole, and therefore the information audiences received, the subcorpus partitions were broken down into the contributions of newsmakers and newsworkers. Newsmakers contribute to the story as protagonists in the form of legitimated persons (henceforth LPs, including political leaders, named experts, and higher military personnel), unnamed, lower ranking military personnel (MIL), and members of the public (VOX, that is, *vox populi*). Newsworkers, on the other hand, are those directly involved in the production and reporting of the news, including newsreaders (henceforth NR), reporters embedded with coalition units (embedded reporters—ERs), so-called *unilaterals* (reporters working within Iraq, but not assigned to coalition forces), journalists reporting from neighbouring countries (WZ, that is, *war zone* reporters), correspondents, special area and studio reporters.

It is interesting to note the small proportion of the physical volume of the news service that is actually taken up by the newsmakers: little more than 12 per cent of the *BBC* and 16.8 per cent of the *CBS* partitions amounting to about 450 words, or three minutes, per day on both channels. Viewers of both channels, therefore, saw little of the leaders Bush and Blair, and heard only brief discussions of the contentious issues behind invasion or debate on an international level. These tended therefore to be glossed over, as equally were the hoped-for benefits of the war, except for the occasional comment by politicians or named military personnel.

A comparison between the two news services shows that the *CBS* comprises a significantly higher proportion of words from MIL (7.8 per cent of the *CBS* partition, compared with *BBC* 2.8 per cent) and VOX (3.5 per cent of the *CBS* partition, compared with *BBC* 2.1 per cent). This reflects a style of coverage on *CBS* during the conflict which emphasises 'home stories', especially from ERs interviewing soldiers, and interviews with ordinary people (VOX) 'back home' (see Chapter 5, this volume). The *BBC* gave slightly more time to LPs, that is, political figures and higher military personnel, than did the *CBS*; LPs such as Bush and Blair contributed an average of just 265 words per *BBC* news programme and even fewer, 147 words (about one minute), on the *CBS*. Over 30 per cent of the words uttered on the *CBS* news (compared with 21.6 per cent for the *BBC*) were spoken by the newsreader who took on a high-profile role by commenting as well as presenting the news. This high profile accorded the newsreader by *CBS* is another structural factor in the difference between the channels (see Chapter 5, this volume).

One of the more significant differences between the news services is the great quantity of words/airtime dedicated to ERs by the *BBC* (18.3 per cent of the total *BBC* partition compared with 11.0 per cent for the *CBS*). Their proximity to both 'sides' put them in the unique position of being part of one 'side', while also seeing the effects of, and on, the 'other', a high-resolution view marred at times by a necessarily narrow angle. They could be considered a hybrid of newsworker and newsmaker, such was the success of the embed program (see Clark 2007). WZs, on the other hand, in positions ranging from Baghdad to Qatar, sometimes had a rather limited or a necessarily skewed view of events—especially those based in Baghdad who could only 'see' one side of the story, often 'guided' by Iraqi authorities. However, ERs and WZs, that is, the correspondents who were in a position to witness and report on war action, contributed to about half the *BBC* coverage and 35 per cent of the *CBS* coverage.

It is not within the scope of this research to discuss the structure of the news programme as a whole, or the individual story in the context of the news programmes. However, some basic differences in format should be noted since they are relevant to the findings. Nor is this study concerned with the visual aspect of the news, although this clearly cannot be disregarded.

6.2.2. Methodology

The overwhelming amount of visual, audio, and textual material generated by the continuously evolving events of the war in Iraq posed problems of organization and analysis of the corpora. The corpus-assisted discourse studies (CADS) methodology, discussed in detail earlier in the current work (see the Introduction and also Chapter 10, this volume), offers an effective framework for managing these large quantities of material in various modes (see Haarman et al. 2002; Partington 2003) by offering a streamlined approach to compiling, accessing, and analyzing a specialized corpus, without losing sight of contextual features.

The present analysis of the *CBS* and *BBC* news services is predominantly quantitative in its initial stages, where we are seeking evidence of words and patterns which may provide an insight into any differences between the news services in their reporting of the same events. It moves then into a more qualitative phase, when we attempt to analyze contextual and cotextual features.

6.3. CORPUS-BASED ANALYSIS

The key to the view of the conflict adopted by the news broadcasters is the representation of the coalition and Iraq as participants, and how the war is portrayed, that is, how military action is reported. The first step is a keyword analysis (*WordSmith Tools*), the aim of which is to provide an insight into any differences in representation of the war for TV news viewers by contrasting the relative word frequencies in the two partitions.[4] At the top of the resulting keyword list are those words with a relative frequency significantly higher in the *CBS* partition, while the so-called negative keywords—those which are more frequent in the *BBC* partition, and notable for their limited frequency in the *CBS* corpus—are found at the bottom.

This analysis of the words characterizing one partition and not the other reveals little to suggest that the *BBC* and *CBS* take profoundly different angles in reporting, or bend any of the journalistic rules of impartiality. However, it does underline several minor points (which perhaps illustrate more the sensitivity of the keyword analysis than the implications of the analysis in the partitions). We note the *CBS* usage of numbers; eleven cardinal and one ordinal number have a high keyness factor, and in nearly all cases these refer to numbers of people (dead, taken prisoner, soldiers, civilians) or kilometres (distances from destination). The first cardinal number (*one*) to be found in the *BBC* has a relative frequency of 0.26 per hundred words, compared with 0.40 for the *CBS*. The same keyword analysis also reveals the keyness of *sandstorm*—entirely absent from the *BBC*. *Sandstorms* are always an impediment; they are *ferocious, brutal, mess with ability*, and *slow down progress* and, in all cases but one, justify the failure to achieve a goal.

In keeping with the research questions, the keyword features investigated were the high keyness in the *CBS* material of {FIGHTERS} (curly brackets are used to indicate words sharing the same semantic field, that is, words related by synonymy, as per Lyons' [1977] usage), that is, *marine(s), army*, and the Iraqi *Fedayin*. As regards the *BBC* keywords, the verbs *say* and *think* were prominent, as were the nationalities *American, British*, and the *coalition*. It would thus appear that the *CBS* tended to cover events in military terms while the *BBC* saw the conflict more on a political level as nations involved in a coalition, and presumably reported more opinions on what was happening.

The individual word lists (produced using *WordSmith Tools*), on which the keyword list is based, provide an overview of the most salient aspects of the news service, that is, the words the audiences heard most often. A number of patterns, although at times tenuous, are revealed, in particular with reference to the second research question, that is, whether the hypothesized differences between the British and US reporting of the conflict is in fact linked to their respective representations of the coalition as morally sound, and of Iraq as a depraved regime.

6.3.1. Representation of the 'Sides'—Coalition

According to mainstream news ideology (see, for example, the 'liberal pluralist' position in Allan 1999:49–50), prime TV news programmes, such as the *BBC* and *CBS*, are generally expected to be impartial, factual, and neutral, as far as possible, presenting viewers with both sides of the story, especially in conflict situations which are closely monitored by both professional agencies and individual viewers for any perceived bias. This implies that reporting the same events should result in very similar, impartial and objective, news reports. On the other hand, it is generally accepted that the reporter's voice, therefore some partiality, is nonetheless evident, mediating and interpreting events (Bell 1991; Fowler 1991; Iedema et al. 1994; Kress 1983:120), constructed by the use of a variety of closely related, and sometimes overlapping, linguistic features such as the use of the pronouns *I* and *we*, intensification, explicit and implicit value judgements and opinions, mental processes, loaded or noncore vocabulary, and modality (Carter 1988; Iedema et al. 1994). These devices also include the nominalization of military action, the use of intransitive and agent-less passive constructions to obscure agency, as well as metaphor (van Leeuwen 2006).

As expected in war reporting, pronouns, as well as lexical items indicating the 'sides', and the 'enemy', can be found very high in the lists of the fifty most frequent words. The pronouns *I*, *we*, and *they* have frequencies per hundred words in the *TVNews* subcorpus of 0.468, 0.591, and 0.957, respectively (all have a relative frequency higher in the *BBC* than in the *CBS* partition). While pronouns feature highly in any corpus, this is significantly higher than the same pronouns in newspapers (*PapNews* partition of *CorDis* corpus) where the frequencies for *I*, *we*, and *they* are 0.224, 0.344, and 0.415, respectively. On the other hand, the absence of items explicitly indicating {WAR} and {FIGHTING} was unexpected. The first reporting verb, *say*, also has a high frequency (lemmatised: *BBC* 0.289, *CBS* 0.347) and occurs within the first fifty words. It is, however, interesting to note that the frequency is significantly lower than in newspapers (*PapNews* partition 0.984).

According to van Dijk (1998:57), opinions are organized according to an 'ideological pattern that polarizes in-groups and out-groups, us vs. them', that is, a strategy of representing the 'self' in positive terms, and the 'other' in negative or contrastive terms. In war reporting, it follows, therefore, that reporter stance will be evident when the representation of 'us' (in this case the coalition), in terms of actions, conquests, and courage, is posited against a representation of 'them' (Iraq) in negative terms—their losses and demise.

This polarization is found in past war reporting, and correspondents in WWI and WWII spoke openly of a total allegiance to, and identification with, the forces on their side (see Gibb 1923; Pyle 1979). More recently, regarding Iraq, Burkeman (2003) reported that reporters 'use the words "we" and "us" profusely, identifying themselves with the military'—in direct conflict with the expected objectivity in reporting mentioned earlier. Within this rationale, *we* should refer to the coalition, and should have a higher frequency in the *CBS* material, in keeping with the supposed patriotic stance of US reporting. In actual fact, however, the relative frequency of *we* was found to be higher in the *BBC* material (0.619 per hundred words compared to 0.541 in the *CBS*). Its relative frequency in the *BBC* was also significantly higher than in the *CorDis* newspaper subcorpora (0.344), as perhaps might be expected. Further, newsworkers used *we* nearly twice as often as newsmakers on both channels. More important than this disparity, however, is the question 'who precisely were *we*?'. It transpires that by far the highest relative frequency of *we* is found in utterances by newsreaders referring to themselves and viewers, followed by MILs who, directly involved in the war, referred to their own actions. This MIL use of *we* does not characteristically reflect an enthusiastic attitude, but rather a sombre and realistic one, such as:

(1)   I wish **we** could do more about it but **we** just don't have the people.

(*BBC* 10 April)

(2)   **we** pick ourselves up and **we** keep going.

(*CBS* 21 March)

What is not found is *we* referring to the coalition as a fighting force, that is, an inclusive *we* referring to the efforts of 'our side'.[5] *We* was not significantly more frequent, nor was it used in triumphant terms on the *CBS*, as might have been expected given the claims of overt patriotism.

The relative frequency of *they* (*BBC* 1.04, *CBS* 0.81) is much greater than in the reference corpus of newspaper texts (the *PapNews* partition of the *CorDis Newspapers* subcorpora) covering the same period (0.415) and in a corpus of spoken language (0.57).[6] Given the conflict circumstances and what was subsequently said about 'biased' or 'patriotic' reporting (see Chapter 10, this volume), it was hypothesized that *they* would refer to the adversary or foe. On a randomized count of 200 instances, it was found that *they* refers in fact more to the {COALITION} than {IRAQ} on both news services.[7] Unexpectedly, Saddam's regime, its armed forces, and its military actions amount to little over 10 per cent of references, while about 70 per cent of instances refer to the {COALITION} and another 10 per cent refer to IRAQI {CIVILIANS}. This finding, when considered with those regarding *we*, suggests that both broadcasters, to similar extents, referred to the {COALITION} with a more neutral *they*, preferring the pronoun *we* to refer to newsmakers. Further, this high frequency of *they* may be justified by the lack of information about Iraq as a result of the limited access to Iraqi civilians and the fact that, except for Baghdad, coalition reporters were almost entirely absent from the Iraqi 'side'.

The keyword analysis comparing the two subcorpora partitions showed a high keyness in the *BBC* partition for *American, British,* and *coalition,* as alternatives to pronouns, suggesting some differences between the partitions. The *BBC* refers more to the United States than the *CBS* does itself, and than the *BBC* refers to the *British.* While the *BBC* refers more often to the *coalition* (relative frequency 0.187 of the total *BBC* subcorpus partition compared with *CBS* 0.028), resulting in very high keyness, the *CBS* totally ignores the existence of a coalition as an abstract entity of governments united in supporting the war effort in Iraq, the only exceptions being when items such as *forces, air strikes,* and so on are premodified. In 20 per cent of instances in the *BBC* partition, *coalition* collocates contiguously to the right with {MILITARY PERSONNEL} (the most frequent cluster: *of the coalition forces*), and is used by newsworkers rather than newsmakers. It is interesting to note that *coalition* does not collocate with *attacks, battles,* or similar, in a span of five words to the left and right of the node word, there being just two instances in the *BBC.* The only verb which collocates with *coalition* functioning as an actor is *advance.*

(3)   Together **coalition** forces are **advancing** day by day in steady progress

(*BBC* 27 March)

(4)   **Coalition** forces **advancing** towards Baghdad

(*BBC* 24 March)

In the CBS material, on the other hand, the rare instances of *coalition* (relative frequency 0.028) collocate, predictably, with {MILITARY PERSONNEL}. The frequency of the similar term *allies* is double on the BBC (0.027 compared with CBS 0.012). On both news services, *allies* collocates frequently with {IRAQI PEOPLE} and, while *coalition* has military connotations, *allies*, as the term itself may suggest, are 'friends', in particular on the BBC:

(5) telling the people there that the **allies** have come as a liberating army

(BBC 24 March)

(6) the **Allies** warn people to stay at home, not to move outside their houses and not to rise up

(BBC 25 March)

The CBS usage of allies tends towards the negative, is more distanced, and is often accompanied by the contrastive *but*:

(7) A fear among local residents that the **allies**, [. . .] are no more committed this time

(CBS 2 April)

(8) The **allies** claim they work well together, but the potential for problems

(CBS 9 April)

The {COALITION} and {ALLIES} as semantic fields comprise the states involved (America, US, Britain, etc.). *Britain* is mentioned on the BBC as a geographical reference (25 per cent of instances), such as *here in Britain*, but more often as a political entity: *Britain and America's legal duty*. The usage is usually metonymic, for example: *Britain wants a prominent role*, and *Britain* collocates with *America* and/or the *United States* in 27 per cent of instances. On neither news service are the individual countries directly related to the conflict itself, that is, Britain and America are not participants in military action, as either actors or goals.

Predictably, the frequency of *Britain* is four times greater on the BBC (0.049 per cent), compared with the CBS (0.013 per cent), where Britain is only referred to (five times) in the cluster *US and Britain*, as an alternative to the *coalition*. In this case, there are predominantly negative connotations:

(9) no way the **US and Britain** will allow the United Nations

(CBS 3 April)

(10) If the **US and Britain** want a short war Saddam wants a long one

(CBS 24 March)

Regarding the *CBS*, *America* appears less as a political entity or power, and is more linked to emotive issues such as: *heroes of America's wars*. Moreover, *America*, on the *CBS*, is a victim of others' evil:

(11) attacks on **America**

(*CBS* 20 March)

(12) Al Qaeda to press the attack against **America**

(*CBS* 17 April)

The analysis also reveals that *America* is not engaged in a conflict. Instead, it has *military might* (*BBC*), and has *unleashed its military fury* (*CBS*), but no results of this power are reported, nor are the 'receivers' of America's actions indicated. Verbs are rarely transactive, and processes are without goals (see Halliday 1994). The frequencies are similar for the *BBC*.

On both channels, as mentioned earlier, the lexical items *America* and *Britain* are predominantly political entities and rarely geographical. Despite the different frequencies mentioned previously, the usage on the two news services of {AMERICA} and {BRITAIN} are very similar, and are not accompanied by overt favourable, or unfavourable, evaluation.

British and *American* collocate almost exclusively with {TROOPS} on both news programmes, although the representation of these troops is rarely transactive, whereby the action passes from the actor to the affected. The keyword analysis also reveals the high keyness of *marines* for the *CBS*, and this item is likewise not associated with transactive or material processes. It is far more common to find the *US*, rather than *American*, as a classifier of military equipment or forces, which in turn, collocate with relational or mental processes, rather than material.

The {COALITION} is a presence, but is not an actor in events, as will be discussed following. Verbs within a span of five words to the right of {COALITION} tend to be relational (that is, encoding an identity or description, such as: *is most anxious, have been in action*) or nontransactive (that is, without an identifiable goal, such as: *going in further, scout around, step up tactics*). Further, very few words at all referring to military action or war are found within a span of five words to the left and right of *British* or *American* on either channel.

6.3.2. Representation of the 'Sides'—Iraq

While in the United States it was frequently suggested in the political arena that the coalition's role in Iraq was to bring an end to the evil and depravity of Saddam's regime, in Britain the government was very clear that its principal aim was 'disarmament' (see Chapter 3, this volume), with the secondary, or flow-on, effect of bringing about the end of Saddam. However, a 'justification' for the conflict in Iraq was not proposed by the news services of either broadcaster. LPs spoke very generally of Saddam as a leader, the coalition's desire to remove him with the backing of the Iraqi people, his responsibility for a *cruel war against Kuwait* (*BBC*), and the aim to *disarm Iraq of its weapons of mass destruction* (*BBC*) but without an overt causal link. Similarly, the concept of an enemy, a *them*, was also largely absent. The relative frequency of the word *enemy* is low (*BBC* 0.025, *CBS* 0.049) although it collocates (in a five-word span either side of the node) with unfavourable situations such as *deception, killing,* and *fighting,* as well as with {COALITION FORCES}. It is interesting to note that the semantic set {ENEMY} (comprising the *Fedayin, fighters, Iraqi troops,* etc.) is rarely the actor in material processes (see Halliday 1994); they are more often sensers in mental processes, such as: *Iraqi soldiers are now pretending to be civilians* (*BBC*). The {ENEMY} do not perform violent actions, nor is the {COALITION} a goal of enemy actions on either channel. In the *BBC* partition, {ENEMY} is a verb complement of *take on, make progress against,* and *try to scare,* while the *CBS* increase the intensity and *deal with, destroy, fight, flush out,* and *kill* the enemy—thus construing a somewhat more decisive and aggressive stance.

The semantic field ENEMY includes the Fedayin, fighters and soldiers, with little difference in frequency, usage, and collocation. The incidence of *fighters* is similar on both news services, as is the context in which they appear, and strong collocation with *loyalty* (to the regime). In rare cases the ENEMY are agents who *ensnarl the British* (*CBS*), *snipe at Americans* (*CBS*), and *shoot their own civilians* according to both channels. Similarly, on both channels, the *regime* collocates frequently with *Saddam,* but is not an actor in material processes against the coalition.

As regards the language used by coalition leaders in sound bites broadcast on TV, President Bush and Prime Minister Blair rarely mentioned Saddam. Blair spoke of *Saddam* a total of nine times on both channels, and Bush just six; however, the same sound bites were repeated on both news services. Saddam was referred to as an individual: *I don't know the whereabouts of Hussein* (Bush, *CBS*) as often as he was as an institutional figure representing the Iraqi regime: *further evidence of the depravity of Saddam's regime* (Blair, *BBC,* and *CBS*). It is interesting to note that LPs on the whole made little reference to *Saddam*: the relative frequency of *Saddam* in the *BBC* LP partition is 0.002 compared with 0.004 for the *CBS* LPs.

Over the entire *TVNews* subcorpus, reference to *Saddam* has a similar relative frequency on both the *BBC* (0.357) and *CBS* (0.422). The majority of instances of the item *Saddam* on both news services are metonymic (*many of them refugees from Saddam Hussein*) or as the classifying genitive (*Saddam's*) referring to his *forces, statue,* or *palaces.* Rarely is Saddam referred to as an individual, except when the identity of the person appearing on TV is questioned. He remains an enigmatic figure. He is not the actor in any processes except a single case of repression: *its people have long been repressed by Saddam* (*BBC*). The only other mentions are that he *might be meeting with his top aides* (CBS), *Saddam Hussein says* (BBC), he *popped up* (CBS), and *seemed less bloated* (CBS). Neither news service echoed the words and feelings of Bush and Blair with regards to Saddam being 'evil'. While the regime and its leader are generally construed in unfavourable terms, even if explicit condemnation is lacking, ordinary soldiers and civilians are portrayed with rather more empathy by both channels.

Iraqi as a modifier is almost entirely reserved for geographical features (such as: *close to the Iraqi border*), but we also find *Iraqi forces* who *turn back*, *put on civilian uniform*, *have abandoned their position*, and have *fled*, on both news services—indicating inadequate preparation. Iraqi forces also *shell*, *control*, and *retreat* on both the CBS and BBC, as well as *fire missiles*, *respond with heavy* [. . .] *fire*, and *battle fiercely*. Overall, however, it is a fairly restrained picture on both channels. *Iraqi fighters*, a stronger term, used more by the BBC, referring to the Fedayin and special forces, *open fire*, *dig in*, and *hold out*, but rarely in transactive clause structures. Yet, with the exception of {FIGHTERS}, *Iraqis* are far more often the goal of coalition actions, as might be expected. The {ENEMY}, in its many forms, has a similar frequency on both channels; it is slightly more 'fierce' on the CBS, although this ferocity is never proposed as a justification for coalition actions, nor is ferocity implied in describing Iraqi actions against us.

Iraqi civilians are mentioned more often on the CBS, where they are *killed*, *die*, and *try to bring order*. Although {IRAQI CASUALTIES} are mentioned just twice on both news services, the CBS makes explicit mention of civilian suffering caused by US 'errors', for example: *a civilian vehicle carrying a family of farmers is attacked by marines* (CBS). The same incident was reported on the BBC without mentioning agency: *the 7 Iraqi women and children killed yesterday in a shooting at a checkpoint* (BBC). The frequency of the item *Iraqi people* is greater on the BBC (0.043 compared with CBS 0.017) and they are generally mentioned in terms of the coalition's need to 'win them over':

(13) It's the first aid shipment of its kind into Iraq, but a crucial weapon in the battle to gain the trust of **the Iraqi people.**

(*BBC* 28 March)

(14) The first step on what is turning out to be a difficult journey to win the support and confidence of **the Iraqi people.**

(*CBS* 26 March)

Both channels recognize the plight of ordinary Iraqis and the need to improve their lot, and present them in sympathetic if, at times, patronising terms. The Iraqi people do not actually perform any actions on either news service; they are not the actors in any material processes. They remain the passive victims of the situation. This view shifts on both news services after 9 April, the date of the so-called Fall of Baghdad, as law-and-order issues came to the fore. On both channels Iraqi civilians became actors, portrayed as engaging in activities evaluated unfavourably:

(15) **ordinary Iraqis** came in and took whatever they could find, all the way down to the mattresses on the gurneys.

(*CBS* 11 April)

(16) Tonight many **Iraqis** in Basra are celebrating but many are also looting, helping themselves from buildings.

(*BBC* 6 April)

(17) **People** are both celebrating and looting.

(*CBS* 8 April)

The item *looting*, however, occurs more often in its nominalized form, thus obscuring agency:

(18) widespread **looting** has continued

(*BBC* 10 April)

(19) the orgy of **looting**

(*BBC* 17 April)

(20) **looting** has been rampant

(*CBS* 15 April)

With this shift in view, both broadcasters present Iraqi civilians as unscrupulous when circumstances permit.

6.3.3. Representation of Military Action

As expected, both the *UK* and the *US* collocate frequently with {MILITARY ACTION} in both partitions. Missing, however, from the higher frequency lists are the words *war* (*BBC* 0.396, *CBS* 0.444) and *conflict* (*BBC* 0.047, *CBS* 0.015).

This was not a *war* (or *conflict*) *with*, *against*, or *on* Iraq. There are just two instances on the *BBC* of the *war against/on Iraq*, and a single more tentative *war with Iraq*. The latter occurs twice in the *CBS* data, and there is just one instance of the *war against*. The frequent use of the intransitive was apparent in many of the collocations of *war* in the *BBC* data: *war comes, begins, unfolds, continues.* and *ends,* and no human element—friend or foe—is causally linked to war. There is no evidence of more emotionally charged words, such as *battle*, except for specific events and where qualified by the location, such as the *Battle for Basra, Nassiriya,* and so on. It becomes clear that *this/the war* or *conflict* is spatially located, stative, and does not occur within the 5L-5R collocation span of *British* and *American*.

The predominant frame of the war coverage was its progress and action, as substantiated in several content analyses (see Media Tenor), which could be expected since over 30 per cent of airtime was attributed to reporters in theatre, either as ERs or WZ reporters. The verb most frequently collocating with *British* is *kill* (0.107 *BBC*, 0.123 *CBS*), although very few cases refer to Iraqis as victims. *Kill* and *die* collocate more frequently with {COALITION FORCES} for both broadcasters, for example, *coalition forces say that thirty British troops have been killed* (*BBC*). The *CBS* goes further than the *BBC* in reporting the deaths of coalition soldiers in action; it does not supply detail, but at the same time makes no suggestion that Iraqis were directly responsible for American deaths. Death happens; it is not causally linked to the enemy on either channel. Limited evidence of sentiment is found on the *CBS*, such as: *more bodies of Americans killed in the war have come home.* In these cases, soldiers are killed in a geographical location, for example, *southern Iraq*, or are killed in action, such as: *killed in a helicopter crash, killed in a car bomb explosion,* but are not killed by Iraqis. However, the cause of death is not always concealed, especially in cases of 'friendly fire' such as: *two RAF pilots have been killed after their Tornado jet was shot down by an American Patriot missile* (*BBC*) and *Stone was killed in a grenade attack by one of his comrades* (*CBS*) where the agent is underlined.

Similarly, on both channels, Iraqis, civilians and military forces, are killed either 'in violent situations' or 'by violent means', but not by the coalition, as in: *three people killed by bombs or missiles* (*BBC*). The *CBS* refers more often to {IRAQI CIVILIANS} as victims of the coalition than the *BBC*, for example:

(21) the US bombing today **killed** at least fifty-eight people in a crowded Baghdad market.

(*CBS* 28 March)

(22) a family of three was **killed,** . . . after the US said the driver of the vehicle failed to stop

(*CBS* 11 April)

Agency is muted, and the location is cited, such as *killed* [. . .] *at a checkpoint* (*BBC*). One of the very few actions within a span of five words to the right of {COALITION FORCES} is *fire*, where explicit action is borne against things not people, such as: *British tanks are now firing into the buildings* (*BBC*). Neither channel, despite accusations to the contrary, obfuscated cases of error:

(23) a British challenger tank **fired** and [. . .] struck another British challenger II tank

(*BBC* 25 March)

(24) the American troops **opened fire** on the vehicle killing seven Iraqi civilians, all women and children

(*CBS* 31 March)

When the coalition are the 'receivers' of *fire*, it is rarely in the active voice, and the agent is omitted: *British troops found themselves under fire* (*BBC*). As a result, the impact is limited as actions on both news services are nominalized, rendering them agentless and dissolving responsibility; viewers hear grammatical metaphors (see Halliday 1994:342–67) such as:

(25) the **attack** on Baghdad

(*CBS* 26 March)

(26) a night time **raid** against the Republican Guards

(*CBS* 28 March)

(27) the apparently rapid American **advance** on Baghdad

(*BBC* 2 April)

On the whole, very few coalition actions are reported by either channel, and when reported they tend to be euphemistic or vague: troops *positioned tanks, patrol roads,* and *push deeper* but do little more. The viewers of both channels were informed of the lead-up to direct confrontation, but not the confrontation itself. Where battle is evident, it is reduced to progress, in euphemistic terms on both channels: allied forces *bear down, push ahead, creeping ever closer,* or even *walk into Mosul.* Bombing too *has been accurate,* although *BBC* and *CBS* viewers receive no further information as to what this accuracy entails.

Television coverage of the conflict described very little military action, and there was little to distinguish the two channels in this regard. Viewers heard of troop movements and positions but generally did not see battles taking place or coalition actions against Iraqis. Visually, the predominant image of 'military action' was that of tanks rolling across the desert towards an undefined goal. Neither news service dwelt upon bloody or ferocious firefights, and exchanges of gunfire were sporadic. Similarly, there were rarely heroics, or rhetorical triumphs. One can ask, therefore, what were reporters reporting? Overall, the *CBS* was slightly more explicit regarding action, in those instances when transactive verbs were expressed, such as: *Apaches hit four tanks,* or *marines and soldiers took on pockets of increasingly desperate defenders* and *we engaged, took out bunkers with grenades, took out the trench line with machine guns.* However, this use of the active voice and transactive verbs to describe military action is limited. Generally, military action is vague, as is the outline of the enemy.

Explicit and informative language in both news services refers almost entirely to distances covered and the speed, obstacles, the weather ,and the geography, such as:

(28) the Americans pushed their tanks to within seven kilometres of the city

(*BBC* 22 March)

(29) they've seized territory north of the city of Kirkuk

(*BBC* 29 March)

(30) visibility was less than a mile

(*CBS* 21 March)

6.3.4. Representation of the Regime

In keeping with van Dijk's construction of *us* and *them*, a further way to highlight 'our' good points is to underline the extent of 'their' bad ones. President Bush justified this conflict by reference to the depravity of Saddam and his regime, and content analyses have shown that this was indeed a secondary frame to TV coverage. Regime depravity was depicted in many forms, one of the foremost being the possession of weapons of mass destruction (WMDs). References in both partitions had very similar frequencies and similar usage. Both channels were cautious in their mention of WMDs, such as: *Saddam's alleged weapons of mass destruction* (*BBC*) and the search for them: *weapons of mass destruction which still have not been found and may not be found* (*CBS*). The possible existence of, and search for, WMDs was not a major point in the reports on either news service. It was either stressed that they had not been discovered, or the issue was avoided altogether. Similarly, chemical weapons were portrayed as a constant, though limited, threat to troops, significantly more so by the *CBS* (*BBC* 0.010, *CBS* 0.028).

Neither news service exploited the supposed evil of Saddam's regime, which could have been expressed in terms of its immoral actions towards *us*, the coalition. The regime, rather than acting against the coalition, is represented as a state of affairs that simply exists. Their supposed depravity is not linked causally to the conflict, nor are their, supposedly immoral, actions towards their own civilians judged explicitly.

6.4. CONCLUSIONS AND DISCUSSION

There is little evidence from this lexical analysis of television news data to indicate that the coalition was exalted by either the *BBC* or *CBS*, or that the Iraqi regime was explicitly condemned as depraved and a source of evil.

A number of other conclusions can, however, be tentatively voiced. Neither of the news stations in this study appeared to follow the call to somehow prove 'either you are with us or you are with them'. The representation of the 'sides' in the conflict, and the military action, on both channels was restrained, and could not reasonably be labelled as either explicitly anti-intervention or pro-war. In contradiction to those who claim that generally US TV coverage was overtly patriotic, the *CBS* partition does not provide evidence of the station being enthusiastically pro-intervention and there were few mentions of heroics and little triumphalism. The results of this lexical analysis suggest, in fact, that it appeared to be no more pro-war than the *BBC*, which, in its turn, was, famously and repeatedly, accused of being anti-intervention, antigovernment and even unpatriotic (see Chapter 10, this volume). Whether or not the *CBS* was entirely representative of US news reporting is, of course, a matter for further study.

Although the restricted size of the *TVNews* subcorpus has limited the nature of the analysis which could be carried out, it was nevertheless clear that the verbal texts produced by the two broadcasters were in ethos very similar, echoing each other in their portrayal of the sides and the conflict itself, although they were clearly framed for local audiences and the news services were structured differently.

There were nonetheless striking differences between the news programmes as Lombardo (Chapter 5, this volume) points out in her study of the stance of news presenters. There is also evidence to be found of an anti-intervention stance in the reporting of *BBC* embeds (Clark 2007) and *BBC* correspondents (Haarman 2006), although this stance is less evident in a lexical analysis of the overall representation of the sides and of military action.

There were also clear differences between the *CBS* and *BBC* reports on the level of the news programme as a whole, that is, in the selection and type of story aired, the structure of the news programme, the narrative, the personalization of reporters, the role of the newsreader (see Chapter 5 this volume), audience design, and visuals, which were not within the scope of this research. The *CBS* included many more home stories, which can be substantiated by the significantly greater number of words (as a percentage of the entire partition) it dedicated to VOX (*BBC* 2.1 per cent, *CBS* 3.5 per cent) and MIL (*BBC* 2.8 per cent, *CBS* 7.8 per cent). It made a point of inviting the military posted in Iraq to address their 'loved ones' left behind, and of interviewing families of forces 'back home', thus anchoring the story in home news.

In short, the *CBS* provided fewer but longer stories based more on a Labovian narrative structure (Labov 1972) recounting an individualized narrative, rather than the objectivized 'news'. The *CBS* newsmakers took on more personalized roles resulting in a less objective appearance. Regarding the visual aspect, which cannot of course be discounted in any investigation of news services, there were several differences between the two broadcasters, a fact which has been documented in media studies and other surveys. Self-censorship was applied by *BBC* and *CBS* newsworkers, although it appeared slightly less evident on the *CBS*. In keeping with Lipson's findings (Lipson 2007), the visuals downplayed violence and death, and dehumanized warfare. Nevertheless the visuals told a story which the verbals tended to hedge, and above all they were not always synchronized, that is, they did not always tell the same story. Viewers who expected action-packed 'militainment' may have been disappointed; according to John Simpson, reporting for the *BBC* as a unilateral, the press were 'desperate for some genuine heroics in a war which seemed disturbingly short of gallantry' (Simpson 2003:313). 'Combat gallantry' was in fact scarce in the verbal representation of the conflict, although an 'ethical' gallantry in the form of good deeds towards civilians was present (Lombardo, 2007). Military action and events were reported in relational and nontransactive terms. Further, what the coalition did was not all good and what Iraq did was not all bad, and there was no attempt to make it seem that way.

The power of TV media may partially explain the initial dichotomy, 'either you are with us or you are with them'. While the war may have been seen by some as 'short on gallantry', this may be because the *BBC* and *CBS* television coverages were not always in a position to report on what gallantry there was. War action, in the form of a detailed account of military engagement, is conspicuously absent from the spoken corpus, limited perhaps by the risks reporters were prepared to take, but also from the visuals (although there is limited footage of the results of military engagement in the form of burnt-out vehicles and distance shots of bodies). Doward (2003) complained that 'pictures were often mundane and repetitive', although reports have cited that the public generally preferred TV to the printed press as a source of information. The Cardiff Commission Report found that 47 per cent of people gave the *BBC* as their preferred choice of information over and above broadsheets (9 per cent) and tabloids (7 per cent) (Brookes and Lewis 2004), although it has also been suggested that serious war watchers turned to quality papers for news. TV provided the pictures, limited as they were, and daily access to the war to a numerous and wide audience, allowing viewers to 'see' what was effectively a carefully planned war. According to Rees-Mogg in the *Times* (24 March 2003), 'television has changed wars; now war is changing television. [. . .] For news of the war [. . .] television has long since overtaken the newspapers'.

NOTES

1. Address to the Joint Session of Congress and the American People, 20 September 2001, after the Al Qaeda 9/11 attacks on New York's Twin Towers.
2. Greg Dyke, (then) Director General of the *BBC*, in a speech given to the University of London Goldsmiths College Journalism Symposium, 24 April, 2003.

3. I make reference to the total words in the subcorpora. Of the total of 105,908 words in the BBC partition, 2,102 (1.9%) were written, whereas of the 60,807 in the CBS partition, 1,762 (2.9%) were written.
4. The keyword analysis compares the frequency of each word in the *CBS* partition with the frequency of the same word in the *BBC* partition, applying a log-likelihood statistical test resulting in a keyness figure.
5. An inclusive *we*, whereby reporters associated themselves with the military was found on the first two days of the conflict, especially by ERs (Clark, 2007). This has also been documented in other studies. Pfau et al. (2004) found that embeds gave more favourable and war-charged stories in the first five days, although there was no overall difference in tone.
6. From a 250,000-word corpus of news interviews conducted on British television, 1999–2000.
7. The randomized count was performed by taking a random selection of 200 instances from the corpus with the node word in the centre, using *Xaira*.

7 Editorials and Opinion Articles in the *CorDis Corpus*
A Transversal Study

Amanda C. Murphy

The research in this chapter builds on previous work that has distinguished linguistic features of the discourse type *opinion articles,* frequently called 'op-eds', from other types in media discourse, such as *editorials* and *newspaper reports.* Starting from Biber's lists of features involved in the 'overt expression of persuasion' (1988:195), Murphy and Morley (2006) documented characteristic features of op-eds in terms of the frequency of first and second personal pronouns, verbs indicating mental and verbal processes, and lexical density. In the present paper, by quantitative and qualitative means, the subcorpora of opinion articles and editorials (*PapOp* and *PapEd*) from the *CorDis Corpus* are compared and contrasted across two different parameters, popular papers versus quality papers, and British versus American papers, with the aim of making finer distinctions between the two discourse types. Three broad issues are approached. Firstly, aspects of spoken discourse such as interjections, vocatives, discourse markers, contracted forms, and first-person imperatives are sought and explored in the two discourse types; this section is a development of research by Murphy and Morley (2006) which reported that, from the point of lexical density, op-eds resemble spoken language more than editorials. Secondly, through an analysis of keywords and headlines, differences are observed across the two types of newspapers, quality and popular, and between American and British papers. Lastly, the phraseology of the two discourse types is examined through comparing clusters of 2, 3, or 4 words in the subcorpora.

7.1 DATA AND METHODOLOGY

The newspaper subcorpora of the *CorDis Corpus* contain op-eds, editorials, and news reports, all on the subject of the Iraq war. The articles date from the first six months of 2003 (19 January–27 June), and are taken from British and American newspapers, with exemplars both from the quality papers, (or, as Conboy 2007 calls them, the elite papers) and the popular range.[1] The corpus was designed to represent a variety of political stances, and accordingly the British quality papers represented are the *Guardian,*

The Times, the *Independent,* and the *Daily Telegraph,* while the populars comprise the *Daily Mirror,* the *Daily Mail,* and the *Sun.* The sister papers published on Sundays (the *Observer,* the *Sunday Times,* the *Independent on Sunday,* the *Sunday Telegraph,* and the *Mirror on Sunday)* are also included. The American quality papers are the *New York Times,* the *Washington Post,* the *Los Angeles Times,* while the populars are the *New York Post* and the *New York Daily News.* The three subcorpora of the *CorDis Corpus*—news (*PapNews*), editorials (*PapEd*), and op-eds (*PapOp*)—each contain articles from the seventeen newspapers, and the software used (*WordSmith Tools* 4.0, Scott 2005) allows the researcher to query partitions of the corpus transversally. For example, it is possible to search for data by selecting only one newspaper, or one UK newspaper, or one popular paper, and so on; it is also possible to make queries within one partition of a single subcorpus, for example, within the editorials in one popular British newspaper. For the purpose of this study, which considered an early, nonfinalized version of the corpus in simple text format, the news reports were discarded, leaving the subcorpora of editorials (473,000) and opinion articles (486,000 words). The fact that the corpus consulted was an early version accounts for the different word counts from those given in other studies in this volume that are based on the *Xaira* version.

As in many other chapters in this volume, the research questions regarding differences between the two discourse types in question are approached through the corpus-assisted discourse studies methodology (Partington 2004a), that is, by combining quantitative and qualitative analysis, using software (*WordSmith Tools* 4.0) for calculating frequencies, seeking collocates, generating wordlists and keyword lists, and, equally importantly, reading the corpus.

7.2. TRACES OF SPOKEN DISCOURSE IN OP-EDS

The starting research point for the present chapter lay in the lexical density index of the *CorDis* op-eds and editorials subcorpora presented in Murphy and Morley (2006:211). According to Ure's study of written and spoken texts (1971), where the lexical density of thirty-four different types of spoken texts was compared to that of thirty-four types of written texts, spoken texts tend to have a lexical density under 40 per cent, and since the *CorDis* op-eds were found to have a density of 31.4 per cent, further research was desirable to ascertain the ways in which op-eds resemble spoken texts.

In the *Longman Grammar of Spoken and Written English,* Biber et al. describe the grammar of conversation in terms of clausal and nonclausal units. The former is defined as 'a structure consisting of an independent clause together with any dependent clauses embedded within it' (1999:1069). A nonclausal unit, on the other hand, while being syntactically independent, cannot be analyzed in terms of clause structure, and may consist of individual words or sentence fragments. In this category, many typical features of speech, such as interjections, contracted forms, vocatives, and question tags, can be found, and nonclausal units were therefore taken as the initial framework within which the similarity of the language of op-eds to spoken language could be gauged. Besides nonclausal units, the use of the first-person imperative *let's* was also examined. The reasons for this will be explained in section 7.2.2.

7.2.1. Nonclausal Units in Op-eds and Editorials: Inserts

Nonclausal units can be broadly divided into what Biber et al. call syntactic nonclausal units (1999:1082), which include questions without a verb, such as *my turn?*, single words, or inserts, which include interjections, attention signals, response elicitors, response forms, hesitators, and discourse markers. For this study, the presence of syntactic nonclausal units was not investigated, and Biber's list of inserts was checked against the list of 'interactional signals and discourse markers' in Stenström (1994:59), and then added to, as more examples emerged while the corpus was read.

The following inserts were found:

- Response forms: *yes, no, doh, oh, ah* (and their combinations, such as *but no, well no, oh yes, ah-ha*), *OK* (British), *okay* (US), *all right* (British), *alright* (US)
- Stronger positive responses: *sure, oh sure, you bet*
- Hesitation markers: *er, um, hmm, hmmm*
- Response elicitors: *eh? right? okay?*
- Attention signals: *hey, look, mind you*

Inserts have a variety of functions (mostly indicated by the name of their categories), but they all indicate interaction with an interlocutor, sometimes introducing an element of emotion or surprise. In written text, they serve to create the semblance of a dialogue with the reader, or with a speaker within the text, or they externalize the author's reaction to something that has been reported in the text, thus creating another level of textual interaction (Hoey 2001).

Interjections

The first type of insert in focus here is interjections, such as *oh* and *ah*, which generally serve to introduce emotion of some kind into a speaker's utterance, and often combine with other inserts such as response forms (e.g., *yes, sure*). The frequency of the various types of interjections is illustrated in Table 7.1, where it can be seen that interjections occur most in op-eds and American papers.[2]

Table 7.1   Relative Frequency of Interjections in the Various Subcorpora per 100 Tokens

UK papers	US papers	Op-eds (UK/US)	Editorials (UK/US)	Qualities (UK/US)	Populars (UK/US)
0.028	0.043	0.050	0.018	0.027	0.038

In example (1), from a quality American op-ed, the writer is imitating someone externalizing their feelings: the initial *hey* is supposed to attract the attention of an interlocutor, and gives the idea of indignation on the part of the person voicing the feeling, wanting the other person to listen to their point of view. Of course, the text is ironic.

(1)   The feeling seems to be: **Hey,** we paid for the destruction. If it weren't for us, there wouldn't be all these roads and bridges that need rebuilding.

(*Washington Post,* 18 April 2003, Quality, Op-ed)

In the second example, the *oh* is supposed to give the idea of someone having a second thought—remembering that the allied forces also include British soldiers. This would be what Aijmer calls the 'boundary' function of *oh*, marking a 'change in perspective' (2002:141). Again, the text is ironic.

(2)   Let's face it, the greatest military power in the history of the world, **oh** and some British soldiers, totally fail to capture two of the top bananas in the axis of evil.

(*Daily Mirror,* 30 May 2003, Popular, Op-ed)

In the third example, *sure* functions as the anticipated agreement with a point of view that declares that many people watching *CNN* do not actually listen to what is being said—the news is not consciously noticed, but is just there, like wallpaper. One feature of the op-eds that emerges strongly from this close reading of the text is the variety of tones that writers can include in their writing, by assuming others' voices or quoting directly, creating a dialogistic type of text.

(3)   As I talked to news junkies as well as those imposing a personal blackout, it became apparent that the living room has become a front all its own. **Sure,** for plenty of folks CNN is just wallpaper. But a whole bunch seem to feel that by watching TV they are actually doing something significant.

(*New York Daily News,* 26 March 2003, Popular, Op-ed)

Discourse Markers

Discourse markers were the second type of inserts investigated. From the total list, which comprised *actually, anyway, basically, I mean, say, like, well, you know, you see, I guess*, the marker *well* is concentrated on, since it occurred far more frequently than any other (seventy-five times in all) and is distributed across all the subcorpora.

In Biber et al.'s categorization (1999:1086), *well* has the general function of a deliberation signal, indicating the speaker's need to give brief thought or consideration to the point at issue. It often indicates a continuation with what precedes it, but marks a contrast, which explains its presence in contexts where there is disagreement. This appears to be the case in the texts when *well* occurs in spoken language that is reported, as in example (4). In the majority of cases, however, rather than indicating a time-taking function, *well* indicates that the speaker's own voice emerges, and that what follows it shows a lack of commitment to the truth of the preceding statements which are attributed to others. This use is illustrated in examples (5) and (6).

(4)   In his discussion of a budget request for the cost of his war, which his staff has said will be sent to Congress only after hostilities begin, Bush said: "In terms of the dollar amount, **well**, we'll let you know here pretty soon."

> (*Washington Post*, 20 March 2003, Quality, Op-ed)

(5)   This war will be prosecuted, says US Admiral Timothy Keating, with "breath-taking speed, agility, precision and persistence". **Well**, we shall see.

> (*Guardian*, 20 March 2003, Quality, Editorial)

(6)   The fall of the dictator will usher democracy into Iraq. Then the contagion of freedom will spread throughout the region, bringing its people prosperity, taking the wind out of the sails of terrorism and securing American interests. **Well**, it may be right. But it may as easily be seriously wrong. The Bush administration has it all planned out. War will lead to the toppling of Saddam Hussein.

> (*Los Angeles Times*, 30 March 2003, Quality, Op-ed)

Both types of example can be read in Schourup's interpretation of this discourse marker, which always shows 'on-the-spot, pointedly epistemic consideration' (Schourup 2001:1056) on the part of the speaker, both in cases of contrast with what has preceded it—see examples (4) and (5)—and when the speaker takes time before continuing—see example (6).

The relative frequencies of *well* in all the subcorpora are illustrated in Table 7.2, where it becomes clear that it is most used in op-eds and popular papers.

Table 7.2   Relative Frequency of the Discourse Marker *Well* in the Various Partitions

UK papers	US papers	Op-eds (UK/US)	Editorials (UK/US)	Qualities (UK/US)	Populars (UK/US)
0.008	0.008	**0.010**	0.006	0.005	**0.014**

Vocatives

The third type of insert examined is that of vocatives, which are a very colourful aspect of the text types under consideration, particularly in the popular papers. Vocatives can take the form of first names, *Tony* for Tony Blair (only in the British corpus), *George* for George Bush, or familiarized forms of names, using nicknames, such as *Rummy* for Donald Rumsfeld, *Saddy* for Saddam Hussein, or deviant spellings which imitate the pronunciation of a name (or initial, in this case) as in *Dubya* or *George Dubya* for George W. Bush. In examples (7) and (8), it emerges that first names for the protagonists in the conflict tend to be used in the subcorpora when the writer is critical of the person's action or stance, or is being patronizing.

(7)   The last thing Britain wants is to be embroiled in another Middle East conflict. You got away with it once, **Tony**. Don't push your luck.

(*Daily Mirror*, 17 April 2003, Popular, Editorial)

(8)   It's simple, **Tony**. In Europe, it's every man for himself. Stick with the friend you can trust through and through—America.

(*Sun*, 14 February 2003, Popular, Editorial).

Generic familiarizers are also used, particularly in American English, examples from the corpus being *buddy, folks, guys, boy chick, college boy, sunshine, Boss*. These terms seem to have a function similar to *well*, discussed previously: the text preceding the generic familiarizer is often a quotation from some other source—see examples (9) and (10)—or voices someone else's thought, and the generic familiarizer indicates a switch to the writer's own voice in which his or her real thought, often in contrast with the previously quoted one, is expressed. In example (11), it can be seen that *folks* actually co-occurs with *well*.

(9)   They did not like to think about a terrorist attack in terms of war, Ms. Conlon said, but more as a disaster like a tornado or earthquake that they could weather. Anyhow, that's just another way of saying, you're on your own, **buddy**, you're an army of one, be all that you can be in the short time that remains.

(*New York Times*, 23 February 2003, Quality, Op-ed)

(10) "It is an earthquake, not just for Iraq, but for the whole region," said Qasem Jaafar, a political commentator for al-Jazeera TV, echoing Gabai's description. "We don't want to believe what happened, we don't want to believe what we saw: American tanks are creating changes in the Arab world." Best to believe it, **guys.**

(*New York Post*, 11 April 2004, Popular, Editorial)

(11) We've all heard the studio-strategists in the media jeering that the Iraqis didn't welcome us with open arms, after all (how about all those cheering Kurds, **folks?**). Well, it happens that our best sources of intelligence in these urban operations are, in fact, Iraqi civilians who can't wait to see the back end of Saddam's regime.

(*New York Post*, 1 April 2003, Popular, Op-ed)

In terms of frequency, as Table 7.3 shows, these vocatives and familiarizers do not occur often, but they characterize popular papers most of all, American papers more than British, and editorials more than op-eds.

7.2.2. Contracted Forms and First-person Imperatives

The final characteristics of spoken discourse investigated were contracted forms and first-person imperatives. The contracted forms, in particular the auxiliary verb *do* (i.e., *don't, doesn't,* and *didn't*), and the American English forms *gonna* and *wanna* proved a fruitful choice. It can be seen in Table 7.4 that contracted forms occur most in popular papers, in op-eds, and in papers from the United States.

As regards first-person imperatives using *let's*, the tendency for this insert to introduce the writer's own voice in a situation of contrast, similar to the use of *well*, can be noted in example (12), which is typical. The writer creates a situation in which there are contrasting views: it is clear that the one presented is different from his or her own, but s/he agrees to accept it provisionally, and prefaces agreement with '*But, OK.*' The use of *let's*

Table 7.3 Relative Frequency of Vocatives and Familiarizers in the Various Partitions

UK papers	US papers	Op-eds (UK/US)	Editorials (UK and US)	Qualities (UK/US)	Populars (UK and US)
0.003	0.004	0.003	0.004	0.001	0.010

Table 7.4 Relative Frequency of Contracted Forms in the Various Partitions

UK papers	US papers	Op-eds (UK/US)	Editorials (UK/US)	Qualities (UK/US)	Populars (UK/US)
0.084	0.125	0.121	0.063	0.062	0.175

invites the reader to adhere to the position the writer is suggesting, and this is particularly significant in a persuasive genre. The writer takes for granted that the reader will agree to adhere to the position, and is persuasive in an unobtrusive way. In the same example, the position assumed (believing that America will behave differently from the way it did in the past, and will attempt to establish democracy in Iraq) is then immediately challenged by the question 'Can that be done down the barrel of a gun?' Example (13), on the other hand, shows another situation of contrast, in which the writer uses *let's* to demand action. Both examples illustrate that *let's* often occurs in pairs and can function as a cohesive link to keep the reader involved in the discourse.

(12) To assume that Iraq will be different is to make a historical leap of faith. But, OK. **Let's** put history aside and believe that, this time, the US will be different. **Let's** say it really will try to establish Iraq as a democracy. Can that be done down the barrel of a gun?

(*Guardian*, 5 February 2003, Quality, Op-ed)

(13) Tony Blair still insists there are weapons of mass destruction in Iraq. **Let's** see them, then. He assures us that intelligence information was faithfully passed on. **Let's** see the full reports, then. He claims that nothing underhand was done. **Let's** have a proper inquiry to confirm that, as there was over the Falklands.

(*Daily Mirror*, 2 June 2003, Popular, Editorial)

In Table 7.5, the figures show that *let's* occurs most of all in popular newspapers and op-eds.

To sum up, it can be seen that, as predicted from the observation about the lower lexical density of op-eds, the features of spoken discourse examined occur more in op-eds than in editorials. The exception to this is the category of vocatives and familiarizers, which occur more in editorials; their highest occurrence, however, is in popular papers. Indeed, with the exception of interjections, all the other features investigated occur more in popular papers than in quality papers.

The next section will concentrate on the distinctions between popular and quality papers in general, and, in particular, on the distinctions that can be made between editorials and op-eds along this parameter.

Table 7.5   Relative Frequency of *Let's* in the Various Partitions

UK papers	US papers	Op-eds (UK/US)	Editorials (UK/US)	Qualities (UK/US)	Populars (UK/US)
0.008	0.009	0.011	0.006	0.006	0.014

7.3. EDITORIALS AND OP-EDS IN THE QUALITY
AND POPULAR PRESS IN ENGLISH

Despite the ubiquity of television, the proliferation of television channels, and the ceaseless sprawling of the Internet, newspapers in Britain and the United States are still important vehicles of information and comment, with circulation varying from approximately 239,000 copies per day for a quality paper like the *Independent* and 1,627,062 for the *New York Times* to as many as 3,158,045 (the *Sun*, a popular British paper).[3] The distinction between quality and popular papers is important from many different points of view, including size (traditionally, the popular press uses smaller-sized paper, but see note 1), the amount of space dedicated to photographs versus written text (the qualities contain more writing, although photographs and colour are an increasingly common feature in quality papers too), their selection of news, and, as Morley (1998) underlines, their attitude to news. A rather simplistic distinction between the two types is that the quality press distinguishes itself by concentrating on hard news (i.e., political, economic, national, and international news and analysis), while the popular press is more concerned with soft news (i.e., celebrities, sport, scandals). Corpora like those under examination here prove one of Morley's points, namely that the relevant distinction is not so much that hard news is not presented and discussed in the popular press, but that the attitude represented in the popular is different: hard news is sensationalized and personalized (Morley 1998:11).

In this section, which focuses on the differences between editorials and signed opinion articles in popular and quality papers, three aspects will be taken into consideration. The comparison deals first with the external aspects of editorials and op-eds and then with the keywords in the popular and quality partitions of the *PapOp* and *PapEd* subcorpora. From the latter analysis, observations about the typical linguistic patterns of the two discourse types are made. Thirdly, the headlines of the popular and quality partitions of *PapOp* and *PapEd* are examined.

7.3.1. External Aspects of Editorials and Op-eds

Interrogating a corpus can sometimes imply that one never sees a complete text, even in cases where the corpus has been compiled exclusively of whole texts. However, in the corpus-assisted discourse studies methodology, which has been widely used in many chapters of this volume, reading whole texts is as fundamental as using the software to interrogate it; some brief remarks about the appearance and length of the texts under consideration are thus obligatory.

The appearance of an editorial or op-ed is an important issue. Some printed op-eds are preceded by the photos of their writer, and followed by an e-mail address to which the interested reader can send a comment. The Web sites of the newspapers in the corpus invariably have photos of their columnists, and online op-eds are now commonly followed by a blog, where readers can post their comments. Indeed, one of the functions of an opinionist's column is to stir up readers' interest and arouse debate, particularly in the online versions. The impression given to the reader is that the op-ed area of the online newspaper is a kind of agora, where personal opinion can be expressed freely and dialogue can take place.

The length of an article is also a distinguishing feature between quality and popular papers, and also between British and American papers. In the quality British papers, the average op-ed article is about 1,080 words long, whereas in the quality American papers, the average op-ed is over 200 words shorter, at around 810. As mentioned previously, the popular papers contain less written text overall, and this is reflected too within both op-eds and editorials: the average British popular op-ed is approximately 745 words long, compared to 560 in the US popular press.

The unique characteristic of editorials is that they have no specific signature (and therefore no corresponding photo) but represent the voice of the paper. The tendency noted for the length of British versus American op-eds is true for editorials too, as is the quality-popular length difference. On average, the editorials in the quality British corpus are 738 words long, the American editorials 557. Editorials in the American popular press are more or less the same length as in their quality press—501 words—whereas the shortest texts are the editorials in the British popular press, which average around 311 words. The *Sun* provides the briefest editorials of all, some amounting barely to 100 words. These data are summed up in Table 7.6.

Table 7.6   Average Number of Tokens in Editorials and Op-Eds

Paper type	Tokens
British Quality Op-eds	1,080
American Quality Op-eds	810
British Popular Op-eds	745
American Popular Op-eds	560
British Quality Editorials	738
American Quality Editorials	557
British Popular Editorials	445
American Popular Editorials	501

7.3.2. Keywords in the Editorials and Op-eds
Subcorpora in Popular and Quality Papers

Using *WordSmith Tools*, word lists of the editorials and op-eds subcorpora were generated and compared in two ways: firstly, comparing the same discourse type across the two varieties of paper—op-eds in popular papers versus quality papers, and editorials in popular papers versus quality papers; secondly, comparing the different discourse types within the same variety of paper: op-eds versus editorials in popular papers, and op-eds versus editorials in quality papers.

The first comparison investigates whether keywords (calculated according to log likelihood) differ within the same discourse type (i.e., within editorials or within op-eds) if the type of newspaper (i.e., quality or popular) changes. This comparison was made using the *Keywords Tool* in *Wordsmith Tools*, taking the qualities corpus as a reference corpus. The results of the comparison are laid out in Tables 7.7 and 7.8, in which the keyness of the words in the table is defined as such by comparison with the qualities corpus. An initial observation regards content: as Morley (2005:221) also pointed out, it emerges from the data that the op-eds in the popular papers have a focus on women, the top keyword being *her,* the third *she,* and the seventh *she's.* This confirms the fairly widely held view reported by Conboy (2007:130) that news in the elite press is essentially male oriented, while the popular press tends to provide more coverage of women and women's issues.

An examination of the concordance lines of *her, she,* and *she's* in the popular op-eds reveals that the women concerned are, in some cases, the politicians involved in the Iraq crisis (Clare Short, for example, resigned from the Cabinet during the war—see Chapter 3, this volume; Margaret Thatcher was consulted on several occasions by Tony Blair, a fact mentioned and commented on several times; American politicians like

Table 7.7   Keywords Comparison: Tabloid Op-Eds vs. Quality Op-Eds

Keyword	Absolute Frequency	Relative frequency	Keyness
her	147	0.11	106.74
our	456	0.35	86.26
she	123	0.10	78.08
Tony	141	0.11	53.59
Blair	260	0.20	48.69
GBP	17	0.01	45.23
she's	19	0.01	43.23

Hillary Clinton and Madeleine Albright also appear on the scene). There are also some objects of gossip (typical 'soft' news) like the wife of the prime minister at the time, Cherie Blair, her aides and confidantes, and a few actresses.

Another keyword worthy of comment, which emerges second in the op-eds popular to qualities investigation, and first in the editorials popular to qualities comparison, displayed in Table 7.8, is the plural possessive pronoun *our*. In both op-eds and editorials, the popular papers emphasize national identity and those fighting on behalf of Britain in the war: this is evident from a look at the first lexical collocates of *our* in both the popular op-eds and editorials corpora, which are *troops* and *forces*. These recurrent phrases, *our troops*, and *our forces*, strengthen a sense of national identity, quite apart from the newspapers' position on the war.

In Table 7.8, which compares keywords in editorials from popular and quality papers, it can be seen that contracted forms, already mentioned in section 2, occur three times in the top 8 keywords: *it's*, *he's*, and *don't*. This points to a key difference in style, rather than content, and provides further evidence (gathered from an alternative angle) for the observation made in section 2.2 that popular papers contain a higher proportion of features related to speech than quality papers.

Lastly, in the keywords comparison in op-eds and editorials within populars and within qualities, no new evidence of differences between the discourse types emerged. Murphy and Morley (2006) had already observed the keyness of first- and second-person personal pronouns (*I, you, my, me, we,* and *our*) in the comparison of the two types, without considering the category of paper (popular or quality); these pronouns emerge as the top keywords even when the comparison is made within the popular or quality partitions of *PapEd* and *PapOp*.

Table 7.8   Keywords comparison: Popular Editorials vs. Quality Editorials

Keyword	Absolute Frequency Populars	Relative Frequency Populars	Keyness Compared to Qualities
our	398	0.30	332.07
America	253	0.19	198.24
he	1,013	0.76	147.17
it's	154	0.11	128.14
Saddam	620	0.46	108.13
GBP	43	0.03	107.84
he's	58	0.04	102.08
don't	96	0.07	97.70

7.3.3. Headlines in Popular and Quality Editorials and Op-eds

Headlines serve three main functions in any paper: they attract attention, give an indication of the content of an article, and also of the news values of the newspaper and its audience (see Galtung and Ruge 1981). It is standard newspaper practice for headlines to be chosen by newspaper subeditors, and not by the person who wrote the article or the editorial (Hodgson 1992); however, headlines are the first thing a reader sees of an article, and they may encourage readers to continue or send them away from the particular article. They are therefore a fundamental feature of the discourse types under scrutiny.

Methodologically speaking, for this part of the analysis, samples of sixty headlines were taken from each partition of the corpus, divided up by discourse type, and analyzed by hand, starting with the editorials. The first analysis is between quality British and American editorials, followed by a comparison of popular British and American editorials; then, the British quality op-eds are compared to American quality op-eds, and, lastly, popular British op-eds to popular American op-eds. The section concludes with some remarks about features of spoken discourse in headlines.

Headlines in Quality British and American Editorials

In the headlines from the editorials in British quality papers, about a quarter of the headlines are constituted by pre-modified noun phrases, for example, *Scare tactics, Serious consequences* or verbal noun phrases: *doing the right thing; rebuilding Iraq.* Another quarter of the sample, which come mostly from the *Independent* and *The Times,* present a declarative sentence, sometimes lengthy and complex, which can end in an interrogative: for example, *Mr Blair and Mr Powell have an agreed line: but will it persuade anyone?* Or *We cannot go to war just because Saddam is a liar—he must also be a threat.* The classic word-playing tools of headline writers, such as alliteration (*death or democracy*), assonance (*Feed the needy*), colloquialisms (*in a bind over Iraq*), subverted proverbs (*No fire without smoke*), intertextual references, such as quotations of or allusions to film or book titles (*Basic Instincts,* or *A Tale of Two Tonys*), or allusions to the Bible (*So shall ye reap*)—which, as Partington noted (1996:45), are normally slightly modified—can be seen in the remaining half of the sample.

In comparison, three-quarters of the headlines of the American editorials in quality papers consist of prosaic pre-modified noun phrases, such as *The case against Iraq, The imbalanced budget,* some of which display alliteration (*Decisive days*). There are no long headlines, such as those found in the *Independent* or *The Times.* A few headlines are imperatives, such as *Tell us why war is needed,* but only ten out of the sixty sample headlines display one or more of the previously mentioned wordplay skills: examples are *Sound and Fury, Uncle Sam as peeping Tom.*

Headlines in Popular British and American Editorials

In the British popular editorial headlines, there is greater syntactic variety than in the quality headlines for editorials, in that alongside modified noun phrases and declaratives, we find imperatives (*Allow our troops to do their job*), interrogatives (*What's the rush to war, Mr. Blair?*), and elliptical requests (*Facts, please*). The American populars have a solid core of modified noun phrases (*cold, hard facts*) and short declaratives, but greater use is made of wordplay skills: *Colin in UN-land; NYPD 2, Terrorists 0; French fry European unity; Mosque masks murder money*. In both the British and the American populars, there is a great variety in the tone of the headlines, and overt criticism, humour, and occasionally vulgarity are voiced, as in *No wonder they call him a Buffhoon* (British popular, criticizing Geoffrey Hoon, British secretary of state for Defence during the Iraq war), *Powell! Right in the kisser!* (US popular), or simply *Two fingers* (British popular), or *Hot air on First Avenue* (US popular). Overall, the headlines in the populars are shorter in both the US and UK partitions than in the equivalent quality paper partitions, as are their articles.

Headlines in Quality British and American Op-eds

Turning to the characteristics of headlines in the op-eds subcorpora, in the British corpus over half the samples are fairly lengthy declaratives, such as *Blair is a Sugar Plum Fairy intent on showing Bush "it is nice to be nice"*, or Wh-declaratives, as in *Why this paper is wrong about Bush and Blair's stance on Iraq*. A quarter of the sample are interrogatives, also generally lengthy, such as *Do troops kill each other by mistake because we trained them too hard?* and there are no short noun phrases. The tone of the headlines is sometimes colloquial, idiomatic, and personal, as in *Why Blair is clearly heading for an early Baath*, or *I predict the pundits will continue getting it wrong*. In the American quality papers, on the other hand, there is again a preponderance of short pre-modified noun phrases, as in *Toxic Talk on War, The Wimps of War*, or short idiomatic phrases, alliterative or allusive, such as *Ready or not . . . , In Doubt We Trust,* and *Desert Spring, Sprung*. There is a clear difference in style here between the headlines in the British and American quality papers: the British headlines are long, complex, and complete, and could almost be part of the text of the op-eds, while the American ones are pithy, and bait the reader, giving just a brief image or hint of an idea.

Headlines in Popular British and American Op-eds

In the British popular headlines, the keywords of the op-eds corpus dominate: the pronouns *you, my, we, our,* and the proper name of *Tony* all stand out. No single syntactic structure dominates: there are interrogatives and exhortations: *The Iraq row? Let's use our intelligence*; pure interrogatives *Why must we crawl to the Yanks?*; direct imperatives aimed at the prime minister: *Face it Tony . . . you're finished*, and declaratives: *we must not betray America*. Humorous puns on song titles or allusions to television programmes or famous speeches abound: *Imagine there's no Tony, it's easy if you try*; or *Good evening, here is the worst possible news*, and *we shall fight them on the wireless*. The tone is varied, if always vehement and direct. In the American populars, once again, modified noun phrases and declaratives dominate, and there is a noticeable lack of humour in the headlines, which was instead present in the quality American op-eds' headlines. Examples of the noun phrases and declaratives in the American populars are, respectively: *anti-war errors, the enemy's smile, Saddam scorns US ultimatum, It's wrong to cover up news about atrocities*. For the op-eds in the popular American papers, it is as though matters—perhaps only in this corpus of articles about the Iraq war—are too serious for humour to be expressed.

Summing up this analysis of headlines across all the subcorpora, it can be said that from the point of view of national differences, headlines in the British papers vary syntactically and in tone, while, with the exception of the quality op-eds, the American headlines are restricted syntactically to noun phrases or short statements, and are generally sober. From the point of view of the discourse type, op-eds in both quality and popular British papers demonstrate features of spoken discourse, having varied syntactic structures including interrogatives and imperatives, and a colloquial, personal tone, with headlines in popular British op-eds often using first-person pronouns and proper names.

7.4. A COMPARISON OF PHRASEOLOGY IN OP-EDS AND EDITORIALS

The last investigation into the differences between op-eds and editorials concerns their phraseology. Murphy and Morley (2006) discussed the keywords of op-eds and editorials in terms of single word forms: personal pronouns and verbs expressing mental processes emerge in op-eds, as opposed to references to recent time, and deontic modals in editorials. For the present research, strings of words were investigated in *PapOp* and *PapEd*, using the word-list function of *WordSmith Tools*. Word lists of the two-grams, three-grams, and four-grams (an n-gram being a recurrent uninterrupted string of orthographic word-forms; see Fletcher 2003–6) in the subcorpora of editorials and op-eds were drawn up, providing evidence of various recurrent traits across the two discourse types. The most revealing search is at the level of four-grams; nevertheless, some observations about phraseology can be made for two-grams and three-grams as well.

7.4.1. Two-grams in the Editorials and Op-eds Corpora

The top ten two-grams for both corpora, illustrated in Table 7.9, illustrate the fact that grammatical items—in this case mostly prepositions attached to the definite article—are the most common two-grams in any corpus. The only lexical items in the top ten two-grams in the op-eds is *the war;* in the editorials subcorpus, the beginnings of either *the United States* or *the United Nations* can be seen.

However, one lexical fact stands out from the word lists slightly lower down: in the editorials corpus, the names and titles of the protagonists of the coalition—*Mr Blair, prime minister,* and *President Bush*—occur much more frequently than in the op-eds. In the editorials corpus, *Mr Blair* occurs 0.150 per hundred words, *prime minister* 0.091, *President Bush* 0.071, compared to 0.042 per hundred tokens for *Mr Blair,* 0.032 for *prime minister,* and 0.030 for *President Bush.* The fact that these men are referred to by their titles indicates respect, at least for their positions, if not for their persons, and this is not surprising since the editorials represent the official voice of a newspaper, whereas opinionists can afford to be more personal, and refer to them by their first names, nicknames, or surnames. In the *WordSmith* concord tool, collocates and clusters of the node word can be called up, and recurrent clusters for both two-grams include the other's name: we find *Bush and Mr Blair, Mr Bush and Mr Blair, Mr Blair and Mr Bush, President Bush and Mr Blair, President Bush and Tony Blair.* These co-occurrences point to the constantly close allegiance that characterized the two politicians during the war.

Table 7.9   Top Ten Two-Grams in the Op-Eds and Editorials

Op-eds	%	Editorials	%
of the	0.687	of the	0.666
in the	0.515	in the	0.462
to the	0.274	to the	0.280
and the	0.218	it is	0.257
on the	0.196	that the	0.235
it is	0.191	and the	0.229
to be	0.186	to be	0.205
that the	0.183	on the	0.201
for the	0.180	the United	0.195
the war	0.141	for the	0.174

7.4.2. Three-grams in the Editorials and Op-ed Corpora

Other differences in the content of the editorials and op-eds will be discussed in the next section on four-grams, but it is worth pointing out that in both the subcorpora, three-grams of lexical groups indicating countries, places, or international bodies all occur within the top ten: *The United States, The United Nations, The Security Council, The Bush Administration* and *The Middle East*. These lexical groups are illustrated in Table 7.10.

In the editorials corpus, a number of recurrent grammatical fragments indicate an important and common function within the text, particularly occurring with the verb BE in various forms, which is that of defining, already pointed out as typical of editorials in one of the fundamental works on language and the news (Fowler 1991:221), and confirmed in previous research on the current subcorpora (Murphy and Morley 2006). Through the investigation of three-grams, another function emerges in the editorials corpus, that of evaluating, expressing a judgement, which could perhaps be understood as a way of defining.

The fragments *But it is, This is a,* and *would be a* all recur more frequently in the editorials than in the op-ed corpus (respectively, *But it is* occurs 0.021% in editorials, compared to 0.011 % in op-eds; *This is a* 0.013 % in editorials and 0.010 in op-eds, and *would be a* 0.013 % in editorials and 0.008 in op-eds) and all three are frequently followed by some form of evaluation. With *but it is*, the most common adjective is *clear*, as in *But it is **clear** that George Bush is doing much for Arab nationalism,* or *But it is **clear** that, had the vote gone against war, British soldiers would have not gone into battle.* Other co-occurrences include indications of epistemic value, such as: *possible, likely, certain, unlikely, hard to believe, impossible;* of importance, such as *essential, a matter of undeniable concern, imperative, important;* and of desirability or otherwise, *a pious hope, a valuable*

Table 7.10   Frequency of Top Ten Three-Grams in the Op-Eds and Editorials

Op-eds	%	Editorials	%
The United States	0.081	The United States	0.104
of mass destruction	0.056	The United Nations	0.087
weapons of mass	0.055	The Prime Minister	0.061
the United Nations	0.041	The Security Council	0.058
the Middle East	0.037	weapons of mass	0.055
one of the	0.031	of mass destruction	0.054
the Bush administration	0.026	the Bush administration	0.049
the Security Council	0.024	there is no	0.031
of the war	0.022	the Middle East	0.030
the Iraqi people	0.021	it is not	0.030

character trait, better than nothing. The pattern *it is* + evaluative group + *that* is recognized in the literature as a common means of expressing stance (Hewings and Hewings 2002; Hunston and Sinclair 2000; Murphy 2004); here, the added adversative conjunction *but* indicates the argumentative style of the text type in which it occurs.

This is a is often followed by a noun phrase pre-modified by an evaluative adjective, as in *a better outcome; a bleak climate, a challenging moment, a considerable achievement, a dangerous conceit. Would be a* is frequently preceded by *it* and followed by the same kind of noun group as *this is a*: as in *this is a bad idea, this is a crazy thing to do, this is a damaging mistake, this is a delicious irony, this is a disaster.* The high frequency of these grammatical fragments followed by an evaluation within the editorial corpus indicates that evaluation in this subcorpus often occurs in an impersonal fashion, more so than in the op-eds corpus.

In the op-eds corpus, on the other hand, one grammatical three-gram stands out as being much more frequent than in the editorials corpus. This is the fragment *in the* + #, which in the op-eds subcorpus stands at 0.018, and in the editorials subcorpus at 0.008. *In the* + # is normally followed by a date, such as *in the 1990s.* The op-ed subcorpus mentions *time* more than the editorial corpus in this way, a fact that also emerges in the analysis of the four-grams in the following section.

7.4.3. Four-grams in the Editorials and Op-eds Corpora

Three observations can be made about the differences in four-grams between the editorials and the op-eds corpus, illustrated in Table 7.11. Firstly, the top four-gram in both subcorpora—a postmodified noun phrase—*weapons of mass destruction*—demonstrates the amount of debate that these weapons (WMDs) created during the crisis, irrespective of the type of article. The search for WMDs was a fundamental issue; indeed, on the British part, the sole official justification for going to war, and both editorials and op-eds gave ample space to it. Secondly, in the editorials subcorpus there is a greater concentration of lexical phrases referring to persons, entities, and countries, as was also evident in the three-gram analysis. Predictably perhaps, the top twenty four-grams in the editorials corpus comprise phrases and proper nouns such as *the United States and, the war in Iraq, United Nations Security Council, The US and Britain, the UN Security Council, the House of Commons.* Thirdly, the op-eds are characterized by a greater frequency of phrases with common general nouns, sometimes headed by prepositions, which link up parts of text, indicating certain types of relations. These are phrases such as *the end of the, the rest of the, at the end of, in the name of, on the other hand* (see Table 7.11), which are also the same types of phrase as the most frequent four-grams in the BNC. Stubbs (2006a:4) points out that "in the whole BNC the most frequent 4-word strings are all parts of nominal and prepositional phrases which express spatial, temporal and/or logical relations".

Table 7.11   Four-Grams in Op-Eds and Editorials

Op-eds	%	Editorials	%
weapons of mass destruction	0.054	weapons of mass destruction	0.054
in the Middle East	0.015	the United States and	0.017
the end of the	0.011	of the United Nations	0.013
the rest of the	0.010	in the Middle East	0.013
at the end of	0.008	Secretary of State Colin	0,012
the United States and	0.008	the rest of the	0.012
the war in Iraq	0.008	the war in Iraq	0.011
of the United States	0.007	United Nations Security Council	0.010
the people of Iraq	0.007	that the United States	0.010
of the United Nations	0.007	the US and Britain	0.010
rest of the world	0.007	the UN Security Council	0.010
for the first time	0.006	the United Nations Security	0.010
of the Iraqi people	0.006	chemical and biological weapons	0.009
of weapons of mass	0.006	of mass destruction and	0.008
in the first place	0.006	the end of the	0.008
in the name of	0.006	of the United States	0.008
in the United States	0.006	of State Colin Powell	0.007
on the other hand	0.006	of the Security Council	0.007
one of the most	0.006	the Bush administration has	0.007

The functions of these common four-grams from the op-eds corpus will be briefly examined. To begin with, the noun *end* within the clusters *the end of the* and *at the end of* refers above all to time (occurring with *the war, our interview, his life, 2001,* etc.), as Forchini and Murphy (2008) also show in a study dedicated to this four-gram. This is another example of the concern with time in the op-eds corpus mentioned in the previous section on three-grams.

The rest of the, also high up in both the editorials and the op-eds frequency list, occurs ninety percent of the time in both corpora with the noun *world,* in contexts where particularly America (but also Britain, as part of the coalition) is set up in contrast to *the rest of the world*. Being common in both sub-corpora, *the rest of the* is not as such a distinguishing mark of the op-eds subcorpus.

The remaining four-grams commented on—*for the first time, in the first place,* and *in the name of*—are worthy of attention because, seen in context, they often indicate more than their literal meaning. The four-gram *for the first time* is clearly linked to the expression of an event in time, but is used pragmatically to draw attention to the importance of something, as Partington and Morley (2004) point out, and as examples (14)–(16) show:

(14) This is a critical moment. **For the first time**, the Palestinians have produced a prime minister, Mahmoud Abbas; a finance minister, Salam Fayyad; and a security chief, Muhammad Dahlan,

(New York Times, 11 May 2003, Quality, Op-ed)

(15) **For the first time in my lifetime**, my countrymen and millions of other citizens of the world are not deaf to what Arabs say or how they feel or what they want.

(Los Angeles Times, 6 April 2003, Quality, Op-ed)

(16) An astonishing event is about to happen. **For the first time in modern history** a city with the population of London is preparing to resist assault from a land army.

(The Times, 28 March 2003, Quality, Op-ed)

For the first time collocates in the corpus with *history* more than any other noun, which emphasizes the uniqueness of the event mentioned, and even sensationalizes what is recounted.

In the first place, on the other hand, brings with it connotations of disagreement or indignation at some action that has been taken, indicating more than just the first in a series of arguments. When it occurs in an interrogative, feeling appears to be added to the question, the sense of indignation is accentuated, and is reminiscent of speech, as the examples (17)–(19) show.

(17) While the inquest into how the six Red Caps were hung out to dry in Iraq gets under way, there's a bigger question which needs to be answered. What the hell were they doing there **in the first place?**

(Sun, 27 June 2003, Popular, Op-ed)

(18) The loudest wish is for the Forces to come home safely. Which rather leaves open the question—if the soldiers' safety is our main concern, why send them into danger **in the first place?**

(The Times, 31 March 2003, Quality, Op-ed)

(19) The tragic deaths of so many British soldiers in Iraq yesterday will once again raise the question: why did we go to war against Iraq **in the first place?**

(Daily Mail, 25 June 2003, Popular, Op-ed)

The strong feeling accompanying the expression can be discerned also through its co-occurrence with the mild expletive *what the hell* in example

(17). The use of this expression can be linked to the speechlike quality of the op-eds.

The phrase *in the name of* in the corpus is often linked to the expression of disagreement, sometimes to the sentiment of indignation, sometimes cynicism. It is rarely used literally with something good or positive, but tends to indicate that the writer does not approve of whatever is being done in the name of X, which, under normal circumstances, would be recognized as something good, as example (20) shows. A cross-check in a selection of newspaper articles amounting to 13,600,000 words (taken at random from the c.150 million words of *SiBol 05*) reveals that in cases where the expression is not used literally, it tends to have negative connotations, which suggests a general trait of its usage, and confirms the evidence from the present corpus.

(20) But he stood tall for what he believed. [. . .]The person who abandons what he thinks, who lives out his life on the basis of what he believes others want him to think, all **in the name of racial loyalty**—or, equally as bad, to suck up to the perceived powerful—is the one whose life has been marginalized. He is the real slave.

         (*Washington Post*, 8 February 2003, Quality, Op-ed)

(21) Provoking chaos **in the name of order,** and resentment instead of gratitude, is something to which all empires are accustomed.

         (*New York Times*, 23 February 2003, Quality, Op-ed)

(22) At the same time, **in the name of national security,** President George W. Bush is putting forward legislation that will make it more difficult for investigators to pry into these matters.

         (*Daily Mail*, 31 March 2003, Popular, Op-ed)

The analysis of four-grams in this section has shown that in the op-eds corpus some common phrases carry attitudes such as sensationalism or indignation or cynicism into the text, over their literal meaning, and do not function merely as linking phrases between parts of the text.

7.5. CONCLUSIONS

On the basis of the multifaceted investigations of the written press sub-corpora in the *CorDis Corpus*, there is ample evidence of the differences between op-eds and editorials. It has been shown that appearance and length of text are distinguishing features between these two discourse types: op-eds encourage readers to send feedback to their writers, and they are longer than editorials in both quality and popular papers. From the point of view of the keywords in these corpora, it has emerged that popular op-eds in particular tend to talk about women, and, at least during the Iraq crisis, also reinforce national identity, by dedicating space to *our troops* and *our forces*. Headlines of British op-eds, more than those of their American counterparts, tend to be frequently dialogic and idiomatic, using a variety of syntactic structures to involve the reader, and popular British op-eds make frequent use of personal pronouns, again inviting the reader to participate.

The phraseology of op-eds, on the other hand, shows a number of four-word clusters, such as *for the first time, in the first place,* and *in the name of,* which have argumentative/rhetorical importance, and communicate attitude such as indignation or cynicism. This can perhaps be linked to the similarity of op-eds to spoken discourse, since the expression of attitude is inherently personal, and op-eds show several features that make them a highly interpersonal type of discourse. Similarly to the way that intonation is one expression of a speaker's attitude, the attitude of the writer seeps through the phraseology of the op-eds under examination here. Further investigations on a larger corpus might shed light on other ways in which the expressive function is realized in this little studied yet ubiquitous discourse type.

NOTES

1. Quality and popular papers have been referred to in the past as broadsheets and tabloids, because of their large or smaller size, but these terms are no longer applicable, since *The Independent* and *The Times*, both quality papers, reduced their size to that of a tabloid in 2003 and 2004, respectively, while the *Guardian* uses a slightly larger size, called the Berliner.
2. Throughout this chapter, since the various subcorpora and partitions are all of different sizes, frequency is relative and expressed in percentages (i.e., per hundred tokens).
3. Source of circulation figures for the British papers: National daily newspaper circulation figures from the Audit Bureau of Circulations, made available via the Media Guardian Web site: http://media.guardian.co.uk/presspublishing/table/0,,2166236,00.html, accessed 13 September 2007. Figures for the American papers in the corpus are high too: the quality paper the *New York Times* sells approximately 1,120,000 copies daily, and the *New York Post* and *New York Daily News* both sell over 700,000. Source: Audit Bureau of Circulation. http://www.accessabc.com/products/top200.htm. Accessed 14 September 2007

8 Interacting with Conflicting Goals
Facework and Impoliteness in Hostile Cross-Examination

Charlotte Taylor

This chapter uses the corpus-assisted discourse studies approach to analyze the Hutton Inquiry from the theoretical perspective of (im)politeness. As with many instances of institutional discourse, in hostile examination it cannot be assumed that conversational norms apply, nor that participants are involved in cooperative facework, and therefore this chapter aims to contribute to the growing body of work on impoliteness in institutional(ized) situations of conflict.

8.1. INTRODUCTION

8.1.1. The Hutton Inquiry

The Hutton Inquiry, described as 'one of Britain's most powerful judicial hearings' (Rogers 2004:ix), started proceedings in August 2003 and ran through to October 2003. Lord Hutton's terms of reference were 'urgently to conduct an investigation into the circumstances surrounding the death of Dr Kelly'.[1] David Kelly was a leading scientific advisor on weapons of mass destruction in Iraq who committed suicide after becoming caught up in conflicts between the government and the *BBC* regarding the government dossier *Iraq's Weapons of Mass Destruction: The Assessment of the British Government* published in September 2002 .[2] The row between the government and the *BBC* centred on *BBC* journalist Andrew Gilligan's claim that the dossier had been 'sexed up'. As the dossier formed part of the government's case for using military force against Iraq, many expected the inquiry to cover issues of use of intelligence and the reasons for going to war.

The Hutton Inquiry heard from seventy-four witnesses over approximately one hundred hours of examination, including testimony from members of the government, the Ministry of Defence, and the *BBC*. The inquiry attracted great amounts of media attention due to interest in both the topics covered and the witnesses called, as it was expected to raise issues of working practice in the government, the MoD, and the *BBC*. The inquiry also became a focus for anger over the war in Iraq. Furthermore, there was almost certainly an element of 'entertainment'; it is interesting to note that the *Daily Telegraph*'s theatre critic covered Tony Blair's appearance,[3] and as a *Scotsman* sketch writer put it: 'One of the joys of the Hutton Inquiry is that people so accustomed to this status find themselves compelled to answer to someone else'.[4] Throughout the inquiry *Sky News* also broadcast reconstructions of each day's proceedings. To give an indication of the amount of coverage the inquiry received, at the time of writing a search for the 'Hutton Inquiry' in the *Daily Telegraph* retrieved 606 articles, the *Independent* 848 articles, the *Daily Mail* 578 articles.

Linguistically, the Hutton Inquiry proved to be an extremely rich source of data, in particular due to the structure of the inquiry. It was divided into two phases: the first stage of the inquiry was intended to be 'devoted to obtaining in a neutral way, by counsel to the inquiry, an account of the events which took place' (Lord Hutton, opening statement, 1 August 2003). In the second stage some witnesses were re-examined by the various counsels. We can, therefore, distinguish between four distinct examination types in the Hutton Inquiry which move along a cline of 'hostility':

- cross-examination by the witness's own counsel, henceforth referred to as friendly examination;
- direct examination by counsel to the inquiry;
- cross-examination by counsel to the inquiry;
- cross-examination by counsel representing persons or bodies who have an opposing view, henceforth referred to as hostile examination.

The effects of these different examination types on the witness discourse are clearly discernible in terms of the amount of talk contributed, as Table 8.1 illustrates. The results show that the lawyers successfully control the quantity of the witnesses' discourse and therefore exert institutional power despite the fact that the witnesses were powerful figures out of the specific context of the inquiry.

Table 8.1   Average Witness Turn Length in Different Examination Types

Examination type	Average no. of words per witness turn
friendly	25.50
direct	17.00
cross	15.49
hostile	13.80

8.1.2. Face and Facework

> The term *face* may be defined as the positive social value a person effectively claims for himself by the line others assume he has taken during a particular contact. Face is an image of self delineated in terms of approved social attributes—albeit an image that others may share.
>
> (Goffman 1967:5)

Goffman's reference to 'approved social attributes' is key to any analysis of facework, given the degree to which it is bound to the discourse context (comprising both the discourse type and social and cultural setting). The notion of face, as used in this paper, predominately draws on Brown and Levinson's definition of face as 'the public self-image that every member wants to claim for himself' (1987:61). Thus, face is seen in terms of the participant's wants, the image that the participant desires to project within a given context. Brown and Levinson's distinction between two related aspects of face is also employed:

> Negative face: the basic claim to territories, personal preserves, rights to non-distraction—i.e. to freedom of action and freedom of imposition.
>   Positive face: the positive consistent self image or 'personality' (crucially including the desire that this self-image be appreciated and approved of) claimed by the interactants.
>
> (Brown and Levinson 1987:61)

For the purposes of this study a further level of delicacy is added by distinguishing between two principal sorts of positive face identified by Partington (2006b): competence face and affective face. Competence face refers to the desire to be seen as capable, authoritative, and in control while affective face refers to the desire to be perceived as 'non-threatening, but also congenial and good to be around' (2006:97).

8.1.3. Facework and Hostile Examination

The amount of attention which the inquiry drew meant that each day's proceedings and the performances of both witnesses and lawyers were analyzed and discussed in the public domain. The witnesses were not only representing themselves in the inquiry but also their respective employers and therefore there were also issues of shared face; individuals were scrutinized and judged on many fronts. Many of the witnesses possessed a high absolute status out of the courtroom context, and were both familiar with and adept at interacting within the constraints of a question-response discourse type, and may therefore be closer to the expert witnesses described in Stygall (2001). Furthermore, as a public inquiry investigating the suicide of David Kelly, it was also a very solemn and serious occasion. The witnesses, either individually or collectively, risked being presented/perceived as responsible for the death of David Kelly, which is undoubtedly a very different and more formidable type of risk from the face threats generally envisaged in most earlier work on conversational facework and politeness.

In courtroom discourse, as in many types of institutional discourse such as the White House press briefings (see Chapter 4, this volume), both turn order and turn type are predetermined by the institutional roles of the participants (Atkinson and Drew 1979). The lawyer is given a 'question' turn and will open and close the interaction, while the witness is given a 'response' turn. Therefore, the structure of the interaction itself means that certain negative face needs have to be suspended. Within these restricted roles the participants interact with the primary function of displaying rather than exchanging information. The resulting interaction has been described as a 'battle between narratives' (Wagenaar 1995:272) as each party attempts, within the constraints of the question-response sequence, to present their macro-narrative to the *beneficiaries* of the discourse. The beneficiaries of the discourse are 'the reason why the discourse is enacted' (Partington 2003:57), as the discourse is ultimately designed for them (Partington 2006:168). In unmarked discourse in the Hutton Inquiry the beneficiaries include Lord Hutton and the media, as well as the wider (voting) public. Within this context it is useful to return to Brown and Levinson, who note that 'in general, persons want their goals, possessions, and achievements to be thought desirable not just by anyone but by some particular others especially relevant to the particular goals' (1987:63), and these *some particular others* may be seen to broadly correspond to the beneficiaries.

Both Goffman (1967) and Brown and Levinson (1987) describe face as something which can be lost, maintained, or enhanced and in this paper the term *facework* is used to refer to this dynamic version. In courtroom discourse, facework is not just a condition of interaction, but also an objective; indeed, the witness's face is part of the narrative(s) presented to the beneficiaries. For example, to use Blair's oft-quoted phrase, whether or not the government team were presented and perceived as 'pretty straight sort of guys' determined the evaluation of their evidence.[5]

In friendly examination the lawyer and witness share a common, although differently motivated, goal or set of wants, and therefore the type of facework enacted is cooperative. The lawyer's competence face, in this context, is dependent on enhancing the face of the witness: either the witness is perceived/presented as honest, trustworthy and so on, or his/her narrative is devalued. In contrast, in hostile examination the two participants in the interaction have opposing and incompatible goals, which means that the facework is aggressive.[6] The lawyer's aim is to threaten the witness's face, to portray him/her as untrustworthy and so on in order to discredit his/her narrative and therefore privilege the lawyer's own narrative. This kind of intentionally aggressive facework lies in direct contrast to the conversational interaction model which dominates Brown and

Levinson's analysis where 'in general, people cooperate (and assume each other's cooperation) in maintaining face in interaction, [. . .] it is in general in every participant's best interest to maintain each others' face' (1987:61).

The important institutional role of such aggressive facework has recently received attention, particularly in the context of parliamentary discourse. Harris, in her 2001 paper on 'Being politically impolite', concludes that 'systematic impoliteness is not only sanctioned in Prime Minister's Question Time but is rewarded in accordance with the expectations of the Members of the House (and the overhearing audience) by an adversarial and confrontational political process' (Harris 2001:466). Perez de Ayala also analysed Question Time and concluded that within this context the 'function of politeness changes: politeness strategies are not the linguistic means necessary to avoid conflict. Question time *is* conflict. Politeness strategies become the means at the Chamber's disposal to be able to work and progress, even in the middle of conflict' (Perez de Ayala 2001:164–65). Christie's (2002) study of UK parliamentary discourse applies Watts's (2003) distinction between polite and politic behaviour and looks at types of transgression and the range of functions of superficially polite behaviour in apologies. Ilie (2004) focuses on a particular type of transgression in her contrastive study 'Insulting as (un) parliamentary practice' in parliamentary discourse in Britain and Sweden, and similarly addresses the systematic nature of impoliteness referring to 'institutionally ritualised confrontational interaction' (2004:81), and also notes that mitigation strategies are used alongside deliberately offensive rhetorical acts in order to avoid being institutionally sanctioned (Ilie 2004:81–2).

As this recent work on institutional impoliteness has highlighted, any aggressive facework towards the interlocutor must be performed within the limitations of appropriate behaviour, both in order for the interaction to continue and to maintain face in the eyes of the beneficiaries. Mullany (2002), in her analysis of a political interview between John Humphrys, a *BBC* journalist and presenter, and Hilary Armstrong, then a government minister, notes that the interviewee uses polite language tactically to avoid conversational breakdown which 'would be damaging both for HA and the Labour Party she represents if she is perceived to be unable to cope with JH's aggressive style' (Mullany 2002:online). Therefore, in order to maintain or enhance face, both participants must demonstrate that they are capable of dealing with the situation. As Goffman states:

> In aggressive interchanges the winner not only succeeds in introducing information favorable to himself and unfavorable to others, but also demonstrates that as interactant he can handle himself better than his adversaries.
>
> Goffman (1967:25).

8.1.4. (Im)politeness

The distinction between cooperative and aggressive facework outlined previously serves as a basis for the analysis of (im)politeness in this chapter. Politeness may be understood as marked cooperative facework, while impoliteness is understood as marked aggressive facework, and thus they are positioned at opposite ends of a continuum. This distinction largely follows Locher's and Watts's descriptions of relational work and (im)politeness (see Locher 2004 and Watts 2003 for volume-length studies). In Locher and Watts (2005), they claim that the research tradition following Brown and Levinson's theory of politeness is concerned with the mitigation of face-threatening acts rather than politeness and posit an alternative concept of politeness in which politeness and impoliteness are considered as discursive concepts and a relatively small part of relational work. They propose a cline for relational work, with negatively marked, inappropriate, impolite behaviour at one end, followed by unmarked, appropriate, nonpolite behaviour, then positively marked, appropriate, polite behaviour, and at the other extreme, negatively marked, inappropriate, overpolite behaviour (see Locher 2004:90 and Locher and Watts 2005:12, for a visual representation).

This conceptualization allows for polite and impolite behaviour to be viewed within the same frame and prioritizes the importance of context in analyzing (im)politeness by describing it as situationally marked behaviour. This focus on context is a common feature of much recent work on impoliteness; Mills (2005) emphasizes that 'it is essential not to see impoliteness as inherent in certain speech acts but rather as a series of judgements made by interactants on the appropriateness of others' actions' (2005:276). For Bousfield 2007, impoliteness:

> constitutes the issuing of intentionally gratuitous and conflictive verbal face-threatening acts which are purposefully performed:
> i. Unmitigated in contexts where mitigation is required, and/or
> ii. With deliberate aggression, that is, with the face threat intentionally exacerbated, boosted or intensified in some way to heighten the face damage inflicted
>
> Bousfield (2007:2186–87)

While, in Culpeper's 2005 definition: 'Impoliteness comes about when: (1) the speaker communicates face attack intentionally, or (2) the hearer perceives and/or constructs behaviour as intentionally face-attacking, or a combination of (1) and (2)' (Culpeper 2005:38).

However, it would appear that one of the difficulties facing work on impoliteness is forming a usefully descriptive definition which may also be operationalized. For instance, one issue raised by Locher and Watts is that their description assumes that the researcher knows a priori what is appropriate to the interaction. Additionally, while many researchers would agree that impoliteness is not accidental, accounts which focus on intentionality create methodological problems in identifying the speaker's motivations. On the other hand, definitions which focus on reception create the same difficulties if there is no explicit marker of evaluation within the text, which is likely to be the case in much institutional discourse. The working definition of impoliteness assumed in this study is returned to in section 3, but, very broadly, the distinction between facework and (im)politeness as marked facework will form the basis for the analysis in this paper, and Culpeper's 'super-strategies' of impoliteness are used to structure and extend the analysis.

Culpeper's model (1996, 2003, 2005) places impoliteness on a parallel with politeness by mirroring the super-strategies of politeness set out in Brown and Levinson (1987). The (nonexclusive) super-strategies of impoliteness Culpeper describes are:

> *Bald on record impoliteness*: the FTA [face threatening act] is performed in a direct, clear, unambiguous and concise way in circumstances where face is not irrelevant or minimized.
>
> *Positive impoliteness*: the use of strategies designed to damage the addressee's positive face wants, e. g., ignore the other, exclude the other from an activity, be disinterested, unconcerned, unsympathetic, use inappropriate identity markers, use obscure or secretive language, seek disagreement, use taboo words, call the other names.
>
> *Negative impoliteness*: the use of strategies designed to damage the addressee's negative face wants, e. g., frighten, condescend, scorn or ridicule, be contemptuous, do not treat the other seriously, belittle the other, invade the other's space (literally or metaphorically), explicitly associate the other with a negative aspect (personalize, use the pronouns "I" and "You"), put the other's indebtedness on record.
>
> *Sarcasm or mock politeness*: the FTA is performed with the use of politeness strategies that are obviously insincere, and thus remain surface realisations.
>
> *Withhold politeness*: the absence of politeness work where it would be expected. For example, failing to thank somebody for a present may be taken as deliberate impoliteness.
>
> (Culpeper 2005:41–42)

8.1.5. Corpus and Methodology

The *Hutton* subcorpus of the *CorDis Corpus* contains 846,634 words in utterances. The subcorpus was created using the official transcriptions of the inquiry and there was no access to prosodic or paralinguistic information. The main partitions used in this study were the different examination types, in particular friendly and hostile, and the partitions which permit the identification of question and response turns. Selecting only interaction between the Queen's Council (henceforth QC) and the witness, there were 112,748 tokens in hostile examination and 69,215 tokens in friendly examination (figures obtained using *WordSmith Tools 3.0*, Scott 1999).

This study makes use of both *WordSmith Tools* and *Xaira*, which means that two corpora containing the same texts were used: one in XML and the other in simple text format. The potential of *Xaira* is set out very clearly in Chapter 1 of this volume and needs no repetition. *WordSmith Tools* was primarily used because of the keywords function which allows for the computerized generation of words and phrases which are statistically characteristic of the texts in one corpus compared to another. This was particularly relevant to the present study which is interested in the features that characterize the different examination types, and it is difficult to see how an a priori selection of terms would have accessed the same information, particularly with reference to 'function' words. A second reason for the use of *WordSmith Tools* at different stages of the research process was for the cluster function, in this context the term clusters being used in the *WordSmith Tools* sense of 'words which are found repeatedly in each other's company' (Scott 1998).

Like most chapters in this volume, the methodology adopted is that of corpus-assisted discourse studies and therefore this section limits itself to describing the ways in which CADS methodologies were put to use in this particular piece of research. In this chapter, *WordSmith Tools* keywords provide the starting point for the analysis, which is then interpreted within the theoretical framework of impoliteness set out earlier. The model of impoliteness also serves to extend the analysis, moving from a primarily data-driven (or perhaps, more appropriately, 'software driven') approach to a more theory-driven approach. In practice, a *more* theory-driven approach in this context may involve the theoretically informed selection of certain terms, phrases, or structures for the concordancer, or alternatively selection through intuition (which is also 'theory' insofar as it is determined by the researcher's priming [Hoey 2005]). The research in this paper was also guided by previous research on the corpus, and in this sense, too, was theory-driven. Indeed, one of the aims of the paper was to bring together research previously conducted on QC discourse (Taylor and Biscetti 2005; Biscetti 2006) and witness discourse (Taylor 2006) in the Hutton Inquiry.

In addition to shunting (see Halliday 1961, in 2002:45) between both quantitative and qualitative positions during the research process, in this chapter both quantitative and qualitative starting points were used. The relatively small size of the subcorpus used in this chapter meant that if, and where, it was considered likely to prove interesting the data could simply be read, not just in extended concordances, but in the full original form. In this case, as I was involved in the 'light encoding' described in Chapter 1 of this volume, I had already read large portions of the text, and rereading the subcategories of hostile and friendly examination was entirely feasible given their size. In corpus linguistics there is a tradition that this is somehow 'cheating', that the researcher may taint his/her data by 'looking inside the box'. While it is certainly true that the data will look different from different viewing perspectives, the two perspectives may offer different and complementary approaches/insights (see also Chapter 10).

8.2. AGGRESSIVE FACEWORK

8.2.1. QC Discourse

Interrogative Structure

As mentioned previously, the starting point for this analysis was through *WordSmith Tools* keywords. In this case the particular partition under study, hostile examination, was not compared with an external reference corpus but with another partition of the same subcorpus, friendly examination. This comparison was chosen in order to highlight the differences between the two extremes on the cline of hostility which had been previously identified. The *WordSmith Tools* keywords for QC discourse during hostile examination are shown in Table 8.2.

As can be seen, the first *WordSmith Tools* keyword was *not,* and the clusters of *not,* as generated by *WordSmith Tools,* are displayed in Table 8.3.

Table 8.2   Keywords for QC Discourse in Hostile Examination Compared to Friendly Examination

	Word	Hostile		Friendly		
		Freq.	*%*	*Freq.*	*%*	*Keyness*
1	Not	869	1.65	131	0.60	148.2
2	He	463	0.88	52	0.24	111.6
3	Let	53	0.10	1		29.2
4	It	994	1.88	295	1.35	26.7
5	Because	102	0.19	11	0.05	25.5

Table 8.3   The First Ten Three-Word Clusters of *Not* in QC Discourse in Hostile Examination

	3-word cluster	*Freq.*
1	is it not	51
2	i do not	49
3	was it not	45
4	did you not	29
5	you did not	29
6	i am not	28
7	do not want	24
8	not want to	22
9	it was not	18
10	do you not	16

Is it not and *was it not* also featured as key clusters in a comparison of hostile and friendly examination, and, like other clusters seen in Table 8.3, indicate the use of negative interrogatives or question tags. In a more detailed analysis, Taylor and Biscetti (2005) found that both negative inter-rogatives and question tags were characteristic of hostile examination com-pared to the other examination types in the Hutton Inquiry.

Heritage (2002:1427) considers the negative interrogative as a limiting case of questioning and suggests that it is 'recurrently produced as, and treated as, a vehicle for assertions'. Therefore it may serve the twin pur-poses of restricting the response turn, and of allowing the questioner to add his/her own narrative with the constraints of a question turn, for example in (1) through the use of evaluative lexis and in (2) through the use of pre-supposition.

(1)   Q. GOMPERTZ: *Do you not* agree that Dr. Kelly was treated shabbily in relation to this episode?
      R. HOWARD: No, I do not agree

(16 September 2003)[7]

(2)   Q. CALDECOTT: *why was it not* put right and *why were you not* con-cerned to put it right?
      R. SCARLETT: Because it was a fleeting moment and then the underly-ing assessment by the media of the dossier was as I have just described, and beyond that, of course, it is not my immediate responsibility to correct headlines and if I did that, I certainly would not have time to do my job.

(23 September 2003)

A similar function may also be seen in the use of question tags, which restrict the response turn and therefore the witness's 'freedom of action' to tell his/her own story.[8] Furthermore, like negative interrogatives, the ques-tion tag allows the insertion of an alternative narrative, which in hostile examination predominately functions as an FTA, as seen in (3).

(3)   Q. SUMPTION: Yes, you watered it down in the statement because you did not wish to be seen to let down the executives. That was the reason for that, *was it not?*
      R. DAVIES: I have never heard such nonsense. We watered it down in the statement because one of our most senior and most respected Gov-ernors thought it was actually actively wrong to give prior notification to No. 10, and

(24 September 2003)

In (4) the evaluation offered by the QC is less overt, but the question tag serves to mark the response, for the beneficiaries, as open to doubt.

(4) Q. CALDECOTT: Yes. But it does represent a judgment—
R. SCARLETT: No it does not.
Q. CALDECOTT: *Does it not?*
R. SCARLETT: No it does not. It is a statement, "Intelligence . . . indi-cates that"

(23 September 2003)

Repetition

From a qualitative reading of the text, the use of repetition was identified as another means of threatening the witness's face, as Gnisci and Pontecorvo (2004) note that the more often lawyers use a question the more coercive it is. The repetition limits the opportunities for response, like the interroga-tive forms discussed earlier, and often also serves to mark the information for the beneficiaries and portray the witness as uncooperative or vague, thus attacking both positive and negative face and indeed both types of positive face. Example (5) also shows how the features discussed here may co-occur as the repetition involves a tag question.

(5) Q. CALDECOTT: *It is clear from this letter, is it not*, that Dr Jones regards his letter to Mr Cragg of at least akin [*sic*] to a formal complaint?
R. HOWARD: The first point is he did not write direct to Mr Cragg, he wrote to his line manager and he copied the minute to Mr Cragg.
Q. CALDECOTT: Can you just answer the question I asked you: *it is clear, is it not*, that Dr Jones viewed his letter as akin to a formal complaint?
R. HOWARD: He wrote formally. He may well have regarded it in that way. But only Dr Jones can answer that clearly as to whether it was a complaint.
Q. CALDECOTT: And *it was also clear, was it not*, that he in fact saw it as a formal complaint?
R. HOWARD: He put it in writing, so I imagine he saw it that way, yes.

(16 September 2003)

Quoting the Witness

As seen in the foregoing examples, features may serve both to threaten negative and positive face, and this dual function is present throughout the corpus, reflecting Penman's (1990) findings on multiple functional utterances. Similarly, the use of attribution by the questioner potentially limits both the quantity and quality of the response turn. Looking at the collocates of *us* in the QC discourse, it becomes clear that with the excep-tion of *let us* (as shown in Table 8.2, *let* was a keyword), *us* is generally exclusive of the witness, and collocates with both *tell* (fourteen occur-rences, 0.012 per hundred tokens) and, more frequently, *told* (twenty occurrences, 0.018). *Tell us* occurs with a higher relative frequency (fourteen occurrences, 0.02) in friendly examination, while *told us* never occurs, thus highlighting the difference in usage, which was confirmed by a closer analysis of the examples. In hostile examination, as in friendly examination, approximately half of the instances formed the cluster *can you tell us* as in example (6).

(6) Q GOMPERTZ: I am not going to spar with you over that. *Can you tell us:* here you were talking to Dr Kelly about the press statement and clearing that with him; right?

(18 September 2003)

In the instances with *told us*, as (7) illustrates, the QC positions himself with the beneficiaries excluding the witness, *us*, thus threatening negative face, and additionally indicates a contradiction in the witness's narrative, *but you just told us*, thus portraying the witness as unreliable or untrustworthy.

(7) Q. SUMPTION: But you just *told us*, Mr Gilligan, that it was not something that Dr Kelly said, it was an inference of yours.
R. GILLIGAN: Yes, it was the—the path which led me to this is clear. Although

(17 September 2003)

In light of these findings, the search was extended to other indicators of attribution in QC discourse. *Said* with *you* within five collocates to the left occurred sixty-nine times in hostile examination (0.061) compared to eighteen times in friendly examination (0.026).

(8) Q. SUMPTION: In your phase 1 evidence *you said* that the *BBC* had to be absolutely clear—these are your words—that they were reporting the words of the source. That is the point that the Governors could have investigated, is it not?
R. DAVIES: Mr Sumption, the word 'investigated' is a strong word here. The Governors

(24 September 2003)

In (8) the threat is intensified with the emphasis on the source of the attribution 'these are your words'.

Querying the Response

A salient feature of the QC discourse which was noted through reading the subcorpus, and which would not have been accessed through the *Word-Smith Tools* keywords analysis, was the higher frequency of progressive forms in hostile examination. There were 175 occurrences of progressive forms with *you* within five words to the left of the node in hostile examination (0.155) compared to eighty-seven (0.125) in friendly examination. Looking at the words in the node it appeared that 'talking about the talk' was characteristic of hostile examination as terms included; *saying* (which was the most frequent progressive word form in hostile examination), *talking, suggesting,* and *speaking* (fifty-nine occurrences in total) as well as *trying.* One frequent function of these forms, in particular with reference to *saying* and *suggesting,* was querying the response.

(9)   Q. CALDECOTT: Are you *seriously suggesting* that the FAC would have thought that there might be a change to the 45 minutes claim included in that prefatory statement 'checked that the text was consistent throughout'?
R. SCARLETT: I can only repeat that

(23 September 2003)

(10)   Q. GOMPERTZ: You think there is no difference between the first draft and the second draft. Is that what you are *really saying*?
R. TEARE: No, I am saying that there is a difference

(18 September 2003)

In the foregoing examples given, the QC's evaluation is heightened by the use of the intensifiers *seriously* and *really.* Recalling that the interaction is enacted for the beneficiaries of Lord Hutton and the media, the querying of the response marks it as inadequate and therefore threatens the witness's positive face.

This section serves to highlight very briefly some of the ways in which the QC performs aggressive facework in hostile examination identified through a CADS approach. It is not intended as an exhaustive list and clearly many evaluative resources have not been taken into consideration.

8.2.2. Witness Discourse

Returning to the *WordSmith Tools* keywords, this time from the witness discourse, we see in Table 8.4 that *not* is also the first keyword for this discourse type. Looking at the cotext reveals that *I* was the most common collocate of *not* in witness discourse, thus indicating the extent to which the witness is involved in denying and rejecting the narrative put forward by the QC.

(11)   Q. SUMPTION: It is pure trouble making, is it not?
R. SAMBROOK: No, I do *not* agree with that.

(17 September 2003)

As in the foregoing examples (1) and (4), in (11) the witness may be seen as performing an FTA by disagreeing and rejecting the QC's view.

Table 8.4 Keywords for Witness Discourse in Hostile Examination

N	Word	Hostile		Friendly		
		Freq.	%	Freq.	%	Keyness
1	Not	1130	2.02	592	1.29	83.3
2	Yes	521	0.93	218	0.47	76.2
3	Is	743	1.33	363	0.79	70.1
4	Do	309	0.55	130	0.28	44.5
5	I	2508	4.49	1683	3.66	43.7
6	What	379	0.68	184	0.40	36.3
7	Correct	86	0.15	18	0.04	36.0
8	Services	39	0.07	2		34.0
9	You	279	0.50	126	0.27	33.3
10	Sumption	27	0.05	0		32.4
11	Am	157	0.28	58	0.13	30.1

However, given the nature of the context I would argue that this cannot be considered to constitute impoliteness because it is entirely appropriate and expected behaviour within the discourse context. Indeed, on at least one occasion, both QC and witness are explicit about the ritualized nature of the interaction.

(12) Q. GOMPERTZ: So if I was to suggest to you, Sir Kevin, that the appearances before the two Select Committees and the briefing session which took place beforehand, that those procedures were thrust upon him, to use a term which you have used elsewhere, *that would be a suggestion you would disagree with, I have no doubt?*
R. TEBBIT: *It will not surprise you to learn that I would strongly disagree with that.*

(13 October 2003)

Watts notes that politic behaviour is 'linguistic behaviour which is perceived to be appropriate to the social constraints of the ongoing interaction' (Watts 2003:19) and this would seem to largely characterize the aggressive facework in the interaction examined so far. However, it is worth emphasizing that the categorization of events as marked or unmarked in this context is based on a cline rather than an either/or distinction, and that in order for impoliteness to be generated there has to be a trigger. In the examples given earlier, rather than listing concordance lines, I have chosen to include fewer instances, but on each occasion accompanied by at least the first part of the response so that the reactions may be seen.

8.3. IDENTIFYING POTENTIAL IMPOLITENESS

In order to identify impoliteness or potential impoliteness, as it is understood in this paper, we need to identify behaviour which, in some way, goes beyond what is expected (Watts 2003:19) or what is considered appropriate within the discourse context. This necessarily involves interpretation on the part of the researcher, which is why it may be more accurate to refer to potential impoliteness. Such behaviour may be identified through analyzing the reception of individual acts and through metadiscursive comments from the participants, or, in the absence of these markers, interpretation may be guided by predictions of expected behaviour. Each of these options will be briefly discussed.

Firstly, within the context of the Hutton Inquiry there were no occasions where communication broke down, or where Lord Hutton overtly intervened in order to reestablish the expected, conventional behaviour. As in Culpeper's 2005 analysis of the TV programme, the *Weakest Link*, it is not clear whether or what sort of social disharmony is present. Like other instances of institutional discourse, in the Hutton Inquiry, the participants will enhance competence face by proving that they are able to successfully participate in the interaction.

Secondly, there were few overt metadiscursive evaluations such as *appropriate, impolite,* and so on, although it was noticeable that one explicit criterion was that the QCs were expected to be *fair,* as illustrated in the examples following (and Concordance 8.2 on page 226):

(13) Q. CALDECOTT: Can we, please, just look at the speaking note at MoD/4/10? Please, Mr Howard, if you think I am being *unfairly* selective, do say so. One of the advantages of a hard copy is it easier to look at the whole document. I want to focus on

(16 September 2003)

(14) R. KELLY: I think Alastair addressed the issue yesterday and really I do not want to second guess what he said in his diary, I do not think that is my role.

Q. GOMPERTZ: If you think it is *unfair* because you were not there on the occasion of the question on 9th July, perhaps you would like to go to 7th July, higher up that same page, the last entry before the date 8th July: "GH wanted to get up source, TK . . ." that is you, is it not?

(23 September 2003)

However, there were not enough references for this to be used to build a picture of perceived *unfairness,* or inappropriate behaviour.

Therefore, the analysis was initially based on the third option described earlier, which in the analysis of institutional discourse like the Hutton Inquiry is made possible because of the highly explicit structure of the setting. Following Brown and Yule (1983), many researchers adopt the 'analytic convenience' of distinguishing between transactional and interactional language: transactional language is primarily used to convey 'factual or propositional information' while interactional language is primarily used to 'establish and maintain social relationships' (Brown and Yule 1983:1–3). Partington proposes describing interactional and transactional as modes rather than functions of language, and notes that they are 'also psychological notions, especially with regard to institutional settings: speakers are in transactional mode when they feel they are doing institutional business' (2006:59). Therefore, although the term *transactional* is used, this is certainly not to suggest that face concerns and facework are irrelevant in this mode, but, as Partington suggests, to indicate that the participants 'felt' they were doing institutional business.

Like much institutional discourse, courtroom discourse is primarily transactional; as previously emphasized, it is a form of interaction in which the talk is enacted for the nonparticipatory beneficiaries and the interaction itself is a type of convention which allows for the display of information. Therefore, when there is a shift towards an interactional mode, it suggests that the interaction is no longer enacted for the original beneficiaries (Lord Hutton etc.). As this shift constitutes a move away from the norms and expected behaviour of the discourse context, it is suggested that identifying movement between transactional and interactional modes offers a way of locating potential (im)politeness in institutional discourse, and a way of approaching the identification of (im)politeness from a CADS perspective.

8.3.1. Potential Impoliteness

You

In Table 8.4, another of the keywords marking witness discourse under hostile examination compared to friendly examination was *you*, which suggests a move towards a more interactional mode and therefore a likely site of (im)politeness. The use of *you* is also noted as a negative impoliteness strategy by Culpeper, in correspondence to Brown and Levinson's negative politeness strategy of 'impersonalize S and H: Avoid the pronouns "I" and "you"' (Brown and Levinson 1987:131). A closer examination of the concordances of *you* in witness discourse showed that on many occasions the witness was threatening some aspect of the QC's competence face. In total there were twenty-two instances of *you* being used to refer to the QC directly in friendly examination (0.032), and 181 in hostile examination (0.161).

In example (15) Hoon, the witness, is seen to mimic the attribution strategy of the QC.

(15) Q. GOMPERTZ: I think I asked her whether she could say whether you did see it.
    R. HOON: No, no, I am quoting *you* directly, **Mr Gompertz**

                                                (22 September 2003)

Example (15) also illustrates the use of a 'polite' address form, *Mr Gompertz*, which was characteristic of both witness and QC discourse in hostile examination. There were 0.086 occurrences of title and surname used as a vocative in hostile examination compared to 0.048 in friendly examination. On the use of titles and names as address forms outside of greetings, hails, and attention-getters, Brown and Levinson comment that 'such usages are also typical in legal proceedings, the title and name accompanying questions that are intended to nail the defendant, for instance, rather than small clarifications of fact' (1987:184). Rather than functioning as a distancing or deferential mechanism, in these instances, the address form accompanies the pronoun *you* in a situation where the identity of the addressee is unequivocal and intensifies the negative face threat by increasing the focus on 'who' is being addressed. This is also illustrated in the following example, in which the witness, Davies, asserts superior knowledge over the QC.

(16) R. DAVIES: I agree with that, **Mr Sumption**; and if *you* knew my colleagues you would not think they were acting as amplifiers to anybody.

(24 September 2003)

Asserting superior knowledge clearly threatens the QC's competence face, and this was accomplished both directly, as in the foregoing example, and indirectly, as in example (17) in which the witness again appropriates the linguistic 'tools' of the QC by introducing the presupposition that the QC has not read the guidance, and is therefore inadequately prepared, which would of course be inappropriate:

(17) R. HATFIELD: No, I do not accept that. When *you* have had the opportunity to look at the very detailed 44-paragraph guidance

(18 September 2003)

Similarly to the use of vocatives, the occurrences of *to you* indicate a negative face threat by focussing on the QC. As the lines in Concordance 8.1 show, this was often accompanied by other means of emphasis such as *just explained, already explained, explained before*. In these instances the witness is seen to attempt to accomplish both face enhancement: anchoring his/her narrative and presenting him/herself as consistent, and face threat: implying that the QC is repetitive, inattentive, slow, and so on.

Examining other patterns of *you*, it became clear that the use of the present progressive was also characteristic of witness discourse in hostile examination (twenty-four instances as opposed to no instances in friendly examination), again marking a shift from the transactional, doing business mode, towards direct negotiation of social relations. In the concordance

I wish to **make that absolutely clear**	to you here today.
make that point. I was **trying to contrast**	to you the difference between a formal d
I have already **explained**	to you, I think that the focus on the notes
No. As I have **explained**	to you before, we saw the core allegation
I think I have just **explained**	to you, Mr Sumption, that it was rather di
answer is the answer that I have just **given**	to you.
count the factors I have already **indicated**	to you.
I have that here. I am simply **indicating**	to you that it is not the whole document.
All I would **say**	to you is that none of these people, who a
As I have **said**	to you before, the problem here is you ar
Let me **explain** something	to you: the Board of the *BBC* cannot oper
e balance which I have already **suggested**	to you.

Concordance 8.1   Concordance of *to you* in response turn in hostile examination (six speakers).

lines the QC is portrayed as: *putting/asking questions, referring, assuming, inviting, making suggestions/points, saying, suggesting,* and *talking* which confirm the shift to focus on the interaction in hand. The following examples show the range of ways in which the FTA is performed; in (18), reference to David Kelly is clearly highly threatening, and the QCs presumed view is contrasted with 'a matter of fact'. In (19) and (20), the witness criticizes the QC and asserts superior knowledge.

(18) R. TEBBIT: Well, we knew that Dr Kelly could not have been one of the senior officials in charge of drawing up the dossier. That was a matter of fact. We knew he was not a member of the Intelligence Services; that was a matter of fact. *You are inviting me* to suspect that Dr Kelly was being untruthful.

(13 October 2003)

(19) R. SCARLETT: *You are talking* as if the assessors sit there and operate in a vacuum. They do not. They are assessing individual intelligence reports against the background of their knowledge.

(23 September 2003)

(20) R. HOON: But I think, **Mr Gompertz**, if I may explain: *you are not properly understanding* the way in which a Q and A document works. A Q and A document is prepared for

(22 September 2003)

Another interesting pattern in the concordance lines of *you + ing* (see Concordance 8.2) was the occurrence of *you are putting*. Although there are few references, too few to be noticeable in the quantitative analysis, the search was widened to *putting* with reference to the QC's actions.

I think that is a very **tendentious** way of	putting it. I was reminding them, as I had
to come out; and, secondly, you are **still**	putting it to me in the context of some st
or repeating the same answer, **but** you are	putting the question in another way. I ha
Well, I think that is **not the fairest** way of	putting this issue. The issue is whether t
from the sort of context in which you are	putting it to me.
I think you are	putting to me the **suggestion** that the me

Concordance 8.2   Concordance of *putting* attributed to the QC in response turns (three speakers).

In each of these examples the witness negatively evaluates the QC's turn not only in representing the QC as 'putting something to him', but also through more overt evaluative markers such as *tendentious, not the fairest, suggestion, still, but.*

Question

In order to identify other instances of 'talk about the talk', or shifts towards an interactional mode, the term *question* was queried. Although it had not emerged as a *WordSmith Tools* keyword, it was more frequent in hostile examination (0.18) compared to friendly examination (0.10). In addition to the frequency, the collocates also differed in the different examination types as *your* did not occur within a five-word span in friendly examination. The concordance lines of *your question* are shown in Concordance 8.3.

The first of the lines clearly rejects the QC's question, and most importantly marks this rejection for the beneficiaries. Like the examples of face-threatening acts co-occurring with polite address forms, as in examples (15), (16), (20), line 1 in Concordance 8.3 is accompanied by the negative politeness form *I am afraid*, and, as in the other examples, it is difficult to interpret these features of negative politeness as mitigating the effect of an unavoidable FTA for the addressee. It would seem to be more reasonable to hypothesize that such mitigation is directed at the beneficiaries of the discourse, showing that the speaker is aware of, and conforming to, what is considered appropriate behaviour in the courtroom.

I am afraid **I do not actually accept**	your question
I have just answered	your question.
That is how you started	your question
The answer to	your question is "yes", and we believe, a
The answer to	your question is no, for good informed re
So I think **strictly the answer to**	your question is that by and large it woul
ely to Gavyn Davies, **I am not sure where**	your question **takes us.**
Sorry, **I do not understand**	your question

Concordance 8.3   Concordance of *your question* in response turns (four speakers).

8.3.2. Surface Politeness

Although several researchers (for example, Fraser and Nolan 1981; Kasper 1990; Watts 2003) have emphasized that no linguistic structure is inherently polite, certain structures continue to be ascribed such values, even though, as is illustrated in the foregoing examples containing 'polite' address forms, the relationship is likely to prove more complex. Surface politeness, referred to as mock politeness or sarcasm in Culpeper's model (2005:41–42), is perhaps one of the most interesting of the impoliteness strategies because it illustrates almost perfectly the risks of assuming that 'polite language' correlates with politeness or even cooperative facework. Indeed, in these instances politeness strategies are an integral part of the impolite utterance. The term *surface politeness* is tentatively used here as an umbrella term since from the data it appeared that not all 'surface realizations', as Culpeper describes them, involve sarcasm or mocking, but some also seem, for example, to involve *patronizing* (Culpeper includes 'condescend' as a realization of negative impoliteness). For instance, Simon Hoggart, the *Guardian* sketch writer, in talking of the examination of Davies by Sumption, comments that 'the phrase "Mr Sumption" was used lavishly, the impression being given of the local toff speaking to a dense rural constable'.[9]

Mock politeness often appears to contain a heavy dose of sarcastic irony which, as described in Partington (2006, 2007), entails some form of reversal of evaluation. Specifically here it involves a reversal of evaluation of the target's face. Therefore, frequently the conventional politeness strategies may be seen to operate along a sort of garden-path mechanism and, by wrong-footing as well as belittling the recipients, the face threat is intensified. Example (21) shows an instance of mock politeness involving the surface realization of positive politeness. In the light of the context of the preceding lines where Scarlett repeatedly threatens the QC's competence face, it is unlikely that the response *No, I sympathise*, superficially showing solidarity, is meant literally, and the impolite force of the utterance come from the conflict between, or reversal of, strategies.

(21) Q. CALDECOTT: I just have to find the passage that I want to show you because, for ease's sake, I had been
R. SCARLETT: This is not the draft, is it?
Q. CALDECOTT: I have found the second but I still need to find—
R. SCARLETT: This is not the draft, this is the covering note
Q. CALDECOTT: Sorry, I still need to find it.
R. SCARLETT: No, *I sympathise*.
Q. CALDECOTT: CAB/31/10. It looks on my copy as though it is contiguous, but it appears not to be.

(23 September 2003)

However, the majority of instances of surface politeness did not involve positive politeness strategies but negative politeness strategies as illustrated in the following examples.

(22) Q. CALDECOTT: Do I understand you to say that you do not correct it because no questions had been asked about it?
R. SCARLETT: No, *you may understand it* but that *would* be wrong, but I have explained that the reason why that was not an issue in my mind was because of the very sober and sensible way in which media coverage of the dossier fell into place immediately after the 25th September.
Q. CALDECOTT: Well, what about the 25th September itself? This is the day

(23 September 2003)

In (22) *you may understand it* could be seen as negative politeness, fulfilling a distancing function. However, if we consider the hypothetical alternatives of *No, that would be wrong* and *No, that is wrong,* it is by no means clear that the actual example is the least offensive. On the contrary, the distancing 'you may understand' suggests that H's view is irrelevant and therefore I would argue that the face threat is actually intensified. The mechanism would seem to be similar to that illustrated by the following examples from the *BNC*:

1. 'May I ride with you this morning, Silas darling?' she cooed in honeyed tones. '*You may ride—but not with me*', he informed her blandly.
2. And the girl was lovely, lovely and fresh and anticipating. "Yes?" ... "I'm Alan Millet, Foreign and Commonwealth" ... "Yes" ... "Can I come in, please?" "*Course you can, but you'll be sitting on your own all day—I'm on my way out*".
3. After that little performance you can hardly deny that you want me. Or *you could, but I wouldn't believe you.* So why don't we take it from there?'

(*British National Corpus*)

Example (23) is typical of many occurrences which proved more difficult to describe without access to sound files.

(23) Q. GOMPERTZ: Oh, I see. Are you not aware of the evidence of Ms Pam Teare?
R. HOON: Yes, I read her evidence very carefully.
Q. GOMPERTZ: That she probably had a copy with her.
R. HOON: I think, *with the greatest respect*, that is a *very* bad point. I cannot anticipate what Ms Teare had with her at the time. I gave you the evidence to the best of my knowledge and recollection. *If I may*

say so, I thought that you *seriously* misled Pam Teare as to the facts before the Inquiry.

Q. GOMPERTZ: I do not seem to be doing very well, Mr Hoon, **in your judgment**.

(22 September 2003)

Although classifying such exchanges as impolite is clearly interpretative, particularly without recourse to the prosody, there are signals that indicate potential impoliteness. The signalling of impolite intent may be seen through the juxtaposition of superficially polite markers and overtly negative evaluations. One of the most frequent of such signals in the subcorpus was the use of intensifiers, in the earlier example *very bad point*, and *seriously misled*, which make the reversal of face evaluation explicit. The presence of the intensifiers following the 'mitigating' devices of *with the greatest respect* and *if I may say so* make it highly improbable that the mitigation is aimed at diminishing the effect of the FTA on the addressee, as Mr Gompertz's closing metadiscursive remark appears to recognize.

8.3.3. Withhold Politeness

A final strategy of impoliteness identified in Culpeper's framework is that of 'withhold politeness'. Example (24) comes from a particularly tense stage of hostile examination where the QC, Caldecott, has to withdraw from his line of questioning. The fact that Lord Hutton has intervened and Caldecott has to publicly accept failure represents a high threat to his competence face. As the example shows, having lost competence face Caldecott then moves into a joking interactional mode, or role, with the comment 'one nil to you'. Scarlett's response rejects the shift in mode from transactional to interactional and therefore negates the QC's attempt to bolster his affective face in recompense for the loss of competence face, a common device in some forms of institutional talk (Partington 2006:97).

(24) HUTTON: I want to be clear. You are not making any point then to Mr Scarlett about these documents.
Q. CALDECOTT: My Lord, I think I have to abandon that.
HUTTON: That can be totally ignored?
Q. CALDECOTT: Yes.
HUTTON: Very well. Thank you.
R. SCARLETT: Thank you.
Q. CALDECOTT: *One nil to you, Mr Scarlett, I think on that document.*
R. SCARLETT: *I did not do anything, I just sat here.*
Q. CALDECOTT: Can I go on to deal very shortly with

(23 September 2003)

8.4. RESPONDING TO IMPOLITENESS

One indication of the ways in which the QCs respond to impoliteness or aggressive facework is apparent in the clusters of the keyword *not* in Concordance 8.4. As well as indications of negative interrogatives and question tags, it contained the clusters *I do not* and *I am not*. The most frequent right collocate of *I do not* was *want* (twenty-two occurrences in hostile examination compared to one in friendly examination) and as can be seen in Concordance 8.4 the majority are turn initial.

Taking the wider cotext of line 1 of Concordance 8.4 (see example (25)), we can see that in the preceding witness turn Hoon appropriates the QC's language and performs a face-threatening act by challenging the QC with an interrogative. The QC then asserts his institutionally more powerful position in rejecting topic direction by the witness and the witness is also negatively framed as potentially wanting *to argue semantics*.

(25) Q. GOMPERTZ: So you did not think it was necessary to get Dr Kelly's consent before his name was released?

R. HOON: The Ministry of Defence did not release his name.

Q. GOMPERTZ: *Well, they did.* In answer to a specific question in the Q and A material his name was confirmed as being correct.

R. HOON: Well, that is not quite the same as releasing it, is it?

Q. GOMPERTZ: *I do not want to argue semantics with you,* **Mr Hoon.** *But* did you consider that he should be told that this strategy was going to be adopted?

(22 September 2003)

	I do not want to **argue semantics** with you, Mr Hoon. But did you
	I do not want to **debate the evidence** with you.
Forgive me,	I do not want to **be at cross purposes.** What I am getting at is ste
	I do not want to **embark upon comparison** of the statement with
Well,	I do not want to **get embroiled** in a discussion of the content of th
previously; and	I do not want to **go over old ground** unnecessarily. But you will
	I do not want to **go all through** it again and I do not propose to do
	I do not want to **go through** evidence which has been given but
	I do not want to **go through** these e-mails in great detail. You hav
So—I am sorry,	I do not want to **interrupt** you.
	I do not want to **interrupt** you but I only have limited time, you u
Yes.	I do not want to **know** what passed between you and the police, b
Mr Scarlett, is	I do not want **any misunderstanding**
been on the run,	I do not want to **overdramatise** it, but escaping from the
	I do not want to **read** more than I have to, but there is an answer o
	I do not want to **spend too much time** on this, but he told the Inq
	I do not want to **take bits out of context,** it is quite a long docum
	I do not want to **take much time** over this. It refers to Sir Ke
Yes.	I do not want to **take up a lot of time** looking at the documents, b
instructions."	I do not want **you to have to take up time** reading out loud the r

Concordance 8.4   Concordance of *I do not want* in question turn in hostile examination (three speakers).

Example (26) also illustrates the explicit rejection of topic direction by the QC where, rather than responding directly to the witness's challenge, he uses his institutional power to pose another question.

(26) R. HOON: **I apologise** for interrupting you. But the suggestion you are making is there is some evidence that I leaked it. **Perhaps** you **would** indicate where it is so that I can comment on it.

Q. GOMPERTZ: *We will come to that in just a moment. What I am going to ask you next* is this, **Mr Hoon.** You say

(22 September 2003)

Example (27) also illustrates the explicit assertion of institutional power, and therefore appropriate roles, where the QC focuses on the institutional roles of the witness *answer the question*, emphasized with the use of *just*.

(27) Q. SUMPTION: Would it be fair to say that both Mr Sambrook and Mr Dyke felt very strongly about this issue?

R. DAVIES: **I think you would have to ask them** how strongly they felt about the issue. I certainly felt strongly that they should give to the Board the right degree of comfort that the source was credible and reliable.

Q. SUMPTION: *I am going to press you* on your view on whether they felt strongly, because you spoke to them. Did they feel strongly about this issue or not?

R. DAVIES: **I think** you **would** have to, **if you do not mind, Mr Sumption**, tell me what aspect of the issue you are talking about.

Q. SUMPTION: Did they feel strongly that the BBC had acted entirely appropriately both in making the original broadcasts and in standing by those broadcasts?

R. DAVIES: I see, so **we** have moved off the source at this point, have **we**?

Q. SUMPTION: That is part of it. *Just answer the question as asked.*

R. DAVIES: They did feel strongly that the *BBC* had acted appropriately in putting the views of this source into the public domain.

(24 September 2003)

Example (27) is shown with rather more cotext than the other examples in order to illustrate the way in which the impoliteness is enacted in the interaction, drawing on Bousfield's (2007) model (based on Culpeper et al. 2003). In the first response the witness seeks to evade the question and portray it as inappropriate 'I think you would have to ask them'. However, the QC persists and explicitly states 'I am going to press you' and follows this with a more coercive interrogative structure, which appears to be a triggering event in Bousfield's (2007) terms. The witness responds using distancing negative impoliteness: *I think, you would, Mr Sumption, if you do not mind*, but, taking into account the wider cotext, these expressions do not appear to be mitigating the speech act in any way and they therefore appear to remain as surface realizations. The QC's next turn seems to accept the challenge and the question is qualified with the extra information. However, in the next response turn the witness continues to treat the whole sequence as a cumulative trigger event and counters with an offensive strategy, challenging the QC's institutional role and therefore competence face with an interrogative form, and additionally employing potential surface politeness with *we* where no solidarity is being shown. Finally, the QC responds and also counters offensively, 'Just answer the question as asked', re-establishing the institutional power roles and marking the witness's behaviour as inappropriate, that is, not answering. Given the greater face threat that any escalation poses to the witness, at this point the episode is resolved as the witness submits to the opponent.

Finally, one of the most effective responses, from the QC's point of view, is not only to draw attention to appropriate behaviour, but, as in (28), to refer explicitly to Lord Hutton.

(28) Q. GOMPERTZ: This was the draft which became the material which was approved for use; yes?
R. HATFIELD: If you tell me it is.
Q. GOMPERTZ: That is the *evidence*. I would like you to *tell his Lordship*, please,

(18 September 2003)

8.5. CONCLUSIONS

This chapter has briefly examined some of the ways in which aggressive facework and impoliteness are played out in hostile examination. It is argued that such analysis needs to consider impoliteness as complementary to politeness, rather than a deviant form, given that institutional discourse is frequently characterized by interaction of participants with conflicting goals. Looking at the *CorDis Corpus* as a whole, aggressive facework is a feature of the interaction in the White House press briefings, the House of Commons, and the House of Representatives subcorpora. However, differentiating between acceptable, or institutionally sanctioned, aggressive facework and impoliteness shows that face needs are only suspended up to a point in the interaction. Secondly, not only is aggressive facework an integral part of the procedure in some instances of institutional discourse but, from the evidence presented here, it is unlikely to lead to a breakdown in communication given the performative nature of the discourse. Any such breakdown would represent a great face threat to both participants; in the Hutton Inquiry the ability to 'handle' the interaction is part of the QC's competence face, while for the witness it is essential to the credibility of his/her narrative.

This chapter has suggested that one means of identifying (im)politeness in institutional discourse is through locating shifts in mode, from transactional to interactional. This is one area where a CADS approach to the study of (im)politeness may prove fruitful, although corpus approaches have a range of potential roles in the field. For example, corpus data can provide information on what is perceived as (im)polite through the querying of metacomments or talk about (im)politeness within a given context.[10] Comparative data following the *WordSmith* approach may help highlight linguistic features characterizing facework in general or (im)politeness in particular within a specified context. Corpus data may also be used to explore the range of functions of 'polite language' and to describe the patterns of use in specified contexts, throwing light on how we are primed (Hoey 2005) to perceive the same structure as polite or impolite in different contexts.

NOTES

1. The terms of reference were set by Lord Falconer, the Lord Chancellor. The letter of confirmation is online. Available at http://www.the-hutton-inquiry.org.uk/content/cf240703.pdf (accessed 1 September 2007).
2. Online. Available at http://www.number10.gov.uk/output/Page271.asp (accessed 1 September 2007).
3. 'Presentation of style over substance, but hey that's showbiz—Tony style'. By Charles Spencer. 28/08/2003. Online. Available at http://www.telegraph.co.uk/core/Content/displayPrintable.jhtml?xml=/news/2003/08/29/nkell229.xml&site=5&page=0 (accessed 28 August 2007).
4. 'Snappy Scarlett Wins Few Fans', by Anne McElvoy, 27/08/2003. Online. Available at http://thescotsman.scotsman.com/index.cfm?id=941772003 (accessed 28 August 2007).
5. Originally said by Tony Blair on BBC 1, On the Record, on 16 November 1997. Transcript available online at http://www.bbc.co.uk/otr/intext/Blair16.11.97.html (accessed 28 August 2007).
6. The terms *cooperative* and *aggressive facework* as used here are not exact equivalents of Goffman's (1967) distinction.
7. The emphasis and use of bold is mine in all examples.
8. For a full discussion of the functional differentiation of types of tag questions see Biscetti 2006.
9. Godzilla, QC, takes on the BBC titan. By Simon Hoggart. 25/09/2003 Online. Available at http://media.guardian.co.uk/huttoninquiry/story/0,,1049149,00.html (accessed 1 September 2007).
10. Referred to as metapragmatic politeness1 in Haugh (2007).

9   Insistent Voices
Government Messages
Alison Duguid

This chapter investigates some patterns in the way speakers represent speech, thought, and writing across the *CorDis Corpus* with particular reference to varieties of voices in the texts. Many frequently occurring lexical items in the word lists of the corpus belong to the semantic fields of speech, thought, and writing (e.g., *talking, conversation, thought, writes, dossier, page, line*). In order to investigate how discourse representation is carried out in the corpus, a number of these were chosen and examined for the way they exemplify different text voices. These words often need lexicalization, as do general nouns such as *point, thing, way,* and, also like general nouns, they have a discourse organizing function (see Francis 1994). There are differences in their distribution and use in the subcorpora which make up the *CorDis Corpus*. Such differences reflect not just the varieties of discourse type but also diverse interests in the representation of voice and different levels of take-up of these insistent messages from government and administration voices. The methodology of corpus-assisted discourse studies is used, as set out in the introduction to this volume.

I will first deal with questions of speech and thought representation and corpus methodology, with a short overview of previous research. Using Thompson's (1996) framework for my description I will give some examples of the key features of the data related to the representation of thought, speech, and writing to be found in the *CorDis Corpus*. Finally I will go on to a consideration of language awareness and language management in politics, and the way in which the relationship between politicians and the media is sometimes played out via the manipulation of speech and thought representation.

9.1. DISCOURSE REPRESENTATION AND CORPUS METHODOLOGY

There are several possible approaches to the way speakers report other discourses or refer to talk and text, and there are a number of reasons why it is a pertinent aspect of the *CorDis* study. Most political action is language action, and speech events become embedded in one another in the process of political action, being passed on to the public via the media. Language is content, tool, and expression of media messages. In politics and in the reporting of politics, language is constantly being reworked and adapted from other speech events: reports, opinions, announcements, reactions, discussions, and what have been called news performatives and performative documents (Bell 1991; Fishman 1980). Such documents have been created not just as part of the political process but also as part of the communication of that process to the public.

Fishman (1980:99) noted, 'Journalists love performative documents because they are the hardest facts they can get their hands on.' Bell (1991:207) stated, 'Journalists love the performatives of politics where something happens through someone saying it. The fusion of word and act is ideal for news-reporting. No other facts have to be verified. The only fact is that somebody said something.' Speech events can of course be reported in a variety of ways. Distance or endorsement, stance signals, signals of interactional resistance, time frames, and values can all be altered to fit a particular political or journalistic purpose. Similar effects can be obtained in interactional situations, such as legal proceedings or briefings, where documents and reported speech and thought are often part of the content. Questions can frame utterances in a particular way and a witness or spokesperson's response can be crafted to answer or evade. All involve different ways of presenting 'voice' in texts.[1]

In British politics, an awareness of these processes has brought about changes in the way politicians handle the communication of their ideas and events to the public via the press, which has been well documented (Jones 2001; Phillis 2004; Rawnsley 2000). Politicians are more self-conscious about how they interface with the news media and this self-consciousness has also meant there is more interest in reactions and evaluations. The reporting of thoughts and feelings also becomes important, and labels describing them become part of the discourse and another facet of 'voice'. Here 'voice' is used in the sense of the originator or source of language which is represented in a text by a report, by direct or indirect speech, by summary or paraphrasing. Thompson uses the term *voice* as a cover term for the variety of sources apparent in language data: a kind of intertextuality which can be signalled in a variety of ways. Sometimes the presence of voice is signalled by means of reporting verbs, sometimes by nouns which might represent speech, thought, or writing.

The *CorDis Corpus* is composed of different discourse types in all of which reporting the words or thoughts of others is crucial, as can be seen in the frequency of lexical items referring to speech, thought, and writing presentation. The most frequent voice-related items (reporting signals such as *claimed, asked*; text nouns[2] such as *dossier, report, paragraph*; and thought-reporting signals such as *felt, wondered*) were selected from the word lists. These signals were compared across the subcorpora, and then compared with a reference corpus. Four hundred forty lexical items with fifty occurrences and over and a relative frequency greater than that in *BNC* were identified from the top of the *CorDis* word list. Their distribution among the subcorpora and their relative frequency are laid out in Table 9.1.[3] Reference will

Table 9.1   Distribution of Reporting Signals among the Subcorpora

Number of word forms expressing reporting signals, by subcorpus	*Subcorpus*	*Incidence of occurrences of reporting signals expressed as relative frequency per 100 tokens, by subcorpus*
206	*HUTTON*	6.805
88	*WHB*	2.449
40	*HoC*	0.659
38	*PapNews*	0.562
24	*HoR*	0.399
17	*TVNews*	0.621
16	*PapEd*	0.135
11	*PapOp*	0.12

also be made to the government and Number 10 partitions of the *HUTTON* subcorpus in which the testimony of government witnesses provides data about their preferences in use of voice.[4]

The two subcorpora drawn from legislative assemblies in the UK and the United States (*HoC* and *HoR*) represent politics in action, through language. The official transcripts of proceedings were used for the collection. The formal context and ritualized proceedings involve a great deal of reflexive language of a particular type and the salient metalanguage items reflect this (the most frequent of these items in *HoR* are *yield, request, allow, urge, hear, add*. In *HoC* the most frequent speech and thought-related items are *agree, decision, ensure, accept, doubt, consider, welcome*).

The *WHB* subcorpus represents the White House press briefings, part of the function of which is to control the source of news, making sure the White House is able to comment first or early in a news cycle; the briefings are given several times a day for breaking news. Partington's detailed studies of the strategies of the participants (2003 and 2006b) have outlined the discourse features and the participant roles. Such press briefings exemplify a discourse type as the site of political action through language. The podium conveys the messages of the president and the administration, as they attempt to angle their presentation of their message in times of conflict, often having to deal with issues they would rather not comment on. The press corps needs to get copy for their editors, to probe as far as possible so that this copy should be interesting but not to probe so far as to risk losing their White House press-corps status. The constant quest for news, for clarity, for evaluations and predictions, explanations and justifications, involves a great deal of language about language. In the absence of hard facts or reportable events, the probing will often involve a request for information in the form of reports that talk has taken place, or information about the expectations, feelings, or attitude of the president, the administration, or even the podium. The frequency of metalanguage, that is, talk about talk, reflects this. *WHB* is a corpus of transcribed spoken language, some of which (the podium's part) we may presume to have been semi-scripted at least in the form of notes. In our analysis we concentrate in particular on the insistent voices signalled by repeated phraseologies.

The newspaper subcorpora contain editorials, news, and opinion pieces (*PapEd*, *PapNews*, and *PapOp*, respectively). They too have a particular configuration of salient lexis, in which past-tense reporting signals are prevalent; in *PapNews* the most frequent speech and thought-related items are *called, found, reported, expected, believed, added*, whereas in *PapEd* we find *opinion, noted, doubts, argued, threatening, refusal*, and in *PapOp* the most frequent reporting signals include *feel, idea, challenge, wonder, argue, convince, scenario, rhetoric*.

The *TVNews* subcorpus was compiled to highlight the characteristics of TV news discourse and the linguistic modalities used to reflect and construct values and cultural identity. The compilers see news discourse as a key site for the transmission of cultural and political values and the choices inherent in the linguistic realization of these values are obviously of interest to researchers. Transcriptions of news programmes are not available and so the corpus had to be transcribed by the research group; it is thus a small subcorpus and so much of the frequency data is limited. However, some patterns are visible, in particular the salience of items referring to 'affect' (Martin and White 2005:45–52).

The Hutton Inquiry (*HUTTON*) constitutes another subcorpus of spoken language with an official transcription, and it provides an example of interaction in an institutional context involving information collecting and adversarial probing. The requirements of the roles of those participating, in particular the roles of witness and inquiry counsel, often mean that the discourse involved conflictual situations in institutional contexts. The amount of language about language, documents and thought processes, is inevitably large in an inquiry which concerned a number of language-related issues, such as attribution, engagement, evaluation, the effects of illocutionary speech verbs, and involved the details of a large number of documents, e-mails, successive drafts of dossiers, discussions of wording, reporters' notes, telephone conversations, and diaries. The Hutton Inquiry was set up because of concerns about the drafting of documents, ownership or attribution of responsibility and false footing, or manipulation of interaction.[5] All have to do with choices made in language reports, and we would expect the inquiry to be very much concerned with this, and to talk about it, and that the signals be identifiable and searchable. Some of the features are connected to politeness conventions: for example, the phrase *I am afraid* frames a face-threatening act (see Chapter 8 in this volume). But other instances which exemplify insistent voice are also discernible.

The actual signals vary in form and distribution. As Table 9.1 shows, the *HUTTON* subcorpus has the highest proportion of the reporting signals for speech and thought and text nouns that were selected from the word lists from the *CorDis Corpus* (206 of the 440 identified items are present in that subcorpus), and the relative frequency of occurrences of these items is higher than in any other subcorpus This is followed by *WHB*, in which eighty-eight of the 440 items are present. Simple quantitative data tell us relatively little, however, and the raw data need to be further investigated by means of concordance searches to find repeated regularities in their cotexts and in patterns of use as part of the methodology of corpus-assisted discourse studies (Partington 2004a).

9.2. SPEECH AND THOUGHT REPRESENTATION

The ways in which language acts can be embedded in other language acts has been examined with reference to three areas of study in particular: fiction, academic discourse, and journalism. In their 1981 *Style in Fiction*, Leech and Short examined the presentation of speech and thought in fiction, deciding that a narratorial interference criterion was the most appropriate to identify a number of categories, from narration to free indirect thought. Different aspects have been highlighted for academic discourse (Charles 2006; Swales 1986, 1990; Tadros 1993; Thompson and Ye 1991) where the focus is on reference to sources and the citation of others and on the conventions which exist for signalling the relationship between texts and parts of other texts; the question of plagiarism and acknowledgment of sources is a key one in this area. The wide range of choices available in reporting accessed voices and thoughts in the journalistic sphere also has become a rich field of study as has discussion of different ways of reporting and choices of source citation (McQuail 1994; Shoemaker1996; Waugh 1995). In journalistic discourse, the issue is that of fidelity to an original, where there is an original text to compare with, leading to considerations of the manipulative aspects of reporting. In the relationship between politics and media, all three issues (narratorial interference, attribution and responsibility, and fidelity to an original) are significant.

Many approaches have made useful and fruitful distinctions, even before the availability of large corpora. Thompson's 1994 volume dealing with reporting was corpus-based and it set out to describe the formal variations using corpus data but gave no quantitative frequency data. Thompson also provided some detailed discussion of reporting in conversation, fiction, academic writing, and newspapers. In 1996 Thompson examined reporting from a discourse point of view. In this discussion he observed:

> Language reports are best approached from a functional rather than a
> structural angle, although it is desirable to draw up—as far as possible—a

list of the structural and lexical features which may be used to signal the reports. Reporting constitutes one of the 'semantic diffusions' or 'semantic motifs' which Martin argues 'permeate the grammar'.

(Thompson 1996:502)

He goes on to say that such a range of different structural forms to realize a group of semantically related meanings needs an approach from above (discourse) rather than from below (structure). He identifies four overlapping areas: voice, message, signal, attitude, which we will use in our analysis of parts of the *CorDis* data. Since we are using a corpus-assisted approach, it is via the different kinds of signal that we get into the data, signals which we can identify via word lists or via quotation marks, which were marked up for *Xaira*. There is therefore no separate discussion of signal as such, but the other three aspects, voice, message, and attitude, are dealt with using salient examples from the various subcorpora. Certain characteristics of voice will be taken up again in section 9.3.4 and 9.4 when we discuss aspects of the political management of attribution and hidden voice.

A later corpus-based study which built on Leech and Short was that of Semino and Short (2004). This is a systematic and detailed annotation of a corpus of written fictional and nonfictional narratives consisting of 258,348 tokens from 120 texts. They extended the descriptive scheme to cover writing and set up a number of other analytical categories. The study involved special markup and tagging of the texts which required detailed qualitative analysis to decide whether a segment involved narrative representation of voice, narrator's representation of speech act, indirect speech, or direct speech, with similar distinctions for thought and writing. Markup decisions and analysis become a major factor with such delicate levels of analysis; each tag marked up was cross-checked by more than one group of researchers. Although we can look on markup as adding value to a corpus, particularly for future researchers, it runs the risk of losing the advantages of the corpus methodology set out by Scott. He points out that modern corpus software

> is capable of ploughing through vast quantities of text in a relatively short time, possibly accessing it remotely, and reordering it to a set of potential patterns [. . .] this ordinary imaginative capacity, that of seeing a pattern [. . .] makes it possible for corpus based methodologies to have a relatively large impact on language theory.

(Scott and Tribble 2006:5)

This impact is lost if an elaborate annotation scheme is required. Certainly a corpus as vast and complex as the *CorDis Corpus* would have been extremely difficult and time consuming to annotate and cross-check to such a level of delicacy.

9.3. VOICES IN THE DATA

As I have said, the frequency counts tell us to some extent the 'aboutness' of texts and our corpus is as much about language as it is about the Iraq conflict. In particular I am interested in the various ways in which voices are signalled in the text, and I take Thompson's (1996) framework as a way to look at the data. For Thompson, voices are signalled in the text when the speaker or writer indicates in some way that another voice is entering the text. The various ways in which this is indicated are identified on functional grounds rather than the more usual structural grounds used to describe language reports (direct and indirect speech, projecting clauses, and so on). I will try to identify factors which influence the choice of one way of introducing a language report over another. Like Thompson, I include reports of opinion, knowledge, feeling, or perception (thought presentation) which cannot strictly be called language reports. Starting from Sinclair's (1986) position that anything that is not attributed is averred and that attribution is a marked option, Thompson sets out four intermeshing dimensions ('voice', 'message' , 'signal', 'attitude'), and, although there is no space here for a complete analysis, we will use these dimensions to highlight particular patterns emerging in the concordance lines, often taking as a starting point a signal of one kind or another found to be salient in a comparison of the different subcorpora.

By 'voice', Thompson means who or what is represented as being the source. He lays out five main groups along a spectrum: 'self', 'specified others', 'unspecified others', 'community', and 'unspecifiable others'.

9.3.1. Voice

Where the voice signalled is that of 'self', *I swore, I promise, I think,* the speaker explicitly attributes the utterance to him- or herself, and assigns to him- or herself the dual roles of utterer and labeller (these are Thompson's terms) with the labeller presenting the utterer's proposition. Framing of this type is thus seen as a signalled choice of 'voice'.

In our data in some cases this voicing comes from a kind of performative usage, prevalent in the House of Representatives data, where the proceedings are highly formalized and there are conventions regarding turns and contributions.

- **add**: *I want to add; I just want to add; I would like to add; might I just add; I want to add one thing*
- **urge**: *I stand here today to urge this President; I urge my colleagues; I urge our colleagues; I urge our Republican colleagues; I urge our colleagues to support; I urge the rejection of this amendment*
- **demand**: *Mr Chairman I demand a recorded vote; Mr Speaker on that I demand the yeas and the nays*
- **yield**: *I yield the balance of my time* (this in particular is a formal procedural performative)

Mostly these items represent what have been called 'achievements' (Vendler 1967): that is, they are conceptualized as being simultaneous with the time of utterance or with some sort of point which results in a change of state (telicity). There is in *HoR* one case where self as source is framed rather anomalously to give another voice: '*I am told I am asking permission to strike the last word*'.

Other functions of using self as source include hedging for politeness to avoid too much face threatening (cf. Partington 2003), or *I wonder/ was wondering* as a frame to introduce a question from the reporters. Markers signalling thought representations can involve privileged access, located in individual subjectivity, *we felt/we thought/I think,* and this has particular advantages for witnesses in an inquiry, as privileged access preempts rebuttal and is not open to contradiction. These are key clusters in the *HUTTON* government partition in comparison with the whole *HUTTON* subcorpus. Thompson characterizes this choice of 'self' as voice 'in the fuzzy area where reporting merges into other areas such as modality' (Thompson 1996:508) and the choices do allow for a modulation of evidentiality, a key issue in an official inquiry. Self as source can be identified through the concordance lines of a variety of node words with a variety of effects and can also be a way of framing a proposition with reference to previous utterances or previous testimony. Frequent clusters in the testimony in the *HUTTON* subcorpus are *as I say* and *as I said in my witness statement, I felt, I thought.* Willingness to respond and openness are often a key strategic need in interaction where there are conflicting aims being performed under public scrutiny. It can be signalled with *I will be glad, I am very glad (WHB), I am delighted (HoC),* as framing for projected clauses, though in the latter case the repetitions lead one to suspect lack of sincerity, sarcasm, or perhaps a way to mark recognition of a friendly question. Sometimes it may be politic to refrain from claiming responsibility for self as voice; a frequent cluster in the *HUTTON* subcorpus is *I can't remember* and *I cannot recall,* the negative can thus serve as an avoidance strategy. In the *WHB* subcorpus, however, this kind of abdication is not used as an avoidance option, as it would be a confession of incompetence on the part of the podium, volition being preferred over ability in the modals. A straight refusal to act improperly as voice is used.

1. I'm **not going to make any comment**; that is legal matter;
2. Ed, I'm **not going to speculate**;
3. And I'm **not going to comment** on any of the specific benchmarks;
4. I'm **not prepared to enter into** any discussions
5. Well, I'm **not going to discuss** intelligence.
6. I'm **not going to go beyond** what the President has said.
7. In terms of President Fox, I'm **not going to try to comment** for him
8. I'm **not going to do it** from this podium.
9. Ken, I **cannot give you** their reasons. **I'm not their spokesman**

The next category is that of 'unspecified others' and when this is the only source of voice signalled, we find a good number of nominalized illocutionary or text items which allow the source to be left unspecified and which give entity status to a grammatical metaphor. The *HUTTON* subcorpus contains a high proportion of these, usually with consistent lexicalization: *claim* refers nearly always to the forty-five-minutes claim in the dossier (that is, the claim that Iran had the capability to deploy weapons of mass destruction within forty-five minutes of an order to do so); *allegation* refers consistently to Andrew Gilligan's allegation, though this is characterized or defined in a variety of ways as being: *an allegation of spin; an allegation of dishonesty; an allegation of conscious wrongdoing; an allegation of bad faith*; and such definitions are contested.

Locative and existential constructions are also frequent with this function in our data and most frequent in the *HUTTON* subcorpus data. In the Number 10 partition of the *HUTTON* data, those testifying (Blair, Powell, and Campbell) seem to prefer existential and locative expressions involving texts, language reports, mental activity verbs, or text nouns as entities, presenting unspecified others as voice in this way (see Table 9.2).

HUTTON shows the highest frequencies for such existential and locative phrasing with thought and speech nouns in the corpus, as Table 9.3 shows.

Table 9.2   Relative Frequencies (per 100 tokens) of Locative and Existential Expressions in Number 10 Partition Compared with All Hutton.

Cluster	Number 10 partition	All Hutton partition
this was	0.19	0.07
that was	0.27	0.15
it was	0.63	0.07
there were	0.27	0.05
there is	0.21	0.09
Total	**1.57**	**0.43**

Table 9.3   Relative Frequencies per 100 tokens of Locative and Existential Expressions in *Hutton* Compared with the *CorDis Corpus*

Cluster	HUTTON	All CorDis
There was	0.138	0.047
There were	0.052	0.022
Total	**0.190**	**0.069**

The following list illustrates examples of existential verbs and locatives combined with a mental activity verb or text noun as 'voice' in *HUTTON:*

- *There was unhappiness*
- *There was a lot of concern*
- *There was some doubt*
- *There were some murmurings about the final wording*
- *There was some discussion*
- *There was a lot of spin on it*
- *There was intelligence on the subject*
- *There were misgivings lower down the chain*
- *There were a number of caveats*
- *There were concerns about its reliability*
- *There were no departmental lines to take on this*
- *My Lord, there were differences of opinion*

Unspecified multiple speakers are sometimes directly quoted, even where the words may not actually have been uttered but are intended to be considered as faithful to the spirit of what people say. We find many examples of the use of *people*—'unspecified others' as a variant of 'voice' found in patterns with quotes (see Concordance 9.1). *People* is a keyword in the Number 10 partition compared with the whole *HUTTON* subcorpus and is salient in the *WHB* subcorpus). Tony Blair in particular frequently favours this kind of simulated direct speech quotation of what 'people' say or think. It should be noted here how the wording changes or the punctuation varies according to the different transcribers making different decisions about the status of the quotations.

The mental processes of others are another source of voice and frequently reported with varying levels of commitment to the proposition and its factuality:

1. **The President wants** to get to the bottom of this
2. I think that's what the **American people want**
3. The **American people want** to see reform at the United Nations
4. The **American people want** us to get to the bottom of this

You know	**people say** I hear what you say
	People would say 'When did you know?; what did
it wasn't as if there were	**people saying** 'don't put it in, don't put it in!
So many	**people saying** 'Well I'm not so sure about that'
at a later time	**people say** 'why on earth did you not give this informatio
So, many	**people will say** 'well, we aren't sure about that'
So many	**people saying** 'well we are not sure about that'

Concordance 9.1 Concordance of unspecified others in the Number 10 partition of *HUTTON.*

5. we think **the American people want** the Senate to put aside the politics and move forward
6. **The American people** are always regretful if it is has come to that
7. **The Iraqi people are determined** to build a brighter future, and I think they've shown
8. **The majority of Iraqi people are committed** to freedom and democracy
9. I think **people are experiencing** the joy of being liberated
10. It was crystal clear **she felt** she had been let down by the PM

Such claims to be able to speak for others' mental processes constitute a claim for authority, the speaker's thoughts about how others think, a claim to estimate others' opinions. There are other kinds of voice: unspecified voice and community, which we will come to later at the end of this section (9.3.4) and when I come to consider language awareness and language management in politics (9.4).

9.3.2. Message

The second aspect Thompson uses for classifying functional aspects of voice is that of 'message'. This is the way in which the communicative function or ideational content is presented. The message can be quoted, or it can be paraphrased, summarized, echoed, or omitted, on a cline of faithfulness in terms of matching or not matching the original. Quotations, although apparently the most faithful, can have a dramatic function rather than a fidelity function. For example, a wish for a higher degree of dramaticity or vividness may be behind the choice of Congress members to quote messages verbatim from their constituents' letters (the reporting signal *writes* is salient in this corpus) and thus we get

1. and are a peace-loving country, **writes** Mr Duckwall.
2. Mr Brad Steinmetz of Columbus, in central Ohio, the State capital, **writes**
3. This is a 20-year-old Navy corpsman, 20 years old and **writes** like that I
4. He **writes** that yesterday in a poor neighborhood, two 14-year-old sisters
5. From Columbus, Ohio, Jason Bennett **writes**, I am appalled at the apparent lack
6. From Ravenna, Ohio, Alan Goldstein **writes**, As you know, I have written many
7. what I teach my students, she **writes**
8. The author **writes** the following paragraph
9. Mark Duckwall of Yellow Springs, southwest Ohio, **writes**
10. The truth will come out one way or another, she **writes**
11. Ken Harlow of Powell, Ohio, in central Ohio, **writes**
12. Please keep our public officials accountable, Ms Steele **writes**

13. in Iraq to get the truth behind the President's claim Mr Bennett
    writes.
14. The American Legion **writes**: This budget defies
15. The mother of a service man **writes**

There are other benefits from fidelity. In the Hutton Inquiry data we can find self-reporting quotations are used when a witness is keen to have the verbatim contents of a witness statement, perhaps composed carefully without the interruptions of oral testimony, heard in court and transcribed by the inquiry.

The degree of fidelity is obviously at issue in an inquiry, and quotations are very frequent in the Hutton Inquiry, which is why the same clusters are found repeated, because citations of the same forms are used so frequently in questions and evidence referring to documents or statements which involve quotations, such as the Gilligan report and the various drafts of the dossier.

The 'paraphrase' function, on the other hand, is frequently exemplified by indirect speech. Direct quotation and indirect speech are often framed by the same reporting signals. Since the categories represent a cline between fidelity (in direct quotation) and paraphrase (indirect speech labelled by the reporter), it is interesting to see when they are close to overlapping. Sometimes the indirect speech paraphrases merge into 'summaries' where the reporting verb itself carries part of the message. In a summary the amount of information about the message can range from minimal to considerable. It can also mark a difference in faithfulness to the original and this can have implications as to 'voice'. The choice of the verb in a summary indicates the reporter's interpretation of events, whereas in paraphrasing the reporter will probably choose more neutral signals, the semantic cover-all terms such as *said, told*. A case in point is that of the illocutionary reporting verb *ordered*, which is most frequent in the news subcorpora and usually involves a particular interpretation of the speech event. In the Hutton Inquiry it assumed particular importance. It occurs twenty-four times in *HUTTON*. Every single occurrence is either relating or quoting the Gilligan assertion that Downing Street 'ordered' the forty-five-minutes claim to be inserted into the dossier. This assertion, which he attributed to Dr Kelly, became a central issue in the inquiry. It is thus the distinction between paraphrase and summary which was critical—was it really an order? Did Downing Street exert undue influence by issuing orders to intelligence staff? For the inquiry, the distinction also means the difference in voice:

(1)   Q. The same is true, is it not, of the word '**ordered**'; that was not something that Dr Kelly had said, it was Gilligan speaking not Kelly, was it not?
      R. Yes. It was my interpretation of what he had said.

                                                              (17 September 2003)

In the White House data there are many challenges and denials which also simultaneously summarize. The durative form of reporting signals like *saying* seems to share both quotation and paraphrase functions, sometimes mixing the two, and along with other signals is often involved in clarification issues, using cleft structures.

1. Well, **what I'm asking is,** is there an effort or a willingness to compromise on this,
2. **What I'm saying is** that from day one we have bent over backwards to provide
3. But **what I'm getting at is** that Americans around the country, as the President
4. **What I'm saying is** that we're continuing to fight for the package as we outline
5. **What I'm saying is** that this was about paying tribute to our sailors and aviators

On the cline of decreasing fidelity to an original message, the next choice in Thompson's framework is that of message omission. There are various examples of omission of content when it has been mentioned that a speech event took place. In the *WHB* subcorpus we find use of *talk, talked, talking* (seen as a positive event), *addressing* and *discussing issues*; *views* are *made known, made clear,* or are *very well known* without mention of their message. This is a marked option, often signalled by the use of durative forms, which present activities rather than accomplishments or achievements, as lexical signals. Other lexical signals are language-event nouns such as *message*. The word *message*, salient in White House briefings (on *message* in the *WHB* subcorpus; see also Chapter 4 in this volume), is treated as an event or material process that is enough in itself. Sometimes it is evaluated, *clear, strong, wrong, tough,* and situated in time by the reporter (see Concordance 9.2).

It seems that the act of sending a message, even to baseball, is in itself significant.

successful in getting the good news	message out
t decided to invade Iraq was to send a	message
We know that the president put out a	message and spoke to President Mbeki
Whatever	message was he trying to send?
It is a terrible	message to send
It sends the wrong	message to the international community
After the President's tough	message we have a greater prospect for peace
North Korea is hearing a clear	message from those countries
ou're going to hear a very welcoming	message
The President sent a very clear	message to baseball as well

Concordance 9.2 Concordance of *message* as summary in *WHB*.

Similar signals are found with many expressions with *'make'*. While in the parliamentary data this kind of message-omission expression is used in the case of formal procedural matters, for example, *he will make a statement,* in the *WHB* subcorpus we find another strategic use. A number of general illocutionary nouns, which do not normally connote formal procedures, are used omitting the message but emphasizing the event (see Concordances 9.3 and 9.4)

the President will give	**remarks** about the war
Yes, he'll make	**remarks**
No, he will not be making	**remarks.**
He's going to be delivering	**remarks** at the Federal Home Loan Bank of
The President made	**remarks** before we departed. You all will hav
He made	**remarks**, via satellite, to the National Society
the President will make	**remarks** on the economy in Appleton, Wisco
The President will make	**remarks** to approximately 20,000 troops and
He will make	**remarks** on the first day of the General Asse
Then the President will make	**remarks** to the troops at Fort Campbell
Then the President will make	**remarks** at a Bush-Cheney 2004 luncheon.
19th, the President will make	**remarks** on the Patriot Act in Hershey, Penns
be focusing a good bit of his	**remarks** on talking about the hopeful period
ill travel to Georgia to make	**remarks** at Fort Stewart
here the President will make	**remarks** at a Barbour for Governor
he President looks forward to making	**remarks** before the United States Hispanic
ited Nations, he will be making some	**remarks** this afternoon
he President looks forward to making	**remarks** on the economy

Concordance 9.3   Concordance of *remarks* as a speech event in *WHB*.

ts to go to the President's Social Security	**conversation** in Colorado
iece that was missing, and that was a final	**conversation** that needed to take place t
ing that, the President will participate in a	**conversation** on the economy and job
President discussed the straightforward	**conversation** he had yesterday with Pres
he will be sitting there with the rest of the	**conversation** participants
n Friday the President will participate in a	**conversation** on job training in Hunting
he'll participate in a	**conversation** on the Patriot Act in Buffal
One, before she left for the area, she had a	**conversation** of matter with President B
the workers there, who will be part of the	**conversation**, as well as in attendance, a
The	**conversation** will include a first-time ho
The President had a good phone	**conversation** with President Chirac yest
Then the President will participate in a	**conversation** on job training and the eco
he President will participate in a	**conversation** on home ownership in Ard
The President had a good	**conversation** with President Hu, of Chi
The President had a very good	**conversation** with the leader of the new
And that was a brief	**conversation**. Then the President had his
And he had a good	**conversation** this morning with the new
No, it was a	**conversation** between Europeans.
ointed out the importance of engaging in a	**conversation** with the rest of the world
esident looks forward to participating in a	**conversation** on the Patriot Act

Concordance 9.4   Concordance of *conversation* as a speech event.

We can see that many of the occurrences of these discourse labels in the *WHB* subcorpus involve the labelling of a noun as an event in itself (for example: *I think there will be some conversations about it*). This is different from normal conversational practice, where it is unusual, for example, to plan future conversations, or to know the participants and topic beforehand; in ordinary life, conversations and remarks tend to be rather more casual forms of communication. The distinction between planned and spontaneous is blurred by the choice of the speech-event noun, but the planned status is clear from the fact that it is part of a scheduling announcement. This also marks the event as detached from content. It is not important what the president said or will say; it is enough to know that *the president made remarks, is looking forward to a conversation*. This choice of omitting content serves also to enhance the importance of the president for whom even remarks and conversations are scheduled events, irrespective of content. There is also a set of other strategies for omitting content while signalling a speech event which seems to serve as a refusal to comment or avoidance of discussion (see Concordances 9.5 and 9.6)

All of these examples illustrate the different ways in which the message or ideational content of a speech event is presented, and where the choice is made to omit the message we also see some rhetorical purpose served, such as enhancement of the role of the president or avoidance of comments which might lead the podium into difficulty; thus implying some kind of

Steve, I think that's kind of	**gettng into** the substance of the discussion
I cannot	**get into** the specifics
I'm not going to	**get into** those conversations
I think it's premature to	**get into** what specific steps we may want to look at
I'm just not going to	**get into** commenting on everything that is said each day
I'm not going to	**get into** hypotheticals
I'm not going to	**get into** specifics
I didn't	**get into** that with him
I can't	**get into** commenting on the things that you're bringing

Concordance 9.5   Concordance of avoidance using *get into*.

So we've	**spoken to** that issue already
And I think we've	**spoken to** that in the past
Well, again, and we've	**spoken to** this, what needs to happen now i
I think that the President has	**spoken to** this recently
I think the interim government has	**spoken to** this issue and talked about how
Prime Ministers Ahern and Blair have	**spoken to** this issue
I think some people have already	**spoken to** that, and I'll leave questions
the Secretary General has previousl	**spoken to** that, or has since spoken to
for the Secretary General has since	**spoken to** that, as well
about some of the coverage, and we've	**spoken to** that
Office of Management and Budget has	**spoken to** this

Concordance 9.6   Concordance of already *spoken to* in WHB.

evaluation, positive in the first case and negative in the second. Speech, thought, and writing presentation also often involves expression of attitude or evaluation, as we will see in the next section.

9.3.3. Attitude

In discussing the evaluation by the present reporter of the message or the original speaker, Thompson calls on the concept of 'attitude', which can be neutral, positive, or negative with respect to truth or validity. In *WHB* and *HUTTON* data there are also evaluations which seep through via the use of aspect and modality. The podium's concern in the briefings data seem to be to emphasize communication in time, in particular stressing continuity: the subtext is 'we are already doing it' (we find such forms as *keeps, continue to, continues, will continue, has already, has always, always, is going to*) talk/ *engage in discussion*. He is also concerned to frame it with aspect, especially durative and nontelic forms, for example, {CONTINUE} *working/to work, talking/to talk, making known/clear, supporting /to support, to urge, to emphasize, to discuss, to believe, to focus on, to consult, to reach out to, to call*.

The Number 10 partition of the *HUTTON* data on the other hand shows concerns with emphasizing deontic modality, *having to* (Number 10, 0.20%: All Hutton, 0.07%), asserting (*knew that, the fact that*), a constraint or suggesting activity forced upon them, or difficulty (Number 10, 0.09%:All Hutton, 0.02%).

1. I think we are going to **have to make it clear** that we are going to publish this dossier
2. I also knew that it **had to be a document** that was owned by the JIC
3. That was what the discussion was about. That it **had to be revelatory** subject of course to the fact that it **had** in the end **to** be the work of the JIC
4. If it was clear that he was in all probability the source then we were going to **have to disclose that**
5. One of the things I was very concerned about was that we **had to have an absolutely copper bottomed reason for not having told the FAC**
6. There has been what has been described as a very **difficult and bloody meeting** with the FAC
7. I would certainly say we were in an extremely **difficult** and unusual set of circumstances
8. It was going to be very **difficult**
9. There were certain **views** that he held which could be uncomfortable or **difficult** for the Government
10. The **Sunday papers** often are even more **difficult** than the daily papers
11. One of the complicating factors which made **our position difficult**
12. Talking about whether **this evidence** was going to be **difficult** for us or unhelpful
13. And it would be **difficult to resist** him being interviewed by them

This last category of Thompson's framework, that of attitude, has features in common with the concept of endorsement in terms of the modality which frames the speech act and can achieve effects of distancing. A particular choice of text noun can also indicate attitude in certain discourse types, for example, some reporting signals which are salient in the *PapOp* subcorpus belong to a set of what might be called 'artefact' or 'literary' text nouns suggesting an attitude of detachment or the role of audience or observer: *fiction, narrative, saga, version, scenario, myth, drama, chorus*.

Other examples of the metonymical use of text words are to be found in the Number 10 partition where 'stories' have a life of their own. *Story* is a keyword in this partition compared to the rest of the *HUTTON* subcorpus.

1. The media were in full pursuit of this **story**
2. This thing was already beginning to build as a very major **story**
3. The **story** of the so-called apology was leading the news
4. This was a **story** that went right round the world
5. I felt the thing was moving away. They were not covering the **story. It was just going away,** as a media thing.
6. It was obvious once the FAC had reported, it was important if possible that **it started to go away as a story.**

Reporter attitude can also be conveyed by the employment of repeated metaphors. It seems that the Number 10 team and the BBC did indeed perceive themselves as being at war: where discourse representation lexis is described metaphorically in terms normally used to refer to war to describe relationships between these two bodies and others involved in the issue, in the Hutton Inquiry.

1. It had then been, as I say, **backed up and really had booster rockets put on** it by the Mail on Sunday article
2. I was exhausted but I felt a lot better and **I had opened a flank** on the BBC.
3. It has been, if you like, a bit of **a turf war** between two Select Committees
4. Sometimes you can just **batten down the hatches** and say: we have absolutely nothing to say.
5. A pretty ferocious **attack** which Alastair Campbell had launched
6. We were under a pretty ferocious **attack** at the FAC
7. Report **attacking** the integrity of the Prime Minister
8. Which was a wholesale **attack** on the story
9. The Government has focussed its **attack** on Andrew Gilligan
10. It was an external **attack** and we had to take some action
11. The BBC had come under a somewhat remorseless **attack**

Other semantic fields can be observed to be preferred representations of 'voice' in particular discourse types. The *TVNews* salient lexis concerned with discourse presentation, for example, is prevalently about affect; the representation of thought is made by recurring reference to emotions: *ashamed, terrified, frightened, furious, anxious, expecting, angry, mood, hoping, worried.*

This concern with the expression of affect and mood is not found to such an extent in the other subcorpora and is thus peculiar to the *TVNews* subcorpus, suggesting that an emphasis on emotional impact is a preferred strategy for this discourse type.

9.3.4. Unspecified Voices

In most of the examples discussed earlier we have been looking at specific signals indicating another 'voice' in the text which is specified in one way or another and which we have thus been able to pick out from the word lists and concordance lines but there are cases where there is no explicit signal. Thompson also has a category of unspecified voice which he calls 'community'—both speaker and hearer know that these words have been used before; there is no need to specify the source, though it could be done if wanted, because the phraseology is felt to be so much common property that the wording can be freely adapted to suit the context. This has a solidarity function for the identification of insiders. It is difficult for computer-assisted discourse studies to identify the category since it is not always clear how the other voice is recognized in the absence of signalling. This concept of shared knowledge, echoes, and repetitions fits into Hymes's hypothesis that members of a speech community are aware of the commonness, rarity, previous occurrence, or novelty of many features of speech and this knowledge enters into their definitions and evaluations of ways of speaking (Hymes 1974:95). The concept of the 'well-known phrase or saying' and the ability to recognize one, even from incomplete samples, is part of the sociocultural competence of the language user (see Council of Europe 2001:5.2.2). An example of such community voices is to be found in many of the newspaper headlines in our corpus. Many of the following partial quotations, all taken from headlines in the corpus, have echoes of previous conflicts in history or literature; others echo political issues:

- *London calling;*
- *Be prepared;*
- *Divided we stand;*
- *Careless talk;*
- *Fit for heroes;*
- *Sound and Fury;*
- *Smoking guns;*
- *Crunch point;*
- *Rebels and causes;*
- *A tale of two Tonies.*

In terms of 'voice' they fit Thompson's labels of either 'community' or 'unspecifiable voice' which depend on shared knowledge rather than identifiable signals. Such sociolinguistic knowledge is a question of priming through previous encounters, and in the context of newspaper headlines a question of interpretation, not everyone will recognize them as representing another voice. They are not signalled formally in any way and therefore are difficult to pick out with quantitative methodology. However, certain items which occur with relatively high frequency might be examples of such echoes. The use of echoes depends upon the subeditor's awareness of how readers may be primed to recognize them even in the absence of overt signals and an awareness of how this might create the feeling of community, shared knowledge, or shared experience. Language technicians can thus use their awareness for the purposes of language management for particular rhetorical effects as we shall see in the next section.

9.4. LANGUAGE AWARENESS, LANGUAGE MANAGEMENT

There is a complex relationship between events and the presentation of such events, and sometimes this complex relationship becomes the subject of discussion and conscious activity. Language management, particularly in terms of issues of attribution and responsibility, both questions of voice, are key factors in both the White House briefings and in the Hutton Inquiry. Those asking the questions are interested in the process of communication as much as the product. Much political action takes place via language, and one would expect to find a great deal of language about language in these two subcorpora. Caution, however, is needed here with reference to frequency data since the subcorpora consist of question-and-answer sequences, increasing the likelihood of the repetition of forms (the dispersion plots frequently show pairs of occurrences). The Hutton Inquiry centred on a number of questions to do with the careful presentation of language events and the process of reaching a presentational form. Attention frequently focused on verbatim testimony, on verbal forms, during the examination by counsel and in the final report. Counsel and witnesses were talking about the same things; documents were presented, quoted from, and referred to. It is therefore not surprising that the *HUTTON* subcorpus has such a large proportion of text nouns, reporting verbs, and illocutionary nouns such as *claim (HUTTON,* 0.029% of the subcorpus), *complaint (HUTTON,* 0.012% of the subcorpus), and *allegation (HUTTON,* 0.025% of the subcorpus). The wide variety of choices possible in the representation of voice is reflected in the high proportion of such items in the *HUTTON* subcorpus word list. What is more, the whole question of the composition and drafting of the dossier, Andrew Gilligan's reporting, the various different accounts of events, and the naming of Dr David Kelly all involve meta-communication. The content of the inquiry itself concerned reflexive language, metalanguage, citation forms, and talk about talk (for example: *they say the document was not sexed up; the wordsmithing was important; I think you'll find my words were; I was just paraphrasing; as I said in my witness statement; say whether it was a complaint; that is a term which is often applied*). The attention is on form as well as content, on process as much as product, the way language is chosen.

Corpus research permits the observation of regularities over a large number of texts from which certain preferences in presentation can emerge as repeated regularities of form (Baker 2006; Partington 1998; Scott and Tribble 2006; Sinclair 2004; Stubbs 1996; Tognini Bonelli 2001). Hoey's concept of priming (2005) is relevant here. Hoey suggests that as a word is acquired through encounters, it becomes accumulatively loaded with the contexts and cotexts in which it is encountered. Through such encounters over a large number of texts, we become primed with certain expectations about its collocations, colligations, semantic and pragmatic associations among other things. Our knowledge, use, and expectations of words are determined by our exposure to words in context. Not all exposure is the result of random personal experience. We can see what we might call *forced* priming, in the sense of frequently repeated messages being deliberately flooded into the discourse for a particular purpose, in a number of contexts: in advertising, foreign language teaching, indeed education in general. Institutions and enterprises appear to find it worth considerable investment to encourage priming through planned repetition. Political spin-doctoring and media manipulation work on similar principles. For this reason it is interesting to examine frequency data in institutional discourse and to examine the voices revealed there. Sometimes we can detect language management through manipulation of the elements of discourse representation.

In an age of mass communication and near instant reproduction of multimedia material, there is an increased care and attention paid by institutions to how their desired messages are conveyed. Fairclough has called this the technologization of discourse (Fairclough 1996:71–83). The people who have the podium role, the so-called spin doctors in the White House, and the special advisers employed by the Labour government in its first two terms, are professionals, discourse technicians. The press constantly deplored the techniques of the Number 10 communications team, while the decisions to use such techniques came from Labour's bitter experience of press hostility during its time in opposition and its awareness of how media representation can lead to distortion of the discourse. From the start, the Blair administration employed technicians from the media as part of its communication strategy. This involved textual practices all involving 'voice': for example, (1) the use of 'on-message' responses known as 'singing from the same hymn-sheet'; here the composer of the message may be a media specialist while the addressers are politicians ostensibly answering questions or making statements or participating in events, with a text which has been pre-prepared and planned for insertion some time before, to be used on many occasions: the hymn-sheet metaphor suggests a bringing together of addresser, message, timing, and attribution to produce a choral effect. Another strategy (2) involved priming in the lobby and the use of nonattributable statements off the record (examples are the Valerie Plame case in the USA, in Britain the description of David Kelly as a 'Walter Mitty character', or the description of Gordon Brown as being 'psychologically flawed') with nonspecific attributions such as, for example, 'sources close to the prime minister'. In the first two cases the original voices were revealed after investigation; in the last case the voice remains anonymous. A further strategy (3) deployed false attribution of statements, which, like (2), involved concealment of the addresser but what also might be called 'false' footing. An example of this third kind of 'voice' would include the two articles with similar wording which appeared at different times in 1998 in the *Sun* newspaper: *Japan says sorry to the Sun for World War II* and *Argentina says 'we're sorry' for the Falklands*. The writers attributed apologies to the Japanese premier and to the Argentinian president, both of whom later denied having apologized; the apologies had been ghostwritten with styling suggestions by Alastair Campbell. It is clear that journalist and spokesman represent a very different footing from premier and president. The perlocutionary effect of the apologies lay principally in the attributed but 'false' footing; either no source is given, or a vague or nonidentifiable source is used to conceal the true source, or a false source is provided. The repetition of the strategy of false attribution indicates an organized intention or orchestration by someone with a requisite amount of language awareness.

As Hoey reminds us (2005), we are primed by our encounters with words and phrases; we see intensified priming around us in advertising and of course in political slogans and sound bites. Such intensified priming consists of planned and concealed extravocalization, that is to say, where there is some kind of quoting or referencing of external sources, other than the ostensible speaker or writer, in terms of their words or points of view. Writers/speakers can also use extravocalization to position themselves dialogistically with respect to their communicative partners, both actual and potential. Having someone pre-prepare possible responses helps a speaker in real-time interaction. Sometimes the sound-bite factor is clear from the less than spontaneous nature in which such pre-prepared phrases are presented; sometimes it is clear from a slight mismatch with the question asked, or in the formulaic nature of many podium responses. When the clusters appear sufficiently often and can be revealed by our software, perhaps the nature of the utterances becomes clear. We might even say we can detect such nonattributed turns of phrase by looking at key clusters or keywords. Let us consider a few examples from the Hutton Inquiry and the White House briefings.

The word *centrally* appeared as a keyword (using *WordSmith* software) when the government partition in the *HUTTON* subcorpus was compared with the subcorpus as a whole (government 0.02%, All Hutton only two occurrences—keyness 34.0, see note 4). It is not a word used frequently enough to appear in the *BNC* lists of words with an overall frequency of at least ten per million words (Leech, Rayson, and Wilson 2001); in comparison with 0.02% in the government testimony its frequency in the *BNC* is in fact 0.00064% or 6.4 per million words. In the *CorDis Corpus*, 60 per cent of the occurrences of *centrally* are from the *HUTTON* subcorpus, and in this it occurred only in government testimony, and is salient enough to appear as a keyword when compared with the subcorpus as a whole. It occurs in a pattern repeated by five different speakers in five different texts (see Concordance 9.7) All these speakers were effectively trying to downplay the role of Dr Kelly in the preparation of the dossier, and they do this by claiming it to have been a peripheral or marginal one, thus simultaneously denying the importance of Gilligan's allegations, a pivotal part of the government's interest. It is difficult to believe that the witnesses had not prepared particular phrases, especially as we accept that people normally do prepare themselves before giving testimony. The issue is the status of the utterance in terms of attribution, since they are ostensibly averrals, but all are speaking with one voice.

Similar traces of forced priming are observable in the other *CorDis* subcorpora and involve clusters which are probably the result of repetition of what the real sources want others to learn, and thus repeat a lot. They are deliberately created collocations. Concordances of *realize* and *reach out* provide examples of insistent voices expressing aims for a wide variety of third parties, spoken by the podium during White House briefings; the interchangeability of contexts suggest insistent voice. *Realize* (0.027 per hundred tokens) seems to have three uses in the *WHB* subcorpus. Five per cent of these relate to cognition, as in '*Ari, I realize it's limited how much you can say*' or *they realize the stakes are very high there*' (this is the use we are most familiar with and in the *HoR* subcorpus all instances are of this use). Another 33 per cent of the occurrences of *realize* have an economic meaning as in *realize a greater rate of return on their savings*. But the majority (61 per cent) in *WHB* are used in a metaphorical extension of the two ideas, cognition and benefit, a somewhat vague expression with a limited and repetitive number of interchangeable accompanying clusters.

Concordance 9.8 displays twenty-five of the ninety-seven instances of this use.

Everyone who was	**centrally**	involved in the dossier knows they are fa
and I knew he was not	**centrally**	involved in the dossier,
and was not	**centrally**	involved in the preparation of the dossie
rrect to say that Dr Kelly was not	**centrally**	involved in decisions surrounding
the Intelligence Services, was not	**centrally**	involved
it was wrong to say that he was	**centrally**	involved in the decisions surrounding
ether this was an official who was	**centrally**	involved in the compilation of the dossie

Concordance 9.7 Concordance of *centrally* in the government partition of the *HUTTON* subcorpus.

is about helping the Iraqi people	**realize** a better and brighter future.
continue to work to help the Iraqi people	**realize** a better future.
move forward to help the Haitian people	**realize** a better future and a more free
Iraqi people and helping the Iraqi people	**realize** a better future.
this is about helping the Iraqi people	**realize** a better and brighter future.
This is about helping the Iraqi people	**realize** a better future
has a stake in helping the Iraqi people	**realize** a better future, realize a free
work together to help the Iraqi people	**realize** a better future
were there to help the Iraqi people	**realize** a better future
has a stake in helping the Iraqi people	**realize** a better future, realize a free
Iraqi people, to help the Iraqi people	**realize** a better future built on democra
working together to help the Iraqi people	**realize** a brighter and better future.
committed to making sure the Iraqi people	**realize** a free and peaceful future
finish the job and help the Iraqi people	**realize** a free and peaceful future
that is ongoing to help the Iraqi people	**realize** a free and peaceful future
work in Iraq, to help the Iraqi people	**realize** a free and peaceful future
their resolve to help the Iraqi people	**realize** a free and peaceful future
ay the course and help the Iraqi people	**realize** a free and peaceful future
We're there to help the Iraqi people	**realize** a free and peaceful future
participate in helping the Iraqi people	**realize** a free and peaceful future
this is about helping the Iraqi people	**realize** a free and peaceful future
This is about helping the Iraqi people	**realize** a free, peaceful, democratic and
in Afghanistan and the people in Iraq	**realize** a much brighter future than what
responsibility for helping the Iraqi people	**realize** a secure, democratic and prosper
future, and helping the Iraqi people	**realize** a sovereign, free and democratic

Concordance 9.8   Concordance of *realize* from the *WHB* subcorpus.

The use is not taken up by any of the newspaper or TV coverage even as quotations; it is a constructed phraseology, used to describe a number of situations (Haiti, Palestine, Iraq). Take-up is apparently nonexistent; the voice is not passed on.

Reach* out is another cluster frequently found in the *WHB* corpus and a favoured way of representing proactive communication (illustrated in Concordance 9.9). There are sixty-six variations on the theme of *reaching out* to others. Again, relatively few examples of *reach out* are found in the newspaper subcorpora. The White House briefing statements represent goals or aims presented through a limited set of phraseologies and repeated across many different circumstances. The subcorpus also reveals that many sets of White House phraseologies vary the reiteration of administration policy by ringing the changes with terms like *continuing, shared goals, working to,*

We continue to	**reach out** to the American people and talk
All across this country	**reaching out** to the American people and engaging
Continue	**reaching out** to the American people and educate them
Continue	**reaching out** to the international community
	Reached out to the administration to make clear

Concordance 9.9   Concordance of *reach out* phrases from the *WHB* subcorpus.

helping, working with. Similar repetitions of clusters can be discerned with this kind of concerted voice in text as we shall see later.

The manipulation of attribution is not usually viewed favourably. In media discourse attribution is important. The *New York Times* style guide (Siegal and Connolly 1999) reads: 'The vivid language of direct quotation confers an unfair advantage on a speaker or writer who hides behind the newspaper, and turns of phrase are valueless to a reader who cannot assess the source.' Similarly, in academic terms, plagiarism occurs when an attribution is not made and something is averred which had its origins elsewhere; it is considered a kind of fraud or stealing of other people's work. And in political discourse the phenomenon of the sound bite also involves attribution which has been hidden for a number of reasons: the nonspontaneous nature of the statement needs to be played down; the footing of the author is perhaps not to be put in the public domain; the timing of composition and the nature of dissemination are not to be made explicit. The so-called forty-five-minutes claim (that Saddam Hussein had weapons of mass destruction that could be ready in forty-five minutes) is an example. It was selected for use in the foreword to the dossier setting out the reasons for war, which was written by Alastair Campbell; it was used by Blair in his speech to a specially re-called Parliament. It was the main headline in the papers the next day (see Hutton report). To give some other examples reiterated in many political biographies and autobiographies and by media commentators (for example, Jones 2001; Rees 2006; Temple 2006), the MP Ron Davies's 1998 'moment of madness' confession leading to his resignation was written for him and the lobby was briefed with the phrase; 'the people's princess' was a phrase pre-prepared for Tony Blair to use as a reply to a press question and was delivered with all the paralinguistic features of deep emotion and searching for phrases as if they were being composed on the spot. They are short, memorable phrases drafted by someone other than the speaker, at a different time from their utterance, for wide dissemination. Sound bites too tend to be evaluated negatively as a form of manipulation. Plagiarism and the sound bite have in common the fact that the addressee is meant to be unaware of the identity of the author; in plagiarism, though, the author too is unaware of the use his or her work is being put to. With the sound bite the author is usually a technician employed specifically to provide such unattributable material.

We have a great deal of information about the processes behind discourse practises from a variety of sources which have documented the New Labour communication strategy (see Chapter 3, this volume, on how the government justified its stance to the House of Commons), a strategy that was adopted from an American model.

A team of briefers work with Blair to prepare for *Prime Minister's Question Time,* they then provide briefing on the lines and phrases to any senior politician appearing on *Question Time, Any Questions,* etc. Written briefings are sent out to all MP's so they too know the phrases to use and the line to take.

(Short 2004:47)

This shows us how clusters are flooded into the discourse for forced priming. The creation of clusters (lines and phrases) which are intended to become collocations is a conscious triggering of the idiom principle. The investment of time and effort suggests that it is considered that such strategies could be a possible factor in changing electoral results and that teams of briefers, who concoct phrases to use and lines to take, are a necessary part of news management, micro-speechwriters in search of memorable metaphors as part of persuasive discourse. An example from American political discourse is the phrase linking *smoking gun* and *mushroom cloud.* The term *smoking gun* was used by the UN weapons inspector Hans Blix. The metaphor linking it with *mushroom cloud* was created by Michael Gerson, a White House speechwriter, and first deployed in a *New York Times* article on 7 September 2002, attributed to unnamed administration officials. It was then used by Condoleezza Rice on 8 September 2002 in an interview with *CNN* ('we cannot wait for the final proof—the smoking gun—that could come in the form of a mushroom cloud. But we don't want the smoking gun to be a mushroom cloud.'). President Bush then used the phrase in a speech on October 7 and on November 12 the *New York Times* article was cited by General Tommy Franks, who warned that inaction might 'bring the sight of the first mushroom cloud on one of the major population centres on this planet'. The phrase became cited as one of the elements in the Bush administration's attempt to deceive the American people (a Google search revealed 480,000 pages containing the phrase on 05.10.07) and the phrase has been used again with reference to Syria and Iran. The cluster *smoking gun* appears eighty times in the corpus without Hans Blix's original quotation always being cited or quotation marks used and thus can be considered an echo or unspecified voice without an explicit signal. A similar much repeated sound bite is 'grave and gathering danger' (1,630,000 pages in a Google search accessed 05.10.07), which might also suggest an echo of 'gathering clouds'. The effects of such technologization of discourse (Fairclough 1996) and the relationship between press, public, and politicians have been the subject of inquiries in the UK (the Phillis Inquiry 2004). The issue of trust and the public perception of politicians and press alike remain a live one. Chibnall says:

the reporter does not go out gathering news, picking up stories as if they were fallen apples, he creates news stories by selecting fragments of information from the mass of raw data he receives and organizing them into a conventional journalistic form.

(Chibnall 1981:76)

This attitude to news creation was put to use by New Labour: journalists were employed as advisers and a team of communication officers had explicit instructions about the creation of 'stories' and the timing of their release to the press. We are told that the prime minister's official spokesman (Alastair Campbell, the former politics editor of the *Daily Mirror*) sent out

> a memo instructing every department that by the end of June they should have drawn up a programme to create 'at least two substantial news stories' every week of August and September to put over 'the government's core message'.
>
> (Rawnsley 2000:381)

We saw previously (9.3.3) how the term *story* was used in the Hutton Inquiry with particular resonance. Politicians and their spokespersons, journalists, lawyers, witnesses, and judges all create versions of reality, construct narratives, and frame them in their utterances. The question is how far does reception become affected by the receiver's awareness of such simulation of the interpersonal function of meanings and forms, and how much awareness of a strategic calculation of effectiveness changes the perlocutionary effect. We react differently when we scent strategy. When an apparently spontaneous gesture, phrasing, emphasis, or hesitation is perceived as being consciously manufactured, it loses its original effect in much the same way as an original figure of speech becomes a cliché. Documents produced at the Hutton Inquiry showed the communication advisers to be very much linguistically aware and to be very careful about possible responses to wording.[6] The process of the dossier presentation, the changes in wording, the strategy of the guessing game to bring Dr Kelly's name into the public arena, all using language awareness, came under public scrutiny. An increased awareness of process which reflects strategic purposes is likely to have made us resistant to that particular kind of priming.

9.5. CONCLUSIONS

Talk about talk and text has a strong presence in the *CorDis Corpus*. Salient lexical items in the subcorpora can be accounted for by choices in the presentation of voice, message, and attitude using a variety of signals. The different alternative modes of framing, reporting, and characterizing utterances and the ends to which they are put are observable over these different discourse types and the quantitative data give us a view of what the preferred forms for each discourse type are. We have seen how the discourse representation in *HoR* reflects the ritualized nature of the proceedings, many of the reporting signals are performatives, and how the *HoC* indicates a concern for the interactional nature of their deliberations. The *WHB* data are also characterized by a high degree of formulaic phraseology suggesting not only insistent voice but also a subtext of continual proactive modality and an emphasized consideration of the importance of the president of the United States. We can see the way specific effects are achieved and how most choices are functional within a discourse type to achieve a particular communicative purpose. *PapNews* constructs its discourse through reporting while *PapEd* and *PapOp* data highlight conflicting and alternative versions of reality, and *TVNews* prefers to highlight matters of affect. Framing and nesting make for a build-up and accumulation of favoured forms in propositions exhibiting the idiom principle, and in some cases the insistent voice of government messages can be heard in repeated phraseologies which ring the changes of a series of forms, as can be seen in the *WHB* podium data and in the government partition of the *HUTTON* subcorpus. Here the pre-prepared nature of communication belies the apparent spontaneity of the interaction. This shows how the interaction is a performance for the benefit of other observers than the participants, and makes such institutionalized discourse so different from normal interaction. We have seen how some significant generalizations can be made about the preferred choices of presentation of voice, message, and attitude through a variety of signals for each of the subcorpora, and how language about language plays a major part, with each one having its own preferences congruent with its interactional features, its aims, and its goals. We have also considered how quantitative data and qualitative methodology can confirm impressions about the orchestration of language. Being aware of the extent to which such choices are made consciously and deliberately for particular effect can make us resistant to compliant interpretations, vaccinate us against forced priming, causing us if not to reject at least to question what we are told.

NOTES

1. The way the utterer indicates that another voice is entering the text; see section 4.
2. For our purposes text nouns refer to texts or parts of texts, e.g., *dossier*, *paragraph*.
3. Most of the work for this study was done using *Xaira* software which produced cross-corpus frequency comparisons to indicate the salience of an item in one particular subcorpus over the rest of the *CorDis Corpus*. Further data were obtained with word lists, keywords, and concordances using *WordSmith Tools*, version 3.1.
4. The Number 10 partition is made up of the testimony of Blair, Campbell, and Powell (39,304 tokens); the government partition is made up of testimony of all government witnesses. These were identified by the counsel chosen to undertake the examination (124,464 tokens). The All Hutton partition is the rest of the inquiry minus these participants' testimony (849,395 tokens).
5. See Chapter 8.
6. For example: '"might" reads very weakly' (AC to JS 17/09/02). The reasons behind changes in the wording of the September dossier were given in a number of e-mails from Alastair Campbell to John Scarlett and justified by him as it being part of his job to produce a carefully worded document that made the 'best case' possible.

10 Evaluating Evaluation and Some Concluding Thoughts on CADS

Alan Partington

This chapter is divided into two halves. In the first, I shall examine how both politicians and newsworkers reported and evaluated the behaviour of rival politicians and news organizations regarding the conflict in Iraq in its initial stages, as evidenced in various *CorDis* subcorpora. The second contains a number of reflections on the nature of corpus-assisted discourse studies (CADS) and its relation to recent theoretical developments in corpus linguistics.

SECTION 1. THE EPIDEICTICS OF REPORTING THE REPORTING

10.1. Fierce Fighting on the Home Front

10.1.1. Epideictics, Evaluation, and Prosody

Aristotle, in Book 1 of his manual *On Rhetoric*, divides his subject matter into three varieties, *political, legal,* and *epideictic*. Taken literally, the term *epideictic* signifies 'for display', 'ceremonial', but the epideictic speaker is concerned with virtue and vice, praising the one and censuring the other (2006: Book 1, Chapter 9) and its current sense is to indicate the rhetoric of praise and blame:

> Epideictic rhetoric, most frequently defined as the persuasive use of praise or blame, plays a central role in negotiating values and belief. Praise and blame are frequently used to define acceptable and unacceptable ways of acting, speaking, or thinking within a culture. Epideictic discourse can intensify the audience's adherence to selected values, fostering the adoption of an attitude [. . .] and increasing the audience's disposition to act in accordance with those values. Thus, examples of epideictic rhetoric are a primary discursive site for negotiating

the values that inform decision-making and orient actions within a culture; they are also involved in constructing both individual subjectivity and social attitudes and beliefs. At the same time, epideictic rhetoric attempts to reduce opportunities for opposition or debate by masking itself as simple praise or blame and by assuming that the rhetor and the audience are already in agreement.

(Summers 2001:25)

To modern eyes this three-part division appears strange, in that epideictic rhetoric also governs the other two; *political* and *legal* seem to be terms governed by field or vocation, whilst epideictics is a general, universal even, function of rhetorical discourse. But in Aristotle's day, public epideictic orations, at funerals and other public occasions, was a more visible category of event and their delivery was a special professional vocation.[1] Nevertheless, Aristotle does to a degree distinguish between them in that the first two are said to exist to 'affect the giving of decisions' in the immediacy of a 'deliberative assembly'. Again, we would object that affecting the decision making of others is the universal *raison d'être* of rhetoric, though not necessarily in the here and now.

In any case, in this chapter we will be dealing with a combination of two of Aristotle's three types of rhetoric, namely, epideictics in politics.[2] Returning to Summers's quote, we can see the relevance of epideictic discourse to news reports and newspapers, which are indeed a 'primary discursive site' for fostering and negotiating ideological values and in constructing individual and social attitudes and beliefs. Many commentators (e.g., Morley 1998; Partington 1998) have also noted how individual newspapers 'groom' their readership, how they, in Summers's words, attempt 'to reduce opportunities for opposition [. . .] by assuming that the rhetor and the audience are already in agreement' by creating a sense of 'collusion'—the 'smugness effect'—between the paper and the readers, flattering and complimenting them on having certain beliefs, values, and personal qualities (Partington 1998:140).

If we move forward circa twenty-four centuries, we can see equally clearly a similarity between epideictics and the basic tenets of evaluation theory, in the version outlined in Thompson and Hunston (2000). The latter goes beyond the feats and defeats in an individual's behaviour and beliefs to include the appraisal of what is good and what is bad about entities, claims, events, and so on. It includes subparameters such as certainty, relevance, and expectedness, and shows how evaluation organizes the discourse. Nevertheless, I shall keep to the narrower Aristotelian focus of the articulation along the good-bad parameter and how this process relates discourse senders to receivers. Not necessarily good or bad in a strictly ethical sense of course (although Aristotle himself tends to concentrate on moral worth and lists a good number of dualities, including vice and virtue, honour and dishonour, calmness and anger, friendship and enmity, confidence and fear, shame and shamelessness, pity and indignation, emulation and envy—the latter three all highly relevant to the conduct of the UK press), but also as favourable or unfavourable in an almost infinite number of wider senses: 'profitable', 'enjoyable', 'sensible', 'efficient' and so on, and their respective opposites.

Evaluation also has a central role in Sinclair's theory of lexical grammar. He makes the claim that the lexical item, by which he means the minimum unit of lexical meaning (2004:24–48, 131–48; others talk of the lexical schema; I myself find the metaphorical concept of the lexical *template* is useful), has five components, three potential and two obligatory. The former are its patterning in terms of collocation, colligation, and semantic preference. The obligatory components, of more interest here, 'are the *core*, which is invariable and constitutes the evidence of the occurrence of the item as a whole, and the *semantic prosody*, which is the determiner of the meaning as a whole' (2004:141). Semantic prosody can be identified with the general evaluative function—good or bad, favourable or unfavourable, pleasant or disagreeable—of a lexical unit (Louw 1993; Morley and Partington 2009; Partington 2004b; Sinclair 2004: 34–38, 144–47). The core constitutes the essential bedrock of the descriptive or referential content of the unit, whilst the prosody, which is diffused throughout the unit, expresses its evaluation (in fact Morley and Partington 2009 explicitly adopt the term *evaluative prosody*); in sum, when we communicate, we have a topic and an attitude to that topic.

We can define epideictic rhetoric, then, as evaluation enacted in social and political spheres. In the following sections we will analyze a few episodes of epideictic reports of reports and 'evaluation of evaluations' in, first of all, the political 'talking-shops' (legislative assemblies in the UK and the United States, White House briefings, and the British judicial investigation, the Hutton Inquiry) as represented in the *CorDis Corpus* in the subcorpora henceforth labelled as *HoC, HoR, WHB,* and *HUTTON,* and then in the US and UK press (*PapNews, PapEd,* and *PapOp*).

10.1.2. Tools and Methods

Given the need to compare the language in different corpora and even different parts of the same corpus, a certain amount of reconfiguration of the corpora was undertaken, especially of the newspapers to enable comparison among UK quality versus UK tabloid, UK quality versus US quality, and so on.

The first step in comparison was the preparation of keywords lists, using *WordSmith Tools,* from which promising items were then concordanced. However, the majority of items concordanced were either intuitively interesting items, such as names of newspapers, TV channels, or political parties, or items which were thrown up serendipitously by previous concordances. Most of the concordancing was performed using *Xaira*'s Query builder, given the greater ease with which it allows the user to call up different (sub)corpora and also the greater clarity of cotext display it offers over *WordSmith*.

10.1.3. The Talking-shops

United States

No instances of heartfelt criticism of any individual newspaper were found in either the *HoR* (House of Representatives) or the *WHB* (White House briefings) subcorpora, the nearest being the following quip from a fellow journalist in a briefings question, which plays on a perceived image of the *New York Times* as ultra-politically correct:

(1)   Q: As the President's media analyst, do you suspect that the *New York Times* would get behind our war effort if only Iraq were to open a males-only golf club, like Augusta, Georgia?

(3 March 2003)

When newspapers are mentioned in *HoR*, the function is overwhelmingly endorsing, either as support for the speaker's own argument or as a way of, a pretext to, introducing it. What was striking, however, were the statistics on which papers were quoted from and by whom, as shown in Table 10.1.

   Given they are cited for endorsement, this is strong though indirect evidence that the two major titles (the *New York Times* and the *Washington Post*) are perceived by both Republicans and Democrats as left-leaning.

   There is, however, some grumbling from several speakers on the Republican side that the TV and papers *taken as a whole* are negative and gloom-mongering (my emphasis):

(2)   A lot of these things we are not going to see on *TV* because the press corps avoids writing about the friendly dealings with the US forces and the local population, and really focuses more on rioting and looting and kind of misrepresenting the nature of things.

(Jack Kingston, Republican, 4 June 2003)

(3)   As we listen to the articles *in the paper and the TV and the radio*, too often we hear that saying, doom and gloom. But there is a different

Table 10.1   Number of References to Major US Newspapers Made by Speakers in the House

	Wton Post	NY Times	LA Times	Wall St J	NY Post	Total
Democrats	66	37	4	9	0	116
Republicans	9	13	2	11	4	39
Total	75	50	6	20	4	145

picture [. . .] Those who have been to Iraq, as I have, and many of my colleagues, have seen a different picture.

(Mark Kennedy, Republican, 23 September 2003)

(4) I went with apprehension because I was concerned that I would find the story of hopelessness, of pessimism because *I had read the papers and I had watched the television* [. . .] but when I returned home, I had great optimism and I had great hope because *what we see on TV and what we read in the papers* is not the real story of Iraq and is not representative of what is actually happening.

(Chris Chocola, Republican, 30 September 2003)

When a concordance was made of the item *TV* in the *HoR* corpus, the word *Hollywood* appeared serendipitously in the textual vicinity more than once. When *Hollywood* in turn was concordanced, it was found to be mentioned twenty-eight times by Republicans but not once by a Democrat. The cotext revealed that, in contrast to the relative mildness of their objections to press coverage, what truly enraged a number of Republican speakers was the political meddling of actors in current affairs. Their comments ranged from the relatively reasonable questioning of qualifications:

(5) for people like Julia Roberts [. . .] they certainly are not masters of foreign knowledge or foreign affairs.
They ought to stick with acting.

(Scott McInnis, Republican, 19 March 2003)

to the utterly vituperative:

(6) Sean Penn, you are a traitor to the United States of America. You gave aid and comfort to the enemy. How many American lives will your little fact-finding trip to Iraq cost?

(7) Why, you bunch of pitiful, hypocritical, idiotic spoiled mugwumps. Get your head out of the sand and smell the Trade Towers burning.

(both Scott McInnis, Republican, 25th May 2003)

United Kingdom

In contrast with US representatives, British MPs are not averse to singling out individual papers for praise or, more usually, blame. The *Guardian* is taken to task twice, once for tendentiousness (Geoff Hoon, Labour) and once for inaccuracy (Denis MacShane, Labour); the *Telegraph* twice also, once for inaccuracy (Hoon) and once simply for being the *Telegraph*

(Caplin, Lab) whilst the *Mail* is accused by both Labour and Conservatives of writing 'pure fiction' (Tony Blair, Labour; Michael Ancram, Conservative), once of running 'populist plebiscites' (Denis MacShane, Labour) and once for its 'isolationist, anti-European traditions' (Denis MacShane again). The *Telegraph* is praised on one occasion for its 'enterprising journalists' (Julian Lewis, Con).[3]

In general, the role and the behaviour of the press is a far more controversial question in the UK Parliament than in the United States. Another inkling we get of this is in a comparison of the—admittedly rather few— questions on embedded reporters. The mentions of embedded reporters in *HoR* reflect how supportive they were of the US war effort, for good if you are pro-intervention:

(8)   If we talk to the **embedded reporters** and listen to our men and women overseas, they want to finish the job

> (Randy Duke Cunningham, Republican, 3 April 2003)

(9)   Martin Savage of *CNN*, **embedded** with the 1st Marine battalion, was talking with four young marines near his foxhole this morning live on *CNN*. He had been telling the story of how well the Marines had been looking out for and taking care of him since the war started.

> (Heather Wilson, Republican, 2 April 2003)

for ill, if you are not:

(10)   We were drowned, literally, in the rhetorical excesses and visual stimulus of **embedded media**, following along with and literally with the troops. We were regaled with admonitions to support the troops by virtue of not questioning the policies that sent those troops in the first place.

> (Neil Abercrombie, Democrat, 3 August 2003)

This can be compared to the open criticism as expressed by Christopher Chope (Conservative) in example (16) and in the following 'friendly' question to the British secretary of state for Defence and his reply:

(11)   KEVIN HUGHES (Labour): Do our military top brass not have better things to do than answer well rehearsed questions from journalists who seem to have first-class honours degrees in hindsight, and most of whom would probably run a mile if a 40 watt bulb popped next to them?
      GEOFFREY HOON (Labour): My hon Friend tempts me [. . .] some **embedded journalists**—who are doing a tremendous job of communicating the details of what is taking place in Iraq back to the UK and elsewhere—have perhaps occasionally exaggerated the nature of the conflict, particularly if they are unused to gunfire.

> (3 April 2003)

Despite the conventional compliment—'doing a tremendous job' (see 10.2)—the 'rhetorical excesses' are here represented as hindering the war effort rather than supporting it.

But exaggeration is the least of the vices attributed to the fourth estate:

(12) That brings me to the current fear and uncertainty. If I belonged to a terrorist organisation in Iraq or Afghanistan, I would like the disunity and division that I see in the United Kingdom press and on *CNN* and *BBC* reports.

(David Burnside, Ulster Unionist, 11 March 2003)

'Disunity' could be taken as a euphemism for 'disloyalty'.[4]

As can be gleaned from the episodes so far, one organization above all is fingered for blame, the *BBC*.

10.1.4. The BBC: *A Particular Case*

Despite its protestations to the contrary and despite the carefully contrived conclusions to the Cardiff Report (see Clark 2007 and 10.2), the overwhelming evidence from the *CorDis Corpus* is that the *BBC* was very widely perceived as a thorn in the side of the pro-interventionist campaign and furnished considerable succour to the antiwar movement.

Starting with the evidence from *HoR*, the *BBC* is cited with approval and in support of their arguments six times by antiwar Democrats (four different speakers), for instance:

(13) all we have to do is read the *BBC*

(Jim McDermott, Democrat, 9 June 2003)

But only once, and antagonistically by a Republican:

(14) or the lower but probably equally preposterous figure of 10,000 [killed] advanced by the British Foreign Secretary and repeated by the *BBC*

(Curt Weldon, Republican, 16 July 2003)

As regards the US press, the *New York Daily News* brackets the *BBC* with *Al Jazeera*:

(15) Even *Al Jazeera* and the *BBC* couldn't spin this story as it played out for the world—including a stunned Arab world—to see. This was fact, not ideological fiction [. . .] a spontaneous declaration of liberation.

(*New York Daily News*, 10 April 2003)

In the UK itself, including in the House of Commons, the criticism was fiercer still:

(16) Does the Secretary of State agree that false claims about civilian casualties have been given credence by the conduct of *BBC* correspondents
in Baghdad? Is it not an insult to *BBC* licence-fee payers that they are,
in effect, being forced to subsidise Saddam's propaganda machine?

(Christopher Chope, Conservative, 3 April 2003)

Some felt that the Corporation not only opposed the war, but was negative
to the point of irresponsibility about the attempts at reconstruction:

(17) The first argument that is made is that post-war Iraq is a mess, that
our forces are unwelcome and that, in the words of that infamous *BBC*
report, ordinary Iraqis are somehow now worse off than they were
under the Saddam regime.

(George Osborne, Conservative, 22 October 2003)

This negativity seems to have been felt even in Iraq:

(18) The new governing council may have its limitations, but at a press
conference on 13 July, Talabani said: "Why do you say its powers are
limited? The *BBC* always tries to distort Iraq's news [. . .]"

(Donald Anderson, Labour, 16 July 2003)

Perhaps the accusation to be debated most seriously is that the *BBC*, rather than
reporting events, arrogated to itself the role of player in the political arena:

(19) Because there is no effective political opposition, certain journalists,
including certain correspondents at the *BBC*, believe that it is their job
to generate a feeding frenzy of a kind that—in their view, as they have
openly been saying—could bring down the Government.

(Mike Gapes, Labour, 4 June 2003)

which, of course, revives the old debate over whether a public service broadcaster, financed by a universal license fee, can justifiably behave like a pri-
vately owned channel or newspaper organization in taking overt stances on
major political issues.[5] In fact, *CNN* was perceived as having a very similar
stance to the war as the *BBC* but was not stigmatized to the same extent.[6]
It also raises the related and equally ancient question of quality, as Andrew
Marr himself, a prominent *BBC* journalist, remarks:

the *BBC* has to offer a gold standard for journalistic integrity and fair-
ness or it is doomed: if the Commons does not believe that the licence
fee buys Britain a range of broadcast journalism that is better and more
reliable than anything the market would provide [. . .] then a core
reason for the Corporation's existence disappears.

(Marr 2004:320)

Turning to the debate around the Hutton Inquiry, in which the *BBC*'s supposed desire to become a major player was certainly requited, one of the more interesting questions was: how would the Conservative press react to Lord Hutton's conclusions in which, though the government was indeed criticized, the main onus of blame was laid at the door of the *BBC*? Would it side with the Labour government or with the odious *BBC*, widely viewed as having been anti-Conservative for quite some time (Aitken 2007)? In the event, the *Telegraph* chose to concentrate its fire on the *BBC*, see box 10.1.

10.1.5. The Papers 1: On Embeds and War Zone Correspondents

Both the US and UK press express considerable interest in embedded and out-of-Baghdad reporting, most of it quite critical. From the personal and professional point of view, attitudes range from the sarcastic (this from a humorous mock dictionary of media war terms):

(20) Embed: Journalist who gets to pretend to be an Army guy and wears cool desert camouflage and writes about riding around in tanks.

(New York Daily News, 5 April 2003)

Box 10.1   The buck mustn't stop with Gilligan

By Alasdair Palmer

Last week's evidence to the Hutton Inquiry was a catastrophe for the *BBC*. Greg Dyke, the *BBC*'s Director-General, Richard Sambrook, its Director of News, and Andrew Gilligan, the Defence Correspondent for Today, all appeared.

    Their testimony amounted to a comprehensive withdrawal of all the main claims which the *BBC* has so doggedly defended since Mr Gilligan first made the infamous broadcast reporting that the Government had "sexed up" its intelligence dossier on Iraq, inserting claims that it knew to be false

    [...]

    The inquiry has shown that the *BBC* was guilty of precisely what it accused the Government of doing: it was the *BBC* that "sexed up" its dossier, and it was the *BBC* which, when the truth became obvious, tried to conceal it.

    It is an appalling indictment against an organisation to whom we all look to be the guardian of the basic journalistic virtue of accuracy.

Daily Telegraph, 21 September 2003

---

to the envious:

(21) The story, for a reporter, is in one of two places: in Baghdad, which it is almost impossible to get to now, or in the southern desert with the Marines. To be there, however, reporters had to "embed" with the Pentagon months ago. Most experienced war reporters balked at the notion of being so controlled and having to obey a 12-page booklet put forth by the American war machine.

"We were all too arrogant, we thought we were too good to embed," complained one veteran war correspondent. "So we gave the slots to the domestic news reporters. Now look at where they are and look at where we are!"

Most of the experienced reporters—John Simpson, Fergal Keane, Allan Little—are marooned on borders everyone thought would open up.

(*The Times*, 27 March 2003)

The US embeds are criticized by both the US and UK press, as well as the occasional politician, for their shortsighted jingoism:

(22) Why have the media bought the administration's propaganda that we come to Iraq with clean hands and virgin swords [. . .] Surely, even embedded journalists recall that it was Reagan administration special envoy Rumsfeld who met with Hussein in the 1980s to guarantee US support for Iraq's war with Iran.

(*Los Angeles Times*, 18 April 2003)

(23) I think in many cases the media got in bed with the war; and "embedded" really had a double meaning.

(Trent Franks, Republican, 19 June 2003)

Much is made of the problems they face, which include, apart from danger, satisfying the demands of real-time TV:

(24) Most journalists simply don't have time to gather enough information before presenters sitting in cosy London studios throw irritating questions at them which they often cannot answer

(*The Times*, 27 March 2003)

and military vetting:

(25) Richard Gainsford, an 'embedded' *BBC* reporter, said recently: 'We have to check each story we have with (the military). And the captain, who's our media liaison officer, will check with the colonel, and they will check with Brigade headquarters as well.'

(John Pilger, *Mirror*, 5 April 2003)

whilst:

(26) In Baghdad, it's even harder. Journalists must comply with the [Iraqi] government-appointed minder who watches their reports. During the excellent broadcasts of Sky's David Chater from the roof of the Ministry of Information, one can practically see the shadow of his minder.

(The Times, 27 March 2003)

But the main discussion is about the politics and efficacy of such reporting. For some, 'embedding' is simply Pentagon suppression and manipulation, a plot to feed us allied propaganda. Others point out that the arrangements of the last Gulf War, where only a 'permitted few' 'pool' journalists were taken along for the ride, made nobody happy, whilst the third possibility, letting everybody go wherever they wish, is hardly feasible: 'OK, it is a problem. But we don't have a fleet of taxis' (Major Blumenfeld, *New York Post*, 8 March). It is also pointed out that reporters who did try to go it alone, so-called 'unilaterals', frequently ran into trouble or worse:

(27) the risks were huge, as the death of the veteran ITN reporter Terry Lloyd showed. I heard that the coalition forces received no fewer than 60 calls from desperate 'unilaterals' travelling alone in the desert who came under fire.

(The Times, 27 March 2003)

But, for the conspiracy theorists, even this is part of the plot:

(28) The threats are now not even subtle, such as this from our Defence Secretary, Geoff Hoon. "One of the reasons for having journalists [embedded]," he said, "is to prevent precisely the kind of tragedy that occurred to an ITN crew; because [Terry Lloyd] was not part of a military organisation." And in those circumstances, we can't look after all those journalists
   Like a mafia boss explaining the benefits of a protection racket, Hoon is saying: do as you are told or face the consequences.

(John Pilger, Independent on Sunday, 6 April 2003)

There is some appreciation of the headaches that the media cause the military as an organization:

(29) This experiment in what the military calls "embedding" entails grafting what amounts to a presidential-campaign-sized press corps onto an army in combat.

As any White House press secretary can tell [the 'military media's front line'], there is no hell quite so annoying as the hell of an infantilized media pack.

(*New York Post*, 8 March 2003)

but very little of the problems faced by the private soldier, whose job is made still more hazardous in keeping embeds out of harm's way (see example 27). When squaddies are mentioned they are simply (as usual) doing a 'good job' (see 10.2): 'I believe the public's understanding of what our troops are achieving is increased by the access we have given the media' (Geoff Hoon, *The Times*, 28 March 2003).

10.1.6. Reporting, Observing, and the Observer's Paradox

The item *truth* occurs 178 times in the newspaper sections of the *CorDis Corpus*, and is the most frequent nonwar or politics-related abstract noun. It is highly likely to feature in keyword lists when comparing these texts to a corpus of any nonjournalistic discourse type. Truth is a commodity which, of course, can be *told, spoken,* and *known* can be *dangerous, undeniabl,e* and a *casualty*, but it can also be *lost, forbidden,* and *buried.* Journalists are obsessed with the idea of truth but they also seem in general to have a very naïve if proprietorial grasp of the concept, philosophically speaking. The 'God's Truth' view of reporting is highly prevalent among journalists, who often like to feel they write 'the first draft of history' (James Cameron, quoted by Pilger, *Independent on Sunday*, 6 April 2003 in an article entitled 'The War for Truth', which truth Pilger duly reveals).

Slightly more sophisticated is the realization that reporting is seeing events though the prism of the reporter and that any lack of awareness of this subjectivity is dangerous:

(30) It's media bias at its most embedded, because those who are guilty of it don't even know they are guilty of it.

(*New York Post*, 23 March 2003)

Note, however, the use of the distancing item 'those'. 'We', of course, are never guilty of media bias.

One of the most sophisticated comments on the topic was the following, which explains how the bias in media organizations can arise, independent of party-political standpoint, through the banding together of the socioculturally like-minded:

(31) Editors do not behave in this way because they are told what to do [. . .] However, producers, editors and presenters of similar views do

flock together. The brisk midmarket populism of *Sky* attracts people who, were they in print journalism, would fit comfortably into the staff of the *Mail*, just as the *BBC* newsrooms attract *Guardian* types. What they choose to show us is what they believe to be true; the bias is in their beliefs.

(William Rees-Mogg, The Times, 24 March 2003)

The same writer is one of the few to show awareness of how war reporting, and especially the embedding of reporters in fighting units, is the very embodiment of the observer's paradox. Embedding not only means a different kind of reporting but that the presence of observers is bound to affect the nature of the event, the war, itself: 'Television has changed wars', he says:

(32) For news of the war, as opposed to analysis and opinion, television has long since overtaken the newspapers.

Television even dominates the strategy of warfare; the whole shock-and-awe doctrine is based on psychological warfare waged by television. Bombs are dropped in order to be filmed and shown on the box.

Wars have always been fought by influencing people's minds, and television is the open road into the minds of allies as well as enemies.

(The Times, 24 March 2003)

We might discern too the note of envy of a paper journalist for the TV colleagues. This sentiment is, however, countered by another print journalist:

(33) My advice, which I intend to follow, is not to spend too much time watching the *BBC* or *Sky* or *CNN*, and more time reading newspapers. Words are calmer and more considered than pictures, and they are often better at conveying the truth.

(Mail, 6 April 2003)

Note, however, how we have come full circle, back to the notion of 'truth'.

10.1.7. The Papers 2: Papers on Papers

At an early stage in the war, the polling agency *YouGov* conducted a survey of UK newspaper readers' attitudes to the war—was it 'right' or 'wrong'; it is reported here in Figure 10.1.

It is interesting to note how the readerships of the *Mirror*, vociferously antiwar, and the *Mail*, by and large pro-intervention, but with sceptical reserves, are split in an identical manner.

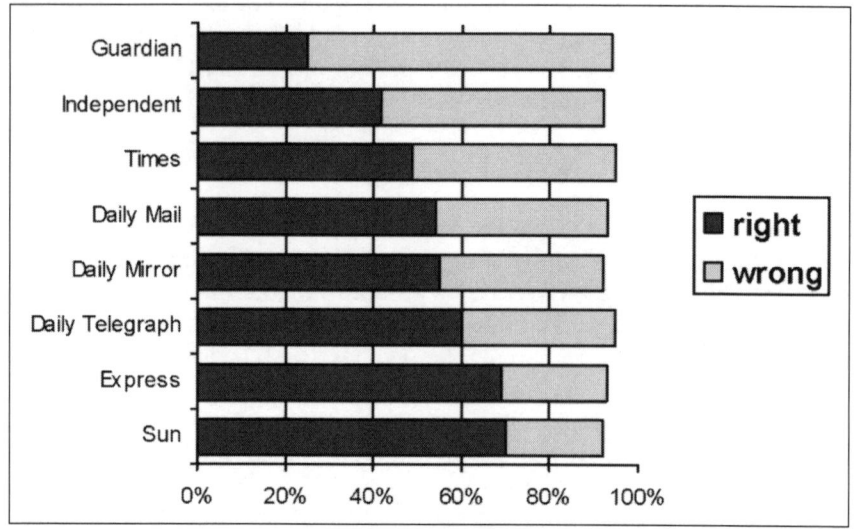

Figure 10.1   Results of the *Telegraph/ITV News* war poll, conducted by *YouGov* March 27–April 1, 2003. The graph reports percentages of British newspaper readers agreeing and disagreeing with the Coalition intervention in Iraq. The sample was 3,682 adults and the national averages were 55 per cent saying it was right and 36 per cent wrong.

In their political content, the *Independent*, the *Mirror*, and the *New York Times* (with the notable exception of William Safire) were more or less univocally antiwar. In contrast, none of the papers in the *CorDis Corpus* was unreservedly pro-intervention. Even right-leaning papers like the *Telegraph*, the *Mail*, and *The Times* (wisely, given the more or less even division among its readers) carried articles of both stances, as well as a good number of pieces which were sceptical or admonitory without being explicitly opposed to war. The most pro-intervention UK paper was, unsurprisingly, the *Sun*, but even this carried the occasional hesitant article, warning perhaps of casualties among 'our lads' and questioning the need for all-out war. A major problem for rightist pro-intervention writers in the UK was to press the case for military action without expressing support for a Labour government. A frequent solution was to maximize attention on Labour antiwar rebels, especially Cook and Short, whilst exhorting Blair to do more. Both camps claimed to have the majority of the people on their side. The most vicious duel was between two redtops, the *Mirror* and the *Sun*, the latter accusing the former of being 'unpatriotic' and 'anti-troops' and inviting its readers to switch papers, to which the former replies:

(34) And our message to the *Sun* is: our readers don't read your paper because you are a nasty little rag that thinks this war's all a bit of a laugh.[7]

(*Mirror,* 8 April 2003)

As regards the broadsheets, the *Guardian*, a newspaper constantly obsessed by the doings of its rivals, is perhaps the most aggressive, as the following edited extract (box 10.2) illustrates:

Box 10.2   Civilian Targets

The *Telegraph* should curb its instincts

At times of war the Daily *Telegraph* comes over all proprietorial, exuding a slight air of offence at the presumption of other media organisations in wishing to play a role. The paper decided not to keep its own correspondent in Baghdad during the recent fighting. No one could possibly criticise the editor for that call. At the same time, it is a little hard to take the persistent sniping at those who did decide to stay in that hellishly dangerous war zone, as well as at other media organisations which do not apparently meet the *Telegraph*'s exacting journalistic standards. Last week the paper accused British journalists in Baghdad of "unintentionally helping Saddam". Much more damagingly, it also argued that the Palestine Hotel, where most western reporters were staying, was being used by the Iraqi regime. This editorial appeared on the day after the building had been shelled, killing two journalists, and came unforgiveably close to implying that the hotel was a legitimate target.

This was followed by a swingeing attack on the *BBC*, which has apparently had "a terrible war"; it was pronounced guilty of bias, vanity, failure to report the news, and of not being in support of our armed forces. The mood among licence-payers was said to be mutinous.

This seems unlikely. Most viewers have been deeply impressed by the courage, the stamina and the cool-headed reporting of Rageh Omaar from Baghdad. Andrew Gilligan, a former *Sunday Telegraph* reporter also in Baghdad, has been outstandingly good on Radio 4. There have been strong supporting roles from such as John Simpson, Frank Gardner, Mark Urban, Philippa Thomas and Brian Hanrahan, never mind the World and Arabic services. Major General Patrick Cordingley, former Commander of the Desert Rats and a military commentator this time around, went out of his way at the weekend to praise the Today programme for its lack of bias and general objectivity.

The truth is that the *BBC* offends all the *Telegraph*'s free market fundamentalism, which is why the paper never misses an opportunity to put the boot in. There is something rather petty and peculiarly graceless about doing it at this time, and in such a fashion.

Guardian, 14 April 2003

The piece is peppered with intensifying epideictic expressions, both 'in blame' of the *Telegraph* and in praise of the *BBC*. The former include: *all proprietorial, persistent sniping, much more damaging, unforgiveably, swingeing attack, free market fundamentalism, put the boot in* and *peculiarly graceless*. The latter include: *deeply impressed, outstandingly good, strong supporting roles* and *went out of his way . . . to praise*. If any were needed, this gives firm substantiation of Aristotle's assertion that amplification is particularly appropriate to epideictic rhetoric. Closely allied to intensification is generalization: *at times of war the Daily Telegraph comes over all proprietorial* and *the paper never misses an opportunity*. It is not sufficient to criticize the rival paper for this particular stance on this particular issue; blame is generalized so that everything about it is rotten due to its *free market fundamentalism*.

Apart from making false and partial allegations, what else is the *Telegraph* accused of? Openly, of presumptuousness, of implying the Palestine Hotel is a legitimate target (that is, the journalists who were killed deserved what they got), of, as we saw, fundamentalism, of hyper-aggressiveness (*never misses* [. . .] *boot in*), pettiness and gracelessness. The covert insinuations are equally grave. Withdrawing your journalists from Baghdad: is that dereliction of duty or actual cowardice? (Note the concessive, in textual rather than grammatical terms): 'No-one could possibly criticise . . . ', immediately followed by the contrastive 'At the same time . . . '.) Meanwhile, the last sentence (*There is . . . fashion*) is a pointed echo of the conventional sentiment that to criticize authority in wartime is tantamount to disloyalty.

If the antiwar journalists were the more aggressive and self-righteous in their attacks on other newspapers, which were projected as more extreme than they actually were and construed as villainous for beliefs they might not actually hold, this is only because the pro-intervention side reserves its vitriol for the left-leaning *broadcast* journalism, which it sees as a better target, as the following edited *Sun* comment demonstrates, see box 10.3.

Epideictic amplification is once more very apparent, with a steady supply of both intensifying modifiers *worst possible* but also innately hyperbolic items such as *hysterical, enormity, pumping out*, and so on.

What are the allegations made against the *BBC, Channel 4,* and the *Independent*? They include partiality, disloyalty, gracelessness (first paragraph), and aggressiveness ('shock troops of the British broadcast media'; the *Independent*'s 'thuggish' columnist). In other words, precisely the same accusations levelled at the *Telegraph* by the *Guardian*. Both articles equally assume that they express the views of the majority of people (*Guardian*: 'most viewers have been deeply impressed . . . '; *Sun*: 'we should have known better'); both essentially present an exaggerated caricature of their opponents and their arguments. The *Sun* article relies far more on humour and a more personal tone (especially in the use of *I* and *we*), but even the *Guardian* makes tactical use of colloquial language ('comes over all . . . ', 'but the

---

Box 10.3   Good evening: Here is the worst possible news

Littlejohn

HYSTERICAL and dishonest in opposition to the war, graceless and defiant in defeat. No, not the Iraqi regime but the shock troops of the British broadcast media.

Here's a story you may have missed. The aircraft carrier Ark Royal, stationed in the Gulf, removed *BBC* News 24 from the channels available on board after complaints from servicemen and women about pro-Saddam bias.

Consider the enormity of this. The pride of the British fleet was forced to take off the air a service provided by the British Broadcasting Corporation because it was pumping out enemy propaganda in wartime.

I'm not arguing that the *BBC* should be the broadcast arm of the British government. But it has a duty to be fair and balanced.

While plenty of individual editors and correspondents have done just that, the overall tone of the *BBC*'s coverage since before a shot was fired has been carping, anti-war, anti-British, anti-American.

They must have a sign in the *BBC* newsroom reading: Accentuate The Negative.

Even the *BBC*'s own defence correspondent was moved to write a memo complaining about his own organisation's coverage after the death of two soldiers was described as "the worst possible news" for the Allies.

[...]

With the Allies in control of Baghdad and Basra, with Saddam's statue toppling, with Iraqis dancing in the streets, with opinion polls swinging firmly behind the military action, a moment of modest rejoicing may have been in order.

If that's what any of us were expecting from [*BBC*'s] Question Time, we should have known better.

On the panel, along with representatives of the three main parties and the head of the CBI, was one Mark Steel, who writes a "humorous" column in The Independent.

What they didn't tell you was that Steel is a leading activist in the thuggish Socialist Workers Party.

Yet there he was given equal billing with democrats and elected politicians [...]

Channel 4 News is just as bad [...] On Monday, when the tanks entered Baghdad and it looked as if the war would soon be over, presenter Jon Snow wore the expression of a man whose dog had just been run over.

There was an air of mourning about the whole programme.

If and when the corpse of Saddam is found, *Channel 4* News will probably slap his official portrait on screen and play nothing but martial music for an hour.

Sun April 11, 2003

boot in'). Both are heavily ironic (*Guardian*: 'other media organisations, which do not apparently meet the *Telegraph*'s exacting standards'; *Sun*: 'the expression of a man whose dog had just been run over', 'play nothing but martial music', and many other instances). Both take care to quote from a *prima facie* 'unlikely'—and therefore all the more persuasive—source: a soldier praising the *BBC* in the *Guardian*, the *BBC*'s own defence correspondent complaining about its defeatism in the *Sun*.

To conclude this first part, then, what is noticeable is how both camps make very similar accusations, blame the other side for much the same things. Firstly, of condoning brutality: the brutality of war for the antiwar writers, the brutality of the psychotic Saddam regime for the pro-interventionists. Secondly, of 'armchair' expertise, that is, sounding off on military matters of which they are not competent (see the discussion in 10.2). And, finally, of being disloyal to 'our lads': of not supporting their brave endeavours for the interventionists, for putting them in harm's way in the first place for the antiwar camp.

SECTION 2. SOME CONCLUDING REFLECTIONS ON CADS RESEARCH: THE ARMCHAIR AND THE MACHINE[8]

Stubbs has lately taken his colleagues somewhat to task, lamenting how 'corpus linguists have generally been very vague about the methods they use' (2006:17). He is not referring to any lack of description of the techniques and technologies employed, which are often, as in this volume, adequately discussed (see also Baker 2006 for a comprehensive summary). He means the consideration of where those techniques fit into wider theoretical questions of the scientific validity and adequacy of what corpus linguists do. And, given the immense variety of things which corpus linguists or, rather, linguists-who-use-corpora do nowadays, as reflected in Teubert and Krishnamurthy's recent compendium (2007) (after, it must be said, a rather inward-looking start, when there was a certain hostility to engaging with other disciplines, even other branches of language study), these questions are urgent.

In modern times, Western scientific practice has drifted among four stances: respect for authority (generally Scripture and Aristotle), rationalist introspection (Descartes: *cogito ergo sum*—I *introspect* therefore I am), 'observationism', characterized by distrust of theory (Francis Bacon: 'The intellect, left to itself, ought always to be suspected'), and, finally, a recognition of the mutually reinforcing hermeneutic interaction of theory and observational data. To its critics (see 10.4), much corpus research has seemed to dwell too stubbornly in the third of these positions: observation for observation's sake. But 'without theory, science is just picking up shells on the beach' (Silver 1998:16). It seems appropriate therefore to conclude this volume with a collection of questions and reflections on the type of research described herein and how it fits into a wider theoretical framework.

10.2. Is CADS Scientific?

Perhaps the greatest of all debates in twentieth-century philosophy of science was over the 'correct' way of describing and prescribing experimentation, with the direct correlation of thus establishing the most valid method by which science can 'proceed'. There was general agreement that there were two overall possibilities, but there was great controversy over their legitimacy and efficacy.

The first school held that the mainstay of science is *induction* (the latinization of ἐπαγωγή, one of the many terms in logic first found in Aristotle), that is: 'the process of inferring a general law or principle from the observation of particular instances' (*OED*), which Ellis (1985) usefully renames 'the research-then-theory approach'. It typically has the following stages:

1. Select a phenomenon for investigation.
2. Collect a relevant data-set.
3. Look inside the data-set for systematic patterns.
4. Formalize significant patterns as rules describing natural events.

To which we must add the vital rider that the theoretical stance of the researcher will, of course, influence the nature of the research question adopted. In corpus linguistics this will tend to include a commitment to the idea that lexis helps organize language structure; in CADS it may well also involve a sociopolitical view of the world.

These procedures sound fairly familiar to researchers into language. We observe one set of data in the hope of discovering recurring patterns (because patterns have meanings), then we analyze another data-set to see whether these patterns recur there too, and so on and so forth, in the search for confirmation of their existence and function. One significant feature of much modern science is that stage 2, the data collection, is not necessarily carried out by the same individuals as steps 1, 3, and 4. The mapping of the human genome, for instance, constitutes a data-set for a whole branch of science. In corpus linguistics we may well decide that a suitable data-set (usually a corpus) for a particular research already exists (perhaps the *British National Corpus* or the *Bank of English*).

However, induction has had its detractors. Popper, famously, attacks it largely on the grounds of its inefficiency and sluggishness. Confirmation, he says, is slow and never certain. He resurrects Hume's objection to induction that predicting future events or the future behaviour of a system on the basis of observations (by definition *past* observations) is not logically justified; something which has held in all 'past futures' will not necessarily hold in 'today's future' or in all 'future futures'. This is especially relevant to a changing system such as language. Popper claimed instead that science advances best by deductive *falsification* of bold conjecture, which is sudden and decisive. This is the process Ellis calls 'the theory-then-research approach', which develops over five stages:

1. Develop an explicit theory (better, hypothesis).
2. Derive a testable prediction from the hypothesis.
3. Conduct a research to test the prediction.
4. Modify (or abandon) the hypothesis if the prediction is disconfirmed.
5. Test a new prediction if the first prediction is confirmed.

Popper reserves the term *corroboration* to define successful prediction testing, though many have argued that in practice it is indistinguishable from the process of confirmation employed in induction.

Occasionally CADS research is hypothesis testing in this way. Clark (2007), for instance, investigates the language use of *BBC* embedded reporters during the early stages of the Iraq war to test the claims of the Cardiff report (*Cardiff School of Journalism, Media and Cultural Studies*), commissioned by the *BBC* itself but not conducted by linguists, that there was no evidence to support the frequent accusations of an anti-intervention, anticoalition and general negative stance in *BBC* reporting. By contrast, she found no lack of such pessimism in the linguistic trace. Similarly, in this volume, Miller and Johnson test G. Lakoff's hypothesis (or 'claims') that politicians of different persuasions tend to favour certain types of metaphors.

For fifty years, from the 1930s to the 80s, Popper's ideas proved highly seductive, but fashions change, even in the philosophy of science, and induction has acquired many defenders. Popperism came under much scrutiny from critics who claim that his procedural approach was not only unduly restrictive but also did not reflect how scientists actually work. Feyeraband (1975), Popper's rebellious pupil, felt that the idea that science can and should be run according to fixed and universal rules was both unrealistic and pernicious. Gardner too is unconvinced: 'Falsifications', he says, 'are much rarer in science than searches for confirming instances'. 'Astronomers', he continues, 'look for signs of water on Mars. They do not think they are making efforts to falsify the conjecture that Mars never had water' (2001:13). We might add that CERN (European Organization for Nuclear Research) has spent billions of euros to build a particle accelerator to search for the Higgs boson in the hope, not of disproving its existence, but of actually finding one. And, surely, catching one will advance subnuclear research rather more swiftly and dramatically than failing to. 'Science operates mainly by induction (confirmation)', concludes Gardner. 'Popper's great and tireless efforts to expunge the word *induction* from scientific and philosophical discourse has utterly failed [. . .] It is hard to think of another philosophical battle so decisively lost' (2001:14). But what Popper was really discussing was the *logic* of scientific methodology (his principal work on the subject is, in fact, entitled *Logik der Forschung, The Logic of Scientific Discovery*), whereas practicing scientists are interested in what actually works. Induction may be faulty logic or no logic at all, but observation of past behaviour, underpinned by a theoretical model of how and perhaps why the system functions as it does, can form the basis for probabilistic predictive statements. It is the best we can do.

How does all this affect the more circumscribed—and decidedly more cash-strapped—world of corpus linguistics? Stubbs claims its 'methods are clearly broadly inductive, in the rough sense that observing large amounts of data leads to the proposal of significant patterns and generalisations' (2006:17). In consequence, anti-inductivist arguments are frequently levelled at corpus linguistics. Statements based on corpus analysis, it is said, are not statements about language, since corpora contain not language but only a form of linguistic trace; language itself is something entirely different and exists in the 'real world'; a corpus is therefore only representative of itself. Moreover, such statements can only be verified by reference to other corpora and so the process is circular. By the time a corpus has been compiled it is already out of date, since language has moved on. As they stand, such arguments are unimpeachable. We can only reply that it is the nature of scientific instrumentation to present an abstraction of the object of study: the Venus probe does not send us Venus or even bits of it. It sends us images. Similarly, the radio telescope supplies us with *representations* of radio waves. They appear to us to be helpful in increasing our knowledge of the object of study. So it is with language and corpora. The distinction between *noumena,* or 'things in themselves', and *phenomena,* our capabilities and efforts to experience them, was raised and discussed by Kant. The second can only ever afford a representation of the former but, again, we try to make the best of things.

It is plain, then, that in a piece of research like the one outlined in Section 1 of this chapter, the initial approach is of the inductive 'research first' type. The starting point is a research question, a phenomenon selected for examination, as Ellis puts it, rather than an explicit hypothesis. At the highest level, the research question is, of course, the CADS-type one informing the entire *CorDis* project—'how was the conflict in Iraq discussed and reported in US/UK political institutions and media?' (and 'how can we use corpus techniques to study it?'). The next step in inductive research generally consists in selecting or compiling a data-set which is appropriate to the research question. In actual practice, as with *CorDis*, this can begin when one has only the most general idea of a research question and the initial relevant data-set collection, at this first, highest level consisted of compiling the various *CorDis* subcorpora.

At the lower level of my more personal project, the research question is embedded in the overall one and slightly more delicate, namely: 'how was the conflict-reporting reported?' As with much CADS research, the initial data-set collection consisted of compiling word lists from the original raw corpus and, since this research was clearly highly comparative in nature (contrasting one news organization's reporting to others, say, or the stance of the members of one political party to that of their rivals), the compiling of comparative keyword lists for manual analysis. One interesting aspect was that a degree of reconfiguration of the original corpora was necessary at this stage—in particular four new newspaper subcorpora were created by lumping together individual papers, namely UK qualities, UK tabloids, US qualities, US tabloids. Purists might well frown on such reconfiguration of the data-set during the process of data investigation, but one of the consequences of the highly serendipitous nature of CADS research is that unforeseen subquestions can arise that require the data-set to be resorted according to investigative requirements to allow new, alternative pathways into it.

In the following sections, then, we will look at two sample investigations, conducted during the piece of research reported in Section 1 of this chapter, of how induction and hypothesis testing combine and interact in corpus-assisted discourse studies.

armchair

Induction, then—the steady, perhaps rather undramatic collection and measurement of observational data leading to a more or less detailed description of a phenomenon—is our default background approach. But it is also frequently interspersed with more decisive moments of experimental hypothesis testing. As an instance from the current research, among the keyword data, the expression *armchair general* stood out. I—intuitively—formulated the twin hypotheses that both *armchair general* and *armchair* itself, used as a modifier, would be *over-the-fence* items (an over-the-fence item being one rarely if ever used by speakers about themselves; Partington 1998:74–76) and also have an unfavourable evaluative prosody (we might also, here, ask ourselves the question of what the difference might be, if any, between a 'hypothesis' and an explicitly formulated intuition).

Concordancing *armchair* in *CorDis*, the first and most obvious observation was that it is only ever used as a modifier. Secondly, there are several variants to *armchair generals*, namely, *armchair generalship, strategists, spectators, warriors,* and even *admiral*. A closer look at the cotext provided much corroboration for both the preceding hypotheses. Regarding the first, its over-the-fence quality, these terms were indeed normally used about others, and the term often indicated the pejorative member of a contrasted pair: *armchair generals* with *real generals*:

(35) It's something that many generals, now he would say armchair generals, have never forgiven him for.

(Matt Frei, BBC, 1 April 2003)

and see example (38), or they are set against *our troops*:

(36) tired, filthy, hungry, shot-at and sleepless, while back home the armchair generals loll before News 24.

(Mail, 4 March 2003)

Its unfavourable epideictic evaluation comes in several forms: it can be used either as an accusation of warmongering: 'may just dull Washington's armchair warriors for new enterprises', or lack of relevant expertise: 'the first casualty of war is the illusions of armchair strategists', or simply overexcitement: 'I am getting some helpful advice [. . .] that the Member for New Forest East has a doctorate in obsessions. I thought it better to suggest he had a doctorate in armchair generalship' (House of Commons, Geoff Hoon, Labour, 27 January 2003). Searches in other corpora, as well as happenchance during my own private reading, threw up quite a number of lexical variations on the same theme: *Mr Bush and his White House warriors* (*Mirror*), *Washington's diplomatic warrior, Colin Powell* (*BBC*), *keyboard warriors* (*Guardian* blog), and *Yankee jim-jam generals* (*Guardian* blog). Again, these variations on a theme tend to be used epideictically, to contrast one unfavourably evaluated entity with another more favourable one:

(37) That's not the taproom consensus of assorted half-pint bombardiers and white wine generals in the Pig and Missile but the considered judgment of the veteran Gulf War commanders William Nash and Barry McCaffery.

(Times, 26 March 2003)

So far, so good. Whether I was really trying to *falsify* (à la Popper) or *reinforce* my original hypotheses is a moot point; they have nevertheless been corroborated. However, there are a couple of flies in the ointment. What should we make of the following?

(38) THIS MUST be my fourth or fifth war as an armchair general.
     But, as any armchair general will tell you, the Second Gulf War is something else. It is the first media war. This means that we experts, safely ensconced on our sofas, possibly with a glass of wine or beer in our hands, can follow battlefield events almost before they happen.
     [But] we armchair generals—let's be honest—know infinitely less about how to fight wars than real generals.

> We armchair generals should back off a bit, and admit that the war being fought in our sitting rooms is not the real war at all, but a kind of media concoction which sometimes takes the form of gruesome entertainment.

> (*Mail*, 26 March 2003)

The term *armchair general* is clearly not an over-the-fence word in this text. But are we to take this as the single negative finding which falsifies our original hypothesis, as Popperism requires? A more realistic interpretation would be that we are confronted with an example of ironic self-deprecation—hardly envisaged in Popper's system.

This may seem a minor point but it has far-reaching repercussions for linguistic theory, particularly lexical priming theory. In brief, lexical priming is a self-reproducing *mental* phenomenon whereby the normal language user learns, by repeated acquaintance with a lexical item and by processes of analogy with other similar items, the typical behaviour of that item in interaction. In particular, we learn which other lexical items it co-occurs with regularly (*collocation*), which semantic sets it occurs with (*semantic association*; other authors would favour the term *semantic preference*), which grammatical categories it co-occurs with or avoids, and which grammatical positions it favours or disfavours (*colligation*), which positions in an utterance or sentence or paragraph or entire text it tends to prefer or to avoid occurring in (*textual collocation*) and whether it tends to participate in cohesion or not. The user then reproduces this behaviour in his/her own linguistic performance.

By metaphorical extension (a process common to all descriptions of grammar), the lexical item itself is said to be primed to behave in these particular ways, and so lexical priming is also regarded as a *textual* phenomenon. Thus, for example, the item *winter* is said to be primed to collocate with *in*, *that*, *during the*, and so on. As regards colligational behaviour, the expression *in winter* is primed to occur with the present tense in clauses expressing relational processes, whilst it displays a semantic preference to occur with expressions of 'timeless truths', for example: 'In winter, Hammerfest is a thirty-hour ride by bus from Oslo [. . .]'. In terms of textual collocation, in some kinds of discourse (e.g., travel writing) *in winter* is probably weakly primed to appear at the beginning of a sentence, as in the preceding.

A hostile critic might argue, however, that lexical priming theory is not proposed in a scientific fashion, in that its main proposition does not allow for the possibility of falsification thanks to the 'get-out clause' of overriding. The linguistic researcher predicts that an item has a particular priming, say, derogatory evaluation, or 'over-the-fence-ness' as in the example here, but when this is not respected in a particular instance of observation, the priming is said to have been overridden. Thus unsuccessful prediction can never falsify the framework.

In an ideal Popperian universe, there is no doubt great merit in expressing a theory in a way that invites falsification/corroboration. But what these 'disrespectful' instances actually prove is that real life is a good deal more complex, messier, and more interesting. Put bluntly: we see for a fact that a priming exists; we see for another fact that it is sometimes overridden. It is the task of the linguistic scientist, through plodding inductive procedures, to (a) elaborate probabilistic data on the likelihood of respect and overriding and (b) attempt to describe the precise circumstances in which it is possible to override a certain priming. What needs emphasizing is the vital role that counterexamples—those disrespectful instances—play; they do not *falsify* the theory of priming but they do lead the researcher to *refine* the description. A burning question in the modern philosophy of knowledge—of great relevance to linguistics—asks whether the interpretation of some issues at least is infinitely refinable. Another asks whether probabilistic statements are *in theory* only universal statements which are not yet sufficiently refined or whether some statements will always remain, even theoretically, probabilistic. Classical science has tended to work on the assumption that the object of enquiry is ultimately describable, but Heisenberg's uncertainty principle and Gödel's incompleteness theorems seem to argue that some matters are ultimately unknowable—and not just in practice because too complex, but even in theory.

It is also, above all, a reminder that linguistics rarely deals in what are known in the philosophy of physics as *universal statements*, such as the famous 'All swans are white' (more precisely 'if something is a swan, it is white'), which, of course, are highly falsifiable, in theory at least. Our questions, instead, tend to be *probabilistic* and *contingent*, roughly of the form 'under circumstances C, what is the statistical probability that, if something is A, then it is X (or displays X characteristics/properties, or has X function)'. Thus a CADS statement looks like: 'in media discussions of war reporting, if the item *armchair* is used as a modifier, then it has a very high probability of displaying an unfavourable evaluative prosody and a high probability of being employed as an over-the-fence term'.

The second insect in the balm becomes apparent when concordancing *armchair* in corpora of other discourse types. In *SiBol 93* and *SiBol 05* (that is, *Siena-Bologna*, the universities where it was compiled: two corpora of UK newspaper texts from, respectively, 1993 and 2005, 100 and 150 million words in size) it was found in a good number of expressions of bad evaluation ranging from the more-or-less indulgent *armchair athletes*, *armchair gardeners*, and *armchair quiz-masters*, to the scathing *armchair experts*, *armchair patriots*, and *armchair insurgents like Michael Moore*, to the comical 'Risk—the *armchair world-domination game*'. But it was also found in *armchair banking*, *armchair investing*, *armchair gambling*, *armchair shopping*, *armchair travelling*, and *armchair fieldwork*, all of which had a favourable prosody, being as fruitful and satisfying as the nonarmchair versions, but easier, quicker, and less hazardous (there is even an *armchair ride*, a semitechnical expression in horse racing indicating an easy victory). How, then, are we to describe the behaviour of *armchair*, which appears to conduct itself in two very different fashions? The distinction is not simply *armchair* + [category of person] = bad versus *armchair* + [activity] = good, as the disparaging nature of *armchair lamentation, armchair criticism,* or *armchair arithmetic* and the frequent complimentary evaluation of *armchair shopper* reveal. If we recall, Sinclair stipulates that a fixed evaluative prosody is one of the two indispensable properties of the lexical unit (10.1.1). We must conclude, therefore, that *armchair banking* is representative of a different lexical unit to *armchair expert*; in other words, *armchair* + [tedium] (good evaluation) is a different item from *armchair* + [military person] or [expert] (bad evaluation). To complicate the issue still further, however, some expressions seem to be able to mean, on different occasions, both types of *armchairing*: *armchair tours/tourist*, for instance, is sometimes good, because convenient, and sometimes bad because not the real thing. Polysemy is a challenging question for all language descriptions. Within lexical grammar, an item is said to have different senses if it displays separate collocational and colligational patternings, that is, primings. But just how different do they have to be, and where do we stop slicing the cake?

job

Word lists are not the only port of departure for serendipitous journeys. Lines from one concordance frequently elicit testable intuitions/hypotheses which lead the researcher on to further concordancing, which can then open up unexpected avenues of exploration, and so on, with, in a very real sense, the data leading the way.

In example (11), we noted the British secretary of state for Defence's use of the expression 'doing a tremendous job':

(39) some embedded journalists; who are doing a tremendous job of communicating the details of what is taking place in Iraq back to the UK and elsewhere

I decided to check my intuition that *job* had an important role to play in epideictic evaluation and in particular to investigate the hypothesis that [intensifier] + *job* was very commonly used in this discourse type (and by this type of speaker) to praise the military in some way, and so applying it to journalists was a marked use requiring explanation. Before beginning the investigation, however, I also felt it would be important to put some figure on 'commonly', in other words, to have an idea of *how* frequent this use was, relative to its overall incidence.

The item *job* was concordanced in the *HoC* subcorpus and, roughly as expected, of 172 occurrences overall, thirty-five (20.2 per cent) had a favourable intensifier in L1 (first item to the left) position. These included *excellent* (six times), *superb* (four), *remarkable, tremendous* (three), *heroic* (two), *fantastic, magnificent,* and *outstanding.* By contrast there were only six seemingly unfavourable intensifiers, namely, *bad* (two), *difficult* (two), *not an easy,* and *wrecking.* I write 'seemingly' because a closer look at *difficult* and *not an easy job* showed that they were in fact embedded inside wider favourable contexts:

(40) The US is doing a tremendously difficult job in tremendously difficult circumstances.

(Edward Garnier, Conservative, 10 September 2003)

It is praiseworthy to be doing a *difficult job* to the best of your ability.

Closer analysis showed that the situation was more complex still. Only fifty of the 172 occurrences were premodified by an adjective and so the thirty-five favourably intensified occurrences comprise 70 per cent of this particular subset, and if we take the template *a(n)* [adjective] *job,* the favourable occurrences account for 86.5 per cent.

It was, furthermore, also very clear that, when the item was not premodified by an adjective, the L1 item was either a possessive or *the.* And these two patterns—*a(n)* [adjective] *job* and [*the*/possessive] *job*—were primed to appear in very different phraseologies. The most frequent collocate of the first was *doing* (eighteen occurrences) and typical phraseologies, revealed partly by eye, partly through *WordSmith*'s cluster tool, were *doing a remarkable/superb/excellent job on behalf of this country/in difficult circumstances.* In this phraseology, those being praised for doing the job are most generally military or police personnel, sometimes *our troops* or *the security services,* sometimes a particular regiment, or sometimes one of our allies or dependents:

(41) Our servicemen and women are doing a remarkable job in difficult circumstances.

(Michael Ancram, Conservative, 10 September 2003)

(42) The Iraqi Red Crescent are doing a fantastic job

(Cheryl Gillan, Conservative, 17 December 2003)

In Hoey's terms, we might say that the pattern *a(n)* [adjective] *job* is primed in this discourse type to have an intensifier in the adjective slot, displays a semantic association/preference for a military actor, and has a pragmatic priming for epideictic praise. In slightly different terms—those of speaker *intentionality*—we might equally say that, whenever a speaker, in these particular discourse circumstances, desires to praise the activities of a military (or associated) actor, there is a strong likelihood they will employ this pattern. The initial intuition-hypothesis was thus largely corroborated.

The most frequent verb collocates of the template [*the*/possessive] *job* were *do* and *get*, with *doing* and *done* following slightly further down the frequency list. Typical patterns were more varied and less emphatic than we saw for *a(n)* [intensifier] *job*, but frequently included *do the job, get on with their job,* and *get the job done,* with wider elements including *properly, can–cannot, enough resources to.* This pattern associates less frequently with military actors but is still most frequently a vehicle for epideictic praise, though not outstanding praise; more for fulfilling a duty rather then exceeding it. Very generally the pattern *a(n)* [intensifier] *job* has a temporal-semantic association with doing an ongoing job in the here and now, whilst the pattern [*the*/possessive] *job* associates with the ability to complete a more circumscribed task in the future, often with the hint of some present hindrance in the way.

As a next step, I also concordanced the plural form *jobs* and, as is often the case, the referential sense of the item and as a consequence the patterns and phraseologies it is found in are very different. *Job* in this discourse type tends to refer to a duty or a particular task, whilst *jobs* means 'waged occupation', 'livelihood'. It co-occurs in the *HoC* data with *new* (three), *civilian, good* (two), *extra,* and *quality.* There was nevertheless still an association with evaluation, *new jobs* and *extra jobs* being a good thing, whilst *killing jobs* (that is, destroying them) is very bad (see also Bayley 2004:237–69).

In *HoR, job* behaved in a similar manner. The *a/an* [adjective] *job* template was relatively even more frequent and there were other intensifiers to add to the list: *admirable, amazing,* and *awesome,* to name but three. But when *job* was analyzed in the other less similar *CorDis* discourse types, its behaviour was quite different. In the 250 occurrences of *job* in *Briefings,* another spoken corpus, the *a(n)* [intensifier] *job* occurs in twenty-three cases (9.2 per cent), all of them expressing epideictic praise and all, without exception, uttered by the podium. Briefings journalists rarely express praise in their questions. Similarly there are traces of the *get the job done* pattern in the podium's turns, but not in those of the journalists. Other patterns also stand out in podium discourse and show how the podium often falls back on rehearsed semifixed descriptions, for instance: *make sure X* [have] [*everything/all the* (*information/resources*)] [*he/it/they*] [need] *to do* [possessive] *job* (fifty-three times), *create* a* [*robust/strong*] *environment* (*as possible*) *for job creation* (*and economic growth*) (twenty-eight times) and (*cannot*) *find a job* (fourteen times).

If we turn to the written newspaper corpora, there are only a couple of instances of the first of our two templates, for example: 'Colin Powell did a superb job of laying out the case against Saddam' (*New York Post,* 6 February 2003). As for the second, the concept of completing a task in the face of hindrance is certainly present in the UK press in, for instance: *to finish their job, more time to do their job,* though sometimes, here, we also find the pattern exploited for criticism as in *should have done the job properly.* By and large, *job* retains a favourable prosody, but in this discourse type, it is also liable to ironic reversal (irony involving reversal of evaluation, Partington 2006b), as in the following:

(43) the administration is already picking and choosing who will be given *the lucrative job* of cleaning up the rubble [9]

(*New York Daily News*, 21 March 2003)

(44) It may seem a waste of good ink to take apart Robin Cook's arguments when he has made such *a good job* of discrediting himself

(*Times*, 8 April 2003)

(45) we already know that there are a lot of unpolished thugs in Saddam's army and *the job of fooling inspectors* is a routine one

(*Mirror*, 6 February 2003)

10.3. Summary of Reflections

CADS Methodology

It is generally accepted that there is a cline between the so-called hard sciences and the social (or human) sciences, rather than a hard-and-fast separation (perhaps as follows: mathematics-physics-chemistry-biochemistry-biology-zoology-ethology-anthropology-sociology and psychology). Linguistics occupies an interesting spot between the two since language belongs partly to the physical and partly to the human world. Corpus linguistics, on the one hand, to a degree objectifies human language behaviour and thus draws close to the harder end of the scale. CADS, on the other, reintroduces a greater focus on social and psychological aspects (see next section) and so borrows approaches from the social sciences. It is no surprise then to find combinations of research methods in play.

Thus, it has frequently been remarked how, in corpus-assisted discourse studies, the researcher combines quantitative and qualitative perspectives of the data. What, however, is less appreciated is how the CADS researcher also frequently exploits and alternates between two research methodologies, namely, inductive and deductive/falsificational methods

Given its exploratory nature, this type of research is both highly data-driven and serendipitous, in the sense that, during the course of the research, the data itself will inevitably dictate to a considerable degree which next steps to take (the corpus researcher as *wanderer* or *picaro*, linguistic vagabonds living off their wits). It is thus inductive in overall approach—Ellis's 'research-then-theory'—in having very general and flexible premises, and investigates some research question rather than testing a well-defined hypothesis. Nevertheless, as we saw in the previous section, there exists the possibility of firmer hypotheses being formulated during the course of the observations and analyses, and these can then in turn be tested against the data, using the Popperian deductive 'theory-then-research' method (the researcher as *traveller*, as *Marco Polo*, who knows where they are going but not what they will find).

Introspection, Intuition, and Judgement

The terms *intuition* and *introspection* are frequently found—and sometimes confusingly misused—in discussions of corpus linguistic methodology. As Stewart (2008) remarks, they are often conflated or used interchangeably, and yet they are two very different, almost opposite, processes. Intuition is defined by the *OED* as 'the immediate apprehension [. . .] by the mind without the intervention of any reasoning process', whilst introspection is described as 'looking within or into one's own mind; examination or observation of one's own thoughts, feelings or mental state'. The one is pre-ratiocination; the other is its embodiment.

Stewart points out how both terms have often received a bad press in corpus linguistics, especially unassisted 'armchair' introspection, at least when it eschews observation and consideration of available data. Fillmore provocatively compares the *modus operandi* of the armchair linguist and a certain type of one-dimensional corpus linguist, implying that the first relies on the mind, the second on the machine:

> the armchair linguist [. . .] sits in a deep soft comfortable armchair, with his eyes closed and his hands clasped behind his head. Once in a while he opens his eyes, sits up abruptly shouting, 'Wow, what a neat fact!', grabs his pencil, and writes something down. Then he paces around for a few hours in the excitement of having come still closer to knowing what language is really like.
>
> the corpus linguist [. . .] has all the primary facts that he needs, in the form of approximately one zillion running words, and he sees his job as that of deriving secondary facts from his primary facts. At the moment he is busy determining the relative frequencies of the eleven parts of speech as the first word of a sentence.
>
> These two don't speak to each other very often, but when they do the corpus linguist says to the armchair linguist, 'Why should I think that what you tell me is true?', and the armchair linguist says to the corpus linguist, 'Why should I think that what you tell me is interesting?'
>
> (Fillmore 1992:35)

And yet knowledge about which parts of speech (or lexical sets) are primed to occur in—and also to avoid—certain grammatical positions (colligational priming, Hoey 2005:13) in a particular discourse type surely counts as a solid set of 'neat facts', and the corpus linguist may well then retire to his or her armchair to reflect upon them. Good corpus linguists—and this, in the end, is Fillmore's point—exploit the interaction of introspection and data observation. Introspective reflection, ratiocination, on what one knows about language, including the differences between what one was conscious of before treating the data and after, will play a part in all stages of research, in analysis, description, interpretation, and explanation. This is certainly the emphasis of CADS, which does not recognize the incompatibility between internalized 'I-language' and externalized or attested 'E-language' approaches that Widdowson complained was inherent in corpus linguistics (Widdowson 2000). Even the most mysterious form of introspection, speculation (a kind of *Act of Creation*, Koestler 1965), has a vital role to play, especially in arriving at the research question. In one section alone of Stubbs's seminal article mentioned earlier (Stubbs 2006) we find all the following hypothetical expressions: . . . *could* be related . . . *may* be reducible . . . *may* also be internally related . . . *seems* to show . . . *might* also provide . . . show how we *could* do real *'ordinary language philosophy'* . There are (hopefully well-informed) introspectional judgements too in deciding what kind of data-set to compile and how.

This leaves the concept of intuition. When we come across statements of the kind that 'even native speakers' "intuitions" about a particular language function are highly suspect', intuition(s) is clearly being used to mean pre-observational introspective judgement(s) (required to be described on the corpus linguist's demand; Stewart 2008). But native and near-native speakers' *intuitional* awareness of how language functions—their communicative competence—far outstrips their ability to rationally analyze it and formulate explicit descriptions. In fact, it is the very task of corpus linguistics to make up some of the ground between intuitive awareness and explicit knowledge of how communication works. The intuitional awareness of and competence in how to use language equates in Hoey's terms with speaker primings, which we acquire naturally and nonconsciously and use intuitively—and by and large faultlessly—in communicating with others but which we could not always explicitly describe accurately (if we ever think about them at all).

If, however, we return to the basic meaning of the term as 'direct or immediate insight' (*OED*), intuition does indeed play an important role. It will be recalled that the inductive research process, 'the research-then-theory approach', includes the stages *select a phenomenon for investigation* and *look inside the data-set for systematic patterns*. Intuition may well play a part both in selecting a potentially interesting phenomenon and in recognizing certain patterns as significant. In CADS work, intuitions can arise from reading or watching parts of the data-set, a process which can help provide a feel for how things are done linguistically in the discourse type being studied. In addition, intuitions themselves deriving serendipitously from data observation can often direct the course of the research.

Serendipity

Returning to the phenomenon of serendipity, not all kinds of language ser-endipity are restricted to corpus linguistics. Armchair linguists too have their felicitous moments (in fact the magnificent 'Yankee jim-jam generals' was not found in the corpus but I happened upon it in a recent *Guardian* blog). Nor is there a *necessary* connection of all serendipity with induction, although induction does create a favourable climate (as when mapping of radio sources led to the 'discovery'—better, hypothesis—of quasars and black holes, changing our view of the universe from a placid to a violent, cannibalistic place), certainly more so than deductive logic, where in a sense the information contained in the conclusion is already to be found in the premises (whereas in science we generally wish to arrive somewhere new). But serendipity certainly occurs during hypothesis testing too, as when I was looking for *armchair* + [expert/general etc.] and came across a second entirely different and unexpected use in *armchair* + [banking etc.].

But there is one particular kind of serendipity which is only possible in inductive research. In the cases cited earlier (quasars and *armchair*), the researcher is looking for something but stumbles across something extra which s/he finds rather interesting. In a second form of serendipity, how-ever, the researcher does not even know what s/he is looking for but is 'playing around' with the data-set, organizing it in new ways, finding new ways to look at it (the whole rationale of corpus linguistics)—when some-thing unexpected crops up. As when Galileo simply turned his telescope on Jupiter and discovered objects—its moons—which clearly didn't revolve around the Earth, or when the expression *armchair general* appeared in a couple of the key cluster lists I had prepared. This particular sort we might perhaps call 'double-blind' or 'picaresque' serendipity.

A final thought on serendipity. It denotes not just a lucky find, but a lucky find that enables fresh questions to be asked in the field. Kuhn argues most convincingly that science advances via moments of revolution (and 'revelation') when a new theoretical model—or paradigm—replaces an older one because of its greater explanatory power. He calls this its 'puzzle-solving' power. But he adds that the new paradigm is also highly likely to suggest many entirely fresh and more intricate puzzles, to show us things we did not even know we did not know ("unknown unknowns" as opposed to "known unknowns").[10] And any self-respecting paradigm will also suggest ways in which at least some of the new puzzles can be tackled (Kuhn 1962/1970:38–39). Serendipity shares this quality—of raising new puzzles—and helps guarantee that the linguistic scientist will never be out of a job. The briefest contemplation of the history of linguistic research reveals that language is today considered to be infinitely more complex than it was felt to be by previous generations (Chomsky 2000:122; Stubbs 2006:26). There is no reason to doubt that we shall continue to discover ever further complexity.[11]

Replicability

Replicability, the requirement that a test be repeatable by other independent observers, is frequently proposed as one of the pillars of the scientific method (Doyle 2005; Stubbs 2001). However, *pure* replicability is only possible on static entities or data-sets, and is generally unworkable in the human sciences. In other words, it is possible to replicate an experiment to test, say, the interaction of one salt with others, but where human behaviour is involved only partial or imperfect replication is normally feasible. For instance, it is not possible to conduct the same experiment twice with the same human subjects, because the conditions have changed: it becomes the second time they have undergone the experience. Changing the subjects undergoing the experiment, on the other hand, inevitably introduces an unwanted variable, because no two sets of individuals are the same. Even in many scientific experiments, pure replication may well be impossible. For example, mapping the 'same' sky for radio sources twice is not possible because time will pass between the two determinations and the object of study may well have altered in the meantime (which of course would be an interesting finding in itself).

This state of affairs has important implications for corpus linguistics and CADS. Whereas it is possible to perform the same test twice on a static, finite, 'finished' data-set like the *British National Corpus*, only partial replication may be feasible with a growing and changing so-called monitor corpus such as the *Bank of English* or, say, a corpus of White House briefings which is periodically being updated with the latest tokens. Doyle (2005) bewails the lack of replication studies so far conducted within corpus linguistics and lists a number of other possible reasons for this, including the lack of public availability of many corpora, changes in, or even disappearance of, searching software over time, and insufficient information supplied by researchers on their original experimental procedures. Nevertheless, very many researches are potentially replicable if the data-set is stable; for instance Stubbs's study of Baden-Powell's *Letters* (1996:81–100). Replicability, of course, only applies to the data collection and procedural parts of research, but not to interpretation of results. In other words, I can give you the recipe and the baking instructions, but you'll have to evaluate the cake yourself.

CADS research, on the other hand, frequently involves another sort of repeatability, which we might term 'para-replication', that is, the replication of an experiment with either a fresh set of texts of the same discourse type or of a related discourse type, 'in order to see whether [findings] were an artefact of one single data set' (Stubbs 2001:124). An example was my para-replication of Best's research on news interviews. Best (1996) found that interviewers, compared to ten years previously, tended to favour the use of polar *yes/no* and narrow '*wh*' questions (that is, with *who, where, when,* and *which*), which generally constrain the respondents' response and can, according to Best, threaten their negative face, over broad '*wh*' questions (*what, why, how*), which by and large encourage an open-ended reply. Conducting a similar experiment on briefings, I found little evidence of any similar phenomenon, with broad questions outnumbering narrow '*wh*' questions by a factor of 7:1 and polar questions by approximately 2.5:1 (Partington 2003:144–5). (Journalists presumably like to keep the podium talking, firstly to obtain copy, and secondly in the hope that, by giving him enough rope, he will hang himself.) This, of course, in no way constitutes a falsification of Best's findings, but it does cast some doubt that narrow questions are becoming a general norm, and gives some indication of how practices in superficially similar discourse types can differ in important ways.

One corollary of these reflections on replication is that we need to develop a terminology of description which goes beyond the simple binary option 'corroboration–falsification'. In the preceding case, had my findings on my data-set been similar to those of Best we would talk of a *corroborative extension* of Best's work; as it turned out, instead, we have to talk of a *failure of corroborative extension*.

Another form of para-replication is exemplified by Clark (2007, forthcoming), where an analyst looks at the same data-set as a previous piece of research and analyzes it using different tools and methodology. In this case, Clark first looked at the research carried out by the Cardiff commission into *BBC* war reporting, which seemed to adopt a critical discourse approach. She instead applied a more systematic CADS methodology. Her conclusions were strikingly different.

Some Limits to Corpus Linguistics and to Corpus-assisted Linguistics

The oldest objection to corpus linguistics is that it is superfluous, given we all have introspection and trained linguists have of course finely honed introspection (see Nelson Francis 1982:7–8 and section 2.4). In this chapter, instead, we are arguing precisely how the two—corpus observation and introspection—can reinforce each other.

However, there may be less superficial and more valid objections to raise. One is that the nature of the corpus skews the view of the object of research. As an example: several studies have relied almost exclusively on newspaper data (e.g., Hoey 2005), and the particular nature of such discourse must inevitably affect the research observations and perhaps even the research questions posed in the first place (studies which actively set out to study newspaper language [Murphy, this volume; Morley 1998] are clearly a different proposition).

Worse still, if a linguistic phenomenon is not present in the corpus, the researcher is effectively 'blind' to it. How does one study *swearing* or *whispering* or *jumbled-up words* if they just are not there (but see McEnery 2005 on swearing)? And, as Baker points out, from an ideological point of view 'sometimes what is not said or written is more important than what is there' (2006:19). The armchair linguist has no such blind spots.

This of course is one of the lacunae which CADS attempts to fill. If there is little trace of the phenomenon in one of the ready-made corpora, the researcher can go out looking for it and make her own corpus which contains it. One then becomes vulnerable to the accusation of data selectiveness. But the observer is always, inevitably, part of the experiment, and is frequently the person who organizes data collection. The lepidopterist leaves home with a butterfly net, not an elephant gun.

Nevertheless, the possibility must be envisaged that some language phenomena may not practicably be open to study using electronic corpora. Corpus-free introspective armchair linguistics may sometimes be the only option.

Finally, *spoken* data of course present very particular problems regarding the potential loss of intonation and speaker and listener kinesics. The work done on briefings (Riccio, Chapter 4, this volume; Partington 2003, 2006), was at least able to study the Internet video information on the speaker, generally the podium. The *CorDis* work on TV broadcast (Clark, Chapter 6, this volume; Lombardo, Chapter 5, this volume; Haarman and Lombardo [eds.] 2009) involved very careful collection and analyses of visual information, alongside the transcripts, but this of course can place human and financial restrictions on the amount of data which can be effectively handled.

Baker (2006:17–21) has an interesting discussion of the strengths and limitations of both corpus methods themselves and their use in discourse analysis.

10.4. CADS and Current Theories in Corpus Linguistics

It is not unusual, within the field, to hear affirmations, protestations even, that corpus linguistics is a set of tools with associated methodology, not a branch of linguistics, still less a separate theory of it. A halfway house vision sees corpus linguistics as a sort of enabler, or perhaps a midwife, easing the birth of a new bottom-up approach to language description, that is, lexical grammar, pattern grammar, or phraseological grammar, whatever we wish to name it (see the discussions in McEnery et al. 2006:7–8 and Teubert and Krishnamurthy 2007:1–10).

But these conservative views fail to appreciate the nature of modern scientific theory as well as current thinking in the philosophy of science. To make such clear distinctions between instruments and enterprise is anachronistic. Firstly, because observation informs theory just as theory informs observation: quasars and black holes, for instance, were hypothesized using mathematical calculations of the behaviour of gravitational fields as observed using the radio telescope, which observations depended on a theory of gravity, which in its turn depended on the legendary (though probably apocryphal) Newtonian observation that apples fall to earth. Secondly, in most modern physical science, the object of observation is only tangible, in a sense only *exists* for an observer (outside a mathematical formula), through the instruments of study, which thus constrain not only what can be perceived but even the very questions that can usefully be put of the physical world. There exists a commonplace heroic narrative of science in which science drives technology.[12] But the reverse is just as true; our knowledge of the world is driven by the technical means we have to observe it. There is a sort of indivisible hermeneutic package—the observer (including mind), observational instruments, observations, object of observation. Alterations in any of the parts will affect the entire system, a process usually known as scientific advance. For instance: (i) the researcher can have a bright new idea of what to search for or how to use a tool in a fresh experimental way; (ii) tools can be constantly refined; (iii) observations can be made wider, deeper, more cohesive; (iv) any change in the observed system gives researchers the chance to fruitfully compare the new with the previous behaviour. Thus it is with corpus linguistics, just as it is for astrophysics or particle science. There is a strong argument, then, that, if not a new *theoretical* model, corpus linguistics embodies a fresh *methodological* paradigm.

But what is the aim and scope of this branch of research? Stubbs has claimed that 'the central programme of corpus linguistics is to develop a theory of meaning' (2001:20). We can divide this massive task into two parts: we must both devise a theory of language as a *system* for potentially communicating meaning, and also attempt a description of how language is actually used for communicating meaning. Stubbs himself would also include the need to develop a theory and description of how language links the mental, the social, and the real worlds (2001:234–8).

In parenthesis, this important question—how language links or distinguishes between real-world, mental, and social facts—would seem to be more a problem for philosophers than for natural language users. In default circumstances, they are all treated in the same manner. Hume and Kant have pointed the way in demonstrating that, in knowing, it is not the mind that conforms to things but instead things that conform to the mind.

By definition we live in a mental world and all facts are mental (mental constructs, that is, thoughts, beliefs, opinions). But we tend to treat, and talk about, facts—whether real-world, mental, or social—as pertaining to the real world: *it's cold*, *I'm not paid enough*, *I love you*, and so on, largely because (like these three examples) they almost always mix up elements of all three spheres, but also because the distinction is not normally useful to us as biological entities (as opposed to philosophers): we are interested in what is relevant, not whether something is real, mental, or social. To use one of Stubbs's examples: that 'money has value' is indubitably a *social* construct. At the same time it 'lives' in people's minds (*mental*). But people treat it as a *real-world* fact because it is useful and reliable (2006:31–32). Conversely, even pure real-world 'facts', such as 'there is no snow on the mountain', are very often interpreted teleologically as, say, 'and so we can't go skiing'. Thus language, being functionally structured, doesn't distinguish the three kinds of fact (as we said, in the end they are all mental anyway), but rather expresses a topic and then evaluates its relevance. Relevance theory, evaluation theory, and Sinclair's insistence that prosody defines the lexical unit (see 10.1.1) all stress this.

Stubbs's own corpus work provides more solid linguistic evidence for the overarching driving force of functional relevance in how people construe the world. He shows how mentions of the days of the week (entirely social entities) are severely skewed, with *Saturday* nearly three times as frequent as *Tuesday* in his corpus (2001:16–17). In the real world there are just as many Tuesdays and Saturdays but the latter are psychologically—mentally—far more salient for social-world reasons. Language users treat the several *parts* of the day (half real-world and half social entities) in an entirely analogous way. In the *SiBol* newspaper corpora, *Monday morning* is nearly three times as frequent as *Tuesday morning*, and even the latter is twice as frequent as *Tuesday afternoon*.

Instead, the vital distinction which is provided for in the language system is that between 'objective' constructs (which are still mental and often not all objective, like 'it's cold' and 'I'm not paid enough') and *explicitly* subjective constructs, where a speaker makes clear that their utterance expresses an opinion or report or a feeling, for example: '*I think I might* be coming down with a cold', or in questions, which have the underlying function of overtly requesting another speaker's view of the world. Halliday (1994) (amongst others) discusses in detail how language makes this distinction. The default is to state something as objective and to express full commitment to it, but language has considerable structural resources enabling us to mark something as a report or a feeling, and so forth, as well as to express myriad degrees of less-than-full commitment to it.

In any case, Stubbs's programmes are undoubtedly both tall orders. Physicists may well have devised the grand unified theory of force before we manage a grand unified theory of meaning in linguistics. Nevertheless, modern corpus-based bottom-up research into grammar by, *inter alia*, Sinclair, Hoey, and Hunston is making impressive and convincing statements as regards the first of these programmes, that is, language as a *system* for potentially communicating meaning. As CADS we are not in the business of articulating similar detailed and highly formulated 'set' theories as such but, since we share the same basic paradigm of lexical grammar, we can have our say on the second of Stubbs's possible programmes, that is, by helping describe how language is actually used for communicating meaning. This indeed involves critical epideictic appraisal, testing, if we prefer, the implications and predictions which are generated by lexical grammar, priming theory, and evaluation as regards how they function in practice in various discourse types. In this enterprise, CADS researchers can be natural Popperians, in other words, potential fault-finders or corroborators with the aim of helping refine these theories.

These overlapping theories all make the explicit predictive and testable statement that language behaves differently across discourse types. CADS is inherently comparative in philosophy and practice (Morley, introduction to this volume), as the present and other *CorDis* reports of research have tried to show. Its apparatus can serve to describe how lexical grammar, priming, and evaluation work in individual discourse types—which include particular sociolects, idiolects and, especially the sort of very special 'technolects', that is, particular occupation-related discourses of the sort analyzed in several of the works in this volume. It can also, conversely, investigate which generalizations about an item's or a pattern's behaviour in the mythical 'language-as-a-whole' are valid and which less so.

However, it can perhaps fulfil a further service. Stubbs also claims that 'corpus linguistics is inherently sociolinguistic' (2001:221). I would hedge and prefer to say corpus linguistics is *potentially* sociolinguistic; it is CADS which is inherently so. Sociolinguistic research is a logical development of corpus linguistics, an entirely reasonable way of using corpus techniques. But historically speaking it was not its main initial rationale. Be this as it may, Stubbs's basic intuition, that the methods of corpus linguistics can be applied to real-world communication and therefore tell us much about human social interaction, power and gender relations, politeness strategies, and so on, is a valid one.

However, the historical concentration on the social aspects of language, most evident in recent British linguistics, has come at a cost. Kuhn has argued very convincingly that although scientific theory does indeed develop—in his vision, more in the evolutionary sense of adapting better to its environment than progressing towards some final teleological goal—whenever one paradigm or theoretical framework is succeeded by another, something is gained but inevitably something is also lost, a phenomenon known as 'Kuhn-loss' (1962/1970:99–100). Most of us would agree that when, in English linguistics in Europe at least, the Hallidayan paradigm was generally adopted at the expense of the Chomskian, many advantages accrued, not least that of creating an auspicious environment for corpus linguistics itself. But there was Kuhn-loss too; the external, social aspects of language were deliberately, systematically, politically privileged over the internal (quasi-)individual psychological ones. One important correlate was that far more attention was paid to the study of linguistic habit than of linguistic creativity.

Many of us felt this was an overreaction, though perhaps an understandable one in its historical context. One of the great achievements of Hoey's lexical priming theory has been to restore due attention to the psychological aspects of language in the sphere of corpus linguistics. It is a theory which re-engages the vital enterprise of building a bridge between the psycholinguistic and the sociolinguistic; it is a framework within which we can investigate just how they interact.

CADS-type studies utilizing specialized corpora can further this enterprise by investigating the primings of speakers (including and especially institutional speakers) in a number of different ways. It is possible to study, say, the primings apparent in the discourse of a podium as individual (as 'Mr Fleischer'), the discourse of a single podium as representative of podiums as a category, or the discourse of all podiums as a group of people with very similar roles and strategies. We are thus using corpus techniques to study the area where the psychological and the social meet, or alternatively where the former begins to turn into the latter.

Evaluation too is interested in this twilight area. In my view, one of the most important points made by Thompson and Hunston is that '(e)valuation which both organizes the discourse and indicates its significance might be said to tell the reader the "point" of the discourse' (2000:12). If discourses have points, then so a priori do speakers, and they are liable to have strategies to achieve them, which various chapters in the current volume examine. To cite just three, Riccio examines the web of semicovert evaluative strategies embroidered by the podium around the simple item *message*(s) over the course not of a single text but an entire field of a discourse type (over a limited period of time, at least). Taylor explores how cross-examiners and examinees perform and evaluate facework, both as individuals and as representatives of their professional categories (lawyers, politicians, etc.). Bevitori studies how one politician over several weeks evaluates her own and opponents' stances to the question of intervention in Iraq.

Specialized corpora and the CADS-type techniques used to interrogate them, then, have a natural role in testing the predictions, corollaries, and implications of modern theories of language. This is especially true in this post-Biber age when language, once viewed as a consistent cohesive monolith, is more accurately considered a huge, growing, and ever-shifting accumulation of interrelated discourse types, sociolects, technolects, and even idiolects. Corpus-assisted discourse studies certainly has its own descriptive ends, but can also serve those of lexical grammar, evaluation, and priming theory.

10.5. On the Virtues of Observation and Data: A Reply

Corpus linguistics doesn't mean anything. It's like saying suppose a physicist decides, suppose physics and chemistry decide that instead of relying on experiments, what they're going to do is take videotapes of things happening in the world and they'll collect huge videotapes of everything that's happening and from that maybe they'll come up with some generalizations or insights. [. . .] My judgment, if you like, is that we learn more about language by following the standard method of the sciences. The standard method of the sciences is not to accumulate huge masses of unanalyzed data and to try to draw some generalization from them. The modern sciences, at least since Galileo, have been strikingly different. What they have sought to do was to construct refined experiments which ask, which try to answer specific questions that arise within a theoretical context as an approach to understanding the world. Go back to Galileo. If you want to understand how bodies fall, Galileo would not have been interested in videotapes of leaves falling and balls going around and rocks rolling down mountains and so on and so forth.

(Chomsky, in Andor 2004:97)

Finally, to end—as we began—with epideictics, let us respond to Chomsky's diatribe—all blame and no praise—against corpus linguistics. In general, he seems to share with Popper the authoritarian desire to lay down the rules of what is permissible in the discipline, to sanction the validity of some approaches and deny that of others. As I have tried to argue, there is room in linguistics for many approaches and combinations of approaches. He also appears to believe that corpus linguistics is simply observation for observation's sake, a reductionist assertion I hope to have answered in this chapter.

The standard method of the sciences, he claims, is not to accumulate masses of observation data in order to draw generalizations from them. But the human genome project, for instance, involved precisely this (it enjoyed the relative good fortune of dealing with a finite universe of data, unlike linguistics). In CADS, in contrast to some other corpus linguistics endeavours, the 'mass' of collected data is, of course, generally specifically related to the research question and is therefore less open to Chomsky's accusation of being 'unanalyzed'. Most curious of all, however, is his exhortation to 'go back to Galileo'. Quite apart from the dubious Virgilian exercise of calling up the shades of the dead in support of one's argument, it is wholly ironic and self-defeating for him to pick, of all people, on Galileo.

First of all, Galileo was anything but a solely armchair thinker. He in particular and the Renaissance spirit in general, for practically the first time in European history (*pace* Roger Bacon), dared to combine science and technology, theory and technique; he was among the very first to exploit the immense productivity of their interaction. Galileo even ground and polished his lenses with his own hands.[13] This is entirely analogous to most modern science, including corpus linguistics (in our rather less heroic fashion), which continuously refines its observational tools—its tools of discovery—including corpora and corpus interrogation tools, as a means to refining knowledge and theory.

Moreover, few in the history of science have given such a fillip and served as such an inspiration to empiricism as Galileo. Of course he combined observation with experimentation—as I hope to have shown, this is also typically the case in CADS—but his experiments were marked by reliance on and good use of real-life data. He collected, in Chomskian parlance, 'performance' data. One suspects, notwithstanding Chomsky, that he would have been enormously 'interested in videotapes of leaves falling and balls going around and rocks rolling down mountains'—especially if they depicted phenomena in places he could not reach and where gravity conditions were different from Earth's—just as he was interested in observing the motion of Jupiter's moons and the phases of Venus.

We have to ponder what kind of linguistic experimentation Chomsky might actually approve of. One common form of experiment involves asking subjects, via questionnaires and the like, to reflect upon their own or others' use of language. Whilst these can be quite informative, they are rarely conducted double-blind and there are clearly issues of contamination to be addressed: the observer paradox in such cases can become extreme. A critic might even suggest they are a little like asking Galileo's various weights to comment on their own 'competence' in reacting to gravity.

What Galileo really showed, then, was that without data there can be little progress or evolution; there is only the obedience to ancient authority or the solipsistic armchair introspection we discussed earlier (and one doesn't discover sunspots by introspection).[14] Linguistic science before electronic corpus use, just as Western science before the Renaissance, was starved of data (Sinclair 2004:9 et passim). Galileo was hungry for data and would never, as Chomsky suggests, have ignored avenues of access to it. As his fellow Tuscan and fellow empiricist, Leonardo, proclaimed:

> There is nothing more deceptive than to rely on your own opinions, without any other proof, as experience [*read* 'data'][15] always proves to be the enemy of the alchemists, necromancers, and other ingenious simpletons.[16]
>
> (Leonardo da Vinci 1956:686)

NOTES

1. Celebrated examples of classical epideictic rhetoric in action include Pericles's famous funeral oration (*praise*) reported in Thucydides and a clear influence on Lincoln's *Gettysburg Address*, and Demosthenes's series of *Philippics* (most definitely *blame*). The latter also worked for a time as a legal speech writer (*logographer*) and was not, according to Plutarch, averse to secretly working for both litigants in the same case. It is one of the small coincidences of history that the great theoretician of rhetoric, Aristotle, and one of its most renowned practitioners, Demosthenes, were exact contemporaries; both were born in 384 BC and both died in 322 BC.
2. Aristotle himself shows he is fully aware of how epideictics serves political rhetoric. He points out in Book 3, for instance, how, in political speeches, narration may be employed to attack someone's character or to eulogize them.
3. They were 'enterprising' in having recovered documents from the Iraqi information minister which the intelligence services had not bothered to collect. *Inter alia* these documents revealed that 'French security services were assisting the Iraqi intelligence agents to deliberately threaten the lives of British

subjects' (Clwyd, Lab). The documents were subsequently adjudged to be of dubious reliability.

4. Surprisingly perhaps, *loyalty* is rarely construed in UK Parliament discourse with an entirely favourable or unproblematic epideictic evaluation. It is frequently contrasted unfavourably with conviction, comprehension, or conscience:

'I will not support the Prime Minister out of loyalty. I will support him out of the conviction';

'The P.M. said he wants people to vote, not out of loyalty, but on the basis of understanding';

'This is a profound matter of conscience, not a loyalty test'.

At its worst it is perceived as almost analogous to sycophancy:

'I do not do so out of sycophancy or blind loyalty';

'Is the Prime Minister not embarrassed to have shown such unstinting loyalty to an American President who regards [. . .] war as an opportunity to dish out contracts to his cronies?'

5. As Robin Aitken, a BBC journalist for 25 years, puts it:

the license fee brings with it a unique *quid pro quo*: it follows that because *everyone* pays for the BBC *everyone* has an absolute right to fair treatment *from* the BBC. That is the bedrock of the contract between the BBC and the country; and it is this contract that has been corroded by the inherent [liberal-left] bias within the BBC's journalism.

(Aitken 2007:16)

It also needs to be remembered that very many *BBC* journalists have 'graduated' to the *BBC* from print journalism. Andrew Gilligan, who precipitated the *BBC*'s fall into hot water over misreporting (see Duguid: Chapter 9, this volume), had also worked for the *Sunday Telegraph* and the *Mail on Sunday*, and was in fact accused of 'Sunday Paper journalism', a notoriously unregulated, not to say irresponsible, scoop-fixated form of the UK newspaper craft.

6. *CNN* was, however, criticized for keeping open its Baghdad office and suppressing information critical of the Iraqi regime, including torture of journalists, out of consideration for staff safety—a decision which 'violated the public trust of journalism [. . .] With an eye on its ratings, CNN had sold its soul' (*New York Times*, 21 April 2003).

7. Stubbs talks of the favourable connotations of *little* in phrases like *beautiful little, charming little,* and *lovely little* (2001:161–4). However, unfavourable combinations like *nasty little* are not hard to find. The 100-million-word newspaper corpus *SiBol 93* supplies, among many others, *wretched little, grubby little, filthy little,* and *vicious little*. The expression *precious little* X exists to express an unfavourable evaluation: 'but they [war reporters] seem to have made *precious little effort* to understand what they are paid to report' (*Telegraph*, 1 April). See also example (6) in this chapter.

8. I am most grateful to Charlotte Taylor for her invaluable comments on Section 2 of this chapter.

9. The modifier *lucrative* always has this unfavourable sense in this data-set; it is often used bathetically: 'Keep in with the big boys [. . .] not a brave motto perhaps but a lucrative one' (*Independent*) or to expose hypocrisy, undermine a façade: 'If America's push for war is motivated by oil, then France and Russia's push for peace is no less so: both have lucrative contracts in the region that they are keen to preserve' (*Guardian*), or humorously 'others [military reporters] are finalizing their lucrative deals to write war books or jockeying for plummy access to Rummy [Donald Rumsfeld], who was jetting around the world on Friday, trying to insult Old Europe at closer range' (*New York Times*).

10. There are known knowns. There are things we know that we know. There are known unknowns. That is to say, there are things that we now know we don't know. But there are also unknown unknowns. There are things we do not know we don't know (Donald Rumsfeld, US defense secretary, press briefing, 12 Feb 2002), http://en.wikipedia.org/wiki/Known_unknown.

11. Again, the analogy with science is striking. At the turn of the century, Albert Michelson famously announced there was nothing left for physics to discover. And Michelson was no fool but one of the greatest physicists ever to draw breath, recipient of the Nobel Prize for measuring the speed of light.

   Today, any physicist with a scrap of humility would have to admit that we don't really know what space and time and gravity are, let alone what happens in black holes, why the universe appears to be expanding at an increasing rate, why matter in the universe has collected into clumps (galaxies, stars, planets, etc.), how many dimensions superstrings are twisted into (should they exist), or where on earth (and everywhere else) all the dark energy has disappeared to.

12. It is, however, a very modern narrative:
   In 1834, during a discussion in the Chambre des Députés, the distinguished French physicist Arago was asked to justify his request for government support for the sciences. His colleagues demanded to know what practical benefits had accrued from the discoveries of science. Arago could only think of one example: the lightning conductor.
                                                                                        (Silver 1998:121)

13. Interestingly, Spinoza too was a lens grinder. Perhaps it was an occupation which afforded plenty of time to think.

14. In fact, famously, Galileo's opponents relied on an introspective theory based on sacred authority to deny that Gods's creation could ever exhibit any such 'blemishes'. A notable exception was the Jesuit mathematician Christoph Scheiner, who also observed sunspots but concluded they must be satellites orbiting the Sun, thus preserving accepted belief in the perfection of holy Creation.

15. The word *empiricism* derives from the Greek *empeiria*, 'experience'. The items *experience* and *experiment* have the same root and experiments consist essentially in devising new ways of experiencing, of observing, data. There is no dichotomy or contradiction, as Chomsky tries to imply, between observational and experimental science, in fact, quite the reverse.

16. 'nessuna cosa è che più c'inganni che fidarsi del nostro giudizio senz'altra ragione, come prova sempre l'esperienza, nemica degli alchimisti, negromanti ed altri semplici ingegni'.

Bibliography

Adams, K. (1999) 'Deliberate dispute and the construction of oppositional stance', *Pragmatics* 9(2): 231–248.

Aday, S., Livingston, S. and Hebert, M. (2005) 'Embedding the truth: a cross-cultural analysis of objectivity and television coverage of the Iraq war', *Press/Politics* 10(1): 3–21.

Aijmer, K. (2002) *English Discourse Particles. Evidence from a Corpus*, Amsterdam and Philadelphia: John Benjamins.

Aitken, R. (2007) *Can We Trust the BBC?*, London: Continuum.

Allan, S. (1999) *News Culture*, Buckingham: Open University Press.

Allan, S. and Zelizer, B. (eds. .) (2004a) *Reporting War: Journalism in Wartime*, London: Routledge.

Allan, S. and Zelizer, B. (2004b) 'Rules of engagement; journalism and war', in S. Allan and B. Zelizer (eds.), *Reporting War: Journalism in Wartime*, London: Routledge, 3–21.

Andor, J. (2004) 'The master and his performance: an interview with Noam Chomsky', *Intercultural Pragmatics*, 1(1): 93–111.

Aristotle (2006) *On Rhetoric*; trans. G. Kennedy, Oxford: Oxford University Press.

Aston, G. and Burnard, L. (1998) *The BNC Handbook: Exploring the British National Corpus with SARA*, Edinburgh: Edinburgh University Press.

Atkins, S., Clear, J. and Ostler, N. (1992) 'Corpus design criteria', *Literary and Linguistic computing*, 7(1): 1–16.

Atkins, B. T. S. Levin, B. and Zampolli, A. (1994) 'Computational approaches to the lexicon: an overview', in B. T. S. Atkins and A. Zampolli (eds.), *Computational Approaches to the Lexicon*, Oxford: Oxford University Press,17–45.

Atkins, B. T. S. and Zampolli, A. (eds.) (1994) *Computational Approaches to the Lexicon*, Oxford: Oxford University Press.

Atkinson, J. M. and Drew, P. (1979) *Order in Court: The Organisation of Verbal Interaction in a Judicial Setting*, London: Macmillan.

Baker, J. P. (1997) 'Consistency and accuracy in correcting automatically tagged data?', in R Garside, G. Leech and T. McEnery (eds.), *Corpus Annotation—Linguistic Information from Computer Text Corpora*, London: Longman, 243–50.

Baker, P. (2006) *Using Corpora in Discourse Analysis,* London: Continuum.

Bakhtin, M. M. (1984) 'Discourse in Dostoevsky', in C. Emerson (ed. and trans.) *Problems in Dostoevsky's Poetics*, Minneapolis: University of Minnesota Press, 181–269.

Baldry, A. and Thibault, P.J. (2006) *Multimodal Transcription and Text Analysis*, London: Equinox.

Bayley, P. (1999) 'Lexis in British parliamentary debate: collocational patterns', in J. Verschueren (ed.), *Language and Ideology: Selected Papers from the 6th International Pragmatics Conference*, vol. 1, Antwerp: International Pragmatics Association, 43–55.

———. (ed.) (2004) *Cross-Cultural Perspectives On Parliamentary Discourse*, Amsterdam and Philadelphia: John Benjamins.

———. (2007) 'Perhaps. . . . . but: expanding and contracting alternative viewpoints', in M. Dossena and A. H. Jucker (eds.), *(Re)volutions in Evaluation*, *Textus* 20(1), 117–35.

Bayley, P. and San Vincente, F. (2004) 'Ways of talking about work in parliamentary discourse in Britain and Spain', in P. Bayley (ed.), *Cross-Cultural Perspectives On Parliamentary Discourse*, Amsterdam and Philadelphia: John Benjamins, 237–269.

Bayley, P., Bevitori, C. and Zoni, E. (2004). 'Threat and fear in parliamentary debates in Britain, Germany and Italy', in P. Bayley (ed.), *Cross-Cultural Perspectives On Parliamentary Discourse*, Amsterdam and Philadelphia: John Benjamins, 185–236.

Beer, F. A. and Hariman, R. (eds.) (1998) 'Post-Realism, just war and the Gulf-War debate', in O. Feldman and C. De Landtsheer (eds.), *Politically Speaking: A World-Wide Examination of Language in the Public Sphere*. Westport (Conn): Praeger, 184–93.

Bell, A. (1991) *The Language of News Media*, Oxford: Blackwell.

Best, A. (1996) 'Political interviewing on the *BBC* Radio Four *Today* programme: a pragmatic analysis of the controversial Anna Ford/Kenneth Clarke interview, 16 September 1996', unpublished MSc thesis in Teaching English, Aston University, Birmingham, UK.

Bevitori, C. (2007) 'Engendering conflict? A corpus-assisted analysis of women MPs' positioning on the war in Iraq', in M. Dossena and A. H. Jucker (eds.), *(Re)volutions in Evaluation*, *Textus* 20(1), 136–58.

———. (2005) 'Attribution as evaluation: a corpus-based investigation of quotations in parliamentary discourse', *ESP Across Cultures*: 2, 7–20.

Biber, D. (1988) *Variation across Speech and Writing*, Cambridge: Cambridge University Press.

Biber, D. and Conrad, S. (1999) 'Lexical bundles in conversation and academic prose', in H. Hasselgard and S. Oksefjell (eds.), *Out of corpora: Studies in Honor of Stig Johansson*, Amsterdam: Rodopi, 181–9.

Biber, D., Johansson, S., Leech, G. Conrad, S. and Finegan, E. (1999) *Longman Grammar of Spoken and Written English*, London: Longman.

Biscetti, S. (2006) 'Tag question in courtroom discourse', in J. Flowerdew and M. Gotti (eds.), *Studies in Specialized Discourse*, Bern: Peter Lang, 209–238.

Blommaert, J. and Bulcaen, C. (eds.) (1998) *Political Linguistics*, Amsterdam and Philadephia: John Benjamins.

Bousfield, D. (2007) 'Beginnings, middles and ends: a biopsy of the dynamics of impolite exchanges', *Journal of Pragmatics*. 39(12): 2185–2216.

British National Corpus, World Edition (2001), Oxford: BNC Consortium.

Brookes, R. and Lewis, J. (2004) 'How British television news represented the case for the war in Iraq', in S. Allan and B. Zelizer (eds.), *Reporting War: Journalism in Wartime*, London: Routledge, 283–300.

Brown, G. and Yule, G. (1983) *Discourse Analysis*, Cambridge: Cambridge University Press.

Brown, P. and Levinson, S. C. (1987) *Politeness: Some Universal in Language Usage*, Cambridge: Cambridge University Press.

Burkeman, O. (2003) 'US television', in *Guardian* 27 March 2003.

Burnard, L. (2004) 'Metadata for corpus work'. Online. Available HTTP: <http://users.ox.ac.uk/~lou/wip/metadata.htm> (accessed: 23 June 2007).

Caldas-Coulthard, C. R. and Coulthard, M. (eds.) (1996) *Texts and Practices. Readings in Critical Discourse Analysis*, London: Routledge.

Carbò, T. (1996) *El discorso parlamentario mexicano entre 1920 y 1950. Un estudio de caso en metolodogia de analisis de discurso* [2 vols], Mexico: CISAS and Collegio de Mexico.

Carletta, J., McKelvie, D,. Isard, A. Mengel, A., Klein, M. and Møller, M. B. (2005) 'A generic approach to software support for linguistic annotation using XML', in G. Sampson and D. McCarthy (eds.) *Readings in Corpus Linguistics*, London: Continuum. Online. Available HTTP: http://homepages.inf.ed.ac.uk/jeanc/readings-in-corpling.final.webformat.pdf> (accessed: 15 July 2007).

Carter, R. (1988) 'Front pages: lexis, style and newspaper reports', in M. Ghadessy (ed.) *Registers of Written English—Situational Factors and Linguistic Features*, London: Pinter, 8–16.

Charles, M. (2006) 'The construction of stance in reporting clauses: a cross-disciplinary study of theses' *Applied Linguistics, 27*(3): 492–518.

Chibnall, S. (1981) 'The production of knowledge by crime reporters', in S. Cohen and J. Young (eds.), *The Manufacture of News: Social Problems, Deviance and the Mass Media*, London: Constable, 75–97.

Chilton, P., Ilyin, M. and Mey, J. (eds.) (1998) *Political Discourse in Transition in Europe 1989–1991*, Amsterdam and Philadelphia: John Benjamins.

Chomsky, N. (2000) *New Horizons on the Study of Mind*, Cambridge, MA: MIT Press.

Christie, C. (2002) 'Politeness and the linguistic construction of gender in parliament: an analysis of transgressions and apology behaviour', *Sheffield Hallam Working Papers on the Web: Linguistic Politeness and Context*. Online. Available HTTP: <http://www.shu.ac.uk/wpw/politeness/christie.htm> (accessed 28 August 2007)

Christopher, P. (1994) *The Ethics of War and Peace*, Englewood Cliffs (NJ): Prentice Hall.

Cirillo, L., Marchi, A. and Venuti, M. (forthcoming) 'The *CorDis* Corpus: Markup and related issues', in *Proceedings from the Corpus Linguistics Conference Series*, vol. 2 no.1.

Clark, C. (2007) 'A war of words: a linguistic analysis of BBC embed reports during the Iraq conflict', in N. Fairclough and G. Cortese and P. Ardizzone (eds.), *Discourse Analysis and Contemporary Social Change,* Bern: Peter Lang,119–140.

——. (2008) 'A CADS analysis of television reports from Iraq: were embeds. "in bed" with the coalition?', in Taylor Torsello, K. Ackerley, E. Castello (eds.) *Corpora for University Language Teachers*, Bern: Peter Lang.

Clayman, S. (1993) 'Reformulating the question: a device for answering/not answering questions in news interviews and press conferences', *Text*, 13(2): 159–88.

Coffin, C. and O'Halloran, K. (2005) 'FINDING THE GLOBAL GROOVE: theorising and analysing dynamic reader positioning using APPRAISAL, corpus, and a concordancer', *Critical Discourse Studies*, 2(2): 143–63.

Cohen, S. and Young, J. (eds.) (1981[1973]) *The Manufacture of News: Social Problems, Deviance and the Mass Media*, London: Constable.

Collins COBUILD *English Collocations on CD-ROM* (1995) London: Harper-Collins.

Collins COBUILD *English Dictionary for Advanced Learners* (2001). Glasgow: HarperCollins.

Conboy, M. (2007) *The Language of the News,* London: Routledge.

Conrad, S. and Biber, D. (2000) 'Adverbial marking of stance in speech and writing', in S. Hunston and G. Thompson (eds.), *Evaluation in Texts: Authorial*

Stance and the Construction of Discourse, Oxford: Oxford University Press, 56–73.

Cooper, C. and McKinnon, J. D. (2005) 'White House Press Room as political stage', *The Wall Street Journal*, 25 February 2005. Online. Available HTTP: <http://www.commondreams.org/headlines05/0225-11.htm> (accessed 7 July 2007).

Coulthard, M. (1985) *An Introduction to Discourse Analysis*, London: Longman.

———. (1994) (ed.) *Advances in Written Discourse Analysis*, London: Routledge.

Council of Europe (2001) *Language Learning, Teaching And Assessment: a Common European Framework*, Cambridge: Cambridge University Press.

Culpeper, J. (1996) 'Towards an anatomy of impoliteness', *Journal of Pragmatics* 25(3): 349–367

———. (2005) 'Impoliteness and entertainment in the television quiz show: The Weakest Link', *Journal of Politeness Research*, 1: 35–72

Culpeper, J., Bousfield, D. and Wichmann, A. (2003) 'Impoliteness revisited: with special reference to dynamic and prosodic aspects', *Journal of Pragmatics*, 35(10–11): 1545–1579.

Cunningham, B. (2003) 'Re-thinking objectivity', *Columbia Journalism Review*, 4 Online. Available HTTP: <http://www.cjrarchives.org/issues/2003/4/objective-cunningham.asp> (accessed 7 July 2007).

De Toqueville, A. (1956) *Democracy in America (1835–1840)*, New York: New American Library.

Diggins, J. P. (1984) *The Lost Soul of American Politics: Virtue, Self-interest and the Foundations of Liberalism*, Chicago and London: University of Chicago Press.

Dimitrova, D., Kaid, L., Williams, A. and Trammell, K. (2005) 'War on the web: the immediate news framing of Gulf War II', *Press/Politics*, 10(1): 22–44.

Don, L. (2007) 'A framework for the investigation of interactive norms and the construction of textual identity in written discourse communities: the case of an email discussion list', unpublished PhD thesis, University of Birmingham.

Dossena, M. and Jucker, A. H. (eds.) (2007) *(Re)volutions in Evaluation, Textus* 20(1).

Doward, J. (2003) 'Sky wins battle for rolling news audience', in *Observer*, 6 April 2003.

Doyle, P. (2005) 'Replication and corpus linguistics: lexical networks in texts'. Online. Available HTTP: <http:/www.corpus.bham.ac.uk/PCLC/COLING_2005_paper.pdf>, (accessed 10 September 2007).

Drew, P. and Heritage, J. (eds.) (1992) *Talk at Work: Interaction in Institutional Settings*, Cambridge: Cambridge University Press.

Dutch, R. A. (ed.) (1962 [1852]) *Roget's Thesaurus of English Words and Phrases*, New York: Dell.

Ellis, R. (1985) *Understanding Second Language Acquisition*, Oxford: Oxford University Press.

Enemark, C., and Michaelsen, C. (2005) 'Just war doctrine and the invasion of Iraq', *Australian Journal of Politics and History*, 51(4): 545–63.

Fairclough, N. (1995a) *Critical Discourse Analysis: The Critical Study of Language*, London: Longman.

———. (1995b) *Media Discourse*, London: Arnold.

———. (1996). 'Technologisation of discourse', in C. R. Caldas-Coulthard and M. Coulthard (eds.), *Texts and Practices. Readings in Critical Discourse Analysis*, London: Routledge, 71–83.

———. (2005) 'Blair's contribution to elaborating a new "doctrine of international community"', *Journal of Language and Politics*, 4(1): 41–63.

Fairclough, N., Cortese, G. and Ardizzone, P. (eds.) (2007) *Discourse Analysis and Contemporary Social Change*, Bern: Peter Lang.

Ferrarotti, L. (2009) 'The news presenter and the television audience: a comparative perspective of the use of *we* and *you*', in L. Haarman and L. Lombardo (eds.), *Evaluation and Stance in War News: A Linguistic Analysis of American, British and Italian Television News Reporting of the 2003 Iraqi War*, London: Continuum, 72–96.

Feyeraband, P. (1975) *Against Method*, Atlantic Highlands, NJ: Humanities Press.

Fillmore, C. (1992) 'Corpus linguistics or computer-aided armchair linguistics', in J. Svartvik (ed.) *Directions in Corpus Linguistics. Proceedings of Nobel Symposium 82, Stockholm, 4–8 August 1991*, Berlin and New York: Mouton de Gruyter, 13–38.

Fishman, M. (1980) *Manufacturing the News*, Austin: University of Texas Press.

Fiske, J.(1987) *Television Culture*, London: Routledge.

Fletcher, W. 2003–6 *PIE: Phrases in English* [database]. Online. Available HTTP: <http://pie.usna.edu> (accessed 14 September 2007).

Flowerdew, J. and Gotti, M. (eds.) (2006) *Studies in Specialized Discourse*, Bern: Peter Lang.

Forchini, P. and Murphy, A. (2008) 'N-grams we live by: 4-grams headed by prepositions in comparable corpora of English and Italian', Special Issue *International Journal of Corpus Linguistics*, 13(3): 351–367

Fowler, R. (1988) 'Notes on critical linguistics', in R. Steele and T. Threadgold (eds.), *Language Topics: Essays in Honour of Michael Halliday*, Amsterdam and Philadelphia: John Benjamins, 481–92.

———. (1991) *Language in the News. Discourse and Ideology in the Press*, London: Routledge.

———. (1996) 'On critical linguistics', in C. R. Caldas-Coulthard and M. Coulthard (eds.), *Texts and Practices. Readings in Critical Discourse Analysis*, London: Routledge, 3–14.

Fowler, R. Hodge, R., Kress, G and Trew, T. (1979) *Language and Control*, London: Routledge.

Francis, G. (1994) 'Labelling discourse: an aspect of nominal group lexical cohesion', in M. Coulthard (ed.), *Advances in Written Discourse Analysis*, London: Routledge, 83–101.

Fraser, B. and Nolan, W (1981) 'The association of deference with linguistic form', *International Journal of the Sociology of Language*, 27: 93–111.

Gaizauskas, R., Burnard, L., Clough P. and Piao, S. (2003) 'Using the XAIRA XML-aware corpus query tool to investigate the METER corpus', in D. Archer, P. Rayson, A. Wilson, and T. McEnery (eds.) (2003) *Proceedings of the Corpus Linguistics 2003 Conference*, Lancaster: UCREL Technical Paper Vol. 16 special issue, 227–36.

Rees, N. (2006) *Brewer's Famous Quotations: 5000 Quotations and the Stories behind them*, London: Wiedenfeld and Nicholson

Galtung, J. and Ruge, M. (1981) 'Structuring and selecting news', in S. Cohen and J. Young (eds.), *The Manufacture of News: Social Problems, Deviance and the Mass Media*, London: Constable, 63–72.

Gardner, M. (2001) 'A skeptical look at Karl Popper', *Skeptical Inquirer*, 25(4): 13–14.

Garside, R., Leech, G. and McEnery T. (eds.) (1997) *Corpus Annotation—Linguistic Information from Computer Text Corpora*, London: Longman.

Geertz, C. (1973) *The Interpretation of Cultures*, New York: Basic Books.

Geis, M. (1987) *The Language of Politics*, New York: Springer.

Gibb, P. (1923) *Adventures in Journalism*, London: Heinemann.

Gnisci, A. and Pontecorvo, C. (2004) 'The organization of questions and answers in the thematic phases of hostile examination: turn-by-turn manipulation of meaning', *Journal of Pragmatics*, 36(9): 965–995.

Goffman, E. (1967) *Interaction Ritual: Essays on Face-to-Face Behaviour*, New York: Pantheon Books.

———. (1981) *Forms of Talk*, Oxford: Blackwell.

Grimshaw, A. (ed.) (1990) *Conflict Talk: Sociological Investigation of Arguments in Conversation*, Cambridge: Cambridge University Press.

Haarman, L. (1999) 'Television talk', in L. Lombardo, L. Haarman, J. Morley and C. Taylor *Massed Medias: Linguistic Tools for Interpreting Media Discourse*, Milano: LED, 157–244.

———. (2004) '"John, what's going on?" Some features of live exchanges on television news', in A. Partington, J. Morley and L. Haarman (eds.), *Corpora and Discourse*, Bern: Peter Lang, 71–87.

———. (2006) 'The construction of stance in *BBC* coverage of the war in Iraq', in J. Flowerdew and M. Gotti (eds.), *Studies in Specialized Discourse*, Bern: Peter Lang, 181–205.

Haarman, L. and Lombardo, L. (eds.) (2009) *Evaluation and Stance in War News: A Linguistic Analysis of American, British and Italian Television News Reporting of the 2003 Iraqi War*, London: Continuum.

Haarman, L., Morley, J. and Partington, A. (2002) '*Habeas Corpus*: methodological reflections of the creation and use of a specialised corpus', in C. Gagliardi (ed.) *Quantity and Quality in English Linguistic Research: Some Issues*, Pescara: Libreria dell'Università Editrice, 55–119.

Hall, S., Chritcher, C., Jefferson, T., Clarke, J. and Roberts, B. (1981) 'A world at one with itself', in S. Cohen and J. Young (eds.), *The Manufacture of News: Social Problems, Deviance and the Mass Media*, London: Constable, 147–156.

Halliday, M. A. K. (1961) 'Categories of the theory of grammar', *Word*, 17: 241–92.

———. (1978) *Language as Social Semiotic: The Social Interpretation of Language and Meaning*, London: Edward Arnold.

———. (1989 [1985]) *Spoken Language and Written Language*, Australia: Deakin University Press, Oxford: Oxford University Press.

———. (1992) 'New ways of meaning: the challenge to applied linguistics', in M. Putz (ed.), *Thirty Years of Linguistic Evolution*, Amsterdam and Philadelphia: John Benjamins, 59–95.

———. (1993) 'Quantitative studies and probabilities in grammar', in M. Hoey (ed.), *Data, Description, Discourse: Papers on the English Language in Honour of John McH Sinclair on his Sixtieth Birthday*, London: HarperCollins, 1–25.

———. (1994 [1985]) *An Introduction to Functional Grammar*, London: Edward Arnold.

———. (2002 [1961]) 'Categories of the Theory of Grammar', in J. J. Webster (ed.), *On Grammar*, Vol. 1 in the collected works of M. A. K. Halliday, London: Continuum, 37–94.

Halliday, M. A. K. and Matthiessen, C. M. I. M. (1999) *Construing Experience through Meaning: A Language-based Approach to Cognition*, London and New York: Cassell.

———. (2004) *An Introduction to Functional Grammar*, 3rd ed., London: Edward Arnold

Hardt-Mautner, G. (1995) 'Only connect. Critical discourse analysis and corpus linguistics', University of Lancaster. Online. Available HTTP: <http://www.comp.lancs.ac.uk/cxomputing/research/ucrel/tech_papers.html> (accessed 23 June 2004).

Harris, S. (2001) 'Being politically impolite: extending politeness theory to adversarial political discourse', *Discourse and Society*, 12(4): 451–472.

Hartley, J. (1982) *Understanding News*, London: Routledge.

Hasan, R. (1978) 'Text in the systemic-functional model', in W. U. Dressler (ed.), *Current Trends in Text Linguistics,* Berlin: Walter de Gruyter, 228–46.
———. (2004) 'Analysing discursive variation', in L. Young and C. Harrison (eds.), *Systemic Functional Linguistics and Critical Discourse Analysis,* London: Continuum, 15–52.
Haugh, M. (2007) 'The discursive challenge to politeness research: An interactional alternative', *Journal of Politeness Research,* 3(2): 295–317
Heritage, J. C. and Roth, A. L. (1995) 'Grammar and institution: questions and questioning in the broadcast news interview', *Research on Language and Social Interaction,* 28(1): 1–60.
Heritage, J. (2002) 'The limits of questioning: negative interrogatives and hostile question context', *Journal of Pragmatics,* 34(10–11), 1427–1446.
Hewings, M. and Hewings, A. (2002) '"It is interesting to note that . . .": a comparative study of anticipatory 'it' in student and published writing', *English for Specific Purposes,* 21: 367–83.
Heywood, A. (2000) *Key Concepts in Politics,* Basingstoke: Palgrave.
Hodgson, F. (1992) *Subediting: A Handbook of Modern Newspaper Editing and Production,* London: Focal Press.
Hoey M. (ed.) (1993) *Data, Description, Discourse: Papers on the English Language in Honour of John McH Sinclair on his Sixtieth Birthday,* London: HarperCollins.
———. (1997) 'From concordance to text structure: new uses for computer corpora', in *PALC 1997, Proceedings of Practical Applications in Language Corpora Conference,* University of Lodz, 2–23.
———. (2001) *Textual Interaction, An Introduction to Written Discourse Analysis,* London: Routledge.
———. (2005) *Lexical Priming: A New Theory of Words and Language,* London: Routledge.
Hoey, M., Mahlberg, M., Stubbs, M. and Teubert, W. (2007) *Text, Discourse and Corpora. Theory and Analysis,* London: Continuum.
House of Commons Official Report, Parliamentary Debates, *Hansard,* vols 397–415, 2003.
Hunston, S. (2002) *Corpora in Applied Linguistics,* Cambridge: Cambridge University Press.
Hunston, S. and Sinclair, J. (2000) 'A local grammar of evaluation', in S. Hunston and G. Thompson (eds.),*Evaluation in Texts: Authorial Stance and the Construction of Discourse,* Oxford: Oxford University Press,74–101.
Hunston, S. and Thompson, G. (2000) *Evaluation in Texts: Authorial Stance and the Construction of Discourse,* Oxford: Oxford University Press.
Hutchby, I. (1996) *Confrontational Talk,* Mahwah, NJ.: Erlbaum.
Hymes, D. (1974) *Foundations in Sociolinguistics: An Ethnographic Approach,* Philadelphia: University of Pennsylvania Press.
Ide, N. and Brew, C. (2000) 'Requirements, tools, and architectures for annotated corpora', in *Proceedings of the EAGLES/ISLE Workshop on Meta-Descriptions and Annotation Schemas for Multimodal/Multimedia Language Resources and Data Architectures and Software Support for Large Corpora.* Paris: European Language Resources Association, 1–6.
Iedema, R., Feez, S., and White, P. R. R. (1994). *Media Literacy.* ('Write it Right' Literacy in Industry Research Project—stage 3). Sydney: Metropolitan East Disadvantaged Schools Program, NSW Department of School Education.
Ilie, C. (2004) 'Insulting as (un)parliamentary practice in the British and Swedish parliaments. A rhetorical approach', in P. Bayley (ed.), *Cross-Cultural Perspectives On Parliamentary Discourse,* Amsterdam and Philadelphia: John Benjamins 45–86.

Jakobson, R. (1960) 'Closing statement: linguistics and poetics', in T. A. Sebeok (ed.), *Style in Language*, Cambridge, Mass.: MIT Press, 350–77.

Johansson, S. (1994) 'Encoding a corpus in machine-readable form: the approach of the Text Encoding Initiative', in B. T. S. Atkins and A. Zampolli (eds.), *Computational Approaches to the Lexicon*, Oxford: Oxford University Press, 83–102.

Johnson J. H. (2006) 'A conflict of minds. A corpus-assisted study of the linguistic positioning of Republicans and Democrats during the Iraq war', unpublished MA thesis, University of Birmingham.

Jones, N. (2001) *Control Freaks: How New Labour Gets its Own Way,* London: Politico's.

Kahrel, P., Barnett, R. and Leech G. (1997) 'Towards cross-linguistic standards or guidelines for annotation of corpora', in R Garside, G. Leech and T. McEnery (eds.), *Corpus Annotation—Linguistic Information from Computer Text Corpora*, London: Longman, 231- 42.

Kasper, G. (1990) 'Linguistic politeness: current research issues'. *Journal of Pragmatics*, 14(2): 193–218.

Kelly, M. (2003) 'Where the media meet the military' in the *New York Post*, 8 March.

Knightley, P. (2004) *The First Casualty*, London: Andre Deutsch.

Koestler, A. (1965) *The Act of Creation*, London: Hutchinson.

Kress, G. and Hodge, R. (1979, second edn., R. Hodge, and G. Kress, 1993) *Language as Ideology*, London and New York: Routledge.

Kress, G. (1983) 'Linguistic and ideological transformations in news reporting', in H. Davis and P. Walton (eds.) *Language, Image, Media*, Oxford: Basil Blackwell, 120–139.

Kuhn, T. (1970 [1962]) *The Structure of Scientific Revolutions*, Chicago: University of Chicago Press.

Kumar, M. J. (2000). *The White House 2001 Project. White House Interview Program. Report no. 31—The Office of the Press Secretary.* Online. Available HTTP: <http://whitehousetransitionproject.org/files/press/PRESS-OD.PDF> (accessed 13 September 2007).

Kurtz, H. (1998) *Spin Cycle: How the White House and the Media Manipulate the News*, New York: Touchstone.

Labov, W. (1972) *Sociolinguistic Patterns*, Philadelphia, PA: University of Pennsylvania Press.

Lakoff, G. (1991). *Metaphor and War: the Metaphor System Used to Justify War in the Gulf.* Online. Available HTTP: <http://lists.village.virginia.edu/sixties/HTML_docs/Texts/Scholarly/Lakoff_Gulf_Metaphor_1.html> (accessed 7 July 2007).

———. (2002) *Moral Politics. How Liberals and Conservatives Think,* Chicago and London: University of Chicago Press.

Leech, G. N. (2005) 'Adding linguistic annotation', in M. Wynne (ed.) *Developing Linguistic Corpora: A Guide to Good Practice*, Oxford: Oxbow Books. Online. Available HTTP: <http://ahds.ac.uk/linguistic-corpora> (accessed: 23 June 2007).

Leech, G. N. (1991) 'The state of the art in corpus linguistics', in K. Aijmer and B. Altemberg (eds.) *English Corpus Linguistics: Studies in Honour of Jan Svartvik*, London: Longman, 8–29.

———. (1997) 'Grammatical Tagging?', in R. Garside, G. Leech and T. McEnery (eds.), *Corpus Annotation—Linguistic Information from Computer Text Corpora*, London: Longman. 19–33.

Leech, G. N, Rayson, P. and Wilson, A. (2001) *Word Frequencies in Written and Spoken English,* London: Longman.

Leech, G. N. and Short, M. H. (1981) *Style in Fiction*, London: Longman.

Leonardo (1956) *Treatise on Painting*, trans. A. McMahon. Princeton: Princeton University Press.

Lewis, J., Threadgold, T., Brookes, R., Mosdell, N., Brander, K., Clifford, S., Bessaiso, E. and Harb, Z. (2003) *Too Close for Comfort? The Role of Embedded Reporting during the 2003 Iraq War: Summary Report*, Cardiff: Cardiff School of Journalism, Media and Cultural Studies.

Lipson, M. (2007) 'The ubiquitous machine: visual texts in the *BBC* coverage of the Iraqi conflict' in N. Fairclough , G. Cortese and P. Ardizzone (eds.), *Discourse Analysis and Contemporary Social Change,* Bern: Peter Lang, 507–530.

Littlejohn, R. (2003) 'You're Salford Shi'ite and you know you are', *Sun,* 28 March 2003.

Locher, M. A. (2003) *Power and Politeness in Action. Disagreements in Oral Communication*, Berlin and New York: Mouton de Gruyter.

Locher, M. A. and Watts, R. J. (2005) 'Politeness theory and relational work', *Journal of Politeness Research*, 1(1): 9–33.

Lombardo, L. (2001) *Selling It and Telling It: A Functional Approach to the Discourse of Print Ads and TV News*, Rome: Istituto di Lingue Moderne, Luiss Guido Carli.

———. (2004) 'That-clauses and reporting verbs as evaluation in TV news', in A. Partington, J. Morley and L. Haarman (eds.), *Corpora and Discourse*, Bern: Peter Lang, 221–238.

———. (2007a) 'The cultural construction of conflict: a comparative study of the language of TV news reporting of the 2003 Iraq war in Italy and the US', *Englishes* 31(11): 59–115.

———. (2007b) 'Downplaying the fall of Baghdad: an analysis of *we* and *you* in *CBS* newsreader talk in reporting the 2003 war on Iraq', in L. Jottini, J. Douthwaite and D. F. Virdis (eds.), *Cityscapes: Islands of the Self. Vol. 2 Language Studies*, Cagliari: CUEC, 403–418.

———. (2009) 'The news presenter as socio-cultural construct', in L. Haarman and L. Lombardo (eds.), *Evaluation and Stance in War News: A Linguistic Analysis of American, British and Italian Television News Reporting of the 2003 Iraqi War*, London: Continuum, 48–71.

Louw, W. (1993) 'Irony in the text or insincerity in the writer?—the diagnostic potential of semantic prosodies', in M. Baker, G. Francis and E. Tognini-Bonelli (eds.) *Text and Technology: In Honour of John Sinclair*, Amsterdam and Philadelphia: John Benjamins, 157–176.

Lukin, A. (2006) 'The "unseen engineer": linguistic patterning in war discourse', *Linguistics and the Human Sciences (LHS)*, 2(1).

Lukin, A., Butt, D. and Matthiessen, C. M. I. M. (2004) 'Reporting war: grammar as covert operation,' *Pacific Journalism Review*, 10(1):11–27.

Lyons, J. (1977) *Semantics*, Cambridge: Cambridge University Press.

MacDougall, C. (1983 [1938]) *Interpretative Reporting*, New York: Macmillan.

Mahlberg, M. (2007) 'Lexical items in discourse: identifying local textual functions of *sustainable development*', in M. Hoey, M. Mahlberg, M. Stubbs and W. Teubert (eds.), *Text, Discourse and Corpora. Theory and Analysis*, London: Continuum, 191–218.

Mahlberg, M. (2009) 'Investigating lexical items and their local textual functions in newspaper story patterns', in L. Lombardo (ed), *Using Corpora to Learn about Language and Learning*, Bern: Peter Lang, 99–132.

Maltese, J. (1992) *Spin Control: The White House Office of Communications and the Management of Presidential News*, Chapel Hill and London: University of North Carolina Press.

Marr, A. (2004) *My Trade: A Short History of British Journalism*, London: Pan Macmillan.

Martin, J. R. (2004) 'Positive discourse analysis: solidarity and change', *Revista Canaria de Estudios Inglese*, 49: 1–37.

Martin, J. R. (2007) 'Comment' *World Englishes*, 26(1): 84–86.

Martin, J. R. and White P. P. R (2005) *The Language of Evaluation: Appraisal in English*, Palgrave Macmillan: Basingstoke, Hampshire.

Mauranen, A. (2001) 'Academic speech corpora: small and special', Unpublished plenary paper given at conference entitled *Academic discourse: small corpora and genre analysis*, Modena, Italy 6–7 December, 2001.

McEnery, T. (2005) *Swearing in English: Bad Language, Purity and Power from 1586 to the Present*. London: Routledge.

McEnery, T. and Wilson, A. (2001[1996]) *Corpus Linguistics: An Introduction*. Edinburgh: Edinburgh University Press.

McEnery, T., Xiao, R. and Tono, Y. (2006) *Corpus-Based Language Studies*, London: Routledge.

McQuail, D. (1994) *Mass Communication Theory*, London: Sage.

Media Research Centre (Vol. Eleven; No. 53) (2006) Online. Available HTTP: <http://www.mediaresearch.org/1996> (accessed 28 March 2007).

Media Tenor (2003) *The War in Iraq on Television: A Split Reality*, study on behalf of *Frankfurter Allgemeine Zeitung*. Online. Available HTTP: http://www.mediatenor.com (accessed 26 June 2006).

Miller, D. R. (1993) 'Model muddle? Some thoughts on the ideological bases of critical discourse analysis', in V. De Scarpis, L. Innocenti, F. Marucci, A. Pajalich (eds.), *Intrecci e contaminazioni, Atti XIV Congresso Nazionale A.I.A.*, Venezia: Supernova, 401–8.

Miller, D. R. (1999) 'Meaning up for grabs: value orientation patterns in British parliamentary debate on Europe', in J. Verschueren (ed.), *Language and Ideology: Selected Papers from the 6th International Pragmatics Conference*, vol. 1, Antwerp: International Pragmatics Association, 386–404.

Miller, D. R. (2000) 'On computing appraisal in a corpus of parliamentary debate, or, ticklish trawling', Unpublished paper delivered to the Systemic Functional Linguistics European Workshop, Glasgow, 19–22 July.

Miller, D. R. (2002a) 'Ways of meaning 'yea' and 'nay' in parliamentary debate as register: a cost-benefit analysis', in M. Bignami, G. Iamartino, C. Pagetti (eds.), *The Economy Principle in English: Linguistic, Literary, and Cultural Perspectives*, Selected Proceedings of the 19th Conference of the Associazione Italiana di Anglistica, Milano: Edizioni Unicopli, 220–33.

Miller, D. R. (2002b) 'Multiple judicial opinions as specialized sites of Engagement: conflicting paradigms of valuation and legitimation in *Bush v. Gore 2000*', in M. Gotti, D. Heller, and M. Dossena (eds.), *Conflict and Negotiation in Specialized Texts*, Bern: Peter Lang, 119–41.

Miller, D. R. (2004) ' "Truth, justice and the American way": The APPRAISAL SYSTEM of JUDGEMENT in the U.S. House debate on the impeachment of the President, 1998', in P. Bayley (ed.), *Cross-Cultural Perspectives On Parliamentary Discourse*, Amsterdam and Philadelphia: John Benjamins, 271–300.

Miller, D. R. (2006a) 'From concordance to text: appraising "giving" in Alma Mater donation requests', in G. Thompson and S. Hunston (eds.), *System and Corpus: Exploring Connections*, London: Equinox, 248–68.

Miller, D. R. (2006b) 'Packaging the presidency: electoral texts in the cultural context of the American Dream', in N. Vasta (ed.), *Forms of Promotion: Texts, Contexts and Cultures,* Bologna: Pàtron Editore, 167–201.

Miller, D. R. (2007) 'Towards a typology of evaluation in parliamentary debate: from theory to practice—and back again', in M. Dossena and A. H. Jucker (eds.), *(Re)volutions in Evaluation, Textus* 20(1). 159–80.

Miller, D. R. and Turci, M. (2006) "Construing the 'social gospel' of M.L. King: a corpus-assisted study of free*", *Linguistics and the Human Sciences*, 2(3), 399–424.

Mills, S. (2005) 'Gender and impoliteness'. *Journal of Politeness Research* 1(2): 263–280.

Morley, J. (1998) *Truth to Tell: Form and Function in Newspaper Headlines*. Bologna: CLUEB.

Morley, J. (2004a) 'Modals in persuasive journalism: an example from the *Economist*', in R. Facchinetti and F. Palmer (eds.) *English Modality in Perspective*, Frankfurt: Peter Lang, 67–82.

Morley, J. (2004b) 'The sting in the tail: persuasion in English editorial discourse', in A. Partington, J. Morley and L. Haarman (eds.), *Corpora and Discourse*, Bern: Peter Lang, 239–255.

Morley, J. (2005) 'The persuasive rhetoric of *Mirror* and *Guardian* editorials on the Iraq war', in M. Bondi and N. Maxwell (eds.) *Cross-Cultural Encounters: Linguistic Perspectives*, Rome: Officina Edizioni, 216–227.

Morley. J. and Partington, A. (2009) 'A few Frequently Asked Questions about semantic or evaluative prosody', *International Journal of Corpus Linguistics* 14(2): 139–158.

Mullany, L. (2002) '"I don't think you want me to get a word in edgeways do you John?" Re-assessing (im)politeness, language and gender in political broadcast interviews', *Sheffield Hallam Working Papers on the Web: Linguistic Politeness and Context*. Online. Available. HTTP: <http://extra.shu.ac.uk/wpw/politeness/mullany.htm> (accessed: 28 August 2007)

Murphy, A. and Morley, J. (2006) 'The peroration revisited' in V. K. Bhatia and M. Gotti, (eds.) *Explorations in Specialized Genres*, London: Routledge, 201–15.

Murphy, A. C. (2004) 'A hidden or unobserved presence? Impersonal evaluative structures in English and Italian and their wake', in A. Partington, J. Morley and L. Haarman (eds.), *Corpora and Discourse*, Bern: Peter Lang, 205–21.

Nelson Francis, W. (1982) 'Problems of assembling and computerizing large corpora', in S. Johansson (ed.) *Computer Corpora in English Language Research*, Bergen: Norwegian Computing Centre for the Humanities, 7–24.

Orend, B. (2000) *War and International Justice: A Kantian Perspective*, Waterloo, Ontario: Wilford Laurier University Press.

OUCS (2006a) 'Indexing with Xaira—Files Used by the Indexer'. Online. Available HTTP: <http://www.oucs.ox.ac.uk/rts/xaira/Doc/indexing.xml.ID=body.1_div.5> (accessed: 23 June 2007).

OUCS (2006b) 'Indexing with Xaira—The Indextools Utility'. Online. Available HTTP:<http://www.oucs.ox.ac.uk/rts/xaira/Doc/indexing.xml.ID=ixtools> (accessed: 23 June 2007).

Partington, A. (1996) 'An all-American villain. A corpus based study of relexicalization in newspaper headlines', *Textus* 9(1): 43–62.

———. (1998) *Patterns and Meanings: Using Corpora for English Language Research and Teaching*, Amsterdam and Philadelphia: John Benjamins.

———. (2001) 'Corpora and discourse strategies in action: from footing to fooling', in PALC 2001, *Proceedings of Practical Applications in Language Corpora Conference*, Frankfurt: Peter Lang, 263–79.

———. (2003) *The Linguistics of Political Argument: The Spin-Doctor and the Wolf-Pack at the White House*, London: Routledge.

———. (2004a) 'Corpora and discourse, a most congruous beast', in A. Partington, J. Morley and L. Haarman (eds.), .), *Corpora and Discourse*, Bern: Peter Lang, 11–20.

———. (2004b) '"Utterly content in each others' company": Semantic prosody and semantic preference', *International Journal of Corpus Linguistics* 9(1): 131–156.

————. (2006a) 'Metaphors, motifs and similes across discourse types: corpus assisted discourse studies (CADS) at work' in A. Stefanowitsch and S. Gries (eds.) *Corpus Based Approaches to Metaphor and Metonymy*, The Hague: Mouton de Gruyter, 267–304.

————. (2006b) *The Linguistics of Laughter: A corpus-assisted Study of Laughter-Talk*, London: Routledge.

————. (2007) 'Irony and reversal of evaluation', *Journal of Pragmatics* 39(9): 1547–1569.

————. (2008) 'The armchair and the machine: Corpus-Assisted Discourse Studies', in C. Taylor Torsello, K. Ackerley, E. Castello (eds.) *Corpora for University Language Teachers*, Bern: Peter Lang, 189–213.

Partington, A. and Morley, J. (2004) 'At the heart of ideology: word and cluster/bundle frequency in political debate' in B. Lewandowska, (ed.) *Practical Applications in Language and Computers*, Bern: Peter Lang, 179–192.

Partington, A., Morley, J. and Haarman, L. (eds.) (2004) *Corpora and Discourse*, Bern: Peter Lang.

Penman, R. (1990) 'Facework and politeness: multiple goals in courtroom discourse', *Journal of Language and Social Psychology* 9(1–2): 15–38.

Perez de Ayala, S. (2001) 'FTAs and Erskine May: conflicting needs.?—politeness in Question Time', *Journal of Pragmatics* 33(2): 143–169.

Pfau, M., Haigh, M., Gettle, M., Donnelly, M., Scott, G., Warr, D., and Wittenberg, E. (2004) 'Embedded journalists in military combat units: impact on newspaper story frames and tone', *Journalism and Mass Communication Quarterly* 81(1): 74–88.

Phillis, R. (2004) *An Independent Review of Government Communications*, London: Cabinet Office.

Pilger, J. (2003) 'The war for truth', in the *Independent on Sunday*, 6 April.

Project for Excellence in Reporting: Embedded reporters: What are Americans getting? (Overview). Journalism.org, 13 Jan. 2004. Online. Available: HTTP: http://www.journalism.org/resources/research/reports/war/embed/default. asp (accessed 12 July 2006).

Pyle, E. (1979) *Here is your War*, Manchester, MA: Ayer.

Ragan, P.H. (2001) 'Classroom use of a systemic functional small learner corpus', in M. Ghadessy, A. Henry and R. L. Roseberry (eds.), *Small Corpus Studies and ELT*, Amsterdam and Philadelphia: John Benjamins, 207–36.

Ravi, N. (2005) 'Looking beyond flawed journalism: how national interests, patriotism and cultural values shaped the coverage of the Iraq war', *Press/Politics* 10(1): 45–62.

Rawnsley, A. (2000) *Servants of the People: The Inside Story of New Labour,* London: Penguin.

Rayson, P. and Garside, R. (1998) 'The CLAWS Web Tagger', *ICAME Journal*, 22: 121–123.

Rees, N. (2006) *Brewer's Famous Quotations: 5000 Quotations and the Stories behind them*, London: Wiedenfeld and Nicholson.

Rees-Mogg, W. (2003) 'Win or lose, there's a TV channel there for you' in *The Times*, 24 March.

Rogers, S. (ed.) (2004) *The Hutton Inquiry and its Impact*, London: Politico's.

Schourup, L. (2001) 'Rethinking *well*', *Journal of Pragmatics* 33(2): 1025–60.

Scott, M. (1998). *WordSmith Tools Manual Version 3.0*. Oxford: Oxford University Press. Online. Available at http://www.lexically.net/wordsmith/version3/manual.pdf (accessed 7 July 2007).

Scott, M. (1999) *WordSmith Tools 3.0*. Oxford: Oxford University Press.

Scott, M. (2005) *WordSmith Tools 4.0*, Oxford: Oxford University Press.

Scott, M. (2005) *WordSmith Tools Manual Version 4.0*, Oxford: Oxford University Press. Available at http://www.lexically.net/downloads/version4/html/index.html?keyness_definition.htm (last accessed 16 June, 2007).

Scott, M. and Tribble, C. (2006) *Textual Patterns: Key Words and Corpus Analysis in Language Education*, Amsterdam and Philadelphia: John Benjamins.

Selby, K. and Cowdery, R.(1995) *How to Study Television*, London: Macmillan.

Semino, E. and Short, M. H. (2004) *Corpus Stylistics: Speech, Writing and Thought Presentation in a Corpus of English Writing*, London: Routledge.

Shoemaker, P. (1996) *Mediating the Message*, London: Longman.

Short, C. (2004) *An Honourable Deception?: New Labour, Iraq, and the Misuse of Power*, London: Free Press.

Siegal, A and Connolly, W. (1999) *The New York Times Manual of Style and Usage*, New York: Times Books.

Silver, B. (1998) *The Ascent of Science*. Oxford: Oxford University Press.

Simpson, J. (2003) *The Wars against Saddam: Taking the Hard Road to Baghdad*, London: Macmillan.

Sinclair, J. (1986) 'Fictional worlds' in D. Coulthard (ed) *Talking about Text: Studies Presented to David Brazil on his Retirement*, Discourse Analysis Monographs no 13, University of Birmingham, 1986, 43–60.

Sinclair, J. (1991) *Corpus Concordance Collocation*, Oxford: Oxford University Press.

Sinclair, J. (2004) *Trust the Text: Language, Corpus and Discourse*, London: Routledge.

Slembrouk, S. (1992) 'The parliamentary Hansard "verbatim" report: the written construction of spoken discourse', *Language and Literature* 1(2): 101–19.

Sperberg-McQueen, C. M. and Burnard, L. (eds.) (2007) *TEI P5: Guidelines for Electronic Text Encoding and Interchange*. Online. Available HTTP: <http://www.tei-c.org/release/doc/tei-p5-doc/html/ST.html> (accessed: 23 June 2007).

Sperberg-McQueen, C. M., Huitfeldt, C. and Renear A. (2000) 'Meaning and interpretation of markup' in Markup Languages: Theory & Practice 2(3), 215-34. Available HTTP: <http://www.w3.org/People/cmsmcq/2000/mim.html> (accessed 15 July 2007).

Stenström, A. (1994) *An Introduction to Spoken Interaction*, London: Longman.

Stewart, D. (2008) 'Amid semantic prosody: Concepts, conceptions, misconceptions'. Paper presented at the seminar Semantic prosody: Has it set in, or should it be budged?, Forlì, Italy, 23 June 2008.

Stubbs, M. (1996). *Text and Corpus Analysis*, Oxford: Blackwell.

Stubbs, M. (2001). *Words and Phrases. Corpus Studies of Lexical Semantics*, Oxford: Blackwell.

Stubbs, M. (2006a) 'Quantitative data on multi-word sequences in English: the case of prepositional phrases'. (Paper given at the Berlin-Brandenburgische Akademie der Wissenschaften).

Stubbs, M. (2006b) 'Corpus analysis: the state of the art and three types of unanswered questions', in S. Hunston and G. Thompson (eds.), *Evaluation in Texts: Authorial Stance and the Construction of Discourse*, Oxford: Oxford University Press, 15–36.

Stygall, G. (2001) 'A different class of witness: experts in the courtroom', *Discourse Studies* 3(3): 327–349

Summers, K (2001) 'Epideictic rhetoric in the *Englishwoman's Review*', *Victorian Periodicals Review*, 34(3): 25–33.

Swales, J. (1986) 'Citation analysis and discourse analysis', *Applied Linguistics* 7(1): 39–56.

Swales, J. (1990) *Genre Analysis: English in Academic and Research Settings.* Cambridge: Cambridge University Press.

Tadros, A. (1993) 'The pragmatics of text averral and attribution in academic texts', in M. Hoey (ed.), *Data, Description, Discourse: Papers on the English Language in Honour of John McH Sinclair on his Sixtieth Birthday*, London: HarperCollins, 98–114.

Taylor, C. (2006) 'Witness strategies in the Hutton Inquiry', in J. Flowerdew and M. Gotti (eds.), *Studies in Specialized Discourse*, Bern: Peter Lang, 263–287.

Taylor, C. and Biscetti, S. (2005) 'Analysing the Hutton Inquiry', paper presented at the Conference on *Corpus Linguistics and the Study of Politics*, Università degli Studi di Siena, 11 February 2005.

Temple, M. (2006) *Blair*, London: Haus Publications.

Teubert, W. (2005) 'My version of corpus linguistics', *International Journal of Corpus Linguistics* 10(1):1–13.

Teubert, W. and Krishnamurthy, R. (2007) 'General introduction', in W. Teubert and R. Krishnamurthy (eds.), *Corpus Linguistics: Critical Concepts in Linguistics*, vol. 1, London and New York: Routledge, 1–37.

Teubert, W. and Krishnamurthy, R. (eds.) (2007) *Corpus Linguistics: Critical Concepts in Linguistics*, vol. 1, London and New York: Routledge.

Thompson, G. (1994) *Reporting,* Collins Cobuild English Guides 5, London: Harper Collins.

Thompson, G. (1996) 'Voices in the text: discourse perspectives on language reports', in *Applied Linguistics*, 17(4): 501–530.

Thompson, G. (2000) 'Corpora, patterns and grammar: is it enough to trust the text?', Unpublished Plenary paper delivered to the Systemic Functional Linguistics European Workshop, Glasgow, 19–22 July.

Thompson, G. and Hunston, S. (2000) 'Evaluation: an introduction', in S. Hunston and G. Thompson (eds.), *Evaluation in Texts: Authorial Stance and the Construction of Discourse*, Oxford: Oxford University Press, 1–27.

Thompson, G. and Hunston, S. (eds.) (2006) *System and Corpus: Exploring Connections*, London: Equinox.

Thompson, G. and Ye, Y. (1991). 'Evaluation in the reporting verbs used in academic papers', *Applied Linguistics,* 12(4): 365–382.

Tognini Bonelli, E. (2001) *Corpus Linguistics at Work*, Amsterdam and Philadelphia: John Benjamins.

Toolan, M. (1997) 'What is critical discourse analysis and why are people saying such terrible things about it?', *Language and Literature* 6(2): 83–103.

Ure, J. (1971) 'Lexical density and register variation' in G. Perren, and J. Trim, (eds.) *Applications of Linguistics*, Cambridge: Cambridge University Press, 443–552.

van Dijk, T. A. (1993) 'Principles of critical discourse analysis', *Discourse and Society*, 4(2): 249–83.

van Dijk, T. A. (1988) *News as Discourse.* Hillsdale, NJ: Lawrence Erlbaum Associates.

van Dijk, T. A. 'Opinions and ideologies in the press', in A. Bell and P. Garrett (eds.) *Approaches to Media Discourse*, Oxford: Oxford University Press, 21–63.

Van Leeuwen, T. (2006), 'War rhetoric' in *Elsevier Encyclopaedia of Language and Linguistics*, Amsterdam: Elsevier, 516–520.

Vendler, Z. (1967) *Linguistics in Philosophy*, Ithaca: Cornell University Press.

Verschueren, J. (ed.), (1999) *Language and Ideology: Selected Papers from the 6th International Pragmatics Conference*, vol. 1, Antwerp: International Pragmatics Association.

Wagenaar, W.A. 1995. 'Anchored narratives: a theory of judicial reasoning, and its consequences', In G. Davies, S. Lloyd-Bostock, M. McMurran and C Wilson (eds.) *Psychology, Law and Criminal Justice*, Berlin: de Gruyter, 267–285.

Walzer, M. (1977) *Just and Unjust Wars: A Moral Argument with Historical Illustrations*, New York: Basic Books.

Watts, R. J. (2003) *Politeness*. Cambridge: Cambridge University Press.

Waugh, L. (1995) 'Reported speech in journalistic discourse: the relation of function and text.', *Text* 15(1): 129–73.

White, P. R. R. (1997) 'Death, disruption and the moral order: the narrative impulse in mass- media "hard news" reporting', in F. Christie and J. Martin (eds.) *Genre and Institutions: Social Processes in the Workplace and School*, London: Continuum, 101–133.

White, P. R. R. (2003) 'Beyond modality and hedging: a dialogic view of the language of intersubjective stance', *Text* 23(2): 259–84.

Widdowson, H. (2000) 'The limitations of linguistics applied', *Applied Linguistics*, 21(1): 3–25.

Williams, R. (1983 [1976]) *Keywords: A Vocabulary of Culture and Society*, New York: Oxford University Press.

Wilson, J. (1990) *Politically Speaking. The Pragmatic Analysis of Political Language*, Oxford: Blackwell.

Wodak, R. (1989) *Language, Power and Ideology: Studies in Political Discourse*, Amsterdam and Philadelphia: John Benjamins.

Wodak, R. (2006) 'Critical linguistics and critical discourse analysis', in J. Verschueren and J.-O Östman (eds.), Handbook of Pragmatics, Amsterdam and Philadelphia: John Benjamins, 1–25.

Wodak, R. and van Dijk, T.A. (eds.) (2000) *Racism at the Top: Parliamentary Discourses on Ethnic Issues in Six European States*, Klagenfurt: Drava.

Wynne, M. (2005) 'Stylistics: corpus approaches', in *Encyclopaedia of Linguistics*, Elsevier. Online. Available HTTP: <http://www.corpus.bham.uk/conference2005/corpora_stylistics.pdf> (accessed: 23 June 2007).

Zelizer, B. and Allan, S. (eds.) (2002) *Journalism After September 11*, London and New York: Routledge.

Contributors

Paul Bayley is Professor of English Linguistics at the Faculty of Political Science "Roberto Ruffilli" of the University of Bologna at Forlì. His research interests are directed towards corpus linguistics, with particular attention to small specialized corpora, discourse analysis within the framework of systemic functional linguistics, paying particular attention to discourse within the institutions.

Cinzia Bevitori is a researcher of English language and linguistics at the Faculty of Political Science "Roberto Ruffilli" of the University of Bologna at Forlì. Her main research interests are in the field of corpus linguistics, discourse analysis within the framework of systemic functional linguistics and appraisal. Particular attention has been focused on institutional discourse, chiefly parliamentary discourse.

Letizia Cirillo is currently a research assistant at the University of Modena a Reggio Emilia. Her research interests include conversation analysis, with particular reference to doctor-patient interaction, and corpus linguistics, with the aim of developing resources, tools, and methodologies for research into linguistics and foreign-language teaching.

Caroline Clark is currently a Researcher in English Linguistics in the Faculty of Political Science of the University of Bologna. Her research interests are mainly in the areas of corpus linguistics and discourse analysis, with particular attention to the areas of appraisal and evaluation, and discourse analysis of specialised corpora. She has recently been working on media coverage of conflict and 'embedded' reporting in particular.

Alison Duguid is Associate Professor of English linguistics at the Humanities Faculty of the University of Siena, where she coordinates the English-language teaching and teacher training programmes. Her research interests are principally in the area of corpus assisted discourse studies and more recently modern diachronic corpus assisted discourse studies applied to media discourse and the resources of persuasive and evaluative language.

Jane Johnson is a researcher at the Political Science Faculty of the University of Bologna and has taught English functional grammar at the Languages and Literature Faculty of the University of Bologna, as well as translation into English at the SSLMIT (Forlì). Her research interests are in corpus-assisted discourse analysis, SFL, and appraisal theory.

Linda Lombardo is Professor of English Language and Linguistics in the Faculty of Political Science of the Luiss Guido Carli University in Rome. Her major research interests are in the area of corpus-assisted discourse analysis within a systemic functional linguistics framework, with particular attention to media discourse.

Anna Marchi is working towards a PhD in linguistics at Lancaster University. She has a background in journalism as an intern at the Italian newspaper *Corriere della Sera* and studied journalism at the University of Texas. Her research interests are in the field of corpus-assisted discourse studies applied to media discourse.

Donna R. Miller is Professor of English Linguistics and Director of the Centre for Linguistic-Cultural Studies (CeSLiC) at the University of Bologna. Her increasingly corpus-assisted research focuses, in an SFL perspective, on register analysis of institutional and literature varieties. Her work specifically explores the grammar of speaker evaluation and stance.

John Morley is Professor of English Language and Linguistics in the Faculty of Political Science of the University of Siena, where he teaches, among other things, media languages and corpus linguistics. His main research interests are connected with analyzing the language of the media.

Amanda Murphy (PhD Birmingham, UK) is a researcher of English Language in the Modern Languages and Literatures Faculty at the Catholic University of Milan. Her major research interests are evaluation in media discourse, applied linguistics, corpus linguistics, contrastive linguistics (English and Italian), and phraseology in native and nonnative speaker texts.

Alan Partington (Bologna University) has published works on phonetics, CALL, lexicology, discourse analysis, humour and irony studies, corpus linguistics, and CADS. He is the author of *Patterns and Meanings* (Benjamins), *The Linguistics of Political Argument* (Routledge), *Persuasion in Politics* (LED), *The Linguistics of Laughter* (Routledge) and is coeditor of *Corpora and Discourse* (Lang).

Giulia Riccio holds a PhD in English for Special Purposes at the University of Naples Federico II. Her main research interests are in the field of corpus-assisted discourse studies, applied to the field of institutional communication and, in particular, to the study of the White House press briefings discourse.

Charlotte Taylor currently researches and lectures in English language and linguistics at the Faculty of Political Science, University of Siena, and is also studying part-time for a PhD at Lancaster University. Her main research interests include the methodology of corpus linguistics, the theory of (im)politeness, and the fields of media, institutional, and computer-mediated discourse.

Marco Venuti, PhD in ESP, is currently a researcher of English language and linguistics at the Faculty of Economics of the University of Napoli Federico II. He is coauthor of *La stampa britannica e la moneta unica* (CUEN 2004). His research interests are mainly in the areas of corpus linguistics and discourse analysis.

Index